A WORLD ON FIRE

DAVID METZLER

Pacific Press®
Publishing Association
Nampa, Idaho | www.pacificpress.com

Cover design resources from iStockphoto | Anson_iStock
Photograph of author by John Levengood
Inside design by Aaron Troia

The author assumes full responsibility for the accuracy of all facts and quotations as cited in this book.

Unless otherwise noted, all Scripture quotations are from the New King James Version®. Copyright © 1982 by Thomas Nelson. Used by permission. All rights reserved.

Scripture quotations marked KJV are from the King James Version of the Bible.

Additional copies of this book may be purchased by calling toll-free 1-800-765-6955 or by visiting AdventistBookCenter.com.

Library of Congress Cataloging-in-Publication Data

Names: Metzler, David, 1951- author.
Title: A world on fire / David Metzler.
Description: Nampa, Idaho : Pacific Press Publishing Association, 2020. | Summary: "A daily
    devotional on the ministry and mission of the apostles"— Provided by publisher.
Identifiers: LCCN 2019052484 | ISBN 9780816366187 (hardcover) |
    ISBN 9780816366194 (kindle edition)
Subjects: LCSH: Apostles—Prayers and devotions. | Church history—Primitive and early
    church, ca. 30-600—Prayers and devotions. | Devotional calendars—General Conference
    of Seventh-Day Adventists.
Classification: LCC BS2618 .M48 2020 | DDC 225.9/2—dc23
LC record available at https://lccn.loc.gov/2019052484

June 2020

Dedication

This book is dedicated to the women of the church.

In this account of the missionary work of Paul, italics have been used to highlight first-century women and their contributions to the fledgling church. Often these women defied the culture of the times and rose above their assigned station in life to make a difference. Women with means sold their properties to advance the cause of the church. Others volunteered their houses as meeting places. They did this at great personal risk. Their homes and real estate could have been forfeited to the state, and they could have been arrested, imprisoned, and martyred for their faith. It took real courage to stand against the wrath of the Sanhedrin and the universal and powerful imperial cult.

While the gospel would have been preached in all the world eventually, had it not been for those women who first supported Jesus' ministry and the others who later assisted the founders of the early church, progress would undoubtedly have been slower. Even the story of Sapphira served a purpose in the early church, showing others that commitments to God are to be honored. For every Sapphira, there was a Dorcas and a Priscilla whose love and devotion carried the church forward.

Do Christian women of this millennium carry forward the work of spreading the gospel that was accelerated by Susanna, Joanna, Priscilla, Lydia, Apphia, Euodia, Syntyche, Junia, Lois, Eunice, Chloe, Rhoda, and Tabitha (Dorcas)? I believe they do, and the church owes them a debt of gratitude for their unselfish contributions to the cause of Christ. I think there was a reason Jesus first appeared to two women after His resurrection, instead of to His disciples. I believe there was a reason He spoke to the Samaritan woman at the well. I believe that He welcomed the mothers bringing their children to sit upon His knee because of His love for them and their burdens. The stories of Christ's interactions with women are numerous if one looks closely. As we study the book of Acts and the letters of Paul, consider the contributions made by women.

Men, we should thank God for our spouses, mothers, sisters, daughters, aunts, and grandmothers! Where would we, or the church, be without them?

Contents

In Appreciation

I extend special thanks to my wife, Margy, for four decades of love and support. Only the spouses of other writers can appreciate Margy's sacrifices. Thanks to all the men and women who nurtured my faith as I grew up in the Adventist message, first at Ukiah Junior Academy in Northern California, then at Rio Lindo Academy in Healdsburg, Pacific Union College at Angwin, La Sierra College, and finally Loma Linda University. (Interestingly, many of those Christian grade-school teachers retired immediately after I left their classrooms.)

Thanks also to the members of the Frederick Seventh-day Adventist Church in Frederick, Maryland (especially the former pastor Dan Goddard and the members of the Faith Sabbath School class), and the members of the Aiea Seventh-day Adventist Church in Aiea (Oahu), Hawaii, and Pastor Lloyd Munson for allowing me to teach, preach, and participate in great Sabbath School discussions. Call me anytime because I love nothing more than sharing and discussing Jesus with you.

I would be remiss if I did not thank Vinnie Springer, Helen Davis, and Cynthia Waters of the Jacksonville Seventh-day Adventist Church in North Carolina for their service to that little church, their ready smiles, their ability to gently keep me in line, their great Southern cooking, and their sharp intellects. I admire all the women of that little church.

Lastly, to Elder Josué Rosado, former principal of Hawaiian Mission Academy, and his wife, Ruth, for their interest, reference material recommendations, steadfast encouragement, and unflagging support in seeing this book written: I thank you both.

Preface

When one proposes to write a biography about an individual, it is generally assumed the story will start at the beginning of the subject's life and progress onward in an orderly fashion to close with his death. Such is a difficult, if not impossible, task when confronted with the life of Paul the apostle. The earliest histories of Paul are fragmentary at best, and many details are simply nonexistent. Luke the physician, author of the New Testament book that bears his name as well as the book of Acts, gave us an incomplete picture of his friend Paul. We know nothing of Paul's early life in Tarsus. There is only conjecture as to how he ended up in Jerusalem, studying at the feet of Gamaliel I, grandson of the great rabbi Hillel and a famous Hebrew scholar in his own right. We have no physical description of Paul, just as we have no physical description of our Lord, Jesus Christ. Scholars have been able to piece together little information relating to Paul's family and his relatives. Was Paul married? And what was the affliction he mentions in his writings? If he was not married, how then could he have been a member of the Sanhedrin? For every question asked, there are three more uncovered that beg answers as well. Paul is a mystery man. Perhaps this is as it should be, for in so doing, Luke kept us from worshiping the man.

Four years of reading and researching the life and times of Paul barely prepared me to tackle his story in a devotional-book format. During that time, my search for crucial biographical details came up empty. Conjecture was everywhere, but information was lacking. Dead ends abounded, and more times than I would like to admit, I set aside the work in frustration. How does one begin a story that has as its main focus an individual who has no historically documented beginning? Where to start? Does one take up the tale in the middle as Luke has done? One day it came to me that perhaps I was approaching the project in the wrong way. Luke had it right after all! Although much of the New Testament is composed of the letters of Paul to the congregations at Corinth, Galatia, Ephesus, Philippi, Colossae, and Thessalonica, the story is not about a person; it is about the spreading of the good news of salvation through belief in Jesus Christ and His sacrifice. The story concerns the mission of Paul to the Gentiles and his perseverance in taking the gospel to "the uttermost part of the earth" (Acts 1:8, KJV). The spread of the gospel is the focus and not Paul. So that is where our story begins.

I am instructed . . . that the whole book of Acts is our lesson book.
All of us need to humble our own individual hearts and be converted daily.
—Ellen G. White, Letter 32, 1910

No man ever lived who was a more earnest, energetic, and self-sacrificing disciple of Christ than was Paul. He was one of the world's greatest teachers. He crossed the seas, and traveled far and near, until a large portion of the world had learned from his lips the story of the cross of Christ. He possessed a burning desire to bring perishing men to a knowledge of the truth through a Saviour's love.
—Ellen G. White, *Sketches From the Life of Paul*, pp. 100, 101

This Gospel Is for Jews

Ministry in Jerusalem

AD 31–34

Acts 1:1–7:60
The Acts of the Apostles, pp. 9–102
Sketches From the Life of Paul, pp. 9–20

The Great Commission

*"And this gospel of the kingdom will be preached in all the world
as a witness to all the nations, and then the end will come."*

—Matthew 24:14

F ollowing Christ's crucifixion, "the sun of the disciples' hope had set, and night had settled down upon their hearts."[1] Jesus' disciples now numbered eleven: "Peter, James, John, and Andrew; Philip and Thomas; Bartholomew and Matthew; James the son of Alphaeus and Simon the Zealot; and Judas the son of James" (Acts 1:13). "His death had come to them as a surprise. . . . When Christ was crucified, they did not believe that He would rise. He had stated plainly that He was to rise on the third day, but they were perplexed to know what He meant. . . .

"Crushed by despondency, grief, and despair, the disciples met together in the upper chamber, and closed and fastened the doors, fearing that the fate of their beloved Teacher might be theirs. It was here that the Saviour, after His resurrection, appeared to them."[2]

During the next forty days, Jesus "spoke of the prophecies concerning His advent, His rejection by the Jews, and His death, showing that every specification of these prophecies had been fulfilled."[3] The words of Jesus now carried unusual weight, for the disciples were hearing One who had literally returned from beyond the grave. "And He opened their understanding, that they might comprehend the Scriptures.

"Then He said to them, 'Thus it is written, and thus it was necessary for the Christ to suffer and to rise from the dead the third day, and that repentance and remission of sins should be preached in His name to all nations, beginning at Jerusalem. And you are witnesses of these things' " (Luke 24:45, 46).

"Christ told His disciples that they were to begin their work at Jerusalem. That city had been the scene of His amazing sacrifice for the human race. There, clad in the garb of humanity, He had walked and talked with men, and few had discerned how near heaven came to earth. There He had been condemned and crucified. In Jerusalem were many who secretly believed Jesus of Nazareth to be the Messiah, and many who had been deceived by priests and rulers. To these the gospel must be proclaimed."[4]

We serve a risen Savior! This year share the good news with others.

---

1. Ellen G. White, *The Acts of the Apostles* (Mountain View, CA: Pacific Press®, 1911), 25.
2. White, *Acts of the Apostles*, 25, 26.
3. White, *Acts of the Apostles*, 26.
4. White, *Acts of the Apostles*, 31.

Preparing to Serve

"But you shall receive power when the Holy Spirit has come upon you; and you shall be witnesses to Me in Jerusalem, and in all Judea and Samaria, and to the end of the earth."

—Acts 1:8

The disciples were to 'wait,' not to 'go a fishing,' as Peter and the others had done a little while before (John 21:3)."[1] Jesus met with the disciples for forty days following His resurrection. These were times of enlightenment. Jesus again set before them the nature of His kingdom. In His name, they were to carry the message of salvation to the world. Their job would not be easy. Christ promised to be with them during difficulties: "Go therefore and make disciples of all the nations, baptizing them in the name of the Father and of the Son and of the Holy Spirit, teaching them to observe all things that I have commanded you; and lo, I am with you always, even to the end of the age" (Matthew 28:19, 20). The disciples were transformed during their forty days with Jesus. Initially discouraged, grief-stricken, and fearful, hiding behind locked doors, they now gained new insights and education that emboldened them.

"As they heard their beloved Master explaining the Scriptures in the light of all that had happened, their faith in Him was fully established. They reached the place where they could say, 'I know whom I have believed.' 2 Timothy 1:12."[2] But they still believed they were on the eve of seeing the Messianic kingdom restored to Israel. Eagerly, they looked forward to the immediate overthrow of Rome. Jesus calmly explained that it was not for them to know the times or seasons that the Father put in His authority. They must wait for the Spirit and then boldly tell others of the salvation found through Jesus Christ!

"The gospel commission is the great missionary charter of Christ's kingdom. The disciples were to work earnestly for souls, giving to all the invitation of mercy. They were not to wait for the people to come to them; they were to go to the people with their message."[3] It was only after the outpouring of the Spirit on the Day of Pentecost that the disciples finally grasped the spiritual nature of the Master's kingdom. Accepting the mercy and salvation Christ offered, they felt compelled to *go* to their relatives with the good news of salvation.

We, likewise, are not to wait for others to approach us. We must work earnestly for souls. Go!

---

1. Francis D. Nichol, ed., *The Seventh-day Adventist Bible Commentary*, vol. 6 (Washington, DC: Review and Herald®, 1957), 121.

2. Ellen G. White, *The Acts of the Apostles* (Mountain View, CA: Pacific Press®, 1911), 27.

3. White, *Acts of the Apostles*, 28.

A Formula for Effective Prayer

These all continued with one accord in prayer and supplication.

—Acts 1:14

The eleven disciples continued to meet in the upper room of a private Jerusalem home. Together with the *women* who supported Christ's ministry, *Mary the mother of Jesus*, His brothers, and others who believed, they strengthened each other's faith. We are not told who owned the house or whether this was the same room in which the disciples had observed Passover with their Master. We know more believers than those mentioned in Acts 1:13, 14 met periodically with the disciples, raising petitions to the Father in the name of Jesus Christ their Lord, because Acts 1:15 records 120 disciples meeting together for prayer and fellowship. Acts 2:1 states that this group was of "one accord" in "one place." Given the cultural downplaying of women in community roles, it is notable that they are mentioned here. These disciples did not pray for personal blessing. They had a conscious burden to save souls who were perishing without a Savior. Their formula for effective prayer consisted of "(1) the petition—they prayed; (2) the perseverance—they continued in prayer; (3) the unanimity—they prayed with one accord."[1] In sharp contrast to the competitive spirit shown during the Last Supper with their Lord (Luke 22:24), the remaining disciples now met in a spirit of unity.

Previously, they had argued among themselves. Who should stoop to wash the other's feet? Now united in purpose, they prayed that the Spirit, the Comforter, would come. Jesus had assured them He would "send the Promise of My Father upon you" (Luke 24:49). The ten days since His ascension were days of humility, true repentance, and confession. "Oh, if they could but have the past three years to live over, they thought, how differently they would act! . . . But they were comforted by the thought that they were forgiven. . . .

". . . Putting away all differences, all desire for supremacy, they came close together in Christian fellowship."[2] Here is the model current believers should emulate. What mighty works for God might be done if congregations put aside differences and with Christian love prayed for the Spirit and each other!

"Our prayers in public should be short, and express only the real wants of the soul, asking in simplicity and simple trusting faith for the very things we need. Prayer from the humble, contrite heart is the vital breath of the soul hungering for righteousness."[3]

---

1. Francis D. Nichol, ed., *The Seventh-day Adventist Bible Commentary*, vol. 6 (Washington, DC: Review and Herald®, 1957), 127.

2. Ellen G. White, *The Acts of the Apostles* (Mountain View, CA: Pacific Press®, 1911), 36, 37.

3. Ellen G. White, "The Prayer That God Approves," *Signs of the Times*, December 3, 1896, 5.

Diversity Becomes "One Accord"

These all continued with one accord in prayer and supplication, with the women *and* Mary the mother of Jesus, *and with His brothers.*

—Acts 1:14; emphasis added

Who were "the women" of Acts 1:14? Some commentators maintain they were the wives of the disciples. They say the mother of Jesus was singled out specifically because she was *not* the wife of a disciple. (It should be noted this is the last biblical mention of Mary, the mother of Jesus. She is described as being united with those who "continued with one accord in prayer and supplication.") Others believe Acts 1:14 refers to the women who aided Jesus during His earthly ministry. This view has wider acceptance as it is based upon Luke 8:2: "And certain *women* who had been healed of evil spirits and infirmities—*Mary called Magdalene*, out of whom had come seven demons, and *Joanna* the wife of Chuza, Herod's steward, and *Susanna*, and many others who provided for Him from their substance" (emphasis added). What a diverse group!

The brothers of Jesus did not accept His divinity during His earthly ministry (John 7:1–9) and are not mentioned as being at the foot of the cross (John 19:25–27). When Jesus was a child in Nazareth, His brothers had tried to intimidate and control Him. "Jesus loved His brothers, and treated them with unfailing kindness; but they were jealous of Him, and manifested the most decided unbelief and contempt. They could not understand His conduct."[1] They disagreed with Him at various times and argued He should observe the teachings of the rabbis more scrupulously, ceasing to antagonize them. The final scenes in Christ's earthly life brought about their rebirth, and they now stood up and were counted among His followers. We are told the brothers of Christ were named James, Joses (Joseph), Simon, and Judas (Matthew 13:55). "No more is heard of Simon and Joses, but James is probably the one who became a leader in the church . . . , and is thought by many to be the author of the Epistle of James. . . . Judas may be the Jude who wrote the brief epistle that bears his name."[2]

"This reference to the mother of Jesus is instructive. Her unique relationship to the ascended Lord justifies her being singled out for special mention, but she is not given any undue pre-eminence."[3]

1. Ellen G. White, *The Desire of Ages* (Mountain View, CA: Pacific Press®, 1940), 87.
2. Francis D. Nichol, ed., *The Seventh-day Adventist Bible Commentary*, vol. 6 (Washington, DC: Review and Herald®, 1957), 127.
3. Nichol, *Seventh-day Adventist Bible Commentary*, vol. 6, 127.

One of Us

"Men and brethren, this Scripture had to be fulfilled . . . concerning Judas, who became a guide to those who arrested Jesus; for he was numbered with us and obtained a part in this ministry."
—Acts 1:16, 17

Peter felt the group needed to address the behavior of Judas. All knew Judas had guided the priests and temple soldiers to arrest Christ in the Garden of Gethsemane. "What a fearful change in occupation! He who had been ordained to lead men to Christ that they might be saved, chose to lead men to Christ that the Saviour might be destroyed."[1] Peter rightly pointed out that while Judas was "numbered with" the disciples, Jesus had never called him to discipleship. Judas had come to the disciples and asked them to intervene with their Master. He came offering his services with the hope that should Jesus be the Messiah, there might be a place in the coming kingdom for one such as him. The man had impressed the other disciples because "he was of commanding appearance, a man of keen discernment and executive ability, and they commended him to Jesus as one who would greatly assist Him in His work. They were surprised that Jesus received him so coolly."[2] Yet, Jesus ordained Judas Iscariot with the other eleven and sent him on a mission with the others (Matthew 10:1–42; Mark 3:13–19; Luke 6:12–16; 9:1–6).

Everyone knew of Judas's role in the plot to arrest Jesus. The disciple John had been present in the judgment hall on the night of Jesus' trial and had witnessed Judas's anguish. During the trial of Christ, Judas was shocked to see that the Master did nothing to free Himself. "As hour after hour went by, and Jesus submitted to all the abuse heaped upon Him, a terrible fear came to the traitor that he had sold his Master to His death."[3] "Judas saw that his entreaties [to Caiaphas on behalf of Jesus] were in vain, and he rushed from the hall exclaiming, It is too late! It is too late! He felt that he could not live to see Jesus crucified, and in despair went out and hanged himself."[4] It was no secret that Jesus had been betrayed by one of His own disciples. It was a topic of discussion throughout Jerusalem, and many were being influenced for Christ as a result.

Those who become Christians for personal gain, fame, or ambition often meet with disaster. Like Judas, many fall headlong from the heights of human acclaim, becoming tragic spectacles.

1. Francis D. Nichol, ed., *The Seventh-day Adventist Bible Commentary*, vol. 6 (Washington, DC: Review and Herald®, 1957), 128.
2. Ellen G. White, *The Desire of Ages* (Mountain View, CA: Pacific Press®, 1940), 294.
3. White, *Desire of Ages*, 721.
4. White, *Desire of Ages*, 722.

Blood Money

"Now this man purchased a field with the wages of iniquity."

—Acts 1:18

S ome believe Luke inserted the description of Judas's betrayal and death by hanging
into the book of Acts to explain the need to select a replacement disciple. Those
present as Peter spoke were well aware of the actions so recently taken by Judas against
their Lord. When Luke wrote, "This man purchased a field," he was not saying Judas
made the purchase personally, but rather, his blood money was used in the purchase.
The thirty pieces of silver that Judas threw at the feet of the high priest were used to
purchase a level field where city potters dumped unused clay. Here Judas had been
buried. "Because of this, or because the money was the price of 'innocent blood,' the
place was called the 'field of blood' (... Matt. 27:3–10)."[1] Peter rightly called to the
minds of his listeners the prophecy found in Psalm 69:25: "Let their dwelling place be
desolate; let no one live in their tents." "Tradition associates the [field of blood] with
Hakk ed-Dumm, on the south bank of the Valley of Hinnom, to the south of Jerusalem.
... The field bought with the 30 pieces of silver was used for burying strangers who
lacked relatives or friends to inter them."[2]

How ironic that the priests refused to return the silver coins to the temple treasury.
They reasoned the blood money was used in the commission of a crime and therefore
was tainted and impure. They refused to see that the innocent blood of their Victim was
a stain on their souls. By entering the house of worship and standing before the people
as paragons of virtue, their sanctimonious behavior was an affront to God. Their lack
of concern for the remorse of Judas, their refusal to show him pity or offer any hope of
forgiveness, showed the haughty callousness of their hearts for all sinners whom they
considered beneath themselves. Remaining aloof from Judas's actions, they saw no
sin in their own conduct. Truly, Jesus described them correctly when He called them
"whited sepulchres" (Matthew 23:27, KJV). Wishing others to think them holy, they
put on a lily-white religious front, but their pious façade hid decaying characters, and
their wicked deeds were recognized. The treachery of Judas, his suicide, the plotting
of the priests, the betrayal of Christ by one of His own disciples, and the Crucifixion
were topics of discussion in Jerusalem on this Pentecostal holiday. The people were
not fooled by the intrigue surrounding the death of Jesus.

Ambition for earthly glory and position clouded Judas's judgment. Motives reveal character.

---

1. Francis D. Nichol, ed., *The Seventh-day Adventist Bible Commentary*, vol. 6 (Washington, DC: Review and Herald®,
1957), 128.

2. Nichol, *Seventh-day Adventist Bible Commentary*, vol. 6, 129.

What Price Jesus?

"And they took the thirty pieces of silver, the value of Him who was priced, whom they of the children of Israel priced, and gave them for the potter's field, as the LORD directed me."
—Matthew 27:9, 10

Matthew's writings characteristically point to prophecy fulfilled as a confirmation of Christ's divinity. Yet the fulfillment of Messianic predictions came about in natural ways, so far as Jesus' contemporaries could discern. Events often were recognized as prophecy fulfilled only many years after they occurred. References to "thirty pieces of silver" and a "potter's floor" are found in Zechariah 11:12, 13. Pronouncements of this event are also found in Jeremiah 18:2–12; 19:1–15; and 32:6–9. New Testament writers often attributed Old Testament prophecies to the more famous of two prophets. Frequently, the Minor Prophets are not annotated, in favor of the Major Prophets. Matthew combines the accounts of Zechariah and Jeremiah and credits them both to Jeremiah. The same literary technique is again seen in Matthew 3:3. Here, Matthew references Isaiah's prophecy foretelling the message and manner of John the Baptist's ministry. While Isaiah 40:3 does speak to the manner and ministry of John the Baptist, Malachi 3:1 also does; however, the prophecy of Malachi is not mentioned.

Let us look closer at the prophecy found in Zechariah 11:12, 13. Here we see Zechariah, representing the Chief Shepherd, asking the flock of Israel to pay him a just wage. In return, the nation offers thirty pieces of silver (shekels), worth approximately $243.37 today. "This very small amount reflected the Israelites' contemptuous thankfulness for what God had done for them. Thirty shekels was the price of a slave."[1] God told Zechariah to cast the money unto the potter as an example of the people's ingratitude for the Lord's blessings. "A change in one letter in the original Hebrew gives the reading 'treasury' instead of 'potter.' . . . Some understand the words 'cast it unto the potter' as merely an expression to denote the contemptuous rejection of the 'pieces of silver' when they were brought to the treasury of the Temple."[2] The low estimation ancient Israel placed upon the gifts of God (Zechariah 11:12) was reflected in the meager amount demanded as payment to betray the priceless gift of His Son (Matthew 26:15).

What value do you place upon God's gifts? Is salvation through Jesus listed among your assets?

1. Francis D. Nichol, ed., *The Seventh-day Adventist Bible Commentary*, vol. 4 (Washington, DC: Review and Herald®, 1955), 1111.
2. Nichol, *Seventh-day Adventist Bible Commentary*, vol. 4, 1111.

Matthias

And they proposed two: Joseph called Barsabas, who was surnamed Justus, and Matthias.
—Acts 1:23

Peter insisted Judas be replaced by quoting Psalm 109:8: "And let another take his office." "Peter apparently thought that the original number of the disciples should be maintained. The apostles doubtless had a concept of 12 as a full number, after the example of the 12 tribes of Israel. In fact, they had been promised 12 thrones from which to govern the tribes (Matt. 19:28), a promise that calls to mind the 12 stars in the crown of the church (Rev. 12:1), and the 12 foundations of the walls of the New Jerusalem, with the names of the 12 apostles on them (Rev. 21:14). Jesus had ordained a company of 12, one of whom was lost. Peter reasoned: The full number is necessary to give testimony concerning all aspects of the Lord's life and works; a mighty task lies before the apostles, and the full quota of witnesses is needed for its accomplishment."[1]

Commentators are divided on whether the next event took place behind closed doors between the 11 disciples or before the entire 120 followers of Jesus that had gathered. In any case, Peter outlined the criteria for a replacement disciple. The man to be chosen must have been with the disciples throughout the life and ministry of Jesus, from His baptism in the Jordan River by John the Baptist to the day He ascended to heaven from the Mount of Olives. Peter was asking for someone who had witnessed the miracles of Jesus with his own eyes, heard the teachings of Christ with his own ears, and believed that Jesus was the Son of man with his whole heart. Only one with these qualifications could tell others what he had seen, heard, and believed.

Only two men met the requirements. Again, commentators disagree on the phrase "they appointed two" (Acts 1:23, KJV). The Greek *estesan duo* may be translated either as "they set two forward" or "two stood." If the first meaning is accepted, the disciples nominated the men. If the second is to be believed, these men were present and stood, indicating they met the requirements as set forth by Peter. Now the disciples prayed for guidance, and they cast lots. The lot fell upon Matthias, and he was numbered with the disciples.

The true disciple of Jesus will have an intimate relationship with the Master.

---

1. Francis D. Nichol, ed., *The Seventh-day Adventist Bible Commentary*, vol. 6 (Washington, DC: Review and Herald®, 1957), 130.

Casting Lots

And they cast their lots, and the lot fell on Matthias.

—Acts 1:26

It seems curious to us today that the apostles would have resorted to what we would call a game of chance in the selection of Matthias. It becomes evident from the scriptural account that the disciples, leading with prayer, expected the Lord to choose the replacement, and Peter's suggestion to use lots was not challenged. The casting of lots certainly had precedent in the Bible. Three of the most common cases were those in which the two goats for the Day of Atonement were selected (Leviticus 16:5–10), the land known as Palestine was apportioned to the various tribes originally (Numbers 26:55; Joshua 18:10), and the land was assigned by lot again after the Captivity (Nehemiah 10:34; 11:1). Repeatedly in the history of Israel, we see lots being cast: "in settling criminal cases where there was uncertainty (Joshua 7:14, 18; 1 Sam. 14:41, 42); . . . in choosing forces for battle (Judges 20:8–10); . . . in appointing to high office (1 Sam. 10:19–21); and . . . in allotting the cities of the priests and Levites (1 Chron. 6:54–65). The method is seen in operation in 1 Chron. 24–26. The Lord was understood to have the final dispensing of lots (Prov. 16:33). Soldiers cast lots on Calvary for the Lord's seamless garment (Matt. 27:35; . . . John 19:23, 24). But the choice of Matthias by lot is the only recorded instance among Christians in the NT [New Testament]."[1]

Ellen White counsels that the casting of lots is no longer an acceptable method of determining the desires of the Lord. "Let none be led from the sound, sensible principles that God has laid down for the guidance of His people, to depend for direction on any such device as the tossing up of a coin. Such a course is well pleasing to the enemy of souls; for he works to control the coin, and through its agency works out his plans. Let none be so easily deceived as to place confidence in any such tests. . . .

"The Lord works in no haphazard way. . . .

"I have no faith in casting lots. . . . To cast lots for the officers of the church is not in God's order."[2] Following Pentecost, "the direct guidance of the Holy Spirit made the casting of lots superfluous (Acts 5:3; 11:15–18; 13:2; 16:6–9)."[3]

Do you want to discern God's will? Study your Bible, pray for guidance, and then move forward.

1. Francis D. Nichol, ed., *The Seventh-day Adventist Bible Commentary*, vol. 6 (Washington, DC: Review and Herald®, 1957), 131.

2. "Ellen G. White Comments—Acts," in Nichol, *Seventh-day Adventist Bible Commentary*, vol. 6, 1054.

3. Nichol, *Seventh-day Adventist Bible Commentary*, vol. 6, 131.

Pentecost—
Celebrating the Harvest

When the Day of Pentecost had fully come, they were all with one accord in one place.
—Acts 2:1

The Greek word *Pentecost* was used for the Feast of Weeks as early as 120 BC. For almost two centuries, Pentecost was the accepted term for this celebration of the wheat harvest. "Each aspect of the old Feast of Weeks presented a symbolic meaning that made it typical of the work now about to be accomplished. As the Feast of First Fruits, it was fitting that it should be the occasion of the first great gathering from the fields that were 'white already to harvest' (Ex. 23:16; John 4:35). At this feast the Israelites, remembering that they had been slaves in Egypt, could feel again the liberty the Exodus had given them (Deut. 16:9–12), and be free of servile work (Lev. 23:21)."[1] Pentecost was a national holiday. No one was expected to work. Entire families were expected to participate, including foreigners. By rabbinical decree, Palestinian Jews were allowed one day for celebration while Jews of the Dispersion were given two days for the feast. "It was therefore a fit time for the outpouring of the Spirit of God; and 'where the Spirit of the Lord is, there is liberty' (2 Cor. 3:17)."[2]

"It is interesting to recall that the rabbis, who computed the interval between the first Passover and the giving of the law on Sinai, concluded that God spoke the law to the people (Ex. 20:1) on the day that was later observed as Pentecost. Through this tradition, the feast is thought to have acquired a commemorative character."[3] "Christ arose from the dead as the first fruits of those that slept. He was the antitype of the wave sheaf, and His resurrection took place on the very day when the wave sheaf was to be presented to the Lord. . . . The sheaf dedicated to God represented the harvest. So Christ the first fruits represented the great spiritual harvest to be gathered for the kingdom of God. His resurrection is the type and pledge of the resurrection of all the righteous dead. 'For if we believe that Jesus died and rose again, even so them also which sleep in Jesus will God bring with him.' 1 Thessalonians 4:14."[4]

Fifty days after the Exodus from Egypt, God gave Israel His commandments at Sinai. Fifty days after Jesus gave us an exodus from sin by His death and resurrection, God gave the early church His Spirit at Jerusalem.

---

1. Francis D. Nichol, ed., *The Seventh-day Adventist Bible Commentary*, vol. 6 (Washington, DC: Review and Herald®, 1957), 134.
2. Nichol, *Seventh-day Adventist Bible Commentary*, vol. 6, 134.
3. Nichol, *Seventh-day Adventist Bible Commentary*, vol. 6, 134.
4. Ellen G. White, *The Desire of Ages* (Mountain View, CA: Pacific Press®, 1940), 785, 786.

Judeo-Christians

And there were dwelling in Jerusalem Jews, devout men, from every nation under heaven.
—Acts 2:5

Jesus ascended to heaven forty days after His Passover resurrection. The festival of the wheat harvest—called the Feast of First Fruits, the Feast of Harvest, the Feast of Weeks, and in New Testament times, the Pentecost (Greek: "fiftieth")—was celebrated on the fiftieth day after Passover. "It was a one-day festival, one of the annual ceremonial Sabbaths (Lev 23:21)."[1] "This was one of the 3 festivals at which all Hebrew men were required to 'appear before the Lord' (Ex 23:17)."[2] "Pentecost, of all feasts of the Jewish year, attracted the largest number of pilgrims from distant lands. The dangers of travel by sea and land in the early spring and late autumn (see Acts 27:9) prevented the coming of people from abroad in any large numbers to the Passover or to the Feast of Tabernacles. But the Pentecostal season was favorable, and at no other feast would there have been present at Jerusalem representatives of so many nations. There was no other time in which the gift of the Spirit was likely to produce such direct, immediate, and far-reaching effects."[3]

Jesus told His followers to begin their witness in Jerusalem. Here, in the center of the greatest hostility toward their Master and themselves, they were to stand up boldly for their Lord and His message. Imagine the turmoil that existed within Judaism (the accepted church) as Christianity exploded onto the scene. As fearful as the disciples were, they still mingled in the temple with the Pentecostal pilgrims. Strange though it seems, the priests did not ban them from the temple. "It must be remembered that the Temple courts were open to all Israelites who did not disturb its peace, partly, perhaps, because there were those in the Sanhedrin, such as Nicodemus, Joseph of Arimathaea, and Gamaliel, who were on the borderline of belief. . . . As for the disciples, they did not think of their religion as a defection from Judaism, but rather as the fulfillment of it. The Christians therefore worshiped with their Jewish blood brothers (Acts 3:1), not only from habit and desire, but also in the hope of seeing them won to the gospel."[4]

Often we are called to witness for the cause of Christ before those who are the guardians of established religion. Your gold standard should always be "Thus saith the Lord."

---

1. Siegfried H. Horn, *Seventh-day Adventist Bible Dictionary*, ed. Don F. Neufeld, Commentary Reference Series, vol. 8 (Washington, DC: Review and Herald®, 1960), s.v. "Pentecost."
2. Horn, *Seventh-day Adventist Bible Dictionary*, s.v. "Pentecost."
3. Francis D. Nichol, ed., *The Seventh-day Adventist Bible Commentary*, vol. 6 (Washington, DC: Review and Herald®, 1957), 134.
4. Nichol, *Seventh-day Adventist Bible Commentary*, vol. 6, 150.

The Spirit Descends

And they were all filled with the Holy Spirit and began to speak with other tongues.
—Acts 2:4

Without warning, there was a sensation of divine breathing in the room where the disciples had gathered. "Luke may have chosen *pnoē* [the Greek word for *wind*] here as describing the supernatural 'breathing' that the disciples were about to experience, and that must have recalled to them their sensations when the Lord 'breathed on them,' and said, 'Receive ye the Holy Ghost' (John 20:22). Now once more they felt the divine impact of the awe-inspiring, divine 'breathing.' "[1] The disciples, men and *women* alike, heard the audible sound and witnessed the visual sign of the coming of the Spirit. An initial body of fire descended and, dividing into many small tongues of flame, settled upon each individual present. Here was the fulfillment of the prophecy of John the Baptist when he announced that he baptized with water but that Christ would baptize with the "Holy Ghost, and with fire" (Matthew 3:11, KJV).

"Even though the fiery-appearing tongues remained upon the believers for only a brief time, the effects of the visitation lasted for the lifetime of the faithful Christians who received the Spirit."[2] We know men and *women* were equally gifted because Peter later referred to the prophecy of Joel (Joel 2:28) to explain the event to those in the Pentecostal crowds. All disciples present were filled with the Spirit. This had not been a casual wind that swept through the room and left. Immediately, these men and women began to speak in tongues. The gift of speaking in tongues was not gibberish as some today define the gift. This was a reversal of Babel!

"Every known tongue was represented by those assembled [for Pentecost]. This diversity of languages would have been a great hindrance to the proclamation of the gospel. . . . The Holy Spirit did for them that which they could not have accomplished for themselves in a lifetime. They could now proclaim the truths of the gospel abroad, speaking with accuracy the languages of those for whom they were laboring. . . . From this time forth the language of the disciples was pure, simple, and accurate, whether they spoke in their native tongue or in a foreign language."[3] At that moment, an international, multilinguistic Christian church was born.

Let us pray that the next outpouring of the Holy Spirit, the prophetic latter rain, will descend soon so we might once again set the world on fire!

---

1. Francis D. Nichol, ed., *The Seventh-day Adventist Bible Commentary*, vol. 6 (Washington, DC: Review and Herald®, 1957), 135.
2. Nichol, *Seventh-day Adventist Bible Commentary*, vol. 6, 137.
3. Ellen G. White, *The Acts of the Apostles* (Mountain View, CA: Pacific Press®, 1911), 39, 40.

Lines Are Drawn

Others mocking said, "They are full of new wine."

—Acts 2:13

The Feast of Weeks called Jews from other countries to worship at the temple. Many spoke only the language of their birth. It was from Jerusalem, the springboard for the gospel, that word of Jesus was to spread into new territories. "And when this sound occurred [the windy descent of the Holy Spirit], the multitude came together, and were confused, because everyone heard them speak in his own language. Then they were all amazed and marveled, saying to one another, 'Look, are not all these who speak Galileans? And how is it that we hear, each in our own language in which we were born?'" (Acts 2:6–8). The languages represented in the crowd were Persian, Elamite, Aramaic, Lycaonian, and various dialects of Greek and Coptic, among others. Imagine the surprise of the priests and native residents of Jerusalem when they heard the simple, unlearned fishermen who had followed Jesus of Nazareth speaking proficiently in these various languages. A false rumor was quickly circulated by the priests that the disciples were drunk; this explained why they were so excited and spoke in what appeared as gibberish to the locals. The priests were experts at adapting disinformation to control opinion.

In a long discourse covered in Acts 2:14–40, Peter refutes the allegation of public drunkenness. "The scene is one full of interest. Behold the people coming from all directions to hear the disciples witness to the truth as it is in Jesus. They press in, crowding the temple. Priests and rulers are there, the dark scowl of malignity still on their faces, their hearts still filled with abiding hatred against Christ, their hands uncleansed from the blood shed when they crucified the world's Redeemer. They had thought to find the apostles cowed with fear under the strong hand of oppression and murder, but they find them lifted above all fear and filled with the Spirit, proclaiming with power the divinity of Jesus of Nazareth. They hear them declaring with boldness that the One so recently humiliated, derided, smitten by cruel hands, and crucified, is the Prince of life, now exalted to the right hand of God."[1]

When we are called to defend our faith, the truth spoken with conviction and feeling allows the Holy Spirit to drive home the message.

---

1. Ellen G. White, *The Acts of the Apostles* (Mountain View, CA: Pacific Press®, 1911), 42.

Repent and Be Baptized

Then Peter said to them, "Repent, and let every one of you be baptized in the name of Jesus Christ for the remission of sins; and you shall receive the gift of the Holy Spirit."
—Acts 2:38

The disciples now possessed a crucial tool needed to spread the gospel. As Peter talked, the disciples translated his words into the languages of those in the crowd. "Some of those who listened to the apostles had taken an active part in the condemnation and death of Christ. Their voices had mingled with the rabble in calling for His crucifixion. . . .

"Now they heard the disciples declaring that it was the Son of God who had been crucified. Priests and rulers trembled. Conviction and anguish seized the people. . . .

"Peter urged home upon the convicted people the fact that they had rejected Christ because they had been deceived by priests and rulers; and that if they continued to look to these men for counsel, and waited for them to acknowledge Christ before they dared to do so, they would never accept Him."[1] "In Jerusalem, the stronghold of Judaism, thousands openly declared their faith in Jesus of Nazareth as the Messiah."[2]

The people were pierced to their hearts with conviction, and in anguish, they cried out, "Men and brethren, what shall we do?" (Acts 2:37). Today's text promises the Holy Spirit as a personal gift to all who believe. We, too, may receive the Holy Spirit. "Note the steps in the blessed experience of becoming a Christian, as outlined in this verse [38]: (1) repentance, (2) baptism, (3) remission of sin, (4) reception of the Holy Spirit."[3] What was accomplished on the Day of Pentecost? The Holy Spirit moved upon those hearing Peter speak of Christ and His mission. "The seed had been sown by the greatest Teacher the world had ever known. For three and a half years the Son of God had sojourned in the land of Judea, proclaiming the message of the gospel of truth and working with mighty signs and wonders. The seed had been sown, and after His ascension the great ingathering took place. *More were converted by one sermon on the day of Pentecost than were converted during all the years of Christ's ministry.* So mightily will God work when men give themselves to the control of the Spirit."[4]

"If the fulfillment of the promise is not seen as it might be, it is because the promise is not appreciated as it should be. If all were willing, all would be filled with the Spirit."[5]

---

1. Ellen G. White, *The Acts of the Apostles* (Mountain View, CA: Pacific Press®, 1911), 42, 43.

2. White, *Acts of the Apostles*, 44.

3. Francis D. Nichol, ed., *The Seventh-day Adventist Bible Commentary*, vol. 6 (Washington, DC: Review and Herald®, 1957), 148.

4. Ellen G. White, MS 85, 1903; emphasis added.

5. White, *Acts of the Apostles*, 50.

The Spark

"However, when He, the Spirit of truth, has come,
He will guide you into all truth. . . . He will glorify Me."

—John 16:13, 14

I t is not a conclusive evidence that a man is a Christian because he manifests spiritual ecstasy under extraordinary circumstances. Holiness is not rapture: it is an entire surrender of the will to God; it is living by every word that proceeds from the mouth of God; it is doing the will of our heavenly Father; it is trusting God in trial, in darkness as well as in the light; it is walking by faith and not by sight; it is relying on God with unquestioning confidence, and resting in His love."[1] Slowly, the Spirit works upon the Christian's heart. The affections are drawn from the earth, and there is an intense desire to be like Christ. As light is shed upon the Word, men and women share their understanding with others, and the power of the Spirit spreads. The words of Jesus—"Let your light so shine before men, that they may see your good works and glorify your Father in heaven" (Matthew 5:16)—take on new meaning when one considers that the Spirit was manifest to the disciples as tongues of firelight. The fire that is kindled by Christ through the Spirit is that which activates all who do His service.

"But near the close of earth's harvest, a special bestowal of spiritual grace is promised to prepare the church for the coming of the Son of man. This outpouring of the Spirit is likened to the falling of the latter rain; and it is for this added power that Christians are to send their petitions to the Lord of the harvest 'in the time of the latter rain.' "[2] There is danger in waiting until one believes the time of the latter rain is near. We must let our lights burn brightly now and not neglect present tasks.

Do you want the Spirit? We are to copy the life of Christ. "His own example is an assurance that earnest, persevering supplication to God in faith—faith that leads to entire dependence upon God, and unreserved consecration to His work—will avail to bring to men the Holy Spirit's aid in the battle against sin."[3] The prayer offered in faith, placing your entire trust in God, offering yourself to His work, is key in forming the partnership!

It takes only a small spark to start a fire. Catch His Spirit, and ignite the world!

---

1. Ellen G. White, *The Acts of the Apostles* (Mountain View, CA: Pacific Press®, 1911), 51.
2. White, *Acts of the Apostles*, 55.
3. White, *Acts of the Apostles*, 56.

$120 \times 25 = 3{,}000$

Then those who gladly received his word were baptized;
and that day about three thousand souls were added to them.

—Acts 2:41

A cts 2 presents a Peter who is entirely different from the one seen in Luke 22. The denial of his Lord and the compassionate look of the Master had broken his heart. The disciple found himself drawn to Gethsemane. Devastated, he had "prostrated himself where he had seen his Saviour's prostrate form. He remembered with remorse that he was asleep when Jesus prayed during those fearful hours. His proud heart broke, and penitential tears moistened the sod so recently stained with the bloody sweat-drops of God's dear Son. He left the garden a converted man."[1] "Some assert that if a soul stumbles and falls, he can never regain his position; but the case before us contradicts this. Before his denial, Christ said to Peter, 'When thou art converted, strengthen thy brethren.' In committing to his stewardship the souls for whom He had given His life, Christ gave to Peter the strongest evidence of His confidence in his restoration. And he was commissioned to feed not only the sheep, but the lambs,—a broader and more delicate work than had hitherto been appointed him. Not only was he to hold forth the word of life to others, but he was to be a shepherd of the flock."[2] "Before Peter's feet slipped, he had not the spirit of meekness required to feed the lambs; but after he became sensible of his own weakness, he knew just how to teach the erring and fallen; he could come close to their side in tender sympathy, and could help them."[3]

Peter finally understood God's purpose in sending His Son to die for sinful humanity. Boldly, he spoke of the deity of Christ. While the other apostles stood by in support (Acts 2:37), Peter drew the multitude close in sympathy with the cause of Christ. Peter urged them to repent—the very message that Christ had commanded be preached (Luke 24:47). Three thousand came forward to be baptized in the ceremonial purification pools outside the temple gates. Imagine! Twenty-five precious souls were baptized for each of the 120 who received the Spirit in the upper room. Josephus has estimated the number of Pharisees in *all* Palestine to be nearly six thousand. Three thousand Jerusalem converts to Jesus was extraordinary!

"For the daily baptism of the Spirit every worker should offer his petition to God."[4]

---

1. Ellen G. White, "Peter's Fall," *Signs of the Times*, November 11, 1897, 3.

2. Ellen G. White, "Peter's Fall and Restoration—No. 2," *Youth's Instructor*, December 22, 1898.

3. Ellen G. White, *Historical Sketches of the Foreign Missions of Seventh-day Adventists* (Basle: Imprimerie Polyglotte, 1886), 121.

4. Ellen G. White, *The Acts of the Apostles* (Mountain View, CA: Pacific Press®, 1911), 50.

The Early Church

And they continued steadfastly in the apostle's doctrine and fellowship,
in the breaking of bread, and in prayers.

—Acts 2:42

The baptized converts possibly remained in Jerusalem and fellowshiped with the apostles and local believers. "Because of the largeness of this number [three thousand souls (Acts 2:31)] it has been urged that the baptism was by pouring or sprinkling, not immersion. Such an assumption is not necessary (see . . . Matt. 3:6). There were adequate supplies of water in and near Jerusalem to provide for the baptism of large numbers of persons, such as the pools at Bethesda (. . . John 5:2) and Siloam (. . . John 9:7), and the pools of Solomon. Furthermore, it need not be thought that the administration of the rite was necessarily confined to the Twelve. Succeeding chapters show that many converts were made from among the Hellenistic Jews who were present at the feast (Acts 6:1) and that few if any of the converts were yet of the local ruling class. . . . Some of these converts went back to the cities whence they had come, and may have been the now unknown founders of the churches in such places as Damascus, Alexandria, or Rome itself."[1] It must be remembered that these new Christians still believed themselves to be devout Jews, worshiping in the temple and observing the feasts to the Lord.

At this stage, the early church had no established tenets, but rather, the term *doctrines* (used in today's verse) may be defined as "teachings." Further lessons were given the new converts regarding the life and teachings of Jesus Christ. Discussions were held with the apostles, and a brotherhood was developed whereby new converts became trusting members of the family of God. Communal meals were shared, in addition to the Lord's Supper. Prayers for each other and for the infant church were offered, and new believers drew strength from fellowshiping with one another. These believers celebrated their connection with Christ in five distinct ways: (1) they listened to the teachings of the apostles (Acts 2:42), (2) they shared meals (verses 42, 46), (3) they prayed for each other and praised God (verses 42, 47), (4) they shared their possessions in a spirit of generosity and benevolence (verses 44, 45), and (5) they cared for the needs of one another (verse 45). Such a united church should be every Christian's goal.

How does your local church measure up to the five criteria of the early apostolic church?

---

1. Francis D. Nichol, ed., *The Seventh-day Adventist Bible Commentary*, vol. 6 (Washington, DC: Review and Herald®, 1957), 148.

At the Temple Gate

Then Peter said, "Silver and gold I do not have, but what I do have I give you: In the name of Jesus Christ of Nazareth, rise up and walk."

—Acts 3:6

I t is three o'clock in the afternoon and time for the evening sacrifice. Peter and John are attending the worship service together. Passing through what some scholars believe to be the Nicanor Gate, or Beautiful Gate, leading from the Court of the Gentiles to the Court of the Women, they saw "a cripple, forty years of age, whose life, from his birth, had been one of pain and infirmity. This unfortunate man had desired to see Jesus, that he might be healed; but he was almost helpless, and was far removed from the scene of the great Physician's labors. His pleadings at last induced some friends to bear him to the gate of the temple, but upon arriving there, he found that the One upon whom his hopes were centered, had been put to a cruel death."[1] Friends continued to bring the man to the temple on a daily basis so that he might beg alms from those coming to worship and thus earn a meager living. Judaism stressed charity, and those donating were highly regarded. Seeing Peter and John pass by, the man asked them for a small donation.

Peter and John stopped and looked down at the cripple. Drawing the man's attention to them, Peter said, "Look at us" (Acts 3:5). The cripple, thinking to receive some money from the two men, gazed up at them. Peter now shattered the man's hopes, saying, "Silver and gold I do not have." The man was crestfallen. But Peter was not through. "But what I do have I give you: In the name of Jesus Christ of Nazareth, rise up and walk" (verse 6). Taking the man by his right hand, Peter raised him up to stand for the first time in forty years on ankles that now were strong and straight. The man instantly came alive, jumping and leaping, shouting praises to God. Stepping outside the courtyards so as not to disturb the prayers, a crowd gathered on Solomon's Porch overlooking the Kidron Valley on the eastern side of the outer court. *The Acts of the Apostles* tells us, "The lame man which was healed held Peter and John."[2] I imagine there was a great deal of rejoicing and hugging going on by all involved. But a crowd was gathering, and with it, a storm of controversy was about to descend upon the shepherds of the little flock of believers.

One gift the Spirit bestows is healing (1 Corinthians 12:9). Oh Lord, help us to believe!

---

1. Ellen G. White, *The Acts of the Apostles* (Mountain View, CA: Pacific Press®, 1911), 57, 58.
2. White, *Acts of the Apostles*, 58.

An Accusation Against the Jews 1

"But you denied the Holy One and the Just, and asked for a murderer to be granted to you, and killed the Prince of life, whom God raised from the dead, of which we are witnesses."
—Acts 3:14, 15

S eeing that the people were amazed by the healing of the crippled man, Peter addressed them and asked, "Men of Israel, why do you marvel at this? Or why look so intently at us, as though by our own power or godliness we had made this man walk? The God of Abraham, Isaac, and Jacob, the God of our fathers, glorified His servant Jesus, whom you delivered up and denied in the presence of Pilate, when he was determined to let Him go. But you denied the Holy One and the Just, and asked for a murderer to be granted to you, and killed the Prince of life, whom God raised from the dead, of which we are witnesses. And His name, through faith in His name, has made this man strong, whom you see and know. Yes, the faith which comes through Him has given him this perfect soundness in the presence of you all" (Acts 3:12–16).

Speaking within the temple grounds, Peter plainly affixed responsibility for the death of Jesus upon the people, their priests, and rulers. Many were aware of the trial, the release of the murderer Barabbas, and the crucifixion of Jesus. Many had believed the rumors, circulated by the priests, that the disciples had stolen the body of their Lord while the Roman guard slept. Now they were being told that God the Father had raised up His Son, the true Messiah. The light slowly dawned upon those who had listened to the words of Christ, and now the Spirit flashed conviction upon their hearts and minds. Jesus of Nazareth was the great I AM. He was the Messiah, the Christ, the Anointed One, the Son of the Living God, the Promised One of Israel, and they had had Him put to death. What must they do now?

"The apostles spoke plainly of the great sin of the Jews in rejecting and putting to death the Prince of life; but they were careful not to drive their hearers to despair."[1] There was still hope through faith in the name of Jesus, just as the crippled man was healed by faith in that precious name. To this theme Peter would repeatedly return during his preaching.

"Neither is there salvation in any other: for there is none other name under heaven given among men, whereby we must be saved" (Acts 4:12, KJV).

---

1. Ellen G. White, *The Acts of the Apostles* (Mountain View, CA: Pacific Press®, 1911), 59.

An Accusation Against the Jews 2

"Yet now, brethren, I know that you did it in ignorance, as did also your rulers. But those things which God foretold . . . , that the Christ would suffer, He has thus fulfilled."
—Acts 3:17, 18

I gnorance did not excuse the actions of the people. "The statement is made that had they known that He was the Prince of life, they would not have crucified Him. But why did they not know? Because they chose not to know. They had no interest to search and study, and their ignorance proved their eternal ruin. They had had the strongest evidence on which to base their faith, and they were under obligation to God to accept the evidence He had given them. Their unbelief made them guilty of the blood of the only begotten Son of the infinite God."[1] "The purpose of all Scripture is to set forth the plan for the salvation of men through Christ's redemptive suffering."[2]

Once the true plight of the Jews was understood, the call was for them to repent of their sinful behavior (Acts 3:19). Repentance leads to conversion. First, one stands condemned and realizes his or her guilt. Second, the individual experiences remorse and turns away from sinful actions. This turning away is termed *conversion.* "Conversion is the basis of a genuine Christian experience. It is distinguished from the new birth (John 3:3, 5) only in that it may be considered as the act of man in turning away from his old life of sin, while the new birth, or regeneration, is the work of the Holy Spirit acting upon man simultaneously with his turning. Neither phase of the experience can be a reality without the Holy Spirit."[3]

Peter reemphasized that the gospel had been given to the children of the prophets, the heirs of the covenant between God and Abraham (Acts 3:25). "This precedence of the Jew as recipient of the gospel is noteworthy. Peter did not as yet know the conditions under which the gospel was to be preached to the heathen, but his words imply a distinct understanding that the message was to go first to the Jews. This sequence was also used by Paul: 'To the Jew first, and also to the Greek' (Rom. 1:16; cf. ch. 2:9, 10)."[4]

Christ said we must be born again. Essentially, we must repent, turn from our sinful habits, and accept the Holy Spirit's guidance in softening and changing our lives to mirror Christ's!

---

1. Ellen G. White, MS 9, 1898.
2. Francis D. Nichol, ed., *The Seventh-day Adventist Bible Commentary*, vol. 6 (Washington, DC: Review and Herald®, 1957), 157.
3. Nichol, *Seventh-day Adventist Bible Commentary*, vol. 6, 158.
4. Nichol, *Seventh-day Adventist Bible Commentary*, vol. 6, 161.

Peter and John Arrested

The priests, the captain of the temple, and the Sadducees came upon them, being greatly disturbed that they taught the people and preached in Jesus the resurrection from the dead.
—Acts 4:1, 2

While Peter and John talked openly of Jesus with worshipers, the priests, Saddu-cees, and the captain of the temple moved into the crowd to quell the distur-bance of evening prayers. Only weeks had passed since the crucifixion of Jesus, and these men had hoped the infant movement would die without a leader. For the first time since the reported resurrection, these men met Christianity, and they were not pleased with what they heard.

Two different captains of the temple are mentioned in Jewish writings. "The *'ish har habbayith*, the 'officer of the temple mount.' . . . This man was not of the soldiery, but had supervision of the guard of priests and Levites who had custody of the Temple, especially at night. As an inspector he made his nightly rounds, visiting all the gates and rousing any slumberers. . . . Another official who more probably is to be identified with the 'captain' in the present passage, was the *segan hakkohanim*, the 'prefect of the priests.' He ranked next to the high priest, assisted him in his official functions, and had general responsibility for the Temple services and the maintenance of order throughout the Temple area." [1]

"The Sadducees are not mentioned frequently in the gospel story. In [Acts] 23:8 they are described as saying, 'that there is no resurrection, neither angel, nor spirit.'

"When they now found His disciples preaching the resurrection, the Sadducees reacted to them as they had to the Lord Himself and became persecutors of the church. There is no record in the NT [New Testament] of any Sadducee accepting the gospel. Not so with the Pharisees, some of whom professed themselves believers." [2] Pharisees were the "doctors of the law" and theologians—self-proclaimed spiritual guides for the nation. While the Pharisees believed in angels, a resurrection, and retribution during a future judgment for those who did evil, they tended to take exception to anyone teaching without training from them or authorization by them to do so. These men had opposed John the Baptist (John 1:19) and Jesus (John 2:18; 7:14, 15), asking both by what authority they taught. Each group had reason to be annoyed with Peter and John's message.

Hearing the gospel brings either conviction and repentance or rejection and hostility.

---

1. Francis D. Nichol, ed., *The Seventh-day Adventist Bible Commentary*, vol. 6 (Washington, DC: Review and Herald®, 1957), 163, 164.
2. Nichol, *Seventh-day Adventist Bible Commentary*, vol. 6, 164.

Trial Before the Sanhedrin

*"Nor is there salvation in any other, for there is no other
name under heaven given among men by which we must be saved."*

—Acts 4:12

The lame man was healed at three o'clock in the afternoon. Jewish law forbade sitting in judgment after eventide, the twelfth hour (six o'clock in the evening). The disciples were therefore held for an early morning trial before the Sanhedrin. Jesus had not been afforded the same legal right. Only weeks before, these very men had convened His illegal night trial. The next morning the seventy members, plus the high priest, took their seats in the semicircular Court of Israel. Peter and John were led in and placed in the center of the august body. "In that very room and before some of those very men, Peter had shamefully denied his Lord. This came distinctly to his mind as he appeared for his own trial. He now had an opportunity of redeeming his cowardice."[1] The question was put to them, "By what power or by what name have you done this?" (Acts 4:7). Here was the opening for which Peter had waited. He would never again deny his Lord. "If we this day are judged for a good deed done to a helpless man, by what means he has been made well, let it be known to you all, and to all the people of Israel, that by the name of Jesus Christ of Nazareth, whom you crucified, whom God raised from the dead, by Him this man stands here before you" (verses 9, 10). Bold words indeed from a supposed coward! The Jewish leaders of the Sanhedrin were appalled at such a courageous defense. They could hardly deny a miracle had taken place. The news had spread throughout Jerusalem, and the healed man stood beside the disciples as a convincing witness.

The disciples were escorted out while the alarmed council deliberated. The Sanhedrin needed to stop all references to Jesus and His resurrection and to stifle all claims that He was the Messiah. Killing the disciples would cause people to riot against the priests and confirm stories of their secret plot that had Jesus crucified. The healing of the lame man was a miracle. A good deed must not be punished. Summoning the disciples, the council threatened them. They must cease speaking and teaching in the name of Jesus at once. Unfazed, Peter gave a classic answer:

"Whether it is right in the sight of God to listen to you more than to God, you judge. For we cannot but speak the things which we have seen and heard" (verses 19, 20).

---

1. Ellen G. White, *The Acts of the Apostles* (Mountain View, CA: Pacific Press®, 1911), 62.

A Praise Service

And being let go, they went to their own companions
and reported all that the chief priests and elders had said to them.

—Acts 4:23

T he apostles had no permanent meeting place. Sometimes they met in the upper
room, sometimes in the temple, sometimes in the homes of fellow believers. It
did not take Peter and John long to find the followers of Christ. Summing up the trial
before the Sanhedrin, they thanked the believers for their prayers. Aware of the priests'
and rulers' savagery directed against Jesus, the believers had prayed without ceasing
during the crisis. They feared Peter and John would be tortured or killed in a manner
similar to Jesus' crucifixion. Now they rejoiced in the salvation of the Lord. This is the
first biblical example of a corporate worship service.

The hymn of praise they chanted is interesting:

"Why did the nations rage,
And the people plot vain things?
The kings of the earth took their stand,
And the rulers were gathered together
Against the LORD and against His Christ"
(Acts 4:25, 26, quoting Psalm 2:1, 2).

The believers saw a parallel between the experience of King David, ready to fight
the enemies of Israel, and Jesus' dealings with His enemies. "For truly against Your holy
Servant Jesus, whom You anointed, both Herod and Pontius Pilate, with the Gentiles
and the people of Israel, were gathered together to do whatever Your hand and Your
purpose determined before to be done" (Acts 4:27, 28).

The believers realized that "even in their sin against the Son of God, the Jews and
Romans had helped to fulfill God's purpose for Christ in His work of salvation. A
divine will manifests itself in the government of the world, and the salvation of individual souls. This does not rule out man's free will. . . . Each man stands or falls by the
part he has taken in the unfolding plan of redemption. . . .

"The man who is surrendered to God works to accomplish His divine will."[1]

It is a comfort when one accepts that God has the whole world in His hands. Each day we have
the opportunity to assist Him, as instruments of His will, in the salvation of precious souls.

---

1. Francis D. Nichol, ed., *The Seventh-day Adventist Bible Commentary*, vol. 6 (Washington, DC: Review and Herald®,
1957), 171.

A Communal Church

Now the multitude of those who believed were of one heart and one soul; neither did anyone say that any of the things he possessed was his own, but they had all things in common.

—Acts 4:32

L uke now offers us a view of the early apostolic church that has confused some and mystified others. It would appear that the church suspended the rights of individuals to own property and forced members to sell assets or pool them. Many modern churches have patterned themselves after this benevolent model with results that have led to infighting, covetousness, competitiveness, and broken agreements. But is it an accurate portrayal of what was happening in the early Christian church? The early church was not setting up an economic system, but rather, believers responded to needs with an outpouring of compassion and generosity.

"Some of the new Christians were persons of substantial means. The genuineness of their brotherly love manifested itself in self-sacrifice for the welfare of their less fortunately situated brethren."[1] "Many of these early believers were immediately cut off from family and friends by the zealous bigotry of the Jews, and it was necessary to provide them with food and shelter."[2] The need was certainly present, yet not all believers possessed property or had the means to contribute. The emphasis was not on everyone being forced to divest himself of his property but rather upon the love expressed by those who could help the less fortunate believers. There was no thought of buying influence or position with the gifts donated to the apostles for the good of the members. There were no strings attached on how the monies should be used. There was no broadcasting by members of how much they had personally given for the relief of the widows. No donor names were affixed to pews or pulpits.

"Thus it will ever be when the Spirit of God takes possession of the life. Those whose hearts are filled with the love of Christ, will follow the example of Him who for our sake became poor, that through His poverty we might be made rich. Money, time, influence—all the gifts they have received from God's hand, they will value only as a means of advancing the work of the gospel."[3]

The motive for giving is judged by God as of more importance than the amount given.

---

1. Francis D. Nichol, ed., *The Seventh-day Adventist Bible Commentary*, vol. 6 (Washington, DC: Review and Herald®, 1957), 173.
2. Ellen G. White, *The Acts of the Apostles* (Mountain View, CA: Pacific Press®, 1911), 70.
3. White, *Acts of the Apostles*, 71.

Barnabas the Levite

And Joses, who was also named Barnabas . . . a Levite of the country of Cyprus, having land, sold it, and brought the money and laid it at the apostles' feet.

—Acts 4:36

L uke introduces his readers to Barnabas in the fourth chapter of Acts. We will not meet Saul, the man Barnabas will travel with on their first missionary tour, until the end of chapter 7. Barnabas was the name given to Joses of Cyprus. The name *Barnabas*, meaning "son of consolation" or "son of exhortation," was a perfect fit. Every time we see Barnabas in Scripture, he is either mentoring or encouraging others in the faith. Barnabas was a Christian others simply liked to be around. Kindly and generous, he always affirmed others. He never ascribed bad motives to their actions. He encouraged them to spread their wings and grow in Christ.

Barnabas was a Jew from the tribe of Levi. We do not know when he converted to Christianity. He may have heard the gospel preached in the temple while he was performing his priestly duties. He may have even heard Jesus speak on one of those occasions. "A tradition recorded by Clement of Alexandria (*The Stromata* ii. 20) lists Barnabas as one of the Seventy sent forth by Jesus (Luke 10:1)."[1] We do know Barnabas was a cousin of John Mark (Colossians 4:10) who lived in Jerusalem and that *Aunt Mary* (Mark's mother) was a believer (Acts 12:12). Most Levites did not own property but rather were supported by the tithes of the people (Numbers 18:20, 21). Such was not the case with Barnabas. Nothing kept a priest or Levite from purchasing or owning land. Jeremiah, another Levite, held land (Jeremiah 32:7–12). At any rate, Barnabas sold his land and brought the money to the apostles.

We will see Barnabas again as he defends and befriends Saul by urging the believers in Jerusalem to accept the former persecutor of the Christians (Acts 9:26, 27). He became a loyal friend to Saul, and being from Cyprus, he had a burning desire to share the message of salvation through Jesus Christ with his countrymen. It is safe to say that without the encouragement and support of Barnabas, Saul would have had a tough time making the contacts necessary to begin his ministry to the Gentiles.

Are you a son or daughter of exhortation? Real Christians do not tear others down but rather lift them up. Real Christians always look for good in fellow believers.

---

1. Francis D. Nichol, ed., *The Seventh-day Adventist Bible Commentary*, vol. 6 (Washington, DC: Review and Herald®, 1957), 174.

Ananias

But a certain man named Ananias, with Sapphira *his wife, sold a possession.*
—Acts 5:1; emphasis added

Among those in the upper room, when the Holy Spirit descended on the 120, were Ananias ("Jehovah is gracious") and *Sapphira* ("beautiful," "sapphire"). Feeling led by the Spirit, the two announced they would sell a piece of real estate and donate the proceeds to the church. But they soon regretted their announcement. This was a costly gift to offer to the cause of Christ. They wanted to keep the money. On the other hand, they coveted the spotlight of praise, for they saw that those who made donations to the poor of the church were held in high esteem. How could they obtain both? They got together and hatched a plan. They would pretend to give all the proceeds from the sale but hold back a large portion of it for themselves. On the surface, they remained generous supporters, but in reality, they lacked the open generosity Barnabas exhibited when he sold his land and brought the disciples his unselfish donation.

When Ananias came with his offering, Peter laid bare the deceit: "Why has Satan filled your heart to lie to the Holy Spirit and keep back part of the price of the land for yourself? While it remained, was it not your own? And after it was sold, was it not in your own control? Why have you conceived this thing in your heart? You have not lied to men but to God" (Acts 5:3, 4). Ananias was not required to give any fixed amount, for the money was his to deal with as he saw fit. His sin lay in bringing a part and saying that it was the whole. This was the lie and the sin.

Covetousness was the exact sin that led to the downfall of Achan during the conquest of the Promised Land. In a sense, Ananias's crime was similar to that of Gehazi (2 Kings 5:20–27), who lied to Naaman to receive payment for a master who wished none, for a healing he had not performed, to gain wealth he alone coveted. Upon hearing Peter expose him before the others (so much for the esteem he craved), Ananias fell down dead. The young men present wrapped him in his robe, took him outside the city walls, and buried him.

"No legal note or bond is more obligatory than a pledge made to the cause of God."[1]

---

1. Ellen G. White, "The Sin of Ananias," *Advent Review and Sabbath Herald*, May 23, 1893, 1.

Sapphira

And Peter answered her, "Tell me whether you sold the land for so much?"

—Acts 5:8

Sapphira waited for her husband to return home, and when three hours had passed, and he did not, she went looking for him. It is interesting that Sapphira was included in the discussion of finances and that her consent was required to sell the property. Most women of this era held few if any legal powers; however, in this case, she was aware of the deception and agreed to it. Here is a dilemma and a lesson for those who shield the sin(s) of a spouse just to keep up appearances before the church or the public. Peter asked Sapphira to confirm the sale price that Ananias had announced. "Peter's forthright question might have warned Sapphira that their scheme was known, but she maintained the lie upon which she and her husband had agreed. She answered glibly, 'Yea, for so much.' "[1] When she spoke these words, Peter said to her, "How is it that you have agreed together to test the Spirit of the Lord? Look, the feet of those who have buried your husband are at the door, and they will carry you out" (Acts 5:9). The outwardly beautiful but inwardly perverse Sapphira died instantly. As a result of these deaths, a new respect for the inviolability of God was gained. "Let truth telling be held with no loose hand or uncertain grasp. Let it become a part of the life. Playing fast and loose with truth, and dissembling to suit one's own selfish plans, means shipwreck of faith."[2] (See Revelation 21:27.)

"God has made the proclamation of the gospel dependent upon the labors and the gifts of His people. Voluntary offerings and the tithe constitute the revenue of the Lord's work. Of the means entrusted to man, God claims a certain portion,—the tenth. He leaves all free to say whether or not they will give more than this. But when the heart is stirred by the influence of the Holy Spirit, and a vow is made to give a certain amount, the one who vows has no longer any right to the consecrated portion. Promises of this kind made to men would be looked upon as binding; are those not more binding that are made to God? Are promises tried in the court of conscience less binding than written agreements of men?"[3]

"Lying lips are an abomination to the LORD" (Proverbs 12:33; see also Proverbs 6:16, 17; 19:9; James 3:3–12)!

---

1. Francis D. Nichol, ed., *The Seventh-day Adventist Bible Commentary*, vol. 6 (Washington, DC: Review and Herald®, 1957), 178.

2. Ellen G. White, *The Acts of the Apostles* (Mountain View, CA: Pacific Press®, 1911), 76.

3. White, *Acts of the Apostles,* 74.

On Solomon's Porch

And they were all with one accord in Solomon's Porch.
Yet none of the rest dared join them, but the people esteemed them highly.
—Acts 5:12, 13

In Jerusalem, where the deepest prejudice existed, and where the most confused ideas prevailed in regard to Him who had been crucified as a malefactor, the disciples continued to speak with boldness the words of life, setting before the Jews the work and mission of Christ, His crucifixion, resurrection, and ascension. Priests and rulers heard with amazement the clear, bold testimony of the apostles. The power of the risen Saviour had indeed fallen on the disciples, and their work was accompanied by signs and miracles that daily increased the number of believers."[1]

In public places, such as the portico in the temple, during the normal hours of prayer, the disciples laid their hands upon the sick, and healing occurred. The promise had been given that the followers of Jesus "will lay hands on the sick, and they will recover" (Mark 16:18). Here was the literal fulfillment of that promise. Many brought beds and couches and laid them in the path of the disciples so that the shadow of these men might fall upon the sick, and by faith in the Lord, the sick might be healed. One cannot but be reminded of the woman who sought to simply touch the hem of Jesus' garment that she might be healed. The message and miracles of Christ were again brought to the memories of the residents of Jerusalem.

In verse 11 of Acts 5, we see the first use of the term *church*. Apparently, by this time, the small community of believers in Jerusalem had organized themselves into a church. By verse 13, we see the beginnings of the split that will tear Judaism and, indeed, the world apart. While many of the people esteemed the followers of Jesus, there were likewise many who chose not to join them. The priests and rulers were in the latter group, as well as those who feared the power of their religious leaders. The Sanhedrin's conflict with Christ had always been about power. The priests and rulers had no intention of allowing these men who preached Jesus Christ as the Messiah to gain in popularity. Christ's disciples now were so bold as to denounce the priests and carry their ministry into the temple itself! Such brazen behavior could not go unchallenged!

Scriptural truth threatens dogma. Doctrinal differences still define and divide churches.

---

1. Ellen G. White, *The Acts of the Apostles* (Mountain View, CA: Pacific Press®, 1911), 77, 78.

Arrested Again

Then the high priest rose up, and all those who were with him (which is the sect of the Sadducees), and they were filled with indignation, and laid their hands on the apostles and put them in the common prison.

—Acts 5:17, 18

The followers of the Nazarene needed to be stopped. "There was resentment because the untutored apostles were presuming to teach the people. Both Pharisees and Sadducees experienced this resentment. But the Sadducees felt a special antagonism because the apostles were teaching that there was a future life—a belief that the Sadducees rejected. The fact that the Pharisees agreed with the apostles on this point did not please the Sadducees."[1] Should the doctrine of the resurrection catch on, the Sadducees foresaw they would cease to exist as a sect. The Pharisees were upset about the disciples' teaching Christ's sacrifice on the cross as the only one a devout Jew needed. These teachings undermined the sacrificial offering system and their lucrative trade in sacrificial animals. Additionally, the apostles had no rabbinical school training, bringing into question the priests' authoritative and unquestioned interpretation of Scripture.

An order went out to arrest *all* the apostles, and this was accomplished. Even though the apostles were taken and held in the public prison, they were not dismayed or discouraged. They recalled Jesus saying, "A servant is not greater than his master. If they persecuted Me, they will also persecute you" (John 15:20). While the apostles were in jail, the Sanhedrin met to draft a strategy. "The priests and rulers had decided to fix upon the disciples the charge of insurrection, to accuse them of murdering Ananias and Sapphira, and of conspiring to deprive the priests of their authority. They hoped so to excite the mob that it would take the matter in hand and deal with the disciples as it had dealt with Jesus. They were aware that many who did not accept the teachings of Christ were weary of the arbitrary rule of the Jewish authorities and anxious for some change. The priests feared that if these dissatisfied ones were to accept the truths proclaimed by the apostles, and were to acknowledge Jesus as the Messiah, the anger of the entire people would be raised against the religious leaders, who would then be made to answer for the murder of Christ. They decided to take strong measures to prevent this."[2]

"But at night an angel of the Lord opened the prison doors and brought them out, and said, 'Go, stand in the temple and speak to the people all the words of this life' " (Acts 5:19, 20; emphasis added).

---

1. Francis D. Nichol, ed., *The Seventh-day Adventist Bible Commentary*, vol. 6 (Washington, DC: Review and Herald®, 1957), 180.

2. Ellen G. White, *The Acts of the Apostles* (Mountain View, CA: Pacific Press®, 1911), 80, 81.

"We Ought to Obey God"

*"Did we not strictly command you not to teach in this name? And look,
you have filled Jerusalem with your doctrine, and intend to bring this Man's blood on us!"*
—Acts 5:28

The apostles had been told by the angel to return to the temple and preach about Jesus. Specifically, they were to preach the resurrection—the words of "this life" that begins here and now and continues into eternity (Acts 5:20). The Jewish rulers had forbidden them to preach any such message or to use Christ's name. Yet there was no conflict in the minds of the disciples. The temple opened at first light. "They entered the temple early in the morning and taught" (verse 21). The Sanhedrin meanwhile sent to the prison for the prisoners. "But when the officers came and did not find them in the prison, they returned and reported, saying, 'Indeed we found the prison shut securely, and the guards standing outside before the doors; but when we opened them, we found no one inside!' " (verses 22, 23). "Doors, even the firmly fastened doors of prisons, are no problem to the angels of God. The apostles were taken out from under the very eyes of the keepers, either under the cover of deep darkness or because the eyes of the guards were 'holden.' . . . The doors were left secured, or were locked again, leaving everything as it had been before the angel came."[1]

About this time, "one came and told them, saying, 'Look, the men whom you put in prison are standing in the temple and teaching the people!' " (verse 25). The captain was sent again to retrieve the apostles and bring them before the council. He did this in a peaceful manner, for the sympathies of the population were with the apostles, and the guards risked being stoned. The apostles came peacefully. When accosted by the high priest and asked why they continued to preach about Jesus, Peter and the others replied, "We ought to obey God rather than men. The God of our fathers raised up Jesus whom you murdered by hanging on a tree. Him God has exalted to His right hand to be Prince and Savior, to give repentance to Israel and forgiveness of sins" (verse 29). "So enraged were the Jews at these words that they decided to take the law into their own hands and without further trial, or without authority from the Roman officers, to put the prisoners to death."[2]

The divine command must supersede the human mandate. A Christian cannot serve two masters.

---

1. Francis D. Nichol, ed., *The Seventh-day Adventist Bible Commentary*, vol. 6 (Washington, DC: Review and Herald®, 1957), 181.
2. Ellen G. White, *The Acts of the Apostles* (Mountain View, CA: Pacific Press®, 1911), 82.

Gamaliel's Advice

"And now I say to you, keep away from these men and let them alone;
for if this plan or this work is of men, it will come to nothing; but if it is of God,
you cannot overthrow it—lest you even be found to fight against God."

—Acts 5:38, 39

G amaliel was the grandson of the famous Hillel . . . , and a renowned teacher and prominent Pharisee in his own right. . . . He was the first to receive the title of Rabban. This indicates the esteem in which his countrymen held him. Jewish tradition reveals him as the ideal Pharisee, a worthy representative of Hillel's school, which was more tolerant and less legalistic than the opposing school of Shammai. Paul was privileged to study under him."[1] Seeing that the violent direction toward which the Sanhedrin was leaning would cause serious repercussions, Gamaliel asked that the prisoners be removed so the council might discuss punishment freely.

Rising, Gamaliel addressed the council. "Men of Israel, take heed to yourselves what you intend to do regarding these men" (Acts 5:35). In other words, be careful! He then went on to relate a short history of men claiming to be the Messiah whose followers came to no success. "For some time ago Theudas rose up, claiming to be somebody. A number of men, about four hundred, joined him. He was slain, and all who obeyed him were scattered and came to nothing" (verse 36). He next cited the history of Judas of Galilee, who moved for complete independence from Rome. Judas urged no taxes be paid to Caesar and raised an armed force to resist. "The war was described as a religious war. Judas and his followers were affiliated with the Pharisees, and his movement, although defeated, and the leader killed, gave origin to the sect, or party, of the Zealots."[2]

All knew of these recent uprisings. While the Sadducees wished to kill the apostles to silence them, the wisdom of Gamaliel was accepted as sound. One wonders why Saul became such a zealot against the Christians when his mentor clearly, on this occasion, urged restraint and caution. Saul was struggling in the midst of the swirling doctrinal turmoil gripping Jerusalem. A respected student of the famed Pharisee Gamaliel, Saul sought to prevent the erosion of Pharisaical authority through violent confrontation with Christians.

Ultimately, the work of God will triumph over the designs of men. The fire cannot be quenched!

---

1. Francis D. Nichol, ed., *The Seventh-day Adventist Bible Commentary*, vol. 6 (Washington, DC: Review and Herald®, 1957), 184, 185.
2. Nichol, *Seventh-day Adventist Bible Commentary*, vol. 6, 185.

A Cheerful Beating

And they agreed with him, and when they had called for the apostles and beaten them,
they commanded that they should not speak in the name of Jesus, and let them go.
—Acts 5:40

The beating of the apostles marks the first persecution of the church. This beating was probably the standard thirty-nine stripes. The Mosaic Law dictated no more than forty lashes were to be administered as punishment. To not exceed that number and for the sake of leniency, thirty-nine were counted off. During the beating, a priest would intone the following words: "If you do not carefully observe all the words of this law that are written in this book, that you may fear this glorious and awesome name, THE LORD YOUR GOD, then the LORD will bring upon you and your descendants extraordinary plagues—great and prolonged plagues—and serious and prolonged sicknesses" (Deuteronomy 28:58, 59).

"The Sanhedrin evidently judged the apostles worthy of punishment, either for disobeying the command of Acts 4:18 [not to speak at all or use the name of Jesus], or for disturbing the peace by preaching in the Temple . . . , or for having escaped from prison—or on all counts."[1] The disciples rejoiced to be counted worthy to suffer for the name of Jesus. The next day, in defiance of the Sanhedrin's order, they were back in the temple, preaching that the Messiah had come in the person of Jesus of Nazareth. Imagine the boldness of these men, willing to again be arrested, imprisoned, beaten, and possibly even killed for declaring their faith in Jesus!

"What was the strength of those who in the past have suffered persecution for Christ's sake? It was the union with God, union with the Holy Spirit, union with Christ. Reproach and persecution have separated many from earthly friends, but never from the love of Christ. Never is the tempest-tried soul more dearly loved by his Saviour than when he is suffering reproach for the truth's sake. 'I will love him,' Christ said, 'and will manifest Myself to him.' John 14:21. When for the truth's sake the believer stands at the bar of earthly tribunals, Christ stands by his side. When he is confined within prison walls, Christ manifests Himself to him and cheers his heart with His love. When he suffers death for Christ's sake, the Saviour says to him, They may kill the body, but they cannot hurt the soul. 'Be of good cheer; I have overcome the world.' . . . John 16:33."[2]

When persecuted, the apostles rejoiced as the final beatitude directs. (See Matthew 5:11, 12.)

---

1. Francis D. Nichol, ed., *The Seventh-day Adventist Bible Commentary*, vol. 6 (Washington, DC: Review and Herald®, 1957), 186.
2. Ellen G. White, *The Acts of the Apostles* (Mountain View, CA: Pacific Press®, 1911), 85, 86.

Saved to Serve

"Therefore, brethren, seek out from among you seven men of good reputation, full of the Holy Spirit and wisdom, whom we may appoint over this business."
—Acts 6:3

As if threats and beatings from the established Jewish religious leaders were not enough, the apostles now were faced with murmuring from within. "The early church was made up of many classes of people, of various nationalities. . . . Among those of the Hebrew faith who were gathered at Jerusalem were some commonly known as Grecians, between whom and the Jews of Palestine there had long existed distrust and even antagonism."[1] It was considered virtuous to be buried in Israel, so foreign Jews would return there to live out their last days and die, leaving a disproportionate number of foreign widows in Jerusalem. Within the church, a process had begun to assist *widows* daily from a common fund. Care of these individuals was encouraged in Scripture (Exodus 22:22; Deuteronomy 14:29; Isaiah 1:17; Luke 18:3). "Probably there was a continuous stream of gifts coming in and of donations being passed out. The drain upon the apostles' time must have been great."[2]

As Palestinian Jews were in the majority, it is quite possible Greek-speaking widows were not being assisted because of the language barriers and different customs. Such was an oversight, not an overt act, by those distributing aid. "Prompt measures must now be taken to remove all occasion for dissatisfaction, lest the enemy triumph in his effort to bring about a division among the believers."[3] The apostles called a church meeting to outline a new plan of organization. By appointing men to oversee the aid distribution (Ellen G. White refers to the men as "deacons" in pages 89 and 90 of *The Acts of the Apostles*), the apostles freed up their time for continual prayer and ministry. The apostles prayed regarding the choice of the seven and then laid hands upon them, dedicating them to and blessing them in their work. The men selected were honest, efficient, and accepted by the Greek believers. All seven had Greek names: Stephen, Philip, Prochorus, Nicanor, Timon, Parmenas, and Nicolas.

"He [God] requires that order and system be observed in the conduct of church affairs today no less than in the days of old."[4]

1. Ellen G. White, *The Acts of the Apostles* (Mountain View, CA: Pacific Press®, 1911), 87.
2. Francis D. Nichol, ed., *The Seventh-day Adventist Bible Commentary*, vol. 6 (Washington, DC: Review and Herald®, 1957), 188.
3. White, *Acts of the Apostles*, 88.
4. White, *Acts of the Apostles*, 96.

Ethnic Tensions

And they stirred up the people, the elders, and the scribes;
and they came upon him, seized him, and brought him to the council.

—Acts 6:12

Jerusalem was ready to erupt. Within the infant church, ethnic tensions between Palestinian and Hellenistic Christians were a microcosm of larger ethnic unrest seen throughout the Roman Empire. Onto this prejudiced stage stepped the new deacon Stephen. "Stephen, the foremost of the seven deacons, was a man of deep piety and broad faith. Though a Jew by birth, he spoke the Greek language and was familiar with the customs and manners of the Greeks. He therefore found opportunity to preach the gospel in the synagogues of the Greek Jews."[1] Stephen actively proclaimed his faith in the Synagogue of the Freedmen.

The Synagogue of the Freedmen consisted of Cyrenians from the north coast of Africa, Alexandrians from Egypt, Cilicians from southeast Asia Minor (Tarsus, Saul's birthplace, was in Cilicia), and Jews of the Dispersion living in the rest of Asia Minor (including Ephesus). Jewish theology was the topic, and these Jews coming from foreign lands were keen and zealous to question and dispute what was truth. "Learned rabbis and doctors of the law engaged in public discussion with him [Stephen], confidently expecting an easy victory. But 'they were not able to resist the wisdom and the spirit by which he spake.' Not only did he speak in the power of the Holy Spirit, but it was plain that he was a student of the prophecies and learned in all matters of the law. He ably defended the truths that he advocated and utterly defeated his opponents."[2]

The Sanhedrin was again confronted with the new teachings of Christianity. Converts were flocking to the new religion. The followers of Christ were not only bold in the proclamation of the gospel but also were attended with miracles, wonders, and signs. Rather than accept the evidence presented, the priests and rulers determined to silence the dissent. If they could not hold the Jews from foreign lands in check, then they were in danger of losing those from Palestine as well. "There must have been something in the teachings of Stephen that made them [the Hellenists] feel that he was lessening, if not supplanting, the singular spiritual importance of the Temple in Jerusalem (see . . . [Acts] 6:13; 7:1)."[3]

Consider: The Hellenists were about to surrender one of their own to prove their loyalties to the ruling system. Religious zealots and fanatics lack love, compassion, and understanding.

---

1. Ellen G. White, *The Acts of the Apostles* (Mountain View, CA: Pacific Press®, 1911), 97.

2. White, *Acts of the Apostles*, 97.

3. Francis D. Nichol, ed., *The Seventh-day Adventist Bible Commentary*, vol. 6 (Washington, DC: Review and Herald®, 1957), 193.

Saul, the Prosecuting Attorney

They also set up false witnesses who said, "This man does not cease to speak blasphemous words against this holy place and the law."

—Acts 6:13

M en were coerced and bribed to lie about Stephen's statements, twisting the truth in much the same manner as had been done during the trial of Jesus. Speaking blasphemy against the temple, against the law, and against Moses were the key charges. Notice the temple was mentioned before God's law. "The legalists were more concerned with their ceremonies than with their God."[1] Stephen "may have taught that the need for a temple had ceased (cf. Acts 7:48), even as Jesus had inferred in talking with the woman of Samaria (John 4:21). This would assail the very foundations of Judaism, and would naturally arouse strong opposition. In the face of such a teaching, Sadducees and Pharisees would unite in opposition. Punishment for blasphemy was death by stoning (Lev. 24:16)."[2] The Sanhedrin now had to take action.

The high priest, the most powerful Jewish official allowed by Rome, led this body of seventy men given permission to deal with all things pertaining to the Jewish religion and, to a certain extent, some civil and judicial matters dealing exclusively with local politics. They could ordain services, enact religious laws, and punish traitorous priests, rebel leaders (messiahs), and false prophets. They had complete control over the temple mount, maintaining their own police force to control crowds and enforce their will. Although Rome prevented the Sanhedrin from administering capital punishment to those found guilty in their court, the council often bribed Roman officials to overlook cases when they had taken the law into their own hands.

On this occasion, the council summoned its most eloquent rising stars to refute the arguments of Stephen. Entering the gospel narrative is a protégé of Gamaliel I and the focus of our devotional. "Saul of Tarsus was present and took a leading part against Stephen. He brought the weight of eloquence and the logic of the rabbis to bear upon the case, to convince the people that Stephen was preaching delusive and dangerous doctrines; but in Stephen he met one who had a full understanding of the purpose of God in the spreading of the gospel to other nations."[3]

Saul's impressive education and impeccable credentials hid a lack of understanding. Prejudice and pride are fatal flaws.

---

1. Francis D. Nichol, ed., *The Seventh-day Adventist Bible Commentary*, vol. 6 (Washington, DC: Review and Herald®, 1957), 193.
2. Nichol, *Seventh-day Adventist Bible Commentary*, vol. 6, 193.
3. Ellen G. White, *The Acts of the Apostles* (Mountain View, CA: Pacific Press®, 1911), 98.

A New Historical Perspective

Then the high priest said, "Are these things so?"

—Acts 7:1

T he prosecution had rested after summing up the charges against Stephen. Now it was the defendant's turn to speak. "As Stephen stood face to face with his judges to answer to the charge of blasphemy, a holy radiance shone upon his countenance, and 'all that sat in the council, looking steadfastly on him, saw his face as it had been the face of an angel.' Many who beheld this light trembled and veiled their faces, but the stubborn unbelief and prejudice of the rulers did not waver."[1]

Stephen continued to relate the history of God's dealings with the Jewish nation but with a twist. The proud Jews still insisted Israel was the chosen nation of God. Their religion, their laws, their country, and their temple were superior to all others, as evidenced by the historical acts of God on their behalf. Stephen now changed their historical perspective. He first pointed out the Hebrew nation was established through Abraham when he dwelt in Mesopotamia, not Palestine (Acts 7:2–5). God had miraculously delivered His people from affliction outside the borders of the Promised Land, in Egypt, at the crossing of the Red Sea, and time and again during the wanderings in the Sinai (verses 9–36). The Decalogue was not delivered from the temple mount but from a mount called Sinai in the wilderness (verse 38)—a mount made sacred by the presence of God, for Moses was instructed to remove his shoes out of respect. God is not found exclusively within the temple or any house built with hands but rather reigns from heaven, and the earth is His footstool (verses 48–50). "The glory of God is His character."[2]

Stephen also quoted Isaiah 66:1, 2 almost word for word. "Isaiah points out that the Most High cannot be confined within human limitations, but will dwell with those who are 'poor and of a contrite spirit.' These words were a rebuke to the Jews who heard them. With their worship centered upon the earthly Temple, they were far from being 'poor and of a contrite spirit.' Stephen's unspoken appeal [was] to accept the Divine One, who had walked among them so humbly, and had shown them their heavenly Father's lovely character."[3]

Is your loyalty directed toward an institution? Your devotion should be only to Christ and His Word.

---

1. Ellen G. White, *The Acts of the Apostles* (Mountain View, CA: Pacific Press®, 1911), 99.
2. Francis D. Nichol, ed., *The Seventh-day Adventist Bible Commentary*, vol. 6 (Washington, DC: Review and Herald®, 1957), 197.
3. Nichol, *Seventh-day Adventist Bible Commentary*, vol. 6, 204.

A "Spirited" Defense

"This Moses whom they rejected, saying, 'Who made you a ruler and a judge?' "
—Acts 7:35

We are spending considerable time expanding the trial of Stephen because it represents a watershed in evangelism. From this point on, the persecution of believers by Jewish authorities would cause the gospel to spread beyond the boundaries of Jerusalem. The early church members would be forced to think outside the walls of their comfort zones. Just as the priests and rulers tended to focus all of their adoration and religious ardor on the temple, early Christians were in danger of focusing too narrowly their outreach just to Jerusalem. Stephen's defense affords insight into early church theology and a study of one believer's character.

Additionally, for the first time, we see Saul mentioned in Scripture. Insert a man such as he: conditioned by a strict legalistic upbringing, educated by none other than the top theologian—Gamaliel—possessing an ardor to protect the traditions and religion of his people, imbued with Jewish arrogance and a pride that brooks no dissent; there we have the makings of a zealot ready to stamp out supposed heresy wherever it may be found. But Saul is now receiving more of an education than he bargained for when he left Tarsus for school in Jerusalem. Saul hears a totally nontraditional reconstruction of Hebrew history by Stephen, and it makes sense.

Did not the Jews remember that Moses gave up his high standing in Egypt to identify with his people? He was appointed to deliver them from bondage, yet they rejected him. Just as Jesus had done signs and wonders, so had Moses. Just as Moses had come as a deliverer, so had Jesus. The implication was clear. "Moses liberated, and so redeemed, his people from Egypt, but Christ liberates, redeems, His people from sin and death."[1] These rabbis now took pride in Moses as a prophet of God, but their fathers had rejected the deliverer and constantly sought to go contrary to his leading. Now they had rejected the Son of God, sent as their Deliverer from sin. Stephen reminded them, "This is that Moses who said to the children of Israel, 'The LORD your God will raise up for you a Prophet *like me* from your brethren. Him you shall hear' " (Acts 7:37; emphasis added). Yet they shut their ears and crucified Him who was the Promised One.

These Jews rejected Jesus, their Savior, just as their fathers had rejected Moses, their deliverer.

---

1. Francis D. Nichol, ed., *The Seventh-day Adventist Bible Commentary*, vol. 6 (Washington, DC: Review and Herald®, 1957), 201.

Hitting the Rabbis Hard

"And they made a calf in those days, offered sacrifices to the idol, and rejoiced in the works of the own hands."

—Acts 7:41

I n words that held the assembly spellbound, he [Stephen] proceeded to rehearse the history of the chosen people of God. He showed a thorough knowledge of the Jewish economy and the spiritual interpretation of it now made manifest through Christ. He repeated the words of Moses that foretold of the Messiah: 'A Prophet shall the Lord your God raise up unto you of your brethren, like unto me; Him shall ye hear.' He made plain his own loyalty to God and to the Jewish faith, while he showed that the law in which the Jews trusted for salvation had not been able to save Israel from idolatry. He connected Jesus Christ with all the Jewish history."[1]

Now Stephen hit the rabbis hard. Of all the history of the Jewish nation, the rabbis were most sensitive concerning the incident of the golden calf. They regarded the construction of this idol at Sinai as perhaps Israel's most shameful and sinful act (Exodus 32:1–6). When infidels would bring up the subject, they were quick to shift blame to the mixed multitude who came out of Egyptian bondage with Israel. Everyone knew the heathen had demanded a familiar idol to worship. Stephen now linked their worship of the temple structure itself to their worship of that golden idol in the desert.

God gave King David the plans for the temple and had blessed the efforts of King Solomon in building it, but God never meant for it to be the object of worship that it had become. The priests, in their pride of the temple mount, had lost sight of the reason for its very existence. "He referred to the building of the temple by Solomon, and to the words of both Solomon and Isaiah: 'Howbeit the Most High dwelleth not in temples made with hands; as saith the prophet, Heaven is My throne, and earth is My footstool: what house will ye build Me?' "[2] Attacking the temple antagonized the council to violence and proved Stephen's point: these men, just like their forefathers, refused to hear the prophets sent to warn them and sought to stifle any view other than their own.

Do you refuse to surrender personally held "sacred cows" when confronted with biblical truth?

---

1. Ellen G. White, *The Acts of the Apostles* (Mountain View, CA: Pacific Press®, 1911), 99.
2. White, *Acts of the Apostles*, 99, 100.

The Defense Rests in Jesus

When they heard these things they were cut to the heart.

—Acts 7:54

Stephen knew by looking that the council members resented his words. Murmuring broke out, and heated arguments arose. "Apparently realizing that his end was near, and that no further discussion would affect the issue, Stephen broke forth in a stern rebuke."[1] "You stiff-necked and uncircumcised in heart and ears! You always resist the Holy Spirit; as your fathers did, so do you. Which of the prophets did your fathers not persecute? And they killed those who foretold the coming of the Just One, of whom you now have become the betrayers and murderers, who received the law by the direction of angels and have not kept it" (Acts 7:51–53). Calling the head clerical body "uncircumcised" implied they were no better than Gentiles!

"When he connected Christ with the prophecies and spoke as he did of the temple, the priest, pretending to be horror-stricken, rent his robe. To Stephen this act was a signal that his voice would soon be silenced forever. He saw the resistance that met his words and knew that he was giving his last testimony. Although in the midst of his sermon, he abruptly concluded it."[2] As they rushed forward like beasts of prey to encircle him, the scene before him faded. Instead, "he, being filled with the Holy Spirit, gazed into heaven and saw the glory of God, and Jesus standing at the right hand of God, and said, 'Look! I see the heavens opened and the Son of Man standing at the right hand of God!' " (verses 55, 56). Stephen stood strong in the midst of a mob, for he did not fear death. As he described the scene before him of the heavenly courts, the priests and rulers shouted for him to be silent. They were no longer open to convincing arguments but rather shouted, "Blasphemy!"

Even the high priest in his rage broke the Levitical law. "Do not uncover your heads nor tear your clothes, lest you die, and wrath come upon all the people" (Leviticus 10:6). "Everything worn by the priest was to be whole and without blemish. By those beautiful official garments was represented the character of the great antitype, Jesus Christ. Nothing but perfection, in dress and attitude, in word and spirit, could be acceptable to God."[3]

While Jesus stood silent before His accusers, Stephen put up a logical and spirited defense. Both trials ended with the same verdict, for nothing had changed in three years.

---

1. Francis D. Nichol, ed., *The Seventh-day Adventist Bible Commentary*, vol. 6 (Washington, DC: Review and Herald®, 1957), 204.
2. Ellen G. White, *The Acts of the Apostles* (Mountain View, CA: Pacific Press®, 1911), 100.
3. Ellen G. White, *The Desire of Ages* (Mountain View, CA: Pacific Press®, 1940), 709.

"Do Not Indict Them"

And they stoned Stephen as he was calling on God and saying, "Lord Jesus, receive my spirit."
—Acts 7:59

Hurrying Stephen outside the walls of the city, the priests and rulers moved to the place of execution. "Before a person might be stoned there must be at least 2 or 3 witnesses, who were to cast the first stones, then all the people were to join in the casting of stones (Deut 17:5–7). The Mishnah ... describes in detail the later procedure followed in stoning: 'The place of stoning was twice a man's height. One of the witnesses pushed him by the hips [so that] he was overturned on his heart. He was then turned on his back. If that caused his death, he had fulfilled [his duty]; but if not, the second witness took the stone and threw it on his chest. If he died thereby, he had done [his duty]; but if not, he [the criminal] was stoned by all Israel....' (Soncino ed. of the Talmud, p. 295)."[1] If the victim's neck wasn't broken by the first fall in the pit or the first heavy stone landing upon his chest, it became a scene of men vying for position to throw heavy rocks at the fallen body of the individual.

Stephen prayed while being stoned. "Then he knelt down and cried out with a loud voice, 'Lord do not charge them with this sin.' And when he had said this, he fell asleep" (Acts 7:60). The similarities between the trials of Jesus and Stephen are startling. From the trumped-up charges, the mock trial, the paid witnesses, and the predetermined guilt to the execution and the prayer for forgiveness directed toward those carrying out the sentence, these two travesties of justice showed that the priests and rulers had not changed their minds about the rightness of their course. "No legal sentence had been passed upon Stephen, but the Roman authorities were bribed by large sums of money to make no investigation into the case."[2] Here again, a bribe was initiated just as it was for the guards at the tomb of Jesus who were paid to say that His disciples came in the night and stole His body. The modus operandi of the Sanhedrin was set in these matters: lie to gain a conviction, murder the innocent, and then cover up the proceedings.

"Throughout his defense Stephen's conduct is in marked contrast with that of his accusers.... The battle is over, the victory is won; God's faithful warrior leaves the tumult and quietly sleeps until the resurrection day."[3]

---

1. Siegfried H. Horn, *Seventh-day Adventist Bible Dictionary*, ed. Don F. Neufeld, Commentary Reference Series, vol. 8 (Washington, DC: Review and Herald®, 1960), s.v. "Stoning."
2. Ellen G. White, *The Acts of the Apostles* (Mountain View, CA: Pacific Press®, 1911), 101.
3. Francis D. Nichol, ed., *The Seventh-day Adventist Bible Commentary*, vol. 6 (Washington, DC: Review and Herald®, 1957), 206, 207.

Coats Versus Conscience

And the witnesses laid down their clothes at the feet of a young man named Saul.

—Acts 7:58

The loose, flowing robes of the witnesses would have impeded their throwing ability, so they removed them and handed them to Saul. He stood by with joy as the object of his legal oratory was executed. No great legal victory on the part of Saul had led to this point; rather, he was witnessing the fury of an uncontrollable mob in action. "At the scene of Stephen's trial and death, Saul had seemed to be imbued with a frenzied zeal. Afterward he was angered by his own secret conviction that Stephen had been honored by God at the very time when he was dishonored by men."[1]

Saul became a man on a mission. "After the death of Stephen, Saul was elected a member of the Sanhedrin council in consideration of the part he had acted on that occasion. For a time he was a mighty instrument in the hands of Satan to carry out his rebellion against the Son of God."[2] Even though Saul was greatly admired by the Jews for his zeal in persecuting the believers of Jesus Christ, he could not shake the impression left upon him by the martyrdom of Stephen. "The mind of Saul was greatly stirred by the triumphant death of Stephen. He was shaken in his prejudice; but the opinions and arguments of the priests and rulers finally convinced him that Stephen was a blasphemer; that Jesus Christ whom he preached was an impostor, and that those ministering in holy offices must be right. Being a man of decided mind and strong purpose, he became very bitter in his opposition to Christianity, after having once entirely settled in his mind that the views of the priests and scribes were right. His zeal led him to *voluntarily* engage in persecuting the believers."[3]

"God does not prevent the plottings of wicked men, but He causes their devices to work for good to those who in trial and conflict maintain their faith and loyalty. Often the gospel laborer carries on his work amid storms of persecution, bitter opposition, and unjust reproach. At such times let him remember that the experience to be gained in the furnace of trial and affliction is worth all the pain it costs."[4]

"Thus God brings His children near to Him, that He may show them their weakness and His strength. He teaches them to lean on Him."[5]

1. Ellen G. White, *The Acts of the Apostles* (Mountain View, CA: Pacific Press®, 1911), 101, 102.
2. White, *Acts of the Apostles*, 102.
3. Ellen G. White, *Sketches From the Life of Paul* (Washington, DC: Review and Herald®, 1974), 21; emphasis added.
4. White, *Acts of the Apostles*, 574.
5. White, *Acts of the Apostles*, 574.

Time's Up

"Seventy weeks are determined for your people and for your holy city."
—Daniel 9:24

The prophecy of the seventy weeks, as delivered to and recorded by Daniel, had its beginning in the year 457 BC when the decree went forth to rebuild and restore Jerusalem (Daniel 9:25). Seventy weeks, or 490 years, stretched down in history to AD 34, utilizing the yardstick for prophetic time that Ezekiel 4:6 gives: "I have appointed thee each day for a year" (KJV). The prophecy stated that Messiah the Prince would come in "seven weeks, and threescore and two weeks" (Daniel 9:25, KJV), or sixty-nine weeks (483 days/years), from 457 BC. Right on time, in AD 27, Jesus was baptized by John in the river Jordan and began His ministry. Daniel also placed a time on the death of the Anointed One: "And he shall confirm the covenant with many for one week [seven years]: and in the midst of the week he shall cause the sacrifice and the oblation to cease" (verse 27, KJV). In the spring of AD 31, exactly three and a half years after beginning His ministry in the fall of AD 27, Jesus, the ultimate Sacrifice and Offering, was crucified.

The seventy-week prophecy of Daniel was nearly over. Yet the prophecy pointed to something of significance happening in AD 34. The angel Gabriel had told Daniel that seventy weeks were set aside for the Jews "to finish the transgression, to make an end of sins, to make reconciliation for iniquity, to bring in everlasting righteousness, to seal up the vision and prophecy, and to anoint the Most Holy" (verse 24, KJV). This the Jews did not do when they rejected the Most Holy and crucified Him instead. The Lord had allotted an additional three and a half years following Christ's death for the Jews to come to a realization of their actions and repent. This they also did not do. At this point, the gospel, which was to be preached to the Jews first, was to be proclaimed to the Gentiles. The final refusal of the Jews to accept the gospel of Jesus Christ was marked by the stoning of Stephen. In AD 34, the cup of iniquity for the Jewish nation was finally full. Further national calamity awaited their country, their temple, and their system of worship. In AD 70, Rome destroyed the most sacred of their affections—their temple.

God controls the affairs of nations. Do not, for a minute, doubt Him. That which He has promised, He is faithful to do!

This Gospel Is for the Gentiles

Ministry in Samaria and Syria

AD 34–44

Acts 8:1–12:23
The Acts of the Apostles, pp. 103–165
Sketches From the Life of Paul, pp. 21–44

The Great Persecution

At that time a great persecution arose against the church which was at Jerusalem; and they were all scattered throughout the regions of Judea and Samaria, except the apostles.

—Acts 8:1

At first, persecution seemed to be limited to Hellenists associated with Stephen. As Saul came from Tarsus in the province of Cilicia, it is possible he worshiped with other Cilicians in the Synagogue of the Freedmen. This synagogue might have been his home church while in Jerusalem, and here, Saul may have first met Stephen. Fellow Greek-speaking Jews offered Stephen up to the authorities, but Saul was called upon by the Sanhedrin to be part of the prosecution team seeking a conviction against him. A respected student of Gamaliel I, a member of the strict Pharisee sect, perhaps a member of the Synagogue of the Freedmen, Saul was ideally suited to prosecute Stephen before a tribunal of fellow Jews.

Interestingly, the apostles were exempt from the "severe" persecution that broke out against the Hellenists. They continued to be well regarded, for they taught observance of accepted religious tradition, and their good works recommended them to the people. This persecution was narrowly focused against those already marginalized by the Jewish faith. Referring to this time, Saul would later say, "Indeed, I myself thought I must do many things contrary to the name of Jesus of Nazareth. This I also did in Jerusalem, and many of the saints I shut up in prison, having received authority from the chief priests; and when they were put to death, I cast my vote against them. And I punished them often in every synagogue and compelled them to blaspheme; and being exceedingly enraged against them, I persecuted them even to foreign cities" (Acts 26:9–11).

Lines were drawn. "At this time of peril Nicodemus came forward in fearless avowal of his faith in the crucified Saviour. . . .

". . . No longer cautious and questioning, he encouraged the faith of the disciples and used his wealth in helping to sustain the church at Jerusalem and in advancing the work of the gospel. Those who in other days had paid him reverence, now scorned and persecuted him, and he became poor in this world's goods; yet he faltered not in the defense of his faith."[1] "The Roman authorities made no special effort to stay the cruel work, and secretly aided the Jews in order to conciliate them, and to secure their favor."[2]

The blood of the faithful has always watered the church, causing it to flourish.

---

1. Ellen G. White, *The Acts of the Apostles* (Mountain View, CA: Pacific Press®, 1911), 104, 105.
2. Ellen G. White, *Sketches From the Life of Paul* (Washington, DC: Review and Herald®, 1974), 20.

Preaching in Samaria

Therefore those who were scattered went everywhere preaching the word.

—Acts 8:4

Since 536 BC, strained relations had existed between Jews and Samaritans. The Samaritan offer to assist in rebuilding Jerusalem following the Babylonian exile had been rejected by the Jews. Understanding that their ancestors had gone into captivity because they had forsaken God, Jewish leaders now sought to "purify" their religion. They didn't want Samaritans, who had mingled the religion of Israel with that of their own ancestors, to taint the reestablished Jewish faith. "As a result of this attitude an increasingly deepening hatred developed between the 2 nations, which was frequently revealed in hostile acts."[1]

Jesus visited Samaria in AD 28 (John 4:3, 4). During a key encounter, He met a *woman* at Jacob's well. Speaking more directly to her regarding the Messiah than He could in Judea, He confessed, "I who speak to you am He" (John 4:26). Rushing back into the city, the woman had brought her neighbors out to hear the Messiah. Crowding around Jesus, they had besieged Him with questions. With infinite patience, He had explained away many of the difficulties they perceived in their religious lives. They had invited Him to stay with them, and for two wonderful days, He remained. Jesus did not narrow down the gospel invitation and offer it to just a few. The message was to be given to all. He referred to that when he told the disciples, "But you shall receive power when the Holy Spirit has come upon you; and you shall be witnesses to Me in Jerusalem, and in all Judea and Samaria, and to the end of the earth" (Acts 1:8).

"Philip, one of the seven deacons, was among those driven from Jerusalem. He 'went down to the city of Samaria, and preached Christ unto them.' . . .

"And when His [Jesus'] disciples were driven from Jerusalem, some found in Samaria a safe asylum. The Samaritans welcomed these messengers of the gospel, and the Jewish converts gathered a precious harvest from among those who had once been their bitterest enemies.

"Philip's work in Samaria was marked with great success, and, thus encouraged, he sent to Jerusalem for help."[2] Five hundred and seventy years after the Jewish attempt to "purify" their religion by excluding Samaritans, similar action by early Christians was initially causing the gospel of Jesus to be offered exclusively to Jews.

How accepting is your congregation?

---

1. Siegfried H. Horn, *Seventh-day Adventist Bible Dictionary*, ed. Don F. Neufeld, Commentary Reference Series, vol. 8 (Washington, DC: Review and Herald®, 1960), s.v. "Samaritans."
2. Ellen G. White, *The Acts of the Apostles* (Mountain View, CA: Pacific Press®, 1911), 106, 107.

Comfortable Religion

Now when the apostles who were at Jerusalem heard that Samaria had received the word of God, they sent Peter and John to them.

—Acts 8:14

The faithful were still active in Jerusalem. Following the death of Stephen, devout men carried Stephen to his burial, making great lamentation over him (Acts 8:2). "Considerable courage must have been required to perform the funeral rites for Stephen, who had fallen before the rage of the Sanhedrin. Indeed, anyone who had been stoned to death on a charge of blasphemy would ordinarily have no funeral honors.... Public lamentation on the part of the 'devout' may have been in the nature of a protest against those who had brought about Stephen's death."[1] Why were the apostles still in Jerusalem? Jerusalem wasn't their home. The Sanhedrin certainly hadn't welcomed them with open arms. The answer may have been that they were simply more comfortable preaching to fellow Jews. Sharing the gospel with Jews was hard but still infinitely easier than having to cross cultural barriers to preach to other nationalities.

Philip, being a Greek-speaking Jew, understood being second-class. The fate of fellow deacon Stephen hit close to home. Philip harbored no cultural fear in going to Samaritans. He was probably safer in Samaria than staying in Jerusalem to face certain death. Not to say it didn't take courage to move away from one's home and comfort zone. As the conflict between the Sanhedrin and Hellenistic Christians grew more hostile and bitter, believers scattered to avoid persecution. Philip's work among the Samaritans had blossomed, and word was relayed back to Jerusalem. Peter and John were sent to verify the report. "There is no evidence here of the supremacy of Peter; he was under the direction of the body of the apostles, who 'sent' him and John on this mission. John, who had once sought to call down fire upon the Samaritans (Luke 9:54), was now, in love, to bring them the baptism of the Holy Ghost and of fire (Matt. 3:11)."[2] Peter and John rejoiced among the new gospel converts, confirming Philip's baptism of the Samaritans and praying they might also receive the baptism of the Spirit. By confession of faith through baptism, the prayer of the apostles, and the laying on of hands, the Holy Spirit now came with power upon the Samaritans. A cultural divide had been crossed!

"Comfortable" Christians warm pews. "Courageous" Christians warm hearts.

---

1. Francis D. Nichol, ed., *The Seventh-day Adventist Bible Commentary*, vol. 6 (Washington, DC: Review and Herald®, 1957), 213.
2. Nichol, *Seventh-day Adventist Bible Commentary*, vol. 6, 217.

A Power Play

And when Simon saw that through the laying on of the apostles' hands the Holy Spirit was given, he offered them money.

—Acts 8:18

S imon was a new Samaritan convert. Philip had baptized him, but for some reason, Simon was not present when the others received the baptism of the Spirit. Being a man who was listened to by his neighbors because of his talent for occult practices, he had achieved a certain amount of notoriety. While the new message Philip taught caused the Samaritans to accept Jesus, it was the wonder-working miracles that attracted Simon. He recognized that here was a power greater than his own. If he could somehow acquire it, his opinions would be even more respected within the community. That others had a new power he did not possess seemed to lessen his status within the fellowship. "He did not desire the Holy Spirit for himself as a spiritual gift to seal his baptism, but that he might use the power to dominate others."[1]

Peter instantly saw the motivation underlying Simon's request and rebuked him. "Your money perish with you, because you thought that the gift of God could be purchased with money! You have neither part nor portion in this matter, for your heart is not right in the sight of God. Repent therefore of this your wickedness, and pray God if perhaps the thought of your heart may be forgiven you. For I see that you are poisoned by bitterness and bound by iniquity" (Acts 8:20–23). While disgusted by Simon's offer of money to purchase the Holy Spirit, Peter didn't close the door completely on Simon's state. He urged him to repent and become converted. "Simon's attitude betrayed a fundamental misapprehension of God's character and the gifts of the Spirit. He had yet to learn that the most precious things in life cannot be bought with money."[2]

A surface reading of Acts 8:24, "Pray to the Lord for me, that none of the things which you have spoken may come upon me," would lead the casual reader to suspect Simon was remorseful and desired Peter to pray for his conversion. Such was not the case. "Simon shows by the nature of his plea that he is not moved by genuine repentance. He shows no sorrow. He sees no need of character. He asks only that he be relieved of the threat of punishment."[3]

"Simony" still means trying to buy or sell church powers or offices.

---

1. Francis D. Nichol, ed., *The Seventh-day Adventist Bible Commentary*, vol. 6 (Washington, DC: Review and Herald®, 1957), 217.
2. Nichol, *Seventh-day Adventist Bible Commentary*, vol. 6, 218.
3. Nichol, *Seventh-day Adventist Bible Commentary*, vol. 6, 218.

Finding "Gaza"

"Arise and go toward the south along the road which goes down from Jerusalem to Gaza." This is desert. So he arose and went.
—Acts 8:26, 27

How I do love Philip! One day, out of the blue, he is told to leave Samaria and go to the least frequented, most desolate route imaginable from Jerusalem to Gaza. With no further instruction than to leave immediately, he instantly obeys. Meanwhile, returning from Jerusalem to northern Sudan after worshiping at the temple is an Ethiopian potentate. As a circumcised eunuch, this individual would have been a unique proselyte. Deuteronomy 23:1 "was explicit concerning the exclusion of eunuchs from the sanctuary of God, but this was doubtless modified in practice. . . . Rank, race, and physical condition are not factors in admission to the family of our heavenly Father (Gal. 3:28, 29; Col. 3:10, 11)."[1]

"During his sojourn in Jerusalem the eunuch had probably heard of Jesus' teaching. The work of the disciples had attracted the attention of the entire city. . . . But many of the discussions he had heard undoubtedly classified Jesus as an impostor, and it is very *unlikely* that he would have seen Isa. 53 in the light of the apostles' preaching."[2] As his chariot driver slowly traced the 750-mile route homeward, the treasurer who served Queen Candace was reading Isaiah from a Greek Septuagint scroll just bought in Jerusalem. Philip was directed to join this royal official by either the audible voice of the Spirit or an inward prodding. Running, Philip overtook the chariot and asked: "Do you understand what you are reading?" (Acts 8:30). The eunuch had to admit he needed someone to explain Scripture to him, specifically, who was the Lamb slaughtered in Isaiah 53:7?

Philip was invited to join the official in his chariot. As the two traveled along, Philip shared the gospel story of Jesus the Messiah and the steps necessary to accept Jesus as one's Savior, including baptism. Upon reaching the *Wadi-el-Hesi*, the Ethiopian commanded his retinue to stop. Turning to Philip, he said, "See, here is water. What hinders me from being baptized?"

Philip replied, "If you believe with all your heart, you may."

The answer came swiftly, "I believe that Jesus Christ is the Son of God" (Acts 8:36, 37). And the two went down into the water, where Philip baptized the first African convert to Christ.

The keeper of the Gaza (treasure) knew value. He found the Pearl of Great Price! So can you.

1. Francis D. Nichol, ed., *The Seventh-day Adventist Bible Commentary*, vol. 6 (Washington, DC: Review and Herald®, 1957), 220.
2. Nichol, *Seventh-day Adventist Bible Commentary*, vol. 6, 221; emphasis added.

The Spirit Leads

Now when they came up out of the water, the Spirit of the Lord caught Philip away.
—Acts 8:39

The Holy Spirit led Philip to meet with the eunuch. The task now complete, the Spirit guided him to another mission field. "When God pointed out to Philip his work, the disciple did not say, 'The Lord does not mean that.' No; 'he arose and went.' He had learned the lesson of conformity to God's will. He realized that every soul is precious in the sight of God, and that angels are sent to bring those who are seeking for light into touch with those who can help them.

"To-day as then angels are waiting to lead men to their fellow men."[1]

Immediately after Philip came up out of the water where he had baptized the Ethiopian by immersion, "the Spirit of the Lord caught [him] away, so that the eunuch saw him no more; and he went on his way rejoicing" (Acts 8:39). "Human feeling would naturally have led the evangelist to remain, to complete his work with the eunuch and to instruct him more fully. But by means of a supernatural power, Philip was literally snatched away from his companion."[2] The eunuch went on his way jubilant, for he accepted the disappearance as a supernatural occurrence and spent no time searching for his mentor. "Eusebius . . . speaks of the eunuch as returning to his native country, and there preaching 'the knowledge of the God of the universe and the sojourn of our Saviour which gives life to men,' and so fulfilling the words 'Ethiopia shall soon stretch out her hands unto God.' (Ps. 68:31)."[3]

Philip appeared in Azotus, the Old Testament town of Ashdod, a city of the Philistines about three miles from the coast and halfway between Gaza and Joppa. Here he preached the gospel of Jesus Christ fulfilling the prophecy found in Psalm 87:4. Moving through Lydda and Joppa, Philip developed Christian communities in these cities and eventually moved on to Caesarea. Herod the Great had developed Strato's Tower, a mere landing place for ships, into a "flourishing port with a harbor as large as that of Piraeus, at Athens. He named the city for his imperial patron Augustus, calling it Caesarea."[4] Caesarea, the official residence of the Roman procurator, was a promising center for missionary work.

"In the experience of Philip and the Ethiopian is presented the work to which the Lord calls His people."[5] *First study Scripture, then, when called, you can effectively explain it to others.*

---

1. Ellen G. White, "The Gospel in Samaria," *Advent Review and Sabbath Herald*, March 2, 1911, 4.
2. Francis D. Nichol, ed., *The Seventh-day Adventist Bible Commentary*, vol. 6 (Washington, DC: Review and Herald®, 1957), 222.
3. Nichol, *Seventh-day Adventist Bible Commentary*, vol. 6, 223.
4. Nichol, *Seventh-day Adventist Bible Commentary*, vol. 6, 223.
5. White, "The Gospel in Samaria," 4.

Roman, Greek, or Jew?

"I am indeed a Jew, born in Tarsus of Cilicia."

—Acts 22:3

W ho was Saul? "Saul of Tarsus was a Jew, not only by descent, but by the stronger ties of lifelong training, patriotic devotion, and religious faith. Though a Roman citizen, born in a Gentile city, he was educated in Jerusalem by the most eminent of the rabbis, and diligently instructed in all the laws and traditions of the Fathers. Thus he shared, to the fullest extent, the hopes and aspirations, the lofty pride and unyielding prejudice, of his nation. . . . He was regarded by the Jewish leaders as a young man of great promise, and high hopes were cherished concerning him as an able and zealous defender of the ancient faith."[1]

He grew up, not in Israel, but in the foreign city of Tarsus. This is important for several reasons. Tarsus was "the chief city of Cilicia, founded by Phoenicians, situated on both banks of the Cydnus River about 12 mi. from the sea, on the important trade route between Syria and western Asia Minor. . . . During the period of the Seleucids it lost much of its Oriental character, because many Greeks settled there. In this period was founded the philosophical school of Tarsus, which in Paul's time was rivaled only by those of Athens and Alexandria."[2] "Famous men who haled from Tarsus were: Athenodorus the Stoic, the teacher of Augustus; Nestor the Platonist, the teacher of Marcellus; the physician Dioscorides; the Stoics Antipater and Archedemus."[3] Paul not only grew up listening to great orators debate life on the streets of his hometown, but he also mingled on a daily basis with citizens of all nations.

Paul's family would have been scrupulous in observance of their religion. There were, however, some Gentile believers to be found observing the Jewish faith. Though considered "second-class" by proud Jews, some of these worshipers had accepted the Torah and been circumcised. Others believed in Israel's God but were still novices to the "true faith." Paul had a much closer religious relationship with these Gentile worshipers in Tarsus than he would have had almost anywhere else in the Roman world. This would be key to his understanding of other philosophies and cultures.

Paul likely would have been familiar with Greek theater and uses frequent references to sporting events in his writings (1 Corinthians 9:24-27; Ephesians 6:12; 1 Timothy 6:12; 2 Timothy 4:7; Hebrews 12:1). Paul dealt with Gentile culture to a greater extent growing up in Tarsus than he would have in Jerusalem.

God often prepares us to serve before He calls us to our mission.

---

1. Ellen G. White, *Sketches From the Life of Paul* (Washington, DC: Review and Herald®, 1974), 10.
2. Siegfried H. Horn, *Seventh-day Adventist Bible Dictionary*, ed. Don F. Neufeld, Commentary Reference Series, vol. 8 (Washington, DC: Review and Herald®, 1960), s.v. "Tarsus."
3. Horn, *Seventh-day Adventist Bible Dictionary*, s.v. "Tarsus."

Tarsus of Cilicia

"I am indeed a Jew, born in Tarsus of Cilicia."

—Acts 22:3

A cts 9:11 is the first mention of Tarsus as the hometown of Saul. "Its physical position guaranteed the importance of Tarsus. Although it stood 10 mi. inland, a safe harbor lay between the city and the sea, and small craft could reach the town. Beyond the city's limits there towered the Taurus Mts., through which the narrow gorge known as the Cilician Gates gave access to the interior of Asia Minor. But the ancient city was noted for more than its strategic site. It was famous as a university town, and was sometimes known as the Athens of Asia Minor. Its scholars were respected for their skill in the sciences, and its philosophers included many noted Stoics, who may have had some influence on Saul's own outlook."[1]

"The philosophers of ancient Greece proposed to solve the problems of the origin, nature, and destiny of man and the natural world by the rational processes, and were thus of a quasi-religious character. . . . During the early part of the 3d [century] B.C., Epicurus and Zeno founded the 2 opposing ethical schools of philosophy known as the Epicureans and the Stoics. Teaching that human knowledge is insufficient to arrive at truth with any degree of certainty, the Skeptics held that man attains to happiness when he realizes he cannot attain to absolute truth and ceases to care about trying to do so."[2] Philosophical uncertainty, in contrast to religious faith, was the conflicted arena within which Saul grew up. He absorbed it all!

Tarsus was conquered first by the Assyrians, then the Medes and Persians, followed by the Greeks under Alexander the Great. Upon the death of Alexander, one of his generals, Seleucus, ruled the area from Syria. "After having belonged to the Seleucids for some time, Cilicia became a Roman province in 102 B.C., but was subsequently reorganized several times. The population consisted of descendants of the Hittites, Greeks, and Jews."[3] Tarsus, lying in the Eastern portion, was a "free city" under Seleucid kings who paid tribute to Rome. Pompey in 67 BC joined Eastern Cilicia with Syria and Phoenicia. This new area was placed under the control of a governor who became the imperial legate stationed in Syria. For the next 140 years, this state of affairs continued. Saul would have known no other geographical reality than that of Syria, Phoenicia, and Cilicia being one Roman province. Saul must have been conflicted.

Perhaps because he was born outside of Palestine and desperately wanted to fit in, Paul may have sought acceptance by being a scrupulously legalistic Pharisee and a religious zealot.

1. Francis D. Nichol, ed., *The Seventh-day Adventist Bible Commentary*, vol. 6 (Washington, DC: Review and Herald®, 1957), 232.
2. Siegfried H. Horn, *Seventh-day Adventist Bible Dictionary*, ed. Don F. Neufeld, Commentary Reference Series, vol. 8 (Washington, DC: Review and Herald®, 1960), s.v. "Philosophy."
3. Horn, *Seventh-day Adventist Bible Dictionary*, s.v. "Cilicia."

What's in a Name?

Paul, an apostle of Jesus Christ by the will of God.

—2 Timothy 1:1

By birth, religion, education, and sentiment Paul was a Hebrew; so much so that in spite of his early contacts with Greek and Roman culture and philosophy he could call himself a 'Hebrew of the Hebrews' ([Philippians] 3:5). He was of the tribe of Benjamin ([Romans] 11:1), and was perhaps a namesake of Saul, the first king of Israel, who was also a Benjamite (1 [Samuel] 9:1, 2; Acts 13:21). His father was a Roman citizen (Acts 22: 28), and probably a Pharisee ([Acts] 23:6). Just how Paul's father gained his Roman citizenship is unknown, but there were certain procedures whereby a prominent Jew in a city such as Tarsus could become a Roman citizen. Assuming that he gained his citizenship through these provisions, we may then also assume that Paul came from a family of some importance. He had at least one sister ([Acts] 23:16)."[1]

Paul was born with coveted citizen rights. Paul's family may have earned citizenship by performing some special service for the state. However obtained, citizenship was Paul's ticket into any city in the empire, and Roman colony cities such as Corinth or Philippi would have opened their doors to a respected citizen of Rome. His social status also came with access to the Roman legal system to address wrongs and grievances. He could travel with safety on Roman roads and join other Citizens or Roman soldiers on a journey.

At birth a newborn had to be registered with the office of the provincial governor within thirty days. A document similar to a passport was issued, and this was priceless. Paul was the name he chose and is the name he uses in all of his writings. "He is introduced in the Bible as Saul (. . . from the Heb. *Sha'ûl*, 'asked [of God],' or 'lent [to God]'; Acts 7:58) and is referred to by that name in the narrative of the book of Acts through [chapter] 13:9. There has been considerable speculation as to why, halfway through the book of Acts, Saul is abruptly referred to as Paul, and is called by that name exclusively from that point on, except when he himself relates the story of his conversion ([chapters] 22:7, 13; 26:14). A simple and plausible answer is that he, like others . . . , had more than one name; in his case a Hebrew name, Saul, and a Grecized Roman name, *Paulos*, or Paul. His Hebrew name was probably commonly used in his home and in his intercourse with Jews. His Greco-Roman name would be in keeping with the Hellenistic influence and environment of the city where he was born, and with his enviable status as a Roman citizen."[2]

The Latin Paulus *means "small." Yet Paul was to become a giant doing the Lord's work!*

---

1. Siegfried H. Horn, *Seventh-day Adventist Bible Dictionary*, ed. Don F. Neufeld, Commentary Reference Series, vol. 8 (Washington, DC: Review and Herald®, 1960), s.v. "Paul."
2. Horn, *Seventh-day Adventist Bible Dictionary*, s.v. "Paul."

A Conflicted Pharisee

Concerning the law, a Pharisee.

—Philippians 3:5

Paul was devout. His family lived outside Palestine, and therefore, religious training took on increased importance. The lives of most Jewish families centered on their local synagogue. The synagogue was both a social meeting place and a church where regular worship services were held each Sabbath. In some synagogues, a rabbi was hired to teach the young boys the Pentateuch. In towns where the Jewish population was small, religious instruction was centered within the family itself. We know Paul was very familiar with the Septuagint, the Scripture written in Greek, for he quotes it often. Paul probably moved to Jerusalem in his early to mid-teen years to study the Torah under Gamaliel, a member of the Sanhedrin.

When it came to the Torah, there were two main schools of pharisaical interpretation. Both schools traced origins back to the time of Herod the Great, and both were convinced they were correct in their exclusive interpretation of Scripture. Saul enrolled in the school of Hillel. Gamaliel was from this more "liberal" school. There was nothing very liberal about a follower of Hillel, but they were more flexible and open to Greek thought. Followers of Hillel cooperated more with Rome and probably were more in line with Saul's experiences in Tarsus and his exposure to Greek thought and culture. He would not have fit in very well in the School of Shammai. Shammaites were extremely conservative in their approach to life and resisted all change, especially the rule of Rome.

To study at the feet of Gamaliel was a monumental honor. He was considered the exceptional teacher of his generation, and one could do no better than to soak up his interpretation of Scripture and the Law. Gamaliel taught an attitude of nonviolence toward Roman authorities and very much believed all things were ultimately to be left to the will of God. It is, therefore, curious that we find Saul dealing with Christians as would an intolerant Shammaite. "Live and let live" was not in his vocabulary when it came to Christians who were polluting the "pure" Jewish religion.

Gamaliel believed in leaving things up to God to work out. Saul didn't learn that lesson very well in Gamaliel's Sabbath School class! Trusting God is a lesson we all must learn.

A Standout Hebrew

Of the stock of Israel, of the tribe of Benjamin, a Hebrew of the Hebrews.
—Philippians 3:5

S aul referred to his Jewish heritage on several occasions. Philippians 3:5 was one of those times. He was making his case before fellow Jews following his arrest at the temple in Jerusalem. The crowd was shocked that he spoke perfect Hebrew. He told them he was of the stock of Israel, meaning his family was directly descended from Abraham. Most Jews of the Diaspora, scattered across the empire, considered themselves to be affiliated with the nation of Israel, whether they could trace descendants back to Abraham or not. But Saul was more than politically affiliated with Israel. His was a genealogical link to the twelve tribes. Saul swore "that he came from the very core of the Jewish nation. The tribes of Benjamin and Judah were closely connected at the time of the revolt of the ten northern tribes (1 Kings 12:21), and they maintained the theocratic continuity of the Jewish race after the Babylonian exile (Ezra 4:1; 10:9). Thus a descendant of the tribe of Benjamin was indeed a 'Hebrew of the Hebrews.' "[1]

"Saul of Tarsus was a Jew, not only by descent, but by the stronger ties of lifelong training, patriotic devotion, and religious faith. . . . He was educated in Jerusalem by the most eminent of the rabbis, and diligently instructed in all the laws and traditions of the Fathers. Thus he shared, to the fullest extent, the hopes and aspirations, the lofty pride and unyielding prejudice, of his nation. He declares himself to have been 'a Hebrew of the Hebrews; as touching the law, a Pharisee; concerning zeal, persecuting the church; touching the righteousness which is in the law, blameless.' He was regarded by the Jewish leaders as a young man of great promise, and high hopes were cherished concerning him as an able and zealous defender of the ancient faith.

"In common with his nation, Saul had cherished the hope of a Messiah who should reign as a temporal prince, to break from the neck of Israel the Roman yoke, and exalt her to the throne of universal empire. He had no personal knowledge of Jesus of Nazareth or of his mission, but he readily imbibed the scorn and hatred of the rabbis toward one who was so far from fulfilling their ambitious hopes; and after the death of Christ, he eagerly joined with priests and rulers in the persecution of his followers as a proscribed and hated sect."[2]

Just because your parents made you go to "their" church is no guarantee you have found the right path.

---

1. Francis D. Nichol, ed., *The Seventh-day Adventist Bible Commentary*, vol. 6 (Washington, DC: Review and Herald®, 1957), 604.
2. Ellen G. White, *Sketches From the Life of Paul* (Washington, DC: Review and Herald®, 1974), 10.

Persecutor of "the Way"

*"I persecuted this Way to the death, binding and delivering into prisons both men and women,
as also the high priest bears me witness, and all the council of the elders."*
—Acts 22:4, 5; emphasis added

Saul "seemed to be angered at his own secret convictions that Stephen was honored of God at the very period when he was dishonored of men. He continued to persecute the church of God, hunting them down, seizing them in their houses, and delivering them up to the priests and rulers for imprisonment and death. His zeal in carrying forward the persecution was a terror to the Christians in Jerusalem. . . .

"Saul was greatly esteemed by the Jews for his zeal in persecuting the believers. After the death of Stephen, he was elected a member of the Sanhedrin council, in consideration of the part he had acted on that occasion."[1]

Saul continued to be troubled, and he came to doubt the rightness of his actions. "In his perplexity he appealed to those in whose wisdom and judgment he had full confidence. The arguments of the priests and rulers finally convinced him that Stephen was a blasphemer, that the Christ whom the martyred disciple had preached was an impostor, and that those ministering in holy office must be right. Not without severe trial did Saul come to this conclusion. But in the end his education and prejudices, his respect for his former teachers, and his pride of popularity braced him to rebel against the voice of conscience and the grace of God."[2]

"The early Church Fathers saw a half-prophetic parallelism between the language of Jacob, 'Benjamin shall ravin as a wolf: in the morning he shall devour the prey, and at night he shall divide the spoil' (Gen. 49:27), and the conduct of one who gloried in being of the tribe of Benjamin (Phil. 3:5), and who bore the name of the tribe's great hero-king."[3] Saul repeatedly tried to get the new Christians to deny Jesus as the Christ, thereby blaspheming His name. This many refused to do, so men and *women* were cast into prison, their property confiscated, their lives forfeited for their belief in their Savior. Saul believed a true Jewish Messiah would someday lift the nation to glory over her conquerors. This man, Jesus Christ, was certainly *not* the promised Messiah. Paul's intense passion on the subject fueled violence against what he saw as a threateningly false Messianism. False Messianic movements needed to be quelled!

Zeal in the pursuit of self-discerned righteousness is a formula for intolerance.

---

1. Ellen G. White, *Sketches From the Life of Paul* (Washington, DC: Review and Herald®, 1974), 20.
2. Ellen G. White, *The Acts of the Apostles* (Mountain View, CA: Pacific Press®, 1911), 113.
3. Francis D. Nichol, ed., *The Seventh-day Adventist Bible Commentary*, vol. 6 (Washington, DC: Review and Herald®, 1957), 225.

Damascus

Then Saul, still breathing threats and murder against the disciples of the Lord, went to the high priest and asked letters from him to the synagogues of Damascus.

—Acts 9:1, 2

S aul was about to journey to Damascus upon his own business; but he was determined to accomplish a double purpose, by searching out, as he went, all the believers in Christ. For this purpose he obtained letters from the high priest to read in the synagogues, which authorized him to seize all those who were suspected of being believers in Jesus, and to send them by messengers to Jerusalem, there to be tried and punished."[1] It seems strange that such a devout Pharisee as Saul would ally himself with the high priest, who was a Sadducee, for there was no love lost between the two factions. However, "the coalition of Sadducees and Pharisees that had earlier been formed against Jesus Christ (Matt. 26:3) was renewed against His followers."[2]

Damascus, a major city of the Decapolis, was an oasis in the desert of Syria. Vitellius, the Roman governor of Syria, ruled from the city. "The river Abana, fed by the snows of the Anti-Lebanon Mts., watered the terrain and made it very productive. . . . Its population was predominantly Aramaic, but the city possessed a large Jewish colony. The narrative (Acts 9:2, 14) implies that there were many 'disciples of the Lord' (v. 1) among them. Of these, many may have been refugees from the persecution in and around Jerusalem, and the local synagogues were doubtless called upon to enforce the decree of the Sanhedrin in Jerusalem. . . .

". . . It is estimated that there may have been 30 or 40 synagogues in the city of Damascus at this time. Doubtless, Christians were still devoutly attending the synagogues, and it was against them that Saul planned to proceed."[3]

We are not told who Saul's traveling companions were, but they were probably members of the temple police who were to escort those arrested back to Jerusalem under guard. Routes to Damascus were limited in the time of Paul. The shortest route forded the Jordan near Jericho and then headed north on the eastern side of the river. The longer route went north through Samaria and then forded the Jordan at Bethsean. Most travelers going from Jerusalem to Damascus would have taken the Jericho road. The trip was about 140 miles and would have taken six or seven days on horseback; even longer by foot. "Paul honestly thought that he was persecuting a weak, ignorant, fanatical sect. He did not realize that he himself was the one deluded and deceived."[4]

Persecution is never justified.

---

1. Ellen G. White, *Sketches From the Life of Paul* (Washington, DC: Review and Herald®, 1974), 21.

2. Francis D. Nichol, ed., *The Seventh-day Adventist Bible Commentary*, vol. 6 (Washington, DC: Review and Herald®, 1957), 225.

3. Nichol, *Seventh-day Adventist Bible Commentary*, vol. 6, 227.

4. Ellen G. White, MS 142, 1897.

Seeing the Light

As he journeyed he came near Damascus, and suddenly a light shone around him from heaven.
—Acts 9:3

On the last day of the journey, 'at midday,' as the weary travelers neared Damascus, they came within full view of broad stretches of fertile lands, beautiful gardens, and fruitful orchards, watered by cool streams from the surrounding mountains. After the long journey over desolate wastes such scenes were refreshing indeed."[1] As it was near noon, the glare of the sun would have been at its most intense. "Paul later says the light he saw from heaven was 'above the brightness of the sun' ([Acts] 26:13). In the midst of this effulgence he so clearly saw the glorified Christ that he includes himself among those who were privileged to behold the Lord after His resurrection (Acts 9:17; 1 Cor. 9:1; 15:8 . . .)."[2]

Saul's companions fell to the ground, blinded by the intensity of the light. They heard a voice but saw no man. The voice spoke in Aramaic (Acts 26:14), saying, "Saul, Saul, why are you persecuting Me?" (Acts 9:4). Jesus here identified Himself with His persecuted disciples. Trembling, Saul answered, " 'Who are You, Lord?'

"Then the Lord said, 'I am Jesus, whom you are persecuting. It is hard for you to kick against the goads' " (verse 5). "This appears to have been a well-known Greek proverb, which might well have been current among any agricultural people, even the Jews. The figure is drawn from the Eastern plowman's custom of using an iron goad to hasten the slow gait of his oxen. . . . The divine message suggests that Paul's conscience had been vigorously resisting the appeals of the Holy Spirit."[3]

Stephen's faith and witness, along with the more moderate teachings of Gamaliel, tormented Saul's conscience. "No doubt entered the mind of Saul that the One who spoke to him was Jesus of Nazareth, the long-looked-for Messiah, the Consolation and Redeemer of Israel. 'Trembling and astonished,' he inquired, 'Lord what wilt Thou have me to do?' And the Lord said unto him, 'Arise and go into the city, and it shall be told thee what thou must do.' "[4]

Saul based his actions on the dogma of others. We need to study to show "ourselves" approved.

1. Ellen G. White, *The Acts of the Apostles* (Mountain View, CA: Pacific Press®, 1911), 114.
2. Francis D. Nichol, ed., *The Seventh-day Adventist Bible Commentary*, vol. 6 (Washington, DC: Review and Herald®, 1957), 228.
3. Nichol, *Seventh-day Adventist Bible Commentary*, vol. 6, 438.
4. White, *Acts of the Apostles*, 117.

In the Dark

Then Saul arose from the ground, and when his eyes were opened he saw no one.
But they led him by the hand and brought him into Damascus.

—Acts 9:8

The brightness of Christ's glory had been too intense for [Saul's] mortal sight, and when it was removed, the blackness of night settled upon his vision. He believed that his blindness was the punishment of God for his cruel persecution of the followers of Jesus. He groped about in terrible darkness, and his companions, in fear and amazement, led him by the hand into Damascus."[1] Saul's companions had not gazed as directly into the light, and their eyesight was not changed. Now the leader became the led. Saul was blind!

"How different from what he had anticipated was his entrance into that city! In proud satisfaction he had neared Damascus, expecting on his arrival to be greeted with ostentation and applause because of the honor conferred upon him by the high priest, and the great zeal and penetration he had manifested in searching out the believers, to carry them as captives to Jerusalem, there to be condemned, and punished without mercy."[2] Saul was literally "in the dark." His pride was reduced to terror and his self-sufficiency to total dependence upon others to lead him. Yet the greatest terror was that which filled his mind and soul. All the time he had thought to be serving God; he now realized he was persecuting Christ.

"The power of Christ's glory might have destroyed him, but Paul was a prisoner of hope. He was made physically blind by the glory of the presence of Him whom he had blasphemed, but it was that he might have spiritual sight, that he might be awakened from the lethargy that had stupefied and deadened his perceptions.

"His conscience, aroused, now worked with self-accusing energy. The zeal of his work, his earnest resistance of the light shining upon him through God's messengers, now brought condemnation upon his soul, and he was filled with bitter remorse."[3] "Helpless, and tortured by remorse, he felt himself to be under sentence of death, and knew not what further disposition the Lord would make of him."[4]

Do you long to see Jesus? "Look up and lift up your heads, because your redemption draws near" *(Luke 21:28). At His second coming, "our eyes" will finally be opened.*

---

1. Ellen G. White, *Sketches From the Life of Paul* (Washington, DC: Review and Herald®, 1974), 25.
2. White, *Sketches From the Life of Paul*, 25, 26.
3. Ellen G. White, MS 23, 1899.
4. White, *Sketches From the Life of Paul*, 26.

A Chosen Vessel

But the Lord said to him, "Go, for he is a chosen vessel of Mine to bear My name before Gentiles, kings, and the children of Israel."

—Acts 9:15

Saul's letters were never delivered to the synagogue leaders in Damascus. He was led instead to the house of Judas on a street called Straight. There he sat for three days in total darkness. Saul neither ate nor drank and hardly thought of food, for "those three days were like three years to the blind and conscience-smitten Jew. He was no novice in the Scriptures, and in his darkness and solitude he recalled the passages which referred to the Messiah, and traced down the prophecies, with a memory sharpened by the conviction that had taken possession of his mind. He became astonished at his former blindness of understanding, and at the blindness of the Jews in general, in rejecting Jesus as the promised Messiah. All seemed plain to him, and he knew that it was prejudice and unbelief which had clouded his perceptions, and prevented him from discerning in Jesus of Nazareth the Messiah of prophecy."[1]

The angel of the Lord now appeared to Ananias of Damascus in vision. We know little of Ananias, but his relationship with the Lord was clearly one of trust. When the Lord called, Ananias answered: "Here I am, Lord." The directions given were (1) go to the house of Judas (2) on the street called "Straight" and (3) find Saul of Tarsus who had been given a vision of Ananias's coming. (4) Put your hands on him that he might receive his sight. Notice how precise the directions are. Ananias wasn't ignorant of the fact that Saul was an enemy. " 'Lord, I have heard from many about this man, how much harm he has done to Your saints in Jerusalem. And here he has authority from the chief priests to bind all who call on Your name.'

"But the Lord said to him, 'Go, for he is a chosen vessel of Mine to bear My name before Gentiles, kings, and the children of Israel' " (Acts 9:13–15). Ananias may have had some initial concerns, but Scripture says he went immediately "and entered the house; and laying his hands on him he said, 'Brother Saul, the Lord Jesus, who appeared to you on the road as you came, has sent me that you may receive your sight and be filled with the Holy Spirit' " (verse 17). Ananias is an inspiration. Who might God challenge you to approach?

"The character will determine the nature of the resolve and the action."[2] Ananias had fidelity!

---

1. Ellen G. White, *Sketches From the Life of Paul* (Washington, DC: Review and Herald®, 1974), 27.
2. Ellen G. White, Letter 135, 1898.

An Effective Witness

Immediately he preached the Christ in the synagogues, that He is the Son of God.
—Acts 9:20

When Ananias laid his hands upon Saul, it was as if scales fell from Saul's eyes, and he was instantaneously cured. That is not to say that he returned to the same condition he had been in before his encounter with Jesus on the road to Damascus. "He was ever to carry about with him in the body the marks of Christ's glory, in his eyes, which had been blinded by the heavenly light."[1] Might this have been the thorn in the flesh to which he refers in Galatians 4:13–15 and 2 Corinthians 12:7–10? Perhaps. After Ananias baptized Saul in the river of Damascus, Saul broke his fast. The Scriptures report, "Saul spent some days with the disciples at Damascus" (Acts 9:19). We do not know exactly how many days he spent there with the followers of Jesus, but it was a time of revelation for the former persecutor of Christians.

Saul now stood in the Diaspora Jewish synagogues of Damascus and preached Jesus Christ as the Messiah. Saul resorted to Old Testament texts to prove Messianic prophecies were fulfilled in the person of Jesus of Nazareth. "Saul's training under Gamaliel stood him in good stead. He could now use his thorough knowledge of Jewish learning for the support of his new-found convictions. His methods commended his faith to those Jews who were sincerely looking for the Hope of Israel; but these, unfortunately, would not be a large proportion of his listeners. The rest of the Jews were 'confounded.' "[2]

"Paul had formerly been known as a zealous defender of the Jewish religion and an untiring persecutor of the followers of Jesus. Courageous, independent, persevering, his talents and training would have enabled him to serve in almost any capacity. He could reason with extraordinary clearness, and by his withering sarcasm could place an opponent in no enviable light. And now the Jews saw this young man of unusual promise united with those whom he formerly persecuted, and fearlessly preaching in the name of Jesus."[3] Devout Jews were at first astonished at Paul's conversion, but soon astonishment turned "into an intense hatred of him, like unto that which they had manifested against Jesus."[4] Saul needed to be silenced!

Saul was a student of Scripture, basing his theology on the sure word of prophecy. Do you?

---

1. Ellen G. White, *Sketches From the Life of Paul* (Washington, DC: Review and Herald®, 1974), 34.
2. Francis D. Nichol, ed., *The Seventh-day Adventist Bible Commentary*, vol. 6 (Washington, DC: Review and Herald®, 1957), 235.
3. Ellen G. White, *The Acts of the Apostles* (Mountain View, CA: Pacific Press®, 1911), 124.
4. White, *Sketches From the Life of Paul*, 33.

Arabian Retreat

I did not immediately confer with flesh and blood, nor did I go up to Jerusalem to those who were apostles before me; but I went to Arabia, and returned again to Damascus.
                                                                    —Galatians 1:16, 17

Little is known of the interval between Saul's conversion in AD 35 and his return to Jerusalem in AD 38. These dates are at best uncertain, yet we know the total period covered three years. It is possible Saul preached the gospel in the synagogues of Damascus for but a few weeks before his life was threatened. "The opposition grew so fierce that [Saul] was not allowed to continue his labors at Damascus. A messenger from heaven bade him leave for a time, and he 'went into Arabia' (Galatians 1:17), where he found a safe retreat.

"Here, in the solitude of the desert, [Saul] had ample opportunity for quiet study and meditation. He calmly reviewed his past experience and made sure work of repentance. . . . Jesus communed with him and established him in the faith, bestowing upon him a rich measure of wisdom and grace."[1] As with Moses and Jesus, Saul pondered his calling in wilderness solitude with God and among fellow believers.

What did Saul do in Arabia? Arabia was ruled by the powerful Bedouin Nabataean king Aretas IV. "His capital was Petra, south of the Dead Sea. . . . The daughter of Aretas IV was married to Herod Antipas, who sent her away when he fell in love with Herodias. Aretas thereupon fought a war of revenge against Antipas, and occupied sections of Perea, east of the Jordan. Upon Antipas' appeal to Tiberius for help, the emperor sent Vitellius, the governor of Syria, to punish Aretas. But Tiberius died and the expedition was not carried out. Caligula seems to have been friendly toward Aretas, and to have given him control of Damascus, which was then administered by an ethnarch in Aretas' name (2 Cor 11:32). The period of Nabataean occupation of Damascus was doubtless between Tiberius' death in AD 37 and the death of Aretas in AD 40."[2] There were many Christians as well as Jews in Arabia and Nabataea. It is possible Saul was forced to leave Arabia after three years because of turmoil in that country.

Saul forsook human wisdom and "determined not to know anything . . . except Jesus Christ and Him crucified" (1 Corinthians 2:2). Our focus should also be to create an unyielding faith in Jesus.

---

1. Ellen G. White, *The Acts of the Apostles* (Mountain View, CA: Pacific Press®, 1911), 125, 126.
2. Siegfried H. Horn, *Seventh-day Adventist Bible Dictionary*, ed. Don F. Neufeld, Commentary Reference Series, vol. 8 (Washington, DC: Review and Herald®, 1960), s.v. "Aretas."

The Tables Are Turned

Now after many days were past, the Jews plotted to kill him. But their plot became known to
Saul. And they watched the gates day and night, to kill him.

—Acts 9:23, 24

After almost three years in Arabia, Saul returned to Damascus and immediately ran into trouble. "When Tiberius died in 37 AD, Vitellius hastened to Rome, and Aretas IV, king of the Nabataeans, seized control of Damascus and governed it by a deputy. Thus matters stood at the time when Saul escaped from the city (2 Cor. 11:32)."[1] "The period of Saul's absence probably witnessed a large growth in the Christian society at Damascus, with a type of discipline and worship similar to that at Jerusalem. So far as is known, no Gentile converts had yet been admitted to the church, and the preaching of the gospel was still restricted to the Jews. With intense affection for his brethren according to the flesh (Rom. 10:1), Saul entered vigorously upon the work of evangelization among them, until their bitter antagonism drove him from Damascus. Saul himself was now tasting the hatred that had been poured out against Stephen."[2]

The Jews of Damascus could not refute the logic or training of Saul, so they sought to silence him by force. "An active part in the plot against Saul was taken by the ethnarch (governor) of the city. . . . The ethnarch apparently wished to court favor with the large Jewish population, and looking upon Saul as a disturber of the public peace, took measures for his arrest and condemnation. From Luke's account it appears that the Jews assumed a large part of the responsibility for Saul's capture. . . . Sentinels were evidently stationed at each gate of the city, through which a fugitive might attempt to pass, in order to prevent Saul's escape."[3]

Things looked bleak for the new apostle of Christ. Friends willingly risked their lives to tell Saul he was in danger. In the middle of the night, they lowered him through a window in the city wall in a large *sarganē*, or wicker hamper. "This experience is mentioned by [Saul] in connection with his 'infirmities' (in which he may have included his traditional smallness of stature) of which he was content to boast (2 Cor. 11:30)."[4] Later references show he considered the ordeal to be a humiliating retreat.

Consider—the believers Saul had sought to persecute three years earlier now saved his life!

---

1. Francis D. Nichol, ed., *The Seventh-day Adventist Bible Commentary*, vol. 6 (Washington, DC: Review and Herald®, 1957), 227.
2. Nichol, *Seventh-day Adventist Bible Commentary*, vol. 6, 235.
3. Nichol, *Seventh-day Adventist Bible Commentary*, vol. 6, 236.
4. Nichol, *Seventh-day Adventist Bible Commentary*, vol. 6, 236.

Barnabas Steps Forward

And when Saul had come to Jerusalem, he tried to join the disciples;
but they were all afraid of him, and did not believe that he was a disciple.
But Barnabas took him and brought him to the apostles.

—Acts 9:26, 27

When Saul had left Jerusalem three years earlier, it was with orders in hand to arrest the followers of Christ in Damascus and return them for trial and punishment. If Saul thought those in Jerusalem he had once persecuted would receive him with open arms, he was to be sadly mistaken. Saul was especially eager to see Peter (Galatians 1:18), but it was difficult to believe that so bigoted a Pharisee, and one who had done so much to destroy the church, could become a sincere follower of Jesus. Like Ananias of Damascus, the disciples found it extremely unlikely that so relentless a foe as Saul could change into a loving, believing brother. Saul wanted desperately "to meet the Galilean fishermen who had lived, and prayed, and conversed with Christ upon earth. It was with a yearning heart that he desired to meet the chief of apostles. As [Saul] entered Jerusalem, he regarded with changed views the city and the temple. He now knew that the retributive judgment of God was hanging over them."[1]

The disciples had cause to be cautious. Persecution had not stopped during the three years Saul was in Arabia. Hellenist believers in Christ were still being detained, arrested, imprisoned, and killed. "Might he [Saul] not be bent on their destruction? They would be cautious until they were sure of his sincerity."[2] "Great was his [Saul's] grief and disappointment when he found that they would not receive him as one of their number."[3] "Barnabas . . . had been acquainted with [S]aul when he opposed the believers. He now came forward and renewed that acquaintance, heard the testimony of [S]aul in regard to his miraculous conversion, and his experience from that time. He fully believed and received [S]aul, took him by the hand, and led him into the presence of the apostles."[4] "Peter and James, who at that time were the only apostles in Jerusalem, gave the right hand of fellowship to the once fierce persecutor of their faith; and he was now as much beloved and respected as he had formerly been feared and avoided."[5] We need more members like Barnabas in our churches!

By all biblical accounts, Barnabas always lived up to his name as a "son of encouragement."

---

1. Ellen G. White, *Sketches From the Life of Paul* (Washington, DC: Review and Herald®, 1974), 35.
2. Francis D. Nichol, ed., *The Seventh-day Adventist Bible Commentary*, vol. 6 (Washington, DC: Review and Herald®, 1957), 236.
3. White, *Sketches From the Life of Paul*, 35.
4. White, *Sketches From the Life of Paul*, 36.
5. White, *Sketches From the Life of Paul*, 36.

Saul—Another Stephen?

And he spoke boldly in the name of the Lord Jesus and disputed
against the Hellenists, but they attempted to kill him.

—Acts 9:29

Finally "the two grand characters of the new faith met—Peter, one of the chosen companions of Christ while he was upon earth, and [Saul], a Pharisee, who, since the ascension of Jesus, had met him face to face, and had talked with him, and had also seen him in vision, and the nature of his work in Heaven.

"This first interview was of great consequence to both these apostles, but it was of short duration, for [Saul] was eager to get about his Master's business. Soon the voice which had so earnestly disputed with Stephen, was heard in the same synagogue fearlessly proclaiming that Jesus was the Son of God—advocating the same cause that Stephen had died to vindicate."[1]

Saul felt sure that the "teachers in Israel, with whom he had once been so well acquainted, were as sincere and honest as he had been. But he had miscalculated the spirit of his Jewish brethren, and in the hope of their speedy conversion he was doomed to bitter disappointment. Although 'he spake boldly in the name of the Lord Jesus, and disputed against the Grecians,' those who stood at the head of the Jewish church refused to believe, but 'went about to slay him.' "[2] Again, Saul was in danger. First, the Diaspora Jews in Damascus and now the Hellenistic Jews in Jerusalem wanted him dead! The disciples urged Saul to flee for his life, but he rejected the idea, thinking that he needed to atone for his part in the martyrdom of Stephen. He redoubled his efforts to reach his former colleagues. Saul was nothing if not brave, and he felt running would look like cowardice.

"Burdened in behalf of those who refused to believe, [Saul] was praying in the temple, as he himself afterward testified, when he fell into a trance."[3] "The Saviour appeared to him in vision, saying, 'Make haste, and get thee quickly out of Jerusalem: for they will not receive thy testimony concerning me' "[4] (Acts 22:18). When the other disciples learned of the vision and the plot to kill Saul, they secretly moved him to the seacoast and urged him to flee Judea.

Despite violent resistance in Damascus and Jerusalem, Saul did not quit preaching the gospel.
Sometimes it takes real courage to be a Christian.

---

1. Ellen G. White, *Sketches From the Life of Paul* (Washington, DC: Review and Herald®, 1974), 36, 37.
2. Ellen G. White, *The Acts of the Apostles* (Mountain View, CA: Pacific Press®, 1911), 129.
3. White, *Acts of the Apostles*, 130.
4. White, *Sketches From the Life of Paul*, 37.

Sent Home

When the brethren found out, they brought him down to Caesarea and sent him out to Tarsus.
—Acts 9:30

How I would have liked to sit in on the initial meetings between Saul and Peter. Imagine what they must have talked about during their two weeks together. Saul was very anxious to meet Peter, one of "the Galilean fishermen who had lived, and prayed, and conversed with Christ upon earth. It was with a yearning heart that he desired to meet the chief of the apostles. As [Saul] entered Jerusalem, he regarded with changed views the city and the temple. He now knew that the retributive judgment of God was hanging over them."[1]

The account we are given by Saul of his visit to Jerusalem is very different from that recorded in the book of Acts. Luke, in Acts 9:28, wanted to show Saul's *acceptance* by the apostles. Saul in Galatians 1:18, 19 drew attention to his *independence* of them. Other than Peter, Saul had met only with Jesus' brother James (verse 19). Saul wanted the Gentiles to know his message had come directly from Christ and was not received secondhand from the disciples. His calling was from Christ, and his message was a unique one structured for them. He did not get his marching orders from Jerusalem! Luke and Saul placed emphasis on this two-week period of meetings to prove separate points—*acceptance* and *independence*.

Now Saul needed to leave Jerusalem—fast! Smuggled out of the capital, he arrived safely in Caesarea, sixty-four miles northwest of Jerusalem. "At Caesarea he would probably find Philip. The two men, one the friend and the other the erstwhile opponent of Stephen, would thus come face to face as brethren" (Acts 8:40).[2] Saul's hometown of Tarsus "may not have been the most comfortable refuge for the apostle. Christ's saying that a 'prophet hath no honour in his own country' (John 4:44) was likely to be painfully true in Saul's case. Not only was he returning to his birthplace; he was going back as a renegade Jew, an apostate from the faith of his fathers, a leader of the despised and persecuted sect of the Christians. His reception may be imagined, and may help to account for his silence on the subject of his family."[3]

Sometimes accepting the gospel means alienation from friends and even family. Saul certainly understood and was willing to sacrifice all for the knowledge of Jesus Christ.

1. Ellen G. White, *Sketches From the Life of Paul* (Washington, DC: Review and Herald®, 1974), 35.
2. Francis D. Nichol, ed., *The Seventh-day Adventist Bible Commentary*, vol. 6 (Washington, DC: Review and Herald®, 1957), 238.
3. Nichol, *Seventh-day Adventist Bible Commentary*, vol. 6, 238.

Tabitha

"Tabitha, arise."

—Acts 9:40

Luke now leaves Saul in Tarsus and shifts his attention to Peter. He does this to emphasize that the gospel was being preached to Jews and Gentiles. It happened that Peter was visiting with believers in Lydda. The town "lay about 10 mi. southeast [inland] of Joppa, and a day's journey northwest of Jerusalem."[1] Here Peter had "healed Aeneas, who for eight years had been confined to his bed with palsy."[2] Philip probably visited Lydda on his evangelistic swing from Azotus to Caesarea (Acts 8:40; 9:32). Not far from Lydda was the town of Joppa by the sea. "The town stood on a hill so high that it was claimed that Jerusalem could be seen from its summit. It was the port nearest to Jerusalem. . . . Here, as in the case of Lydda (. . . Acts 9:32), the raising up of a Christian company was probably accomplished by Philip."[3]

In Joppa lived *Tabitha*, from the Hebrew name Zibiah. Her Greek name, Dorcas, meant "gazelle." Dorcas was a deaconess in the Joppa church. She may have been in charge of caring for the widows. "Dorcas' benevolence expressed itself in two principal ways: she gave her services in 'good works'; she gave her means in 'almsdeeds.' "[4] Ellen White says of Dorcas, "Her skillful fingers were more active than her tongue."[5]

Suddenly Dorcas took sick and died. The members of the church, realizing Peter was in nearby Lydda, sent a delegation urging him to come to Joppa at once. Peter left Lydda immediately on the four-hour return. Meanwhile, the women tenderly washed the body and waited, knowing that burial must precede sunset. Upon arrival, Peter entered the room where Dorcas lay covered. Widows tearfully showed him the many garments Dorcas had skillfully made for them. Following the example of Jesus when He raised Jairus's daughter, an act Peter had personally observed, Peter asked everyone to cease weeping and leave the room. In silence, he knelt down and fervently prayed that Dorcas might be restored to life and health. "Turning to the body, he said, 'Tabitha, arise. And she opened her eyes: and when she saw Peter, she sat up.' "[6]

How interesting that Joppa was the port from which Jonah put to sea to avoid service (Jonah 1:3) and the same city where Dorcas was raised to continue serving.

1. Francis D. Nichol, ed., *The Seventh-day Adventist Bible Commentary*, vol. 6 (Washington, DC: Review and Herald®, 1957), 241.
2. Ellen G. White, *The Acts of the Apostles* (Mountain View, CA: Pacific Press®, 1911), 131.
3. Nichol, *Seventh-day Adventist Bible Commentary*, vol. 6, 242.
4. Nichol, *Seventh-day Adventist Bible Commentary*, vol. 6, 242.
5. White, *Acts of the Apostles*, 131.
6. White, *Acts of the Apostles*, 132.

Cornelius

There was a certain man in Caesarea called Cornelius, a centurion of what was called the Italian Regiment, a devout man and one who feared God with all his household.

—Acts 10:1, 2

C ornelius was a Roman citizen and a minor officer in command of 80 to 100 men, or a century—a small part of a larger five-hundred- to one-thousand-man regiment, or cohort. A century usually formed 1/60th of a Roman legion (six thousand men). Cornelius commanded within the elite Italian Regiment. "This was probably the *Cohors II. Italica*, which is known to have been stationed in Syria during the Jewish-Roman War, and apparently was there earlier, at the time of the present narrative. This cohort is thought to have been made up of freedmen, or at least of men who were non-Roman in origin. It was an auxiliary cohort of archers."[1] Military service was a tough career path. Of those who signed up for a twenty-year enlistment, half would not survive. If one did survive, the rewards were large. Noncitizens were not allowed to join legions but became auxiliary troops. These received citizenship upon discharge from their term of enlistment.

Cornelius was "a man of wealth and noble birth, and his position was one of trust and honor. A heathen by birth, training, and education, through contact with the Jews he had gained a knowledge of God, and he worshiped Him with a true heart, showing the sincerity of his faith by compassion to the poor."[2] His actions call to mind another centurion of whom the Jews said, "He loves our nation, and has built us a synagogue" (Luke 7:5). "The conversion of Cornelius marks a new stage of expansion in the growth of the church. Cornelius was a Roman officer, but he was not completely a heathen. He was 'devout' and 'feared God,' and gave alms to the people. . . . Even so, in Jewish eyes he was a Gentile, for he was uncircumcised. Consequently his admission into the church marks a new stage in the expansion of Christianity."[3]

Luke, in referring to Cornelius's "household," would certainly have known Rome did not allow military personnel to marry. Luke includes servants or emancipated slaves as a "household" in keeping with the times. A regular soldier might pay one-third of his annual pay for a low-priced slave. Centurions received up to fifteen times the pay of noncommissioned soldiers.

Cornelius was stationed in Caesarea, the administrative capital of the Roman province of Judea. Under the very nose of the Roman procurator, he bravely adopted the religion of the Jews!

---

1. Francis D. Nichol, ed., *The Seventh-day Adventist Bible Commentary*, vol. 6 (Washington, DC: Review and Herald®, 1957), 246.

2. Ellen G. White, *The Acts of the Apostles* (Mountain View, CA: Pacific Press®, 1911), 132.

3. Nichol, *Seventh-day Adventist Bible Commentary*, vol. 6, 246.

"Send for Peter"

"Your prayers and your alms have come up for a memorial before God. Now send men to Joppa, and send for Simon whose surname is Peter. He is lodging with Simon, a tanner, whose house is by the sea. He will tell you what you must do."

—Acts 10:4–6

Cornelius was waiting for the Messiah to come but had no knowledge of Jesus Christ. He had adopted the Jewish hours of prayer and was praying at three o'clock, or the ninth hour of the day, when suddenly he received a vision. Standing before him was an angel. Seeing this man in bright clothing (Acts 10:30) frightened Cornelius, but quickly, he recovered his composure and asked, "What is it, Lord?" The reply is our text for today. "In the tenth chapter of Acts we have still another instance of the ministration of heavenly angels, resulting in the conversion of Cornelius and his company. Let these chapters [8–10] be read, and receive special attention. In them we see that heaven is much nearer to the Christian who is engaged in the work of soul-saving than many suppose. We should learn through them the lesson, also, of God's regard for every human being, and that each should treat his fellow man as one of the Lord's instrumentalities for the accomplishment of His work in the earth."[1]

Note how specific are the instructions given to Cornelius to bring him into contact with Peter. The directions given tell us something of the wisdom and power of God. Have you ever felt alone? You aren't, you know. "Consider that the Lord knows every one of us by name, and just where we live, and the spirit we possess, and every act of our life. The ministering angels are passing through the churches, noting our faithfulness in our individual line of duty."[2] God knew exactly where Peter was staying at that moment. Just as He intervened with Ananias and Saul in their Damascus meeting, He now directed this meeting between Peter and Cornelius.

Joppa lies thirty miles south of Caesarea. If Cornelius's messengers left sometime after three o'clock in the afternoon (the ninth hour—verse 3), they would have had to travel part of the night on foot and sleep in the open. Estimating three miles per hour for a man on foot, they approached Joppa at the "sixth hour," or noon (verse 9).

"God reveals Himself to those who are striving to form characters that He can approve."[3]

---

1. Ellen G. White, MS 17, 1908.
2. Ellen G. White, Letter 20a, 1893.
3. Ellen G. White, "The Pearl of Great Price," *Advent Review and Sabbath Herald*, August 8, 1899, 501.

All Food Is Clean?

"What God has cleansed you must not call common."

—Acts 10:15

Peter was now lodging in Joppa with Simon, the tanner. "The occupation of tanner was one that repelled strict Jews. This was either because it would require coming in contact with carcasses and hides of dead beasts, with the risk of ceremonial defilement (see Lev. 11:24, 25), or because it was in general a repulsive and unpleasant business. . . . This tanner's house was 'by the sea side' (Acts 10:6). It would be easy for Peter, during his long stay with the humble but hospitable Simon, to return to his old occupation of fishing, and thus earn his living. The fact that he was willing to take up his abode with a tanner indicates that the apostle was already tending to abandon Jewish prejudices."[1]

Peter was on the flat roof of the dwelling, engaged in a midday prayer. Quite possibly, he had not eaten yet that day and was offering his afternoon prayer early to follow the rule stating one must not eat just before prayer. Peter was hungry. While praying, he saw heaven open, and a sheet let down containing all manner of forbidden foods. A voice told him to "Rise, Peter; kill and eat" (verse 13). Peter was shocked! "Not so, Lord! For I have never eaten anything common or unclean." The voice spoke to him again, saying, "What God has cleansed you must not call common" (verse 15). Peter was puzzled. He could not imagine eating nonkosher food. And while he pondered the meaning of the vision, the men sent by Cornelius were knocking at Simon's gate seeking Peter. An outer gate would indicate Simon was a man of some means. "The messengers doubtless were Gentiles, like Cornelius himself, and so would hesitate to enter a Jewish house without giving notice of their presence."[2]

The angel told Peter, "Behold, three men are seeking you. Arise therefore, go down and go with them, doubting nothing, for I have sent them" (verse 19). Three times the sheet had been let down, just as three times Peter had been told by His Lord to " 'Feed my lambs' or 'Feed my sheep' (John 21:15–17), an injunction that now was to take on a new and fuller meaning to him."[3] The Spirit now impressed Peter to connect his vision with the arrival of this delegation.

Some try to excuse the eating of unclean foods by citing this message to Peter. It is well for all to remember that the vision "did not concern food, it concerned men."[4]

---

1. Francis D. Nichol, ed., *The Seventh-day Adventist Bible Commentary*, vol. 6 (Washington, DC: Review and Herald®, 1957), 243.
2. Nichol, *Seventh-day Adventist Bible Commentary*, vol. 6, 250.
3. Nichol, *Seventh-day Adventist Bible Commentary*, vol. 6, 250.
4. Nichol, *Seventh-day Adventist Bible Commentary*, vol. 6, 250.

No Partiality

"In truth I perceive that God shows no partiality. But in every nation whoever fears Him and works righteousness is accepted by Him."

—Acts 10:34, 35

Peter came down the outside staircase from the rooftop and introduced himself with great reluctance. "To Peter this was a trying command, and it was with reluctance at every step that he undertook the duty laid upon him; but he dared not disobey."[1] Jewish teachers often talked with Gentiles hoping to convert them to Judaism, but a strict Jew would never enter a Gentile's house nor allow a Gentile entrance to theirs. Peter, therefore, faced a significant cultural problem. He was invited to a Gentile's home! Peter has a second, more immediate problem. While a Pharisee would never offer overnight lodging to a Gentile, eating with them was forbidden on the principle that they were wicked company. Peter invited the Gentile envoys to spend the night in the home of Simon because it was too late in the day to return the thirty miles to Caesarea.

In the morning, Peter called together six Jewish Christians to accompany him, and together with the two servants and soldier whom Cornelius had sent, they all set out for Caesarea. They passed the night on the road, and early the following morning arrived at Cornelius's door. Cornelius had called together citizens and friends to hear Peter's message. When he saw Peter, he bowed down to him, showing he recognized Peter as a messenger of God. Peter quickly raised him up, assuring him that he was a man and not a god. After a brief discussion in the entryway of the house, Peter took the next bold step, entering the Gentile's home. Peter, regarding his vision, had briefed the six Jewish Christians, and they entered right behind him!

Peter told Cornelius of the vision he had received and stated he had put aside his initial prejudices and come without objection to the home of the Gentile. Now, "I ask, then, for what reason have you sent for me?" (Acts 10:29) Cornelius told of his own visit from the heavenly messenger and how he had been told to send for Peter. "So I sent to you immediately, and you have done well to come. Now therefore, we are all present before God, to hear all the things commanded you by God" (verse 33). Peter's response is today's devotional text.

Thank God He sent His Son to die for all who believe (John 3:16)!

---

1. Ellen G. White, *The Acts of the Apostles* (Mountain View, CA: Pacific Press®, 1911), 137.

The Spirit Breaks Barriers

Then Peter answered, "Can anyone forbid water, that these should not be baptized who have received the Holy Spirit just as we have?"

—Acts 10:46, 47

Peter had seen in his Master an absence of 'respect of persons,' whether the distinctions were of social rank, or knowledge, or wealth. This even His enemies acknowledged (Matt. 22:16). . . . Peter needed to learn that the full application of this great principle called for the Jewish Christians to accept those of other races into equal fellowship with themselves. Paul, the champion of Gentile Christianity, stresses this principle in Rom. 2:9–11. From Cornelius' vision, parallel to his own, Peter was learning that God makes Himself known to all aspirants to righteousness, whether they are Jews or Gentiles."[1] "Then to that company of attentive hearers the apostle preached Christ—His life, His miracles, His betrayal and crucifixion, His resurrection and ascension, and His work in heaven as man's representative and advocate. As Peter pointed those present to Jesus as the sinner's only hope, he himself understood more fully the meaning of the vision he had seen, and his heart glowed with the spirit of the truth that he was presenting."[2]

Suddenly the Holy Spirit descended upon the Gentiles. "The descent of the Holy Spirit upon the Gentile Cornelius and his family before their baptism directly fulfilled, for Peter's companions, Christ's promise that the Holy Spirit 'will guide you into all truth' (John 16:13). In spite of Peter's vision they still were unprepared to accept Gentiles fully into the church (Acts 10:45), until the coming of the Holy Spirit demonstrated that Gentiles were acceptable to God."[3] These were uncircumcised Gentiles and not full-fledged Jewish proselytes. This made no difference now to Peter, who commanded that the Gentiles should be baptized. The implication is "that Peter himself did not baptize these converts. Jesus (John 4:1, 2) and Paul (1 Cor. 1:14–16) refrained from baptizing converts. . . . Paul declares that he refrained generally from baptizing, lest factions arise and Christian unity be broken by men dividing into parties under the names of those who had baptized them."[4] Peter consented to stay several days with the new believers, eating and drinking with them without fear of defilement. This marked a turning point in Peter's life and a watershed for the church. Cornelius accepted Jesus. Peter accepted Cornelius.

Both teacher and student benefit when sharing is encouraged in the Sabbath School class discussion.

---

1. Francis D. Nichol, ed., *The Seventh-day Adventist Bible Commentary*, vol. 6 (Washington, DC: Review and Herald®, 1957), 253, 254.

2. Ellen G. White, *The Acts of the Apostles* (Mountain View, CA: Pacific Press®, 1911), 138, 139.

3. Nichol, *Seventh-day Adventist Bible Commentary*, vol. 6, 256.

4. Nichol, *Seventh-day Adventist Bible Commentary*, vol. 6, 257.

Peter, What Were You Thinking!

And when Peter came up to Jerusalem, those of the circumcision contended with him, saying, "You went in to uncircumcised men and ate with them!"

—Acts 11:2, 3

Peter had not left Caesarea before news of his behavior regarding Cornelius reached Jerusalem. Sometimes it seems no matter what one does, there are those who delight in spreading tales and making things appear in the worst light. The story that reached Jerusalem was that, for the first time, uncircumcised Gentiles had been baptized and taken into church fellowship. That Peter would eat with Gentiles, who did not discriminate regarding what they ate or how it was prepared (nonkosher), was also a real concern. The news was met with incredulity, opposition, and hostility. At this time, those who would become known as *Judaizers* or the *circumcision party* had not yet formed. Once established, however, these pious, self-righteous, exclusionary, prejudiced Jews would make life miserable for Saul and anyone seeking to bring salvation to Gentiles on any other basis than what they decreed.

"Those who had been born Jews, and who had neither heard of Peter's vision nor seen the gift of the Holy Spirit poured out upon Cornelius and his household, are to be pardoned if their scruples caused them to challenge Peter's conduct. When these had heard his story they were satisfied (see [Acts 11:]18), but many Jewish Christians elsewhere continued to make this a matter of contention."[1] "The contenders insisted the difference between Jew and Gentile should still be maintained. That is, that Christians should hold fellowship only with those who had become proselytes to Judaism and gave due obedience to the ritual law. . . . The prejudice that had grown up among the Jews through generations of ceremonial observance makes this comprehensible."[2]

"Peter laid the whole matter before them."[3] He related the visions given Cornelius and himself. He told of the Holy Spirit being bestowed upon the Gentiles. He reminded the leaders that Jesus had said they would be baptized with the Holy Ghost (John 14:26), and as such, how could he, Peter, contend with God? Peter produced the brethren who accompanied him to Caesarea and called them to witness. The majority of Jewish Christians in Jerusalem were persuaded! God had convincingly shown that both Jews and Gentiles might be saved on the same terms.

It is a sin when self feels the proud exclusivity that would deny others the gospel and salvation.

---

1. Francis D. Nichol, ed., *The Seventh-day Adventist Bible Commentary*, vol. 6 (Washington, DC: Review and Herald®, 1957), 259.

2. Nichol, *Seventh-day Adventist Bible Commentary*, vol. 6, 260.

3. Ellen G. White, *The Acts of the Apostles* (Mountain View, CA: Pacific Press®, 1911), 141.

Phoenicia, Cyprus, and Antioch

Now those who were scattered after the persecution that arose over Stephen traveled as far as Phoenicia, Cyprus, and Antioch, preaching the word to no one but the Jews only.

—Acts 11:19

Persecution in Jerusalem caused many Hellenist Christians to drift north to Phoenicia. Phoenicia, modern-day Lebanon, consists of a narrow coastal strip of flat land sandwiched between the Lebanon Mountains and the Mediterranean Sea. Numerous small headlands exist where the mountains recede from the sea. Each bluff boasted a seafaring city, the principal of these being Tyre and Sidon. "Phoenicia was rich in grain, fruit, and wine, and as the principal exporter of cedar wood from the mountains . . . , it became the commercial clearinghouse of the ancient world.

"The Greek name for the land, Phoenicia, is related to one of its principal exports, a purple-colored dye material called *phoinix*, 'purple,' or 'crimson.' However, they called themselves *Kena'ani*, that is, Canaanites, and their country Canaan, which agrees with Gen. 10:15–19."[1]

Cyprus, the birthplace of Barnabas, is a large island in the Mediterranean approximately sixty miles from the Phoenician coast. It is 160 miles long and from six to sixty miles wide, possessing a fertile central plain. "The copper ore in its mountains made it the main copper-producing area for the ancient world. This gave it its name Cyprus, which means 'copper.' "[2] Cyprus, while still mainly populated with Greeks, was a Roman senatorial province ruled by a proconsul.

Antioch, the capital of Syria, was located on the Orontes River about fifteen miles inland from the Mediterranean and the port of Seleucia. "Following Rome, Alexandria, and Ephesus, Antioch was the greatest city of the Roman Empire."[3] "Antioch was headquarters for the Roman prefect, or propraetor, of Syria. Christianity found itself at Antioch in closer contact with Greek culture than at Jerusalem or Caesarea. Here also it encountered heathenism in its most tempting and debasing forms. Its groves to Daphne were famous for their voluptuous, idolatrous worship. It was an amazing victory that the church was able to make Antioch one of its principal headquarters."[4] The infant church may have been crossing borders, but it was still only approaching Jews! Why is it that map borders are often easier to cross than ethnic borders?

Reaching out to other cultures often means moving beyond your comfort zone to embrace souls.

---

1. Francis D. Nichol, ed., *The Seventh-day Adventist Bible Commentary*, vol. 2, rev. ed. (Washington, DC: Review and Herald®, 1976), 68.

2. Siegfried H. Horn, *Seventh-day Adventist Bible Dictionary*, ed. Don F. Neufeld, Commentary Reference Series, vol. 8 (Washington, DC: Review and Herald®, 1960), s.v. "Cyprus."

3. Francis D. Nichol, ed., *The Seventh-day Adventist Bible Commentary*, vol. 6 (Washington, DC: Review and Herald®, 1957), 262.

4. Nichol, *Seventh-day Adventist Bible Commentary*, vol. 6, 262.

Barnabas Recruits Saul

Then Barnabas departed for Tarsus to seek Saul.

—Acts 11:25

Just as Peter and John had been sent to Samaria, Barnabas was sent from Jerusalem to strengthen the work in Antioch. Barnabas was a good choice to encourage the believers in Antioch. In some respects, Barnabas was uniquely qualified to bridge the gap between the mother church in Jerusalem and the new church in Antioch. On the one hand, Barnabas had long associated with the apostles in Jerusalem (Acts 4:36, 37; 9:27). He was a cousin to John Mark, and Mark's family was from Jerusalem (Colossians 4:10; Acts 12:12). On the other hand, Barnabas was a Diaspora Jew from Cyprus (Acts 4:36), and many of the Christian leaders in Antioch were Greek Cypriots. Barnabas probably knew many of them quite well (Acts 11:20). "A man of character like Barnabas, eminent among Greek Jews of Antioch, would have a great influence among both Jews and Greeks in the city."[1]

Even though Antioch was a city of luxury and vice, the gospel was being well received. Upon his arrival, Barnabas saw the work was greatly blessed, and he pitched in with enthusiasm. As the work progressed and AD 44 dawned, Barnabas saw he needed help. Immediately his thoughts turned to Saul, who was somewhere around Tarsus in Cilicia preaching the gospel to Gentiles (Diaspora Jews and proselytes). "Why did Barnabas receive Saul when the other disciples feared him? The answer may be found in his character, which appears to have been of a kindly, generous nature. . . . Many commentators suggest that Barnabas championed Saul because of previous acquaintance."[2]

Years had passed; could Barnabas find Saul? If he could, would Saul agree to come to Antioch to serve? It was more than a hundred miles from Antioch to Tarsus, and there were no guarantees Saul would be easy to find or recruit. Barnabas set about to try. What was Saul doing during these "silent years"? He writes: "Afterward I went into the regions of Syria and Cilicia. And I was unknown by face to the churches of Judea which were in Christ. But they were hearing only, 'He who formerly persecuted us now preaches the faith which he once tried to destroy.' And they glorified God in me" (Galatians 1:21–24).

Obscure years spent in Arabia, Syria, and Cilicia, suffering unrecorded hardships and dangers, refined Saul's talent for reaching people effectively. He wasn't a big-name evangelist overnight.

---

1. Francis D. Nichol, ed., *The Seventh-day Adventist Bible Commentary*, vol. 6 (Washington, DC: Review and Herald®, 1957), 265.
2. Nichol, *Seventh-day Adventist Bible Commentary*, vol. 6, 237.

Antioch

And the disciples were first called Christians in Antioch.

—Acts 11:26

S aul agreed to accompany Barnabas to Antioch, and there the two apostles labored side by side for souls in a Gentile world. Luke is exact in his account of the time spent here. "So it was that for a whole year they assembled with the church and taught a great many people" (Acts 11:26). Almost as a footnote, Luke adds that disciples in Antioch became known as "Christians." The badge "those belonging to Christ" is thought by many commentators to have been a tag of ridicule bestowed upon the new sect by the Gentiles of Antioch. While the name "Christian" clearly separated them from Judaism, "the name was given them because Christ was the main theme of their preaching, their teaching, and their conversation."[1]

"When these new Gentile converts joined the church at Antioch, none of the former names would embrace the entire cosmopolitan body. They were no longer all Nazarenes or Galileans or Greek Jews, and in the eyes of the people of Antioch they must have seemed a strange mixture. Therefore, the hybrid term 'Christians,' a Greek word with a Latin termination, would seem to fit them. At a later time, what had been at first a taunt became a name in which to glory: 'If any man suffer as a Christian, let him not be ashamed' (1 Peter 4:16)."[2] The new term is found two places in the book of Acts: in today's text, and in Acts 26:28, where King Agrippa tells Paul, "You almost persuade me to become a Christian." Obviously, the term was widely accepted by that time and was in general use, and why not? "It was God who gave to them the name of Christian. This is a royal name, given to all who join themselves to Christ."[3]

"The example of the followers of Christ at Antioch should be an inspiration to every believer living in the great cities of the world today. While it is in the order of God that chosen workers of consecration and talent should be stationed in important centers of population to lead out in public efforts, it is also His purpose that the church members living in these cities shall use their God-given talents in working for souls."[4]

"God is calling . . . to consider the needs of the unwarned cities. Time is rapidly passing, and there is much to be done."[5]

---

1. Ellen G. White, *The Acts of the Apostles* (Mountain View, CA: Pacific Press®, 1911), 157.
2. Francis D. Nichol, ed., *The Seventh-day Adventist Bible Commentary*, vol. 6 (Washington, DC: Review and Herald®, 1957), 266.
3. White, *Acts of the Apostles*, 157.
4. White, *Acts of the Apostles*, 158.
5. White, *Acts of the Apostles*, 159.

Famine Relief

Then one of them, named Agabus, stood up and showed by the Spirit that there was going to be a great famine throughout all the world, which also happened in the days of Claudius Caesar.
—Acts 11:28

The gift of prophecy was important to the early church. Paul placed the gift second in importance following that of apostleship: "And God has appointed these in the church: first apostles, second prophets, third teachers, after that miracles, then gifts of healings, helps, administrations, varieties of tongues" (1 Corinthians 12:28). Agabus was a prophet of some note. Acts 21:10, 11 record his warning to Paul not to go up to Jerusalem. While predicting a famine was not a far stretch for civilization during any year, this particular famine was predicted to be extensive and extreme. "The reign of Claudius lasted from AD 41 to 54, which period was memorable for frequent famines. (Suetonius *Claudius* xviii. 2; Tacitus *Annals* xii. 43)."[1] This particular famine "may be seen as a partial fulfillment of Jesus' prophecy in Matt. 24:7."[2] "It appears safe to conclude that the famine mentioned in Acts 11 occurred sometime between AD 44 and 48."[3] The church at Antioch decided to take up a collection for the church in Jerusalem.

When Luke speaks of a "worldwide" famine, he is speaking of the Roman Empire as a whole during the imperial period. Much of the Roman Empire could not grow enough food to sustain life. The empire had to depend upon areas where crops could be grown in abundance. Egypt, in particular, became known as the "Breadbasket of the Empire." Crop failure due to insect infestation, drought, and transportation disruption—all could and did drive up prices, making what little food existed all but unaffordable to the masses dependent on the supply lifeline. A failure in one part of the empire was felt in all parts within a matter of weeks. Many Jerusalem Christians were already poor, and a long famine would hit them hard. They would be unable to afford the spiraling cost of food, and many would starve. Barnabas had already given a gift to the believers in Jerusalem, so he was acquainted with their pressing need (Acts 4:36, 37). The gift from Antioch was hand-carried by Saul and Barnabas to the "elders" (Acts 11:30) of the Jerusalem church. They were gratified to receive this gift from their fellow believers.

Christians of Antioch helping Christians of Jerusalem—a great example for our churches today.

---

1. Francis D. Nichol, ed., *The Seventh-day Adventist Bible Commentary*, vol. 6 (Washington, DC: Review and Herald®, 1957), 266.

2. Nichol, *Seventh-day Adventist Bible Commentary*, vol. 6, 266.

3. Nichol, *Seventh-day Adventist Bible Commentary*, vol. 6, 98.

Herod Agrippa I

Now about that time Herod the king stretched out his hand to harass some from the church.
—Acts 12:1

Herod Agrippa I was the son of Aristobulus and Berenice, grandson of Herod the Great and the Hasmonaean Princess Mariamne, and brother of the Herodias who appears in the story of John the Baptist. . . . After his father had fallen a victim in 7 B.C. to the suspicions of his grandfather, Herod the Great . . . , he was sent to Rome, partly as a hostage and partly to keep him out of involvement in intrigues. There he became an intimate of Caligula and Claudius, both of whom later became emperors."[1] Herod Agrippa I voiced support for Caligula to become emperor rather than Tiberius. For his vocal opinion, he was cast into prison when Tiberius came to power, and there he remained until Tiberius died. "Tiberius' adopted son, Gaius, generally known as Caligula, or 'Little Boots,' now became emperor. . . . Caligula was a weak, nervous, dissipated young man who all too readily accepted Agrippa's tutelage in the despotic ways of the East, and thereby laid an unfortunate foundation for his future exercise of imperial power."[2]

Caligula remembered his loyal friend imprisoned by his stepfather, Tiberius. "He loaded his friend Agrippa with honors, gave him the tetrarchies, first of Philip and then of Lysanias (Luke 3:1), and bestowed upon him the title of king. When Antipas was deposed [another interesting story of political intrigue] . . . , Agrippa fell heir to his territories also."[3] Herod Agrippa I ruled with his friend Claudius's backing, and wishing to be considered a "devoted Jew," he curried favor with mainstream Jewish religious leaders. Following their wishes, he began persecuting the rapidly growing Christian movement. The apostles, once looked upon with favor, now were regarded with alarm as a threat to the state-sanctioned religion.

Agrippa took polls before making political moves. Good Christians base decisions on principles and are not swayed by popularity. One should obey God, not vacillate and sacrifice principles to gain favor with friends!

---

1. Francis D. Nichol, ed., *The Seventh-day Adventist Bible Commentary*, vol. 6 (Washington, DC: Review and Herald®, 1957), 269.
2. Nichol, *Seventh-day Adventist Bible Commentary*, vol. 6, 78.
3. Nichol, *Seventh-day Adventist Bible Commentary*, vol. 6, 269.

James Slain

Then he killed James the brother of John with the sword.

—Acts 12:2

James, the brother of John and one of the Sons of Thunder (Mark 3:17), had continued to preach the gospel in Jerusalem with zeal. Herod Agrippa caused him to be arrested and then, without trial, beheaded (a Roman form of execution rather than the Jewish form of stoning). Just as Herod Antipas had caused the beheading of John the Baptist, now Herod Agrippa I killed James in the same manner. "James filled a short ministry of only 13 years after Christ's ascension. Of the apostles, he died first."[1] "It was during the Passover that these cruelties were practiced. . . .

"Herod's act in putting James to death was applauded by the Jews, though some complained of the private manner in which it was accomplished, maintaining that a public execution would have more thoroughly intimidated the believers and those sympathizing with them. Herod therefore held Peter in custody, meaning still further to gratify the Jews by the public spectacle of his death. But it was suggested that it would not be safe to bring the veteran apostle out for execution before all the people then assembled in Jerusalem. It was feared that the sight of him being led out to die might excite the pity of the multitude."[2]

"The Jews resented Christianity for numerous reasons. They feared lest the Christians would bring the wrath of the Romans down upon the Jews themselves. They hated the Christians' Christ as a rival to their expected Messiah. They hated Christians the more because they took Gentiles into their fellowship. Hence, at every opportunity the Jews made trouble for the Christians, in so far as it was in their own power to persecute them in the land of Palestine, and elsewhere, by stirring up mobs to riot against the Christians."[3] The Christian church now endured the combined wrath of religious zealots and the complicity of the state. In Herod, the Sanhedrin found a replacement for Saul, their lost persecutor. Agrippa held and used the power of life and death that Rome denied the Sanhedrin. Life became difficult for Christians: property was seized, believers were imprisoned and killed, goods were vandalized, businesses boycotted. Jewish synagogues became known as "fountains of persecution."[4]

"Blessed are ye, when men shall revile you, and persecute you, and shall say all manner of evil against you falsely, for my sake" (Matthew 5:11, KJV).

---

1. Francis D. Nichol, ed., *The Seventh-day Adventist Bible Commentary*, vol. 6 (Washington, DC: Review and Herald®, 1957), 269.

2. Ellen G. White, *The Acts of the Apostles* (Mountain View, CA: Pacific Press®, 1911), 144.

3. Nichol, *Seventh-day Adventist Bible Commentary*, vol. 6, 61.

4. Nichol, *Seventh-day Adventist Bible Commentary*, vol. 6, 61.

Arise Quickly!

And because he saw that it pleased the Jews, he proceeded further to seize Peter also.
—Acts 12:3

It was during the Passover that Peter was cast into prison. James had just been beheaded. "The death of James caused great grief and consternation among the believers. When Peter also was imprisoned, the entire church engaged in fasting and prayer."[1] Fearing Peter would make a fiery appeal to the Passover crowds, the priests and elders pressed Herod to postpone the execution until after Passover. Herod agreed to hold Peter over for execution, but he remembered the miraculous escape of the apostles on a previous occasion, and he took no chances of a repeat occurrence. Four quaternion (squads) of four men were detailed to guard the prisoner at all times. "In his cell he [Peter] was placed between two soldiers and was bound by two chains, each chain being fastened to the wrist of one of the soldiers. He was unable to move without their knowledge. With the prison doors securely fastened, and a strong guard before them, all chance of rescue or escape through human means was cut off. *But man's extremity is God's opportunity.*"[2]

It is the night before his execution, yet Peter sleeps the sleep of a trusting servant of God. Suddenly, the strong gates swing open silently without human assistance. "The angel of the Most High passes through, and the gates close noiselessly behind him. He enters the cell, and there lies Peter, sleeping the peaceful sleep of perfect trust. . . .

". . . Not until he feels the touch of the angel's hand and hears a voice saying, 'Arise up quickly,' does he awaken sufficiently to see his cell illuminated by the light of heaven. . . . Mechanically he obeys the word spoken to him, and as in rising he lifts his hands he is dimly conscious that the chains have fallen from his wrists."[3]

Instructed to put on his sandals, take his outer cloak, and follow, Peter obeys. "They step over the guard and reach the heavily bolted door, which of its own accord swings open and closes again immediately, while the guards within and without are motionless at their post."[4] In this noiseless manner, they traverse two more locked and guarded doors. "No word is spoken; there is no sound of footsteps. The angel glides on in front, encircled by a light of dazzling brightness, and Peter, bewildered, and still believing himself to be in a dream, follows his deliverer."[5] Once they are out on the street, the angel suddenly disappears, and Peter is alone.

"For He shall give His angels charge over you, to keep you in all your ways" (Psalm 91:11).

---

1. Ellen G. White, *The Acts of the Apostles* (Mountain View, CA: Pacific Press®, 1911), 144.
2. White, *Acts of the Apostles*, 146; emphasis added.
3. White, *Acts of the Apostles*, 146, 147.
4. White, *Acts of the Apostles*, 147.
5. White, *Acts of the Apostles*, 147.

Rhoda

And as Peter knocked at the door of the gate, a girl named Rhoda came to answer.
—Acts 12:13

P eter found himself alone on the open street with the cool night air jolting him from what must have felt like a dream. It took him a few moments to realize he was free, and he was not dreaming. He immediately headed for the house of *Mary*. "This Mary was related to Barnabas. . . . Mary may have been a widow. Like Barnabas . . . , she apparently possessed means, for she was able to have a house which was large enough to serve the church as a meeting place for prayer."[1] Here the faithful had gathered to pray and fast for Peter's deliverance. Arriving, Peter knocked quietly at the courtyard gate. A young servant girl named Rhoda (Rose) hastened to the door. In hushed tones, Peter announced himself. Excitedly, Rhoda ran to tell the others that Peter was outside. Not willing to believe her, they told her she was mad! Perhaps it was his Galilean accent or the hours she had spent listening to Peter teach that gave her absolute certainty that she was right and they were wrong. No, she argued, it *is* Peter! Sadly, those praying for Peter's deliverance didn't seem to believe God could—in fact, already had—answered their prayers.

While the debate took place, Peter was left standing in the middle of the street, knocking ever louder, demanding entrance. Fearing the commotion would awaken neighbors, the group finally opened the door. There, to their astonishment, stood Peter. Immediately he asked that James, the brother of Jesus and the presiding elder of the church, be notified of his deliverance. "In the morning a large concourse of people gathered to witness the execution of the apostle. Herod sent officers to the prison for Peter, who was to be brought with a great display of arms and guards in order not only to ensure against his escape, but to intimidate all sympathizers and to show the power of the King. . . .

"When the report of Peter's escape was brought to Herod, he was exasperated and enraged. Charging the prison guard with unfaithfulness, he ordered them to be put to death. Herod knew that no human power had rescued Peter, but he was determined not to acknowledge that a divine power had frustrated his design, and he set himself in bold defiance against God."[2]

Do you believe your prayers to be unanswerable? Keep a prayer journal and discover that God is faithful!

---

1. Francis D. Nichol, ed., *The Seventh-day Adventist Bible Commentary*, vol. 6 (Washington, DC: Review and Herald®, 1957), 271.

2. Ellen G. White, *The Acts of the Apostles* (Mountain View, CA: Pacific Press®, 1911), 149.

Usurping God's Praise

And the people kept shouting, "The voice of a god and not of a man!" Then, immediately an angel of the Lord struck him, because he did not give glory to God.

—Acts 12:22, 23

Following his embarrassment in Jerusalem, Herod retired to his palace in Caesarea. Here he received a delegation from Tyre and Sidon, two coastal Phoenician cities he had been blackmailing into paying tribute by withholding trade. The delegation arrived at court on a feast day set aside to honor Caesar. "With great pomp and ceremony Herod appeared before the people and addressed them in an eloquent oration. Clad in a robe sparkling with silver and gold, which caught the rays of the sun in its glittering folds and dazzled the eyes of the beholders, he was a gorgeous figure.... Their senses already perverted by feasting and wine drinking, they were dazzled by Herod's decorations and charmed by his deportment and oratory; and wild with enthusiasm, they showered adulation upon him, declaring that no mortal could present such an appearance or command such startling eloquence. They further declared that while they had ever respected him as a ruler, henceforth they should worship him as a god."[1]

"The Jews had refused to receive Christ, whose garments, coarse and often travel-stained, covered a heart of divine love. Their eyes could not discern, under the humble exterior, the Lord of life and glory, even though Christ's power was revealed before them in works that no mere man could do. But they were ready to worship as a god the haughty king whose splendid garments of silver and gold covered a corrupt, cruel heart."[2] Herod knew he did not deserve the title or praise belonging to Jehovah, but pride caused him to bask in their adulation. "Suddenly a terrible change came over him [Herod]. His face became pallid as death and distorted with agony. Great drops of sweat started from his pores. He stood for a moment as if transfixed with pain and terror; then turning his blanched and livid face to his horror-stricken friends, he cried in hollow, despairing tones, He whom you have exalted as a god is stricken with death."[3] "The same angel who had come from the royal courts to rescue Peter, had been the messenger of wrath and judgment to Herod. ... Herod died in great agony of mind and body, under the retributive judgment of God."[4] Herod died in AD 44 at the age of fifty-three, in the seventh year of his reign.

Beware of flattery, for it can lead to pride. We all know pride often precedes a fall!

---

1. Ellen G. White, *The Acts of the Apostles* (Mountain View, CA: Pacific Press®, 1911), 150.
2. White, *Acts of the Apostles*, 150.
3. White, *Acts of the Apostles*, 151.
4. White, *Acts of the Apostles*, 152.

Set Apart

"Now separate to Me Barnabas and Saul for the work to which I have called them."
—Acts 13:2

While the death of James and the imprisonment and deliverance of Peter were happening in Jerusalem, Saul and Barnabas had been quietly working together in Antioch. After the excitement had calmed, Barnabas and Saul brought the Antioch famine relief fund to Jerusalem. Not tarrying long, they decided to set out on the return trip to Antioch, some four hundred miles distant by way of the eastern coast of the Mediterranean. John Mark, hearing of their impending missionary trip, begged to go with them, and the two men agreed to take him with them back to Antioch. John Mark was the son of *Mary*. Colossians 4:10 refers to John Mark as the "sister's son to Barnabas"(KJV); however, the Greek expression means "cousin to Barnabas."[1] Ellen White calls John Mark "his [Barnabas's] nephew."[2]

The church at Antioch had more fully grasped the international vision of Christ (Matthew 24:14; Acts 1:8) to preach the gospel to the ends of the earth than did the church at Jerusalem. Early on, the disciples had led the Jerusalem church, but gradually they began to leave on missions of their own. Following the pattern of all Jewish synagogues, Jewish elders were appointed to direct the church. The church at Antioch differed in that it enjoyed a more "cosmopolitan leadership. Barnabas was a Cypriote; Lucius, a Cyrenian; Manaen, apparently a Palestinian aristocrat; and Saul, a rabbi from Tarsus in Cilicia."[3] These men were all prophets and teachers. "Both [Saul] and Barnabas had been laboring as ministers of Christ, and God had abundantly blessed their efforts; but neither of them had previously been formally ordained to the gospel ministry by prayer and the laying on of hands."[4] Being moved by the Spirit, the leaders laid hands upon Saul and Barnabas, setting them apart and ordaining them to their special work of preaching salvation to the Gentiles. This was an important step. Until now, Barnabas and Saul had been teachers and prophets within the church. Now they were being set apart and sent on a distinct missionary journey to preach salvation to the Gentiles.

Saul believed his ordination was extremely important. Henceforth he would call himself "a servant of Jesus Christ, called to be an apostle, separated unto the gospel of God" (Romans 1:1, KJV).

---

1. Francis D. Nichol, ed., *The Seventh-day Adventist Bible Commentary*, vol. 6 (Washington, DC: Review and Herald®, 1957), 271.
2. Ellen G. White, *Sketches From the Life of Paul* (Washington, DC: Review and Herald®, 1974), 48.
3. Nichol, *The Seventh-day Adventist Bible Commentary*, vol. 6, 279.
4. White, *Sketches From the Life of Paul*, 42.

Paul's First Missionary Journey

With Barnabas and John Mark to
Cyprus, Perga, Antioch of Pisidia,
Iconium, Lystra, and Derbe

AD 45–47

Acts 13:1–14:28
The Acts of the Apostles, pp. 166–187
Sketches From the Life of Paul, pp. 44–63

Cyprus

So, being sent out by the Holy Spirit, they went down
to Seleucia, and from there they sailed to Cyprus.

—Acts 13:4

M ost commentators refer to the event described in Acts 13:4 as Paul's first missionary journey. As we have seen, this was certainly not his first. He had traveled
to Damascus and worked there. He had worked silently in the area of his hometown
of Tarsus. He had spent three years working in Arabia. What set this new venture apart
was the direct command he received from the Holy Spirit to move westward. "Under
the leading of the Holy Spirit the prophets and teachers of Antioch ordained Barnabas
and [Saul] and sent them out."[1]

Evidently, the idea to first go to Cyprus had been a part of the direct command given
by the Holy Spirit (verse 4). "If the missionaries were not specifically directed, doubtless
they chose this first point of call because Cyprus was the birthplace of Barnabas. Its
population was largely Greek. It claimed Aphrodite, or Venus, as its patron goddess. Her
chief center of worship was at Paphos, which was conspicuous for the licentiousness
of the harlot-priestesses of her temple. The metal *cuprum*, 'copper' took its name from
the island, and the copper mines, lying only a short voyage from Syria, had attracted
many Jews. Probably it was among these that the gospel had been preached already by
itinerant Christian evangelists ([Acts] 11:19). It is probable, too, that some of those from
Cyprus who were converted in Jerusalem on the day of Pentecost took the Christian
message back to their homeland."[2]

Sixteen miles west of Antioch lay the city's seaport of Seleucia at the mouth of the
Orontes River. Barnabas, Saul, and Mark set sail across the Mediterranean for Cyprus.
A direct west-southwest course of seventy miles brought them to the main eastern
port on the island, Salamis. With a large Jewish population, Salamis must have had
several synagogues. As visiting teachers skilled in the Torah, Barnabas and Saul would
have been asked to speak. Preaching the message of the crucified and risen Savior,
Jesus Christ, the three worked their way across the island to the city of Paphos on the
extreme western side.

Saul loved taking the gospel to new lands. He felt danger, hardship, and toil were a small price
to pay for souls in need of saving! We need the same dedication today.

---

1. Francis D. Nichol, ed., *The Seventh-day Adventist Bible Commentary*, vol. 6 (Washington, DC: Review and Herald®,
1957), 29.
2. Nichol, *Seventh-day Adventist Bible Commentary*, vol. 6, 281, 282.

Sergius Paulus

Now when they had gone through the island to Paphos, they found a certain sorcerer, a false prophet, a Jew whose name was Bar-Jesus, who was with the proconsul, Sergius Paulus, an intelligent man.

—Acts 13:6, 7

A t Salamis, they preached in the Jewish synagogues. Taking the southern Roman road from Salamis to Paphos, 115 miles distant, they arrived in town and began their work among the Jews. Sergius Paulus, the Roman proconsul on the island, soon heard of these visitors. As deputy of the country, he was a prudent man and had a sincere desire to hear the word of God. Sharing the gospel with Sergius Paulus was not going to be easy, for Barnabas and Saul came up against "a certain sorcerer, a false prophet, a Jew, whose name was Bar-jesus. . . . But Elymas the sorcerer (for so is his name by interpretation) withstood them, seeking to turn away the deputy from the faith."[1] The Jewish wizard Elymas "feared the loss of the influence he thought himself exercising over the proconsul. He saw his victim emancipating himself, passing from credulity toward the sorcerer to faith in the gospel, and that change Elymas was determined to check."[2] Elymas, standing close to Saul, ridiculed his every word.

"Although sorely beset by Satan, [Saul] had the courage to rebuke the one through whom the enemy was working. 'Filled with the Holy Ghost,' the apostle 'set his eyes on him, and said, O full of all subtlety and all mischief, thou child of the devil, thou enemy of all righteousness, wilt thou not cease to pervert the right ways of the Lord? And now, behold, the hand of the Lord is upon thee, and thou shalt be blind, not seeing the sun for a season. And immediately there fell on him a mist and a darkness; and he went about seeking some to lead him by the hand. Then the deputy, when he saw what was done, believed, being astonished at the doctrine of the Lord.' "[3] Just as Moses had to confront the magicians of Pharaoh, so too did Saul have to meet the powers of Satan in the court of a ruler. His reference to Moses resisting Jannes and Jambres in the court of Pharaoh (Exodus 7:11, 22) may be found in 2 Timothy 3:8.

Must Christians be meek when confronted by sin? Saul certainly minced no words at Paphos!

1. Ellen G. White, *Sketches From the Life of Paul* (Washington, DC: Review and Herald®, 1974), 44.
2. Francis D. Nichol, ed., *The Seventh-day Adventist Bible Commentary*, vol. 6 (Washington, DC: Review and Herald®, 1957), 283.
3. Ellen G. White, *The Acts of the Apostles* (Mountain View, CA: Pacific Press®, 1911), 168.

Saul Becomes Paul

Then Saul, who also is called Paul, filled with the Holy Spirit, looked intently at him.
—Acts 13:9

I n the midst of the story of Elymas, a subtle change takes place. Almost as an aside, Luke mentions the "Saul" he has written about is called "Paul" by others. "At this point for the first time the name is introduced by which the apostle to the Gentiles is best known."[1] Now that Paul is moving into predominantly Roman territory, he begins to use his Roman name. The more astute of Luke's readers recognize for the first time that Luke is writing about someone of whom they have already heard. "Luke shows his awareness of the apostle's two names, Saul and Paul. Prior to Acts 13:9, he has portrayed him in a predominantly Hebrew environment, and has therefore used his Hebrew name, Saul. Now, in ch. 13:9, Luke sees him face to face with a Roman official, who would naturally ask him such questions as, 'What is your name?' 'Where is your home?' To such queries the Roman citizen would not reply, 'Saul, a Pharisee of Jerusalem,' but 'Paul, a Roman citizen of Tarsus.' "[2]

The Holy Spirit moved through Paul to affect Elymas just as it moved through Peter to affect Ananias. "The death of Ananias and Sapphira (Acts 5:1–11) and the blinding of Elymas (ch. 13:8–11) were instances of the exercise of apostolic authority accompanied by special divine acts of punishment."[3] The proconsul had earnestly been seeking truth when he summoned Paul and Barnabas. His questions to Elymas regarding the Jewish faith had previously been met with blurring and deception. Realizing the superiority of the gospel of Jesus Christ and the power of God in rebuking Elymas, Sergius Paulus became a Christian.

Some believe Paul had to look intently at Elymas because the bright light on the road to Damascus had permanently affected his vision. How fitting "the form of Elymas' punishment stands in striking contrast with the apostle's own previous experience. Paul had become blind to outward light, but had been illuminated inwardly by a light from heaven (. . . [Acts] 9:9). Elymas, blinded for a time, might be able yet to receive the Light that lights every man (John 1:9)."[4]

Christians still must confront the devil and his agents to advance the gospel. Be bold for Christ!

---

1. Francis D. Nichol, ed., *The Seventh-day Adventist Bible Commentary*, vol. 6 (Washington, DC: Review and Herald®, 1957), 283.
2. Nichol, *Seventh-day Adventist Bible Commentary*, vol. 6, 209.
3. Nichol, *Seventh-day Adventist Bible Commentary*, vol. 6, 925.
4. Nichol, *Seventh-day Adventist Bible Commentary*, vol. 6, 284.

John Mark Goes Home

Now when Paul and his party set sail from Paphos, they came to Perga in Pamphylia; and John [Mark], departing from them, returned to Jerusalem.

—Acts 13:13

Note that the dynamic within the group has changed! Luke now refers to Paul as the party leader. In Acts 13:7 it was *Barnabas and Saul*, but now, six verses later, it is *Paul and* his *party*. From here on, Paul takes center stage in the book of Acts as the main character. "Pamphylia was a small region about midway on the south coast of Asia Minor [modern-day southern Turkey]. In A.D. 43, just before Paul's visit, it was combined with Lycia, its western neighbor, to form an imperial province. Perga was its chief city, situated on the river Cestrus, about 8 mi. from the sea. Luke records no evangelistic work in the city at this time, perhaps because there were no synagogues. . . . They did preach in Perga on the return journey."[1] Upon reaching Perga, John Mark had had enough!

We have no idea why John Mark decided to leave Paul and Barnabas at this point to go home to Jerusalem. "Perhaps he feared the perils and hardships of the journey into the interior."[2] We are blessed to have Ellen G. White's prophetic explanation for his departure. She writes, "Paul and his company continued their journey, going to Perga, in Pamphylia. Their way was toilsome; they encountered hardships and privations, and were beset with dangers on every side. In the towns and cities through which they passed, and along the lonely highways, they were surrounded by dangers seen and unseen. But Paul and Barnabas had learned to trust God's power to deliver. . . . As faithful shepherds in search of the lost sheep, they gave no thought to their own ease and convenience. . . . They had in view but one object—the salvation of those who had wandered far from the fold.

"It was here that Mark, overwhelmed with fear and discouragement, wavered for a time in his purpose to give himself wholeheartedly to the Lord's work. Unused to hardships, he was disheartened by the perils and privations of the way. He had labored with success under favorable circumstances; but now, amidst the opposition and perils that so often beset the pioneer worker, he failed to endure hardness as a good soldier of the cross."[3]

As tempting as it is to criticize John Mark, being Paul's assistant must have been no picnic!

---

1. Francis D. Nichol, ed., *The Seventh-day Adventist Bible Commentary*, vol. 6 (Washington, DC: Review and Herald®, 1957), 284, 285.
2. Nichol, *Seventh-day Adventist Bible Commentary*, vol. 6, 285.
3. Ellen G. White, *The Acts of the Apostles* (Mountain View, CA: Pacific Press®, 1911), 169, 170.

Antioch in Pisidia

But when they departed from Perga, they came to Antioch in Pisidia, and went into the syna-
gogue on the Sabbath day and sat down.

—Acts 13:14

The defection of John Mark "caused Paul to judge Mark unfavorably, and even severely, for a time. Barnabas, on the other hand, was inclined to excuse him because of his inexperience. He felt anxious that Mark should not abandon the ministry, for he saw in him qualifications that would fit him to be a useful worker for Christ. In after years his solicitude on Mark's behalf was richly rewarded, for the young man gave himself unreservedly to the Lord and to the work of proclaiming the gospel in difficult fields. Under the blessing of God, and the wise training of Barnabas, he developed into a valuable worker."[1] Again we see Barnabas, son of exhortation, mentoring and heartening those in the faith. The gift of support is sorely needed in all churches!

"To reach Antioch they 'passed through' the whole breadth of Pamphylia and the southwestern corner of Galatia. . . .

". . . [Antioch] lay on the lower slopes of the Taurus Mts. at an elevation of 3,600 feet above sea level. Its people had been granted a form of Roman citizenship under Augustus. Antioch probably had attracted a considerable Jewish population, which apparently had led the Gentiles to acquire an interest in Judaism. . . .

"Perhaps on this journey Paul and his companion were exposed to 'perils of robbers,' of which he speaks in 2 Cor. 11:26. Pisidia, through which they passed to reach Antioch, was a mountainous country, rising gradually toward the north. Strabo . . . speaks of much brigandage in those regions."[2]

As was his custom, Paul rarely missed a Saturday service in a local synagogue. He consistently met first with the Jews of any area through which he might pass to meet with fellow Jews who might be open to the gospel of Jesus Christ and to keep the Sabbath day holy (Luke 23:56; Exodus 20:8–11). "Although Paul was the declared apostle to the Gentiles, he always went first to the synagogues . . . , which frequently afforded visitors an opportunity to speak."[3] Generally, these synagogues had no priest. Once the congregation knew a Pharisee trained by Gamaliel was present, it was inevitable Paul would be asked to expound on Scripture.

Paul initially judged Mark severely! Barnabas worked with him and developed the valuable worker who wrote the Gospel of Mark for future generations. Be like Barnabas—be a mentor!

1. Ellen G. White, *The Acts of the Apostles* (Mountain View, CA: Pacific Press®, 1911), 170.
2. Francis D. Nichol, ed., *The Seventh-day Adventist Bible Commentary*, vol. 6 (Washington, DC: Review and Herald®, 1957), 285.
3. Nichol, *Seventh-day Adventist Bible Commentary*, vol. 6, 285.

The Gospel Is for Jews

And after the reading of the Law and the Prophets, the rulers of the synagogue sent to them, saying, "Men and brethren, if you have any word of exhortation for the people, say on."
—Acts 13:15

Paul stood and waved his hand for silence. He started his discourse much as Peter had his sermon on the Day of Pentecost and Stephen had during his defense before the Sanhedrin. "He proceeded to give a history of the manner in which the Lord had dealt with the Jews from the time of their deliverance from Egyptian bondage, and how a Saviour had been promised, of the seed of David, and he boldly declared that 'of this man's seed hath God according to His promise raised unto Israel a Saviour, Jesus.' "[1] Paul spoke as if he expected his audience to at least be familiar with Jesus and His work. He spoke without hesitation of the condemnation and rejection of Jesus by the priests and rulers in Jerusalem and how they had put Him to death on the cross. "Paul put forward the resurrection as proof that God was fulfilling the promise made to Abraham and to David, of the 'seed' in whom all nations of the earth should be blessed (Gen. 12:1–3). . . . As with every argument the apostles put forward in these early days of the beginning church, the resurrection is necessary in the development of the gospel argument. The resurrection is proof that Jesus is the Messiah."[2]

"And now, having spoken plainly of the fulfillment of familiar prophecies concerning the Messiah, Paul preached unto them repentance and the remission of sin through the merits of Jesus their Saviour. . . .

"The Spirit of God accompanied the words that were spoken, and hearts were touched. The apostle's appeal to Old Testament prophecies, and his declaration that these had been fulfilled in the ministry of Jesus of Nazareth, carried conviction to many a soul longing for the advent of the promised Messiah."[3] "Forgiveness of sins is the happy news of the gospel, bringing rejoicing to every sin-burdened heart (see 1 John 1:9). It was the keynote of Paul's preaching (see Acts 26:18), as it was of Peter's (chs. 2:38; 5:31; 10:43). It had been the burden of John the Baptist (Mark 1:4) and of Jesus Himself (Matt. 9:2, 6; Luke 7:47, 48; 24:47)."[4]

Paul's message is for all. We are forgiven and saved through faith in Jesus! "And if you are Christ's, then you are Abraham's seed, and heirs according to the promise" (Galatians 3:29).

---

1. Ellen G. White, *The Acts of the Apostles* (Mountain View, CA: Pacific Press®, 1911), 171.
2. Francis D. Nichol, ed., *The Seventh-day Adventist Bible Commentary*, vol. 6 (Washington, DC: Review and Herald®, 1957), 288.
3. White, *Acts of the Apostles*, 172, 173.
4. Nichol, *Seventh-day Adventist Bible Commentary*, vol. 6, 290.

The Gospel Is Also for Gentiles

"It was necessary that the word of God should be spoken to you first; but since you reject it, and judge yourselves unworthy of everlasting life, behold, we turn to the Gentiles."

—Acts 13:46

When the synagogue service was over, Paul and Barnabas were begged by many of the Jews and proselytes (Greek believers who had grown up following Jewish customs) to return on the next Saturday to speak on the same topic. The record reports, "And the next sabbath day came almost the whole city together to hear the word of God" (Acts 13:44, KJV). "It is evident that the Jewish synagogue where the meeting was held on this 'next Sabbath' could not contain the crowd, and accordingly we must picture the listeners thronging around the doors and windows while the apostles were inside speaking or else gathered in some open space near the synagogue, addressed from its entrance."[1]

Many Gentiles came to hear the "good news." "But when the Jews saw the multitudes, they were filled with envy, and spake against those things which were spoken by Paul, contradicting and blaspheming."[2] "The Jews of Antioch doubtless were chagrined that newcomers such as Paul and Barnabas should attract so much interest among the Gentiles. They also realized that these Gentiles were being invited to the same religious privileges as themselves, and this was abhorrent to them. They had felt too long that they were exclusively the children of God, to be content to have Gentiles invited to salvation on the same terms with themselves. They could accept a message as sent of God, and could endure some changes in their teachings and way of worship, but they could not endure having Gentiles made equal in God's sight with His chosen people. This practical repudiation by Paul and Barnabas of the exclusive privileges upon which the Jews prided themselves was more than they could bear."[3]

Paul and Barnabas, noting the shift in Jewish attitude, met the resistance with today's text. "In turning to the Gentiles in Antioch of Pisidia, Paul and Barnabas did not cease laboring for the Jews elsewhere, wherever there was a favorable opportunity to gain a hearing.... But their chief energies were henceforth directed toward the building up of the kingdom of God in heathen territory, among peoples who had but little or no knowledge of the true God and of His Son."[4]

Beware pride and bigotry, for both point to an elitist. There will be no dividing walls in heaven.

---

1. Francis D. Nichol, ed., *The Seventh-day Adventist Bible Commentary*, vol. 6 (Washington, DC: Review and Herald®, 1957), 291.
2. Ellen G. White, *The Acts of the Apostles* (Mountain View, CA: Pacific Press®, 1911), 173.
3. Nichol, *Seventh-day Adventist Bible Commentary*, vol. 6, 292.
4. White, *Acts of the Apostles*, 174, 175.

They Shook Off the Dust

But the Jews stirred up the devout and prominent women *and the chief men of the city, raised up persecution against Paul and Barnabas, and expelled them from their region.*
—Acts 13:50; emphasis added

During the life of Christ on earth he had sought to lead the Jews out of their exclusiveness. The conversion of the centurion, and of the Syrophenician woman, were instances of his direct work outside of the acknowledged people of Israel. The time had now come for active and continued work among the Gentiles, of whom whole communities received the gospel gladly, and glorified God for the light of an intelligent faith. The unbelief and malice of the Jews did not turn aside the purpose of God; for a new Israel was grafted into the old olive tree. The synagogues were closed against the apostles; but private houses were thrown open for their use, and public buildings of the Gentiles were also used in which to preach the word of God.

"The Jews, however, were not satisfied with closing their synagogues against the apostles, but desired to banish them from that region. To effect this purpose, they sought to prejudice certain devout and honorable women, who had great influence with the government, and also men of influence. This they accomplished by subtle arts, and false reports. These persons of good repute complained to the authorities against the apostles, and they were accordingly expelled from that district."[1]

Of all the disappointments faced during his ministry, failure by a major share of the Jewish people to accept Jesus Christ as their Messiah was Paul's most heartbreaking reality. In town after town, his methodology was the same. First, he would attempt to preach to the Jews in their synagogue, and failing that, he would move out into the streets and preach to the Gentiles. The *women of Antioch* who aided in banishing the apostles were certainly not the norm. Following the admonition of Jesus (Matthew 10:14, 15; Mark 6:11; Luke 9:5; 10:11), the apostles shook the dust off their feet as a witness against the unbelievers at Antioch in Pisidia and moved on; rejoicing in those who did believe.

It is thought the Gentile women of Antioch feared their status within the synagogue would be threatened by the inclusion of all their neighbors in the salvation Paul preached. Sad, if true.

---

1. Ellen G. White, *Sketches From the Life of Paul* (Washington, DC: Review and Herald®, 1974), 51.

Iconium—A City Divided

But the multitude of the city was divided: part sided with the Jews, and part with the apostles.
—Acts 14:4

Paul and Barnabas trudged east along the imperial road from Antioch headed for Lystra, about one hundred miles to the southeast. Thirty-five miles out, they came to a fork in the road. Here they turned north toward Iconium. Whereas Antioch and Lystra were Roman colonies, Iconium was not, and this held promise of Jewish converts. "This place was a great resort for pleasure-seekers, and persons who had no particular object in life. The population was composed of Romans, Greeks, and Jews. The apostles here, as at Antioch, first commenced their labors in the synagogues for their own people, the Jews. They met with marked success."[1] They stayed in Iconium a "long time" (Acts 14:3), several months, and, as at Antioch, they met with initial success.

"Numbers of both Jews and Greeks accepted the gospel of Christ. But here, as in former places where the apostles had labored, the unbelieving Jews commenced an unreasonable opposition to those who accepted the true faith, and, as far as lay in their power, influenced the Gentiles against them.

"The apostles, however, were not easily turned from their work, for many were daily embracing the doctrine of Christ. They went on faithfully in the face of opposition, envy, and prejudice. Miracles were daily wrought by the disciples through the power of God; and all whose minds were open to evidence were affected by the convincing power of these things."[2] The new Christian converts "were doubtless in the minority and probably came from the lower classes of society as was commonly the case in the early days of the church."[3]

The apostles were accused of holding secret meetings in which dangerous plans for revolt were being discussed. The city magistrates, fearing an insurrection, repeatedly interviewed the apostles but found their message "calculated to make men virtuous, law-abiding citizens."[4] Next, the Jews decided to incite a riot to stone the apostles for preaching "blasphemy." Unbelieving friends warned Paul and Barnabas, and secretly they fled the city before the plan could be carried out, thus obeying Jesus' command (Matthew 10:23). A six-hour journey to the southwest took them up a plateau to the city of Lystra.

"Do you suppose that I came to give peace on earth? I tell you, not at all, but rather division" (Luke 12:51). Those preferring the status quo often cast the gospel in a negative light.

1. Ellen G. White, *Sketches From the Life of Paul* (Washington, DC: Review and Herald®, 1974), 52.
2. White, *Sketches From the Life of Paul*, 52, 53.
3. Francis D. Nichol, ed., *The Seventh-day Adventist Bible Commentary*, vol. 6 (Washington, DC: Review and Herald®, 1957), 296.
4. White, *Sketches From the Life of Paul*, 53.

Zeus and Hermes

"The gods have come down to us in the likeness of men!"

—Acts 14:11

D riven by persecution from Iconium, the apostles went to Lystra and Derbe, in Lycaonia. . . .

"In Lystra there was no Jewish synagogue, though a few Jews lived in the town. Many of the inhabitants of Lystra worshiped at a temple dedicated to Jupiter."[1] Here in Lystra, Paul located the family of Timothy, a young man with a Gentile father and a Jewish mother. Timothy "had been brought up to know the [Old Testament] from his childhood (2 Tim. 3:15)."[2] Timothy was a common Greek name meaning "honored of God." It is possible Paul and Barnabas stayed with the family of Timothy for two years previously. They had visited Lystra and always sought out members of the local Jewish community with whom to reside.

Just as Peter met and healed a lame man at the gate called Beautiful in Jerusalem (Acts 3:2–10), Paul now came upon a man, lame from birth, at the city gate to Lystra. Sensing the man possessed the faith to be healed, Paul commanded him, "Stand up straight on your feet!" (Acts 14:10). Previously "the sufferer had been able to take a sitting posture only, but now he instantly obeyed Paul's command and for the first time in his life stood on his feet. Strength came with this effort of faith, and he who had been a cripple 'leaped and walked.' "[3] The heathen residents of Lystra immediately believed Paul and Barnabas had to be supernatural beings.

Believing the two missionaries were Greek gods was easy for the superstitious Lystrians. Local legend stated that "Zeus and Hermes (Jupiter and Mercury) had come in human guise and been received by the aged couple Philemon and Baucis, to whom they presented gifts (*Metamorphoses* viii. 626–724)."[4] The Lystrians did not intend to miss this opportunity in the case of Paul and Barnabas. Chief among the gods was Zeus "and his son Hermes, the herald and messenger of the gods, and patron of eloquence. . . . Barnabas may have been of more impressive bearing than Paul, and thus to him was assigned the title of [Zeus] Jupiter. Since Paul had done much of the speaking, he was identified as [Hermes] Mercury."[5]

In Iconium, Paul and Barnabas had been called fanatic insurrectionists. In Lystra, they were honored as gods! Ethnic experiences and historical and classical training form our perceptions.

---

1. Ellen G. White, *The Acts of the Apostles* (Mountain View, CA: Pacific Press®, 1911), 179, 180.

2. Francis D. Nichol, ed., *The Seventh-day Adventist Bible Commentary*, vol. 6 (Washington, DC: Review and Herald®, 1957), 323.

3. White, *Acts of the Apostles*, 181.

4. Nichol, *Seventh-day Adventist Bible Commentary*, vol. 6, 297.

5. Nichol, *Seventh-day Adventist Bible Commentary*, vol. 6, 297, 298.

Left for Dead

Then Jews from Antioch and Iconium came there; and having persuaded the multitudes,
they stoned Paul and dragged him out of the city, supposing him to be dead.
—Acts 14:19

Then the priest of Zeus, whose temple was in front of their city, brought oxen and garlands to the gates, intending to sacrifice with the multitudes.

"But when the apostles Barnabas and Paul heard this, they tore their clothes and ran in among the multitude, crying out and saying, 'Men, why are you doing these things? We also are men with the same nature as you, and preach to you that you should turn from these useless things to the living God.' . . . And with these sayings they could scarcely restrain the multitudes from sacrificing to them" (Acts 14:13–18).

"But, after much persuasion on the part of Paul, and explanation as to the true mission of the apostles, the people were reluctantly led to give up their purpose. They were not satisfied, however, and led away the sacrificial beasts in great disappointment that their traditions of divine beings visiting the earth could not be strengthened by this example of their favor in coming to confer upon them special blessings which would exalt them and their religion in the estimation of the world.

"And now a strange change came upon the fickle, excitable people, because their faith was not anchored in the true God."[1] Some days would pass before the next challenge.

Jews from Antioch and Iconium banded together and traveled the twenty-four miles south of Iconium to Lystra to oppose the apostles and "save" the poor heathen. "The disappointment that the Lystrians had suffered in being refused the privilege of offering sacrifice to the apostles, prepared them to turn against Paul and Barnabas with an enthusiasm approaching that with which they had hailed them as gods. Incited by the Jews, they planned to attack the apostles by force. The Jews charged them not to allow Paul an opportunity to speak, alleging that if they were to grant him this privilege, he would bewitch the people."[2] "The Lystrians rushed upon the apostles with great rage and fury. They hurled stones violently; and Paul, bruised, battered, and fainting, felt that his end had come. The martyrdom of Stephen was brought vividly to his mind, and the cruel part he had acted on that occasion."[3] We are not told how Barnabas escaped harm.

"Those who believe and teach the truths of God's word in these last days, meet with similar opposition from unprincipled persons who will not accept the truth."[4]

---

1. Ellen G. White, *Sketches From the Life of Paul* (Washington, DC: Review and Herald®, 1974), 59.
2. Ellen G. White, *The Acts of the Apostles* (Mountain View, CA: Pacific Press®, 1911), 183.
3. White, *Sketches From the Life of Paul*, 60, 61.
4. White, *Sketches From the Life of Paul*, 60.

Retracing Steps

They returned to Lystra, Iconium, and Antioch, strengthening the souls
of the disciples, exhorting them to continue in the faith.

—Acts 14:21, 22

Imagine. The Antiochian Jews hated Paul enough to travel more than a hundred miles to destroy his influence! "The disciples stood around the body of Paul, lamenting over him whom they supposed to be dead, when he suddenly lifted his head, and arose to his feet with the praise of God upon his lips. To the disciples this seemed like a resurrection from the dead, a miracle of God to preserve the life of his faithful servant. They rejoiced with inexpressible gladness over his restoration, and praised God with renewed faith in the doctrine preached by the apostles."[1]

"Among those who had been converted at Lystra, and who were eyewitnesses of the sufferings of Paul, was one who was afterward to become a prominent worker for Christ and who was to share with the apostle the trials and the joys of pioneer service in difficult fields. This was a young man named Timothy. When Paul was dragged out of the city, this youthful disciple was among the number who took their stand beside his apparently lifeless body and who saw him arise, bruised and covered with blood, but with praises upon his lips because he had been permitted to suffer for the sake of Christ."[2]

Paul and Barnabas left the next day for Derbe in Galatia, where many received Jesus as their Savior (Acts 14:20, 21). "It would have been a much simpler matter to proceed east to Tarsus, and return by ship to Antioch in Syria. But Paul and Barnabas chose a long, weary way, traveling some 250 mi. on their return journey to the sea. But by going back over the ground they had covered, they had opportunity to scatter still further the seed of the word they had earlier sown at such personal peril. The hostility of the Jews at Antioch and Iconium must have subsided to enable the apostles to revisit those cities without further personal danger."[3] Paul and Barnabas had suffered much for the gospel in these cities, and they wanted the churches to understand "all that will live godly in Christ Jesus shall suffer persecution" (2 Timothy 3:12, KJV; Revelation 1:9; 7:14). Turning back to their previous fields of endeavor, they picked elders to shepherd these newly formed churches.

"Organization is essential for maintaining the spiritual life and growth of the church."[4]

---

1. Ellen G. White, *Sketches From the Life of Paul* (Washington, DC: Review and Herald®, 1974), 61.
2. Ellen G. White, *The Acts of the Apostles* (Mountain View, CA: Pacific Press®, 1911), 184, 185.
3. Francis D. Nichol, ed., *The Seventh-day Adventist Bible Commentary*, vol. 6 (Washington, DC: Review and Herald®, 1957), 300.
4. Nichol, *Seventh-day Adventist Bible Commentary*, vol. 6, 301.

Mission Complete!

From there [Attalia] they sailed to Antioch, where they had been commended to the grace of God for the work which they had completed.

—Acts 14:26

With the new congregations placed on a sound footing, Paul and Barnabas now could return home to Antioch, the church that had sent them forth in the first place to evangelize the Gentiles. In every place where they had planted a new church, Paul and Barnabas had established proper order, appointed elders, encouraged and strengthened the brethren, and bound the work together.

"Now they could return to their home congregation with the satisfaction that their commission was fulfilled. Though they had only begun their preaching to the heathen, yet what they had done was done well. . . .

". . . It was fitting that the apostles should report to this church the results of their First Missionary Journey.

". . . During the interval of the missionary tour the Christians had probably heard little or nothing from the apostles, and we may well picture the eagerness with which they now gathered to listen to the report. . . .

". . . The gospel privileges had been given to everyone who believed. This freedom was first offered to the Gentiles at Antioch, where Paul had assisted Barnabas and others in the work ([Acts] 11:20–26). The gospel had now been carried to the Gentiles over a much wider field. Paul was fulfilling his commission to go to the Gentiles (ch. 22:21)."[1]

Paul and Barnabas had indeed broken new ground by venturing outside Jewish synagogues to approach Gentiles (Acts 13:46, 47). When encouraging Gentiles to accept the gospel, certain uniquely Jewish requirements (such as circumcision and the rigid observance of Jewish ceremonial law) had not been stressed as binding upon new converts. Although the first missionary journey had been a resounding success, there were those of the Jewish faith who were concerned for the "purity" of the new Christian movement within the larger belief of Judaism. While the glowing missionary report of the apostles was met with enthusiasm in the church at Antioch, the report received a decidedly cool response by Judaizing teachers claiming to speak for the church in Judea.

Sadly, when it comes to tolerance, liberals and conservatives still battle over "purity" within our churches. While truth should never be compromised, love should reconcile differences of opinion.

---

1. Francis D. Nichol, ed., *The Seventh-day Adventist Bible Commentary*, vol. 6 (Washington, DC: Review and Herald®, 1957), 302.

The Council of Jerusalem

Jew and Gentile

AD 49

Acts 15:1–35
The Acts of the Apostles, pp. 188–200
Sketches From the Life of Paul, pp. 63–72

Judaizing Teachers

And certain men came down from Judea and taught the brethren, "Unless you are circumcised according to the custom of Moses, you cannot be saved."

—Acts 15:1

Paul and Barnabas spent considerable time in Antioch following their return from the churches in Galatia and Pisidia. But a crisis was brewing within the new Christian church. "And certain men came down from Judea and taught the brethren, 'Unless you are circumcised according to the custom of Moses, you cannot be saved'" (Acts 15:1). "Paul and Barnabas had not required their Gentile converts to be circumcised. Here opens the account of the first major controversy in the Christian church. It was certain to arise as soon as Christianity spread beyond Palestine. The first converts to Christianity were Jews, but they retained most of the practices and prejudices of the religion in which they had been reared. Therefore they were shocked to see Gentiles come into the Christian church without first having become full proselytes to Judaism. . . . Those who now set forth objections may have been willing to accept Cornelius and his household into the church. But they probably argued that the leading of the Holy Spirit had brought about an exception in Cornelius' case that did not vitiate the rule of circumcision. Hence they declared that those who were brought into the church through baptism, under the clear leading of the Holy Spirit, should now be circumcised."[1]

"Before his conversion Paul had regarded himself as blameless 'touching the righteousness which is in the law.' Philippians 3:6. But since his change of heart he had gained a clear conception of the mission of the Saviour as the Redeemer of the entire race, Gentile as well as Jew, and had learned the difference between a living faith and a dead formalism."[2] If the Judaizer's assertions were accepted, most of the believers in Antioch, as well as those in the new Pisidia and Galatia churches just established by Paul and Barnabas, were not saved Christians. The Judaizers "purpose was to influence believing Jews against Paul because of his indifference to the requirements of the ceremonial law.

". . . Their pretended friendliness had a sinister motive—jealousy of the 'freedom' of Gentile converts."[3] The Judaizers wanted religion to be restrictive!

Churches struggle to keep souls when "pious" members, favoring direct criticism over loving guidance, threaten evangelistic efforts by taking new members to task for minor infractions.

---

1. Francis D. Nichol, ed., *The Seventh-day Adventist Bible Commentary*, vol. 6 (Washington, DC: Review and Herald®, 1957), 305.

2. Ellen G. White, *The Acts of the Apostles* (Mountain View, CA: Pacific Press®, 1911), 190.

3. Nichol, *Seventh-day Adventist Bible Commentary*, vol. 6, 945.

Christians: By Faith or Culture?

Therefore . . . they determined that Paul and Barnabas and certain others of them should go up to Jerusalem, to the apostles and elders, about this question.

—Acts 15:2

T he church at Antioch decided to send Paul and Barnabas to Jerusalem to settle the question of the status of new Gentile believers. "The Jews had prided themselves upon their divinely appointed services; and they concluded that as God once specified the Hebrew manner of worship, it was impossible that he should authorize a change in any of its specifications. They decided that Christianity must connect itself with the Jewish laws and ceremonies. They were slow to discern to the end of that which had been abolished by the death of Christ, and to perceive that all their sacrificial offerings had but prefigured the death of the Son of God, in which type had met its antitype rendering valueless the divinely appointed ceremonies and sacrifices of the Jewish religion."[1] Paul understood this better than most. He instinctively knew requiring Gentiles to become Jewish proselytes before they could become Christians was a huge roadblock. Additionally, Romans considered circumcision mutilation of the flesh, and Gentiles found Jewish obsession on three things, circumcision, their strict Sabbath observance, and their food laws, to be mere superstition. Jews' refusal to eat pork was especially baffling.

Food laws and table fellowship were critical church issues. A Gentile could easily sit down to a meal with a Jew, but a devout Jew could not partake of the nonkosher food at a Gentile table. "Peter had eaten with men among whom there would ordinarily be no regard as to kinds of food and ways in which it was prepared—things very important to the Jew."[2] The experience of Peter and Cornelius was now reexamined. While Peter's explanation had been accepted by the leadership in Jerusalem (Acts 11:15–18), the table fellowship issue was far from settled in the minds of conservative Christian Jews. Even Peter still seemed to be conflicted. Just *after* the Jerusalem Council, Paul would write, "Now when Peter had come to Antioch, I withstood him to his face, because he was to be blamed; for before certain men came from James, he would eat with the Gentiles; but when they came, he withdrew and separated himself, fearing those who were of the circumcision. And the rest of the Jews also played the hypocrite with him, so that *even Barnabas* was carried away with their hypocrisy" (Galatians 2:11–13; emphasis added).

Consider: "The fact that Peter could be militantly challenged demonstrates that he was not considered the head of the church, nor the 'chief of the apostles,' and certainly not infallible."[3]

1. Ellen G. White, *Sketches From the Life of Paul*, (Washington, DC: Review and Herald®, 1974), 64, 65.
2. Francis D. Nichol, ed., *The Seventh-day Adventist Bible Commentary*, vol. 6 (Washington, DC: Review and Herald®, 1957), 260.
3. Nichol, *Seventh-day Adventist Bible Commentary*, vol. 6, 260.

A Private Jerusalem Meeting

Then after fourteen years I went up again to Jerusalem with Barnabas, and also took Titus with me. And I went up by revelation, and communicated to them that gospel which I preach among the Gentiles, but privately to those who were of reputation.
—Galatians 2:1, 2; emphasis added

In Galatians 2, Paul writes a slightly different version of his Jerusalem trip than does Luke in Acts 15. According to Paul, before the main meeting was called, a "private meeting" was held with a select group of leaders present to hear Paul and Barnabas relate their concerns. Paul's description of that meeting is today's text. "Wisely, Paul sought to avoid unnecessarily stirring up opposition to the course of action to which God had called him, yet at the same time took counsel with the recognized leaders of the church."[1] Paul "feared that the brethren in Jerusalem might disapprove of his gospel ministry among the Gentiles. This would be a major victory for his Judaizing opponents and a serious obstacle to his plans for evangelizing the Gentiles. Had the Judaizers been able to oppose Paul with official letters from the twelve apostles condemning him and his gospel, he would have been cast in the role of an apostle of error."[2] The future of Christianity hung in the balance during this critical meeting. Paul wished a quiet consensus rather than an inflamed confrontation. It was not to be.

Into the meeting slipped the false brothers who argued in favor of circumcision. Paul called them "spies." They interrupted Paul, shouting that his Gentile converts must be circumcised. Titus stood unabashedly before them as an uncircumcised Christian Gentile. Paul was so angered by their tactics that he seemed to lose his train of thought (Galatians 2:4–6). Refusing to yield the floor, he finally agreed to put the question to the full church. Paul realized as he addressed James, the presiding officer of the church in Jerusalem, that he had a tough position to defend. The agitators who had come to Antioch claimed to be speaking in the name of James. Only later, when a decision had been reached, did "James distinctly [deny] having authorized them to do this [Acts 15:24]. However, inasmuch as he seems to have been a stickler for Judaic ritual and custom in his personal life (cf. Gal. 2:12), they probably felt justified in identifying him with their teaching."[3] Paul was once a strict Pharisee himself. He could certainly relate.

Those who shout the loudest aren't necessarily in the right. Passion is no excuse for rudeness.

---

1. Francis D. Nichol, ed., *The Seventh-day Adventist Bible Commentary*, vol. 6 (Washington, DC: Review and Herald®, 1957), 944.
2. Nichol, *Seventh-day Adventist Bible Commentary*, vol. 6, 944.
3. Nichol, *Seventh-day Adventist Bible Commentary*, vol. 6, 305.

The Jerusalem Council

*"But we believe that through the grace of the Lord Jesus Christ
we shall be saved in the same manner as they."*

—Acts 15:11

On their way to Jerusalem from Antioch, Paul and Barnabas had shared their missionary successes with the churches of Phoenicia and Samaria. They had countered the influence of the Judaizers by explaining that they were going to put their questions to a "fair" vote in Jerusalem. It must be remembered that Paul and Barnabas, as delegates from the church in Antioch, were putting forward their cultural questions voluntarily. They had not been summoned. Paul wanted the question of circumcision settled because it affected the recognition of his God-given mission to the Gentiles. Now his questions had moved from a select committee of leaders to the entire assembly, where it "was warmly discussed."[1] "The various points involved in the settlement of the main question at issue seemed to present before the council insurmountable difficulties. But the Holy Spirit had, in reality, already settled this question, upon the decision of which seemed to depend the prosperity, if not the very existence, of the Christian church."[2]

Peter rose to speak. He recounted his experience with the call to go to Cornelius and the descent of the Holy Spirit upon the Gentiles. He closed by saying, "So God, who knows the heart, acknowledged them by giving them the Holy Spirit, just as He did to us, and made no distinction between us and them, purifying their hearts by faith. Now therefore, why do you test God by putting a yoke on the neck of the disciples which neither our fathers nor we were able to bear? But we believe that through the grace of the Lord Jesus Christ we shall be saved in the same manner as they" (Acts 15:8–11). "There is no such contrast as is often claimed to exist between the Old and the New Testament, the law of God and the gospel of Christ, the requirements of the Jewish and those of the Christian dispensation. Every soul saved in the former dispensation was saved by Christ as verily as we are saved by Him to-day. Patriarchs and prophets were Christians. The gospel promise was given to the first pair in Eden, when they had by transgression separated themselves from God. The gospel was preached to Abraham. The Hebrews all drank of that spiritual Rock, which was Christ."[3]

Peter had his theology right!

---

1. Ellen G. White, *The Acts of the Apostles* (Mountain View, CA: Pacific Press®, 1911), 191.
2. White, *Acts of the Apostles*, 192.
3. Ellen G. White, "Obedience Better Than Sacrifice," *Signs of the Times*, September 14, 1882, 409.

The Council's Decision

"On that day I will raise up
The tabernacle of David, which has fallen down,
And repair its damages;
I will raise up its ruins,
And rebuild it as in the days of old;
That they may possess the remnant of Edom,
And all the Gentiles who are called by My name,"
Says the LORD who does this thing.

—Amos 9:11–12

Peter, the leading apostle, had spoken to the issue of circumcision and ruled that it was not necessary for Gentiles to first become Jews in order to become Christians. Now James, the brother of Jesus and the leading elder in Jerusalem, rose to speak to the issues. He quoted today's text. James saw the text as a prophecy of the Messiah and further that it spoke exactly to the inclusion of the Gentiles among those who would come to the Savior. There should be no stumbling blocks placed before Gentile converts. Paul and James agreed on this first issue.

James now put forward a potential solution to the second issue, the problem of Jewish and Gentile Christians eating together at the same table. He suggested Gentiles be requested by letter to abstain from four things: (1) food polluted by idols, (2) sexual immorality, (3) meat strangled, and (4) blood (Acts 15:20). Three of the four restrictions were related to food. All four prohibitions are found in Leviticus 17 and 18. To understand the suggestions of James regarding food, one needs to realize that most meat sold in markets was first offered to idols; "consequently a strict Jew never bought meat in the open market, but only of a Jewish butcher."[1]

Jews believed the life of the animal was its blood. "The prohibition against the use of blood as food was made as soon as animal food was permitted for men (Gen. 9:4), and it was frequently reiterated in the Mosaic law (Lev. 3:17; 7:26; 17:10; 19:26). . . . Food prepared with blood was common on the tables of both Greeks and Romans."[2] "Ancient Jewish tradition declared that when the neck of an animal was broken the blood flowed into the limbs in such a way that it could not be brought out, even with the use of salt."[3] "Idolatry and fornication sometimes were related in pagan cults. . . . Prostitution was often a part of idolatry."[4]

Jewish Christians wanted Gentile converts to embrace high morals, respect for women, and rejection of idolatry in all its forms. A change in lifestyle still marks a "born again" Christian.

---

1. Francis D. Nichol, ed., *The Seventh-day Adventist Bible Commentary*, vol. 6 (Washington, DC: Review and Herald®, 1957), 311.
2. Nichol, *Seventh-day Adventist Bible Commentary*, vol. 6, 312.
3. Nichol, *Seventh-day Adventist Bible Commentary*, vol. 6, 312.
4. Nichol, *Seventh-day Adventist Bible Commentary*, vol. 6, 312.

The Right Hand of Fellowship

And when James, Cephas, and John, who seemed to be pillars, perceived the grace that had been given to me, they gave me and Barnabas the right hand of fellowship, that we should go to the Gentiles and they to the circumcised. They desired only that we should remember the poor, the very thing which I also was eager to do.

—Galatians 2:9, 10

The Jerusalem conference was extremely important for Paul's subsequent mission. It was here that Paul was recognized as *the* apostle to the Gentiles. The Jerusalem leaders encouraged him to continue his efforts to win Gentiles for Christ. Critically, the grounds of Gentile acceptance into the church were established. Paul's principle of "faith in Christ alone" was acknowledged. Gentiles would not be saddled with the requirement to be circumcised, nor did they have to live by the Torah. "Paul insisted that the Gentile converts be free. The man who was justified by faith would in no way be helped heavenward by legalistic practices."[1] It is important to remember this decision by the Jerusalem Council pertained only to Gentile believers. Jewish Christians were still not released from the ritual law.

The leaders of the church at Jerusalem entered into a formal and friendly agreement with Paul during this meeting, and he received from them the "right hand of fellowship" (Galatians 2:9). This was important, for it established him as an equal in the Christian ministry. His gospel was accepted as worthy of being preached. Their consent to his continuing mission to the Gentiles meant that he did not run "in vain" (Galatians 2:2), but rather he had gained their "stamp of approval" on his ministry. Paul was to hold in high esteem his relationship with the Jerusalem church. He routinely, from this point forward, returned to Jerusalem at the end of every mission. He referred to his ministry as beginning in Jerusalem and spreading as far as Illyricum (Romans 15:19). He selected Barnabas and Silas to accompany him on his journeys. Both had ties to the church at Jerusalem. And his all-consuming task at the end of his ministry became gathering a collection for the saints in Jerusalem. He risked everything to take it there in person. He saw the Jerusalem congregation as the model for which he worked—a church composed of Gentiles and Jews, working together, united under the banner of Christ Jesus.

Peter and Paul believed and taught that all united in church capacity should be "subject one to another" (1 Peter 5:5, KJV). When we "unite," the latter rain will fall. It's time to come together!

---

1. Francis D. Nichol, ed., *The Seventh-day Adventist Bible Commentary*, vol. 6 (Washington, DC: Review and Herald®, 1957), 403.

Conflict Out of Victory

For it seemed good to the Holy Spirit, and to us, to lay upon you no greater burden than these necessary things: that you abstain from things offered to idols, from blood, from things strangled, and from sexual immorality.

—Acts 15:28, 29

The Judaizers "had struck at the very basis of Christian experience and belief—the fact that salvation is not gained by outward observances or by being identified with a certain group of people."[1] Many Christians even today have difficulty accepting the concept that "by grace, [we] have been saved through faith, and that not of [ourselves]; it is the *gift* of God, not of works, lest anyone should boast" (Ephesians 2:8; emphasis added). The "whole" (Acts 15:22) Jerusalem church agreed with the suggestions of James and voted to urge the Gentiles "to keep the commandments and to lead holy lives. They were also to be assured that the men who had declared circumcision to be binding were not authorized to do so by the apostles."[2] Those who favored Gentile circumcision were frustrated and angry. Their position had been struck down, and they had not even been allowed to vote. Salvation by outward observances had been found to be inconsistent with the gospel of grace and salvation by faith. They were resolved, however, not to give up so easily. They would continue the fight and sow seeds of discontent in Paul's churches for years to come.

The reason was simple. "The entire body of Christians was not called to vote upon the question. The 'apostles and elders,' men of influence and judgment, framed and issued the decree, which was thereupon generally accepted by the Christian churches. Not all, however, were pleased with the decision; there was a faction of ambitious and self-confident brethren who disagreed with it. These men assumed to engage in the work on their own responsibility. They indulged in much murmuring and faultfinding, proposing new plans and seeking to pull down the work of the men whom God had ordained to teach the gospel message. From the first the church has had such obstacles to meet and ever will have till the close of time."[3] "In his ministry, Paul was often compelled to stand alone. He was specially taught of God and dared make no concessions that would involve principle. At times the burden was heavy, but Paul stood firm for the right."[4]

"The advance of the gospel message must not be hindered by the prejudices and preferences of men, whatever might be their position in the church."[5]

1. Francis D. Nichol, ed., *The Seventh-day Adventist Bible Commentary*, vol. 6 (Washington, DC: Review and Herald®, 1957), 314.
2. Ellen G. White, *The Acts of the Apostles* (Mountain View, CA: Pacific Press®, 1911), 195.
3. White, *Acts of the Apostles*, 196, 197.
4. White, *Acts of the Apostles*, 199.
5. White, *Acts of the Apostles*, 200.

Paul's Second Missionary Journey

With Silas and Timothy to Cilicia, Lystra, Galatia, Troas,
Philippi, Thessalonica, Berea, Athens, and Corinth

AD 49–52

Acts 15:36–18:22
The Acts of the Apostles, pp. 201–280
Sketches From the Life of Paul, pp. 72–128

Paul and Barnabas Have "Words"

Then the contention became so sharp that they parted from one another.

—Acts 15:39

The Jerusalem Council sent two of their own to Antioch with Paul and Barnabas to confirm that "the decrees adopted might come from lips other than those of these two men, who were so personally involved in the question. Thus there would be no chance of some recalcitrant Judaizer charging Paul and Barnabas with forgery."[1] The two selected to accompany the apostles to Antioch were Judas surnamed Barsabas and Silas (Acts 15:22). One can appreciate the "eager excitement as the letter was solemnly opened and read aloud, with perhaps murmuring on the one side, and applause on the other, as sentence after sentence repudiated the teachings of the Judaizers and confirmed the stand taken by Paul and Barnabas. To the Gentile believers at Antioch this epistle was a charter of freedom, won after a real struggle."[2]

"After spending some time in ministry at Antioch, Paul proposed to his fellow worker that they set forth on another missionary journey. 'Let us go again,' he said to Barnabas, 'and visit our brethren in every city where we have preached the word of the Lord, and see how they do.'"[3] "Barnabas was ready to go with Paul, but wished to take with them Mark, who had again decided to devote himself to the ministry. To this Paul objected. He 'thought [it] not good to take . . . with them' one who during their first missionary journey had left them in a time of need. He was not inclined to excuse Mark's weakness in deserting the work for the safety and comforts of home. He urged that one with so little stamina was unfitted for a work requiring patience, self-denial, bravery, devotion, faith, and a willingness to sacrifice, if need be, even life itself. So sharp was the contention that Paul and Barnabas separated, the latter following out his convictions and taking Mark with him. 'So Barnabas took Mark, and sailed unto Cyprus; and Paul chose Silas, and departed, being recommended by the brethren unto the grace of God.'"[4] "The warmth of a long-standing friendship sealed by Barnabas' help to Paul when he stood most in need of a human friend . . . , as well as the mutual prosecution of a great work, and the successful securing of a great decision, made the breach between Barnabas and Paul the more painful."[5]

Paul and Barnabas, who had faced so much together, parted over John Mark. Human relationships are hard to maintain when opposing personal opinions are not surrendered.

---

1. Francis D. Nichol, ed., *The Seventh-day Adventist Bible Commentary*, vol. 6 (Washington, DC: Review and Herald®, 1957), 313.

2. Nichol, *Seventh-day Adventist Bible Commentary*, vol. 6, 315.

3. Ellen G. White, *The Acts of the Apostles* (Mountain View, CA: Pacific Press®, 1911), 201.

4. White, *Acts of the Apostles*, 202.

5. Nichol, *Seventh-day Adventist Bible Commentary*, vol. 6, 317.

Barnabas and John Mark

And so Barnabas took Mark and sailed to Cyprus.

—Acts 15:39

L uke is very open about recording the shortcomings of Paul and Barnabas. In his depiction of their disagreement, we see two strong men with cherished opinions who differ on how to get a job done. Neither was 100 percent right, and neither was 100 percent wrong. Luke wanted to believe God was blessing the new Paul-Silas team, but at the same time, He did not approve of the dispute between Paul and Barnabas. It is especially painful when a successful team breaks up over personalities. There was wisdom in the decision of Paul and Barnabas, even though it meant breaking up a winning team. Barnabas stood by Mark, and his steadfast loyalty was not in vain. Paul eventually "received John Mark as a fellow worker (Philemon 24), and Paul learned to recognize in John Mark one who was 'profitable' to him 'for the ministry'(2 Tim. 4:11)."[1] Mark would go on to work with Peter (1 Peter 5:13).

"Both Paul and Barnabas had a tender regard for those who had recently accepted the gospel message under their ministry, and they longed to see them once more. This solicitude Paul never lost. Even when in distant mission fields, far from the scene of his earlier labors, he continued to bear upon his heart the burden of urging these converts to remain faithful, 'perfecting holiness in the fear of God.' 2 Corinthians 7:1. Constantly he tried to help them to become self-reliant, growing Christians, strong in faith, ardent in zeal, and wholehearted in their consecration to God and to the work of advancing His kingdom."[2] This makes Paul's inflexible refusal to travel with Mark even more difficult to understand. Paul usually saw the good in everyone and tried to help them. Here he was deviating from his usual nature. Perhaps the high standard he set for himself was lacking in the young John Mark, but what better reason to labor all the more intensely to salvage him? There has to be more to the story than we are told. John Mark's desertion apparently struck Paul to his very core. So the two apostles agreed to disagree. "This is the last mention in Acts of either Barnabas or Mark."[3]

Were Paul's standards of acceptance too high? Consider: If Barnabas hadn't accepted Saul in Jerusalem and presented him to the church leaders, would we be studying the life of Paul now?

1. Francis D. Nichol, ed., *The Seventh-day Adventist Bible Commentary*, vol. 6 (Washington, DC: Review and Herald®, 1957), 317.
2. Ellen G. White, *The Acts of the Apostles* (Mountain View, CA: Pacific Press®, 1911), 201.
3. Nichol, *Seventh-day Adventist Bible Commentary*, vol. 6, 317.

Paul and Silas

But Paul chose Silas and departed, being commended by the brethren to the grace of God.
And he went through Syria and Cilicia, strengthening the churches.
—Acts 15:40, 41

Judas Barsabas had returned to Jerusalem sometime after the presentation of the Jerusalem Council decree. Silas must have remained in Antioch to work with Paul. Silas "may be an Aramaic name, or a contraction of the Roman Silvanus."[1] Now, following the disagreement between Paul and Barnabas, Silas was chosen to accompany Paul back to the churches Paul and Barnabas had established. Why did Paul select Silas? There is speculation that Paul chose Silas because he was a member of the Jerusalem church and would strengthen ties between that church and the missionary team. Silas later became affiliated with Peter, serving as Peter's secretary, who wrote down Peter's first epistle (1 Peter 5:12).

Silas was a good choice. An impartial representative who had been present in Jerusalem during the circumcision debate, he would be able to refute the charges of the Judaizers who had been busy among the churches of Cilicia during Paul's absence. Now no one could accuse Paul of twisting the council decision to fit his opinion. Also, Silas was interested in evangelism among the Gentiles. "He was well fitted as was Barnabas, for he had the gift of prophecy. Silas could now claim the title of apostle, in its broader sense of 'missionary,' as he was sent forth by the church of Antioch."[2] Paul and Silas now headed north from Antioch then turned west to visit the churches established during the first mission. The road led them to Tarsus, Paul's home. From there, they turned north and passed through the Cilician Gates in the Taurus Mountains. Once on the plain north of the mountains, they turned west again for Derbe, Lystra, and Iconium.

"As Paul had not visited his home province of Cilicia on the first journey, it is probable that the churches there were founded by him during his years at Tarsus following his conversion (see [Acts] 9:30; 11:25). But the Judaizers had been active in the two provinces named, and the presence of Paul, with Silas as one of the emissaries from the council, must have helped to allay any doubts or questionings in the minds of either Jews or Gentiles in the churches they now visited."[3] Paul was returning to Tarsus. Was he on speaking terms with his family? Had they converted to Christianity? Did the Jewish community at large in Tarsus accept him?

In choosing to follow Jesus, Paul sacrificed everything he had previously considered important.

---

1. Francis D. Nichol, ed., *The Seventh-day Adventist Bible Commentary*, vol. 6 (Washington, DC: Review and Herald®, 1957), 313.

2. Nichol, *Seventh-day Adventist Bible Commentary*, vol. 6, 317.

3. Nichol, *Seventh-day Adventist Bible Commentary*, vol. 6, 317.

Timothy Recruited

Then he came to Derbe and Lystra. And behold, a certain disciple was there, named Timothy, the son of a certain Jewish woman who believed, but his father was Greek.
—Acts 16:1; emphasis added

In company with Silas, Paul again visited Lystra, where he had been greeted as a god by the heathen; where the opposing Jews had followed on his track, and by their misrepresentation had turned the reverence of the people into insult, abuse, and a determination to kill him. Yet we find him again on the scene of his former danger, looking after the fruit of his labors there.

"He found that the converts to Christ had not been intimidated by the violent persecution of the apostles; but, on the contrary, were confirmed in the faith, believing that the kingdom of Christ would be reached through trial and suffering."[1]

"Here Paul again met Timothy. . . .

". . . In Timothy Paul saw one who appreciated the sacredness of the work of a minister; who was not appalled at the prospect of suffering and persecution; and who was willing to be taught. Yet the apostle did not venture to take the responsibility of giving Timothy, an untried youth, a training in the gospel ministry, without first fully satisfying himself in regard to his character and his past life.

"Timothy's father was a Greek and his mother a Jewess. From a child he had known the Scriptures. The piety that he saw in his home life was sound and sensible. The faith of his *mother* [Eunice] and his *grandmother* [Lois] in the sacred oracles was to him a constant reminder of the blessing in doing God's will. The word of God was the rule by which these two godly women had guided Timothy. The spiritual power of the lessons that he had received from them kept him pure in speech and unsullied by the evil influences with which he was surrounded. Thus his home instructors had cooperated with God in preparing him to bear burdens.

"Paul saw that Timothy was faithful, steadfast, and true, and he chose him as a companion in labor and travel."[2] Timothy was quite young when Paul chose him to be his assistant. Most commentators believe he was eighteen to twenty years of age, "but his principles had been so established by his early education that he was fitted to take his place as Paul's helper. And though young, he bore his responsibilities with Christian meekness."[3]

"As the lessons of the Bible are wrought into the daily life, they have a deep and lasting influence upon the character."[4]

---

1. Ellen G. White, *Sketches From the Life of Paul* (Washington, DC: Review and Herald®, 1974), 72.
2. Ellen G. White, *The Acts of the Apostles* (Mountain View, CA: Pacific Press®, 1911), 202, 203; emphasis added.
3. White, *Acts of the Apostles*, 203, 204.
4. White, *Acts of the Apostles*, 205.

Timothy Circumcised

Paul wanted to have him go on with him. And he took him and circumcised him because of the Jews who were in that region, for they all knew that his father was Greek.

—Acts 16:3

L uke gives no clear information concerning the religion of Timothy's father. That he was 'a Greek' may indicate that he was a heathen Gentile, in which case his marriage with Eunice would not have been acknowledged by the Jews; or, he may have been a Gentile 'that feared God.' However, apparently he was not a full proselyte, for his son, Timothy, had not been circumcised."[1] "Paul, with his usual good judgment, caused Timothy to be circumcised; not that God required it, but in order to remove from the minds of the Jews an obstacle to Timothy's ministration. Paul was to labor from place to place in the synagogues, and there to preach Christ. If his companion should be known as an uncircumcised heathen, the work of both would be greatly hindered by the prejudice and bigotry of the people. The apostle everywhere met a storm of persecution. He desired to bring the Jews to Christianity, and sought, as far as was consistent with the faith, to remove every pretext for opposition. Yet while he conceded this much to Jewish prejudice, his faith and teachings declared that circumcision or uncircumcision was nothing, but the gospel of Christ was everything."[2]

Paul probably performed the services of a Jewish *mohel* himself. "This act seems at first inconsistent with Paul's conduct respecting Titus, whom he refused to circumcise (. . . Gal. 2:3), and with his general teaching concerning circumcision (. . . 1 Cor. 7:18, 19, Gal. 5:2–6). But there is a distinct contrast between the cases of Titus and Timothy. Titus was a Greek, and to have him circumcised would have yielded a principle that Paul was not prepared to yield. The mixed parentage of Timothy made him a Jew, for the rabbinical code held that the child of a Jewish mother was reckoned as a Jew. . . . Had both his parents been faithful Jews, he would have been circumcised on the eighth day (Lev. 12:3), but religious differences between his parents doubtless prevented this. . . .

". . . If uncircumcised, he would be a source of difficulty to the Jews, who would think that a bad Jew could not be a good guide as a Christian."[3] Circumcising Timothy was consistent with Paul's philosophy (1 Corinthians 9:20).

We, like Paul, must constantly watch that our actions do not give cause for another to stumble.

---

1. Francis D. Nichol, ed., *The Seventh-day Adventist Bible Commentary*, vol. 6 (Washington, DC: Review and Herald®, 1957), 324.

2. Ellen G. White, *Sketches From the Life of Paul* (Washington, DC: Review and Herald®, 1974), 73.

3. Nichol, *Seventh-day Adventist Bible Commentary*, vol. 6, 324.

The Spirit Leads West

*Now when they had gone through Phrygia and the region of Galatia,
they were forbidden by the Holy Spirit to preach the word in Asia.*

—Acts 16:6

After visiting the churches he had established at Derbe, Lystra, Iconium, Antioch, and the other cities of Lycaonia, Paul headed northwest toward Bithynia (on the southern shore of the Black Sea). This was the part of western Asia Minor known as Phrygia. Here the group turned more directly north toward Galatia. Some argue Paul took a "northern" route through Galatia, while others argue strongly for a "southern" route. The *Seventh-day Bible Commentary* advocates a "modified northern version," claiming that the churches of Galatia to which Paul would later write were to be found between Phrygia and Bithynia and Mysia (on the southern shore of the Sea of Marmara and the Hellespont). This is only important for serious students of Paul and his writings. "The divergence of opinion on this problem is not vital to the integrity of the book of Acts."[1] Yet it is of interest to know to whom Paul wrote his Epistle to the Galatians. "Phrygia possesses a special interest for Christians because it later included the churches of the Lycus Valley, Colossae and Laodicea."[2] We are not told how the Spirit directed Paul, but he was told *not* to travel to western "Asia, with its teeming cities such as Ephesus, Smyrna, and Sardis, which had large Jewish communities, and were great centers of idolatrous worship. Such cities must have made a strong appeal to Paul, but he was completely obedient to the Spirit's commands."[3] Areas Paul was not to enter were later evangelized by Peter (1 Peter 1:1).

"In Gal. 4:13–15 . . . Paul refers to his visit to Galatia, where he seems to have been detained by a serious illness, possibly some affliction of the eyes. Many commentators have understood Paul's statement about a 'thorn in the flesh' (2 Cor. 12:7 . . .) as referring to an eye malady. Probably this led to a longer stay in this region than Paul at first intended. During this illness, the Galatians had opportunity to show themselves singularly devoted to him. He declares that they would have 'plucked out' their 'own eyes,' if it had been possible to replace his own with them, and thus relieve his suffering."[4] Paul gave them a vision of Jesus. He told them about the cross! "Christ's death proves God's great love for man. It is our pledge of salvation. To remove the cross from the Christian would be like blotting the sun from the sky."[5]

How's your spiritual "eyesight"? You can best see the Son in the shadow of the cross!

---

1. Francis D. Nichol, ed., *The Seventh-day Adventist Bible Commentary*, vol. 6 (Washington, DC: Review and Herald®, 1957), 338.

2. Nichol, *Seventh-day Adventist Bible Commentary*, vol. 6, 325.

3. Nichol, *Seventh-day Adventist Bible Commentary*, vol. 6, 325.

4. Nichol, *Seventh-day Adventist Bible Commentary*, vol. 6, 325.

5. Ellen G. White, *The Acts of the Apostles* (Mountain View, CA: Pacific Press®, 1911), 209.

A Vision at Troas

And a vision appeared to Paul in the night. A man of Macedonia
stood and pleaded with him saying, "Come over to Macedonia and help us."
—Acts 16:9

We do not know the route Paul and his companions took through Galatia. Forbidden to travel further north or to the Southwest, the trio moved directly west toward the coast. Leaving the rugged mountainous interior of present-day Turkey, Paul and his companions found themselves in Troas, a major settlement on the Aegean Sea. "The town of Alexandria Troas, so named in honor of Alexander the Great, was at this time reckoned as a Roman colony and a free city. The site of ancient Troy lay a few miles to the north of Troas. But Paul doubtless had little interest in Homer's account of the siege of the old Greek town. The questions occupying his thoughts now concerned the best means of proclaiming Christ as Saviour, that the inhabitants of Troas might find eternal life. Such thoughts undoubtedly expressed themselves in Paul's prayers, and in answer to those prayers came the vision recorded in v. 9. There is no mention of any missionary work done by Paul at Troas at this time, but Scripture gives ample evidence that a church was later established there (. . . Acts 20:5–12; 2 Cor. 2:12, 13; 2 Tim. 4:13)."[1]

While at Troas, Paul received the vision recorded in Acts 16. Macedonia was "originally a country north of classical Greece. It rose quickly to power under Philip (359–336 b.c.) and Alexander the Great (336–323 b.c.). In 142 b.c., however, it became a Roman province and preserved that status through Paul's day. . . . Many of its flourishing towns held large Jewish communities, which would provide excellent bases for Christian evangelism."[2] "This is one of the crucial moments in history. Much of Europe's future depends on Paul's response to the appeal. Europe can well be thankful that the courageous apostle did not hesitate to answer the call that now came to him. Hitherto, he had been prevented from fulfilling his great desire to evangelize in Asia and Bithynia; but now a whole continent beckons him, and he cannot fail to have seen the reason that lay behind the divine prohibitions he had so faithfully obeyed."[3]

"Your young men shall see visions, your old men shall dream dreams" (Acts 2:17).

---

1. Francis D. Nichol, ed., *The Seventh-day Adventist Bible Commentary*, vol. 6 (Washington, DC: Review and Herald®, 1957), 326.
2. Nichol, *Seventh-day Adventist Bible Commentary*, vol. 6, 326.
3. Nichol, *Seventh-day Adventist Bible Commentary*, vol. 6, 327.

Luke's Medical Mission

Now after he had seen the vision, immediately we *sought to go to Macedonia, concluding that the Lord had called* us *to preach the gospel to them.*
—Acts 16:10; emphasis added

I n Troas, Paul, Silas, and Timothy accepted a fourth person into their party. "When a narrative is being related in the third person, and the first person of the pronoun is suddenly introduced, the inference is plain that the author has become an actor in the events recorded. Most commentators conclude that Luke, the author of the Acts . . . , joined the missionary party at Troas, rather than that he wrote artificially from the point of view of Silas or Timothy. Since Luke does not mention his own conversion, it is reasonable to suppose that it had taken place some time before this junction at Troas. Since he includes himself in the phrase 'the Lord had called *us* for to preach the gospel,' Luke must also be counted as one of the evangelists."[1]

Paul and his three companions—Silas, Timothy, and Luke—departed at once for Macedonia. "Therefore, sailing from Troas, we ran a straight course to Samothrace, and the next day came to Neapolis, and from there to Philippi, which is the foremost city of that part of Macedonia, a colony. And we were staying in that city for some days" (Acts 16:11, 12). Perhaps Luke joined the party because Paul was in need of a physician. This would seem to be the most logical explanation for his accompanying the party.

"Some Asia Minor men went to Alexandria to study medicine, but there were distinguished schools on the peninsula: the Asclepium of Cos, the Herophileian school of Men Carou near Laodicea, the Asclepium of Pergamum, a school at Smyrna, and one at Ephesus. These schools contributed much to the development of medicine in Asia Minor. There were private physicians, but some cities also maintained public physicians—which formed a real 'health service' directed by master physicians."[2] "Medical education involved, first and foremost, the writings of Hippocrates, though much of this body of material was written later. Instruction included how to behave in the sickroom. There were groups of physicians offering instruction in some of the major cities, but essentially the trainee did his apprenticeship under a practicing physician. Students went with the physician as he made rounds and examined his patients. This was not a 'quick fix.' One might study this way in several cities over a period of time. The famous Galen of Pergamum studied in this manner for eleven years."[3] So must have Luke.

The practice of medicine and ministry go hand in hand. Christ, the Great Physician, epitomized both forms of outreach.

1. Francis D. Nichol, ed., *The Seventh-day Adventist Bible Commentary*, vol. 6 (Washington, DC: Review and Herald®, 1957), 327.
2. H. I. Marrou, *A History of Education in Antiquity* (New York: New American Library, 1964), 263.
3. Marrou, *History of Education in Antiquity*, 265.

Philippi

Therefore, sailing from Troas, we ran a straight course to Samothrace, and the next day came to Neapolis, and from there to Philippi, which is the foremost city of that part of Macedonia, a colony. And we were staying in that city for some days.

—Acts 16:11, 12

C asting off the hawsers holding the ship to the pier, the group set sail westward toward the island of Samothrace. Samothrace lay halfway across the Aegean between Asia Minor and Greece. The mountainous island was visible from both Asia Minor and Greece because of its five-thousand-foot peak. It could be reached in a single day of westerly sailing with a following breeze, and most ships stopped there for the night. A contrary wind could make the crossing difficult, and Paul on a return trip took five days to make the transit against the wind (Acts 20:6). Neapolis, or "new town," was the port for Philippi, "which lay about ten mi. to the northwest. . . . It was the eastern terminus of the Egnatian Way, the great road that connected the Aegean and the Adriatic.

". . . At Neapolis they probably left their ship and went overland to their immediate goal, Philippi.

". . . Originally known as Krenides, 'place of small fountains,' the city was rebuilt by Philip of Macedon (359–336 B.C.), father of Alexander the Great, and named in his honor."[1]

"Macedonia became a Roman province in 146 B.C. In 42 B.C. the great battle between Octavian and Antony, the avengers of Caesar, and Brutus and Cassius, his murderers, took place in the vicinity of Philippi [on the Plains of Philippi to the southwest of the city]. Octavian and Antony were victors [naming the city *Colonia Victrix Philippensium*] and later enlarged the city and elevated it to the status of a colony (*Colonia Julia Philippensis*). Still later it was granted the *ius italicum*, which meant that its citizens received a form of Roman citizenship. Since many Roman veterans had been settled there, about half of its population was of Latin descent in [New Testament] times."[2] "In this way the colony was closely united with Rome. These colonies were sometimes described as the 'bulwarks of an empire' . . . or 'miniatures, as it were, and in a way copies' of the people of Rome. . . . The spirit of a colony was therefore intensely Roman. Thus in this Macedonian city Paul, himself a Roman citizen, came directly in contact with a flourishing example of Roman imperial organization."[3]

Paul will discover that those he considers to be fellow "countrymen" will turn out to be persecutors.

---

1. Francis D. Nichol, ed., *The Seventh-day Adventist Bible Commentary*, vol. 6 (Washington, DC: Review and Herald®, 1957), 328.

2. Siegfried H. Horn, *Seventh-day Adventist Bible Dictionary*, ed. Don F. Neufeld, Commentary Reference Series, vol. 8 (Washington, DC: Review and Herald®, 1960), s.v. "Philippi."

3. Nichol, *Seventh-day Adventist Bible Commentary*, vol. 6, 328.

Lydia

Now a certain woman named Lydia *heard us. She was a seller of purple from the city of Thyatira, who worshiped God. The Lord opened her heart to heed the things spoken by Paul.*

—Acts 16:14; emphasis added

O n Sabbath, Paul and his companions went looking for a synagogue in Philippi. "They had been there some days, but when the Sabbath came they would naturally long to be with fellow Jews with whom they could worship and to whom they could impart their good news of salvation."[1] Searching, they found no synagogue. This was not surprising. "A minimum of ten Jewish men was necessary to constitute a regular synagogue and thus indicated a city where Jewish people would be likely to form their own community; this number of Jewish men may not have lived in Philippi. But in places with no official synagogue, Jewish people preferred to meet in a ritually pure place near water; ritual washing of hands before prayer seems to have been standard in Diaspora Judaism, and excavations show the importance of water to synagogues. The nearest body of flowing water, the Gangites (a tributary of the Strymon), is about one and a quarter miles from Philippi. It was thus more than a 'sabbath day's journey' by Pharisaic standards, suggesting that they were more concerned with assembling near a pure place than with the technicalities of Palestinian legal ideals."[2]

Here the missionaries found a circle of devout Gentile women assembled to pray. Among them was Lydia. "She was an attendant at the Jewish place of worship, having been sufficiently influenced by the Jewish religion to be called one who 'worshipped God,' a technical term for converts to Jewry who had not become full proselytes (Acts 16:14). She became one of Paul's earliest converts and his hostess during his stay at Philippi before and after his prison experience (vs 15, 40)."[3] Being the owner of her own business, selling expensive purple cloth from the Lydian city of Thyatira in Asia, she was a woman of substance. Eagerly she invited the apostles to stay as her guests while in Philippi. Paul said "thank you, but no." Lydia continued to press until Paul finally yielded. "*Euodias and Syntyche, and other women of Philippi* who 'laboured' with Paul 'in the gospel' ([Philippians] 4:2, 3), may have been among the 'women' of v. 13. The group formed the first Christian church in Europe founded by Paul. By its loving hospitality and steadfast adherence to the faith it won a special place in Paul's affections."[4]

Start a prayer circle! Who knows, it might develop into a church. Wouldn't that be great!

---

1. Francis D. Nichol, ed., *The Seventh-day Adventist Bible Commentary*, vol. 6 (Washington, DC: Review and Herald®, 1957), 328.

2. Craig S. Keener, *The IVP Bible Background Commentary—New Testament* (Downers Grove, IL: InterVarsity Press, 1993), 368.

3. Siegfried H. Horn, *Seventh-day Adventist Bible Dictionary*, ed. Don F. Neufeld, Commentary Reference Series, vol. 8 (Washington, DC: Review and Herald®, 1960), s.v. "Lydia."

4. Nichol, *Seventh-day Adventist Bible Commentary*, vol. 6, 330; emphasis added.

Fortune-Telling

Now it happened, as we went to prayer, that a certain slave girl possessed with a spirit of divination met us, who brought her masters much profit by fortune-telling.
—Acts 16:16; emphasis added

The second story Luke relates as taking place during their Philippi visit also involved a woman. "As the messengers of the cross went about their work of teaching, a woman possessed of a spirit of divination followed them, crying, 'These men are the servants of the most high God, which show unto us the way of salvation. And this did she many days.'

"This woman was a special agent of Satan and had brought to her masters much gain by soothsaying. Her influence had helped to strengthen idolatry. Satan knew that his kingdom was being invaded, and he resorted to this means of opposing the work of God, hoping to mingle his sophistry with the truths taught by those who were proclaiming the gospel message. The words of recommendation uttered by this woman were an injury to the cause of truth, distracting the minds of the people from the teachings of the apostles and bringing disrepute upon the gospel, and by them many were led to believe that the men who spoke with the Spirit and power of God were actuated by the same spirit as this emissary of Satan."[1]

The girl was a valuable find, and multiple owners held shares in her ability to make money by telling fortunes. Luke described her as having the spirit of a python. "In Greek mythology Python was a dragon or serpent who was thought to have guarded the oracle at Delphi and to have been killed by Apollo, who was subsequently known as the Pythian Apollo. Python was worshiped at Delphi as a symbol of wisdom. . . . It is clear that the local population believed that the slave possessed supernatural abilities, and doubtless her wild cries were noted and received as oracles. Her masters took advantage of her supposed inspiration, and made the girl give answers to those who made inquiries of her."[2] "There is a limit to what even a Christian can passively endure when the Lord's work is being hindered."[3] Paul finally became exasperated! Turning to the slave girl, he said to the spirit, " 'I command you in the name of Jesus Christ to come out of her.' And he came out that very hour" (Acts 16:18). "It is surely permissible to think that she became a Christian . . . and found shelter with the *women* who 'laboured' with the apostle (Phil. 4:3)."[4]

Many today consult those with "psychic" powers. Christians know Satan pulls those strings!

---

1. Ellen G. White, *The Acts of the Apostles* (Mountain View, CA: Pacific Press®, 1911), 212.
2. Francis D. Nichol, ed., *The Seventh-day Adventist Bible Commentary*, vol. 6 (Washington, DC: Review and Herald®, 1957), 330.
3. Nichol, *Seventh-day Adventist Bible Commentary*, vol. 6, 331.
4. Nichol, *Seventh-day Adventist Bible Commentary*, vol. 6, 331; emphasis added.

Before the *Praetorés*

"These men, being Jews, exceedingly trouble our city; and they teach customs which are not lawful
for us, being Romans, to receive or observe."
—Acts 16:20, 21

D ispossessed of the evil spirit and restored to her right mind, the woman chose
to become a follower of Christ. Then her masters were alarmed for their craft.
They saw that all hope of receiving money from her divinations and soothsaying was
at an end and that their source of income would soon be entirely cut off if the apostles
were allowed to continue the work of the gospel.

"Many others in the city were interested in gaining money through satanic delusions,
and these, fearing the influence of a power that could so effectually stop their work,
raised a mighty cry against the servants of God. . . .

"Stirred by a frenzy of excitement, the multitude rose against the disciples. A mob
spirit prevailed and was sanctioned by the authorities, who tore the outer garments
from the apostles and commanded that they should be scourged. 'And when they had
laid many stripes upon them, they cast them into prison, charging the jailer to keep
them safely: who, having received such a charge, thrust them into the inner prison,
and made their feet fast in the stocks.' "[1] A Roman lictor "carried bundles of rods as
symbols of their office."[2] Paul may have protested that as a Roman citizen he could
not be flogged, but the mob may have drowned out his defense. In any case, the
lictor zealously flogged the two men according to the sentence handed down by the
praetorés. No limitation existed, as with the Jewish limit of thirty-nine stripes. Paul
and Silas were forced to lie on bruised and bleeding backs.

"The scene is filled with local color. It is a Roman colony, a little island of Rome in
the Macedonian sea—complete with Roman magistrates, Roman police, and Roman
law. The irony, of course, is that the law enforcers become the lawbreakers by flogging
the two Roman citizens Paul and Silas without a proper hearing. The charges brought
by the owners should not be missed ([Acts 16:] 20-21). There was nothing illegal with
being a Jew; so the first charge had no substance. 'Throwing [the] city into an uproar'
was little more than rhetorical hyperbole, and the officials knew it meant nothing. The
charge that got their attention was 'advocating customs unlawful for us Romans.' It,
too, was nebulous, but it was the type of appeal to patriotic sentiments that was bound
to evoke a response of indignation in the populace of the proud Roman colony."[3]

Paul and Silas, the two leading members of the missionary group, were Jewish. Did Luke and
Timothy escape the same fate because they looked more like Gentiles?

1. Ellen G. White, *The Acts of the Apostles* (Mountain View, CA: Pacific Press®, 1911), 213.
2. Francis D. Nichol, ed., *The Seventh-day Adventist Bible Commentary*, vol. 6 (Washington, DC: Review and Herald®,
1957), 332.
3. John B. Polhill, *Paul and His Letters* (Nashville, TN: Broadman & Holman, 1999), 162.

Midnight Prayer Meeting

But at midnight Paul and Silas were praying and singing hymns to God,
and the prisoners were listening to them. Suddenly there was a great earthquake.

—Acts 16:25, 26

Paul and Silas were placed in stocks, "an instrument of torture, a wooden frame with holes into which head and feet and hands were thrust, thus placing the prisoner in a most uncomfortable position. . . . With Paul and Silas the feet only were fastened, and the rest of the body was left lying on the ground, a particularly agonizing position for men punished as the apostles had been."[1] "The apostles suffered extreme torture because of the painful position in which they were left, but they did not murmur. Instead, in the utter darkness and desolation of the dungeon, they encouraged each other by words of prayer and sang praises to God because they were found worthy to suffer shame for His sake. . . .

"With astonishment the other prisoners heard the sound of prayer and singing issuing from the inner prison. They had been accustomed to hear shrieks and moans, cursing and swearing, breaking the silence of the night; but never before had they heard words of prayer and praise ascending from that gloomy cell. Guards and prisoners marveled and asked themselves who these men could be, who, cold, hungry, and tortured, could yet rejoice.

"Meanwhile the magistrates returned to their homes, congratulating themselves that by prompt and decisive measures they had quelled a tumult. But on the way they heard further particulars concerning the character and work of the men they had sentenced to scourging and imprisonment. They saw the woman who had been freed from satanic influence and were struck by the change in her countenance and demeanor. In the past she had caused the city much trouble; now she was quiet and peaceable. As they realized that in all probability they had visited upon two innocent men the rigorous penalty of the Roman law they were indignant with themselves and decided that in the morning they would command that the apostles be privately released and escorted from the city, beyond the danger of violence from the mob.

". . . All heaven was interested in the men who were suffering for Christ's sake, and angels were sent to visit the prison. At their tread the earth trembled. The heavily bolted prison doors were thrown open; the chains and fetters fell from the hands and feet of the prisoners; and a bright light flooded the prison."[2]

"For He shall give His angels charge over you, to keep you in all your ways" (Psalm 91:11).

---

1. Francis D. Nichol, ed., *The Seventh-day Adventist Bible Commentary*, vol. 6 (Washington, DC: Review and Herald®, 1957), 333.
2. Ellen G. White, *The Acts of the Apostles* (Mountain View, CA: Pacific Press®, 1911), 213–215.

Do Yourself No Harm

And the keeper of the prison, awaking from sleep and seeing the prison doors open, supposing the prisoners had fled, drew his sword and was about to kill himself.

—Acts 16:27

The earthquake had awakened the on-site prison warden. "Starting up in alarm, he saw with dismay that all the prison doors were open, and the fear flashed upon him that the prisoners had escaped. He remembered with what explicit charge Paul and Silas had been entrusted to his care the night before, and he was certain that death would be the penalty of his apparent unfaithfulness. In the bitterness of his spirit he felt that it was better for him to die by his own hand than to submit to a disgraceful execution. Drawing his sword, he was about to kill himself, when Paul's voice was heard in the words of cheer, 'Do thyself no harm: for we are all here.' Every man was in his place, restrained by the power of God exerted through one fellow prisoner. . . .

"The jailer dropped his sword, and, calling for lights, hastened into the inner dungeon. He would see what manner of men these were who repaid with kindness the cruelty with which they had been treated. Reaching the place where the apostles were, and casting himself before them, he asked their forgiveness. Then, bringing them out into the open court, he inquired, 'Sirs, what must I do to be saved?' "[1]

"Compare his question with Saul's query on the Damascus road ([Acts] 9:6). Little did the heathen jailer know how effective his own inquiry would be in leading countless others also to find eternal life. . . .

". . . Circumstances did not permit a profound theological discussion. The fearful man needed succinct directions for salvation. His situation might be compared with that of the thief on the cross (. . . Luke 23:39–43). . . . They impressed on the suppliant the truth that salvation depends on personal belief in the redeeming life and work of Jesus."[2]

Paul and Silas were direct: " 'Believe on the Lord Jesus Christ, and thou shalt be saved, and thy house,' they answered; and 'they spake unto him the word of the Lord, and to all that were in his house.' The jailer then washed the wounds of the apostles and ministered to them, after which he was baptized by them, with all his household. A sanctifying influence diffused itself among the inmates of the prison, and the minds of all were opened to listen to the truths spoken by the apostles. They were convinced that the God whom these men served had miraculously released them from bondage."[3]

"Paul and Silas had the spirit of Christ, not the spirit of revenge."[4] What spirit do you have?

---

1. Ellen G. White, *The Acts of the Apostles* (Mountain View, CA: Pacific Press®, 1911), 215, 216.
2. Francis D. Nichol, ed., *The Seventh-day Adventist Bible Commentary*, vol. 6 (Washington, DC: Review and Herald®, 1957), 334.
3. White, *Acts of the Apostles*, 217.
4. White, *Acts of the Apostles*, 216.

Uncondemned Romans

*But Paul said to them, "They have beaten us openly, uncondemned Romans,
and have thrown us into prison. And now do they put us out secretly?
No indeed! Let them come themselves and get us out."*

—Acts 16:37

T he magistrates may have considered the punishment to have been sufficient, or
they may have felt that they had acted hastily in punishing the accused without a
regular trial or an inquiry into their backgrounds. Probably the earthquake had alarmed
the magistrates. The Holy Spirit also may have aroused within them an uneasy sense
of wrongdoing. In any event they wished to release the two prisoners as quickly and
as quietly as possible."[1] Paul was having none of it. When the jailer heard the apostles
were to be released, he expected they would eagerly leave the prison. Imagine his
surprise when Paul refused to leave, instead demanding a public apology. The disciples
had been tied to a *palus*, or public whipping post, and humiliated before the entire city.
" 'To bind a Roman citizen is a crime, to flog him is an abomination.' (*Against Verres*
v. 66. 170; Loeb ed., *Verrine Orations*, vol. 2, p. 655)."[2]

Paul and Silas had received no trial. They were afforded no chance to mount a
defense. Of even greater concern, they were Roman citizens! "Paul includes Silas as
being a Roman citizen. A false claim to Roman citizenship was a capital offense."[3]
Punishment had been handed down to prisoners who had not even been found guilty.
A rush to judgment had jeopardized the reputation of the city, and if Rome found out,
repercussions would be swift and sure. The "wrongful punishment of a Roman citizen
could have caused the magistrates' removal, degradation, and inability to hold other
positions of responsibility. . . . A plea of ignorance of the victims' citizenship would not
be sufficient defense for their illegal actions. They could only hope to persuade Paul
and Silas to accept a discreet settlement for the injustice done them."[4] Graciously the
apostles did so. "So they went out of the prison and entered the house of Lydia; and
when they had seen the brethren, they encouraged them and departed" (Acts 16:40).

And so the story of Philippi ends in the home of *Lydia*, where it began. Paul's
insistence upon an apology may have been "to ensure better treatment for Philippian
converts, many of whom probably were Roman citizens. Not Paul's personal honor,
but that of the gospel, was at stake."[5]

When a sincere apology is offered, the Christian accepts it with grace.

---

1. Francis D. Nichol, ed., *The Seventh-day Adventist Bible Commentary*, vol. 6 (Washington, DC: Review and Herald®, 1957), 335.
2. Nichol, *Seventh-day Adventist Bible Commentary*, vol. 6, 336.
3. Nichol, *Seventh-day Adventist Bible Commentary*, vol. 6, 336.
4. Nichol, *Seventh-day Adventist Bible Commentary*, vol. 6, 336.
5. Nichol, *Seventh-day Adventist Bible Commentary*, vol. 6, 336.

Thessalonica

Now when they had passed through Amphipolis and Apollonia,
they came to Thessalonica, where there was a synagogue of the Jews.

—Acts 17:1

T he sixteenth chapter of Acts, just finished, presented "a vivid picture of the beginning of Christian work in Europe. The conversions recorded were dramatic and of widely differing types. There was *Lydia*, a settler from Asia, apparently a woman of wealth and refinement. There was probably also the *slave girl*, who was delivered from demonic possession. . . . [Then] follows the conversion of a jailer, a heathen and doubtless a Roman citizen, of a stern and hardened type, who would be thought least likely to respond to the gospel. In this mixed group of converts was contained a promise of future gospel triumphs on the continent of Europe."[1] These were the nucleus of believers forming the church at Philippi. Remember them well, for we will later read Paul's epistle to the same Philippians.

Now, traveling to the southwest, Paul and Silas passed through Amphipolis (thirty-three miles southwest of Philippi), then Apollonia (thirty miles southwest of Amphipolis), arriving in Thessalonica. Thessalonica is known today as Salonika, an important Greek city. In Paul's time, this was already a busy city of commerce where many Jews lived. Thessalonica "was an important commercial city and military station on the *Via Egnatia* (Egnatian Way), which crossed the whole of Macedonia from west to east."[2] Situated at the crossroads of land and sea lanes, Thessalonica boasted an outstanding natural harbor. There was a temple established here to venerate Julius Caesar, and by the time of Paul, a cult had been established for the worship of the goddess Roma.

"The city experienced its greatest expansion under the Romans, into whose hands it fell after the battle of Pydna in 168 B.C. When the province of Macedonia was organized in 146 B.C., Thessalonica became the provincial capital as well as the capital of the 2d district of the 4 into which the province was divided. After the battle at Philippi (42 B.C.), Thessalonica was made a free city, administered by magistrates called *politarchai*, 'rulers of the city,' in Acts 17:8, an expression attested also by a Greek inscription on the arch in Thessalonike."[3]

The term "politarchs" used by Luke is confirmed by archeology. The Scriptures may be trusted!

---

1. Francis D. Nichol, ed., *The Seventh-day Adventist Bible Commentary*, vol. 6 (Washington, DC: Review and Herald®, 1957), 335; emphasis added.

2. Siegfried H. Horn, *Seventh-day Adventist Bible Dictionary*, ed. Don F. Neufeld, Commentary Reference Series, vol. 8 (Washington, DC: Review and Herald®, 1960), s.v. "Thessalonica."

3. Horn, *Seventh-day Adventist Bible Dictionary*, s.v. "Thessalonica."

How Paul Taught

*Then Paul, as his custom was, went in to them, and for three
Sabbaths reasoned with them from the Scriptures.*

—Acts 17:2

Paul and Silas were "given the privilege of addressing large congregations in the Jewish synagogue. Their appearance bore evidence of the shameful treatment they had recently received, and necessitated an explanation of what had taken place. This they made without exalting themselves, but magnified the One who had wrought their deliverance."[1] Paul appealed to the minds of his audience by reasoning from Old Testament prophecies concerning the Messiah. According to Ellen White, his texts included Genesis 3:15; 22:18; 49:10; Deuteronomy 18:15, 18; Psalms 16:9, 10; 22:6–8, 17, 18; 69:8, 20; Isaiah 11:1–3; 42:1–4; 50:6, 53:1–10, 12; 55:3–5; 61:1–3; Jeremiah 23:5, 6; 33:17, 18; Micah 5:1, 2; and Zechariah 13:6. Paul's method of outreach was repeated in every new town he visited. First, he would seek out large commercial cities set at crossroads of travel and commerce. Next, he would look for communities of Jews within these cities. Seeking Jews first, he would then preach the gospel of Jesus Christ. He would teach that Jesus was *the* Messiah, reasoning with them from Scripture to prove his point. God-fearers and proselytes would be first to accept his message. Initial successes would threaten the synagogue status quo. Resistance would build, and in time violence would force him to leave town, but not before he had established a core of Christian believers.

"For three successive Sabbaths Paul preached to the Thessalonians, reasoning with them from the Scriptures regarding the life, death, resurrection, office work, and future glory of Christ."[2] "That Paul was allowed to preach for three Sabbaths in succession shows the respect accorded him as a rabbi, and his earnest eloquence."[3] A minority of the Jews believed Paul's message. Most of his converts were Gentile. "These Gentiles were not hampered by the prejudices that clung so closely about those who were born Jews."[4] A sizeable number of the new believers were *women*. "These may have been economically and socially independent, like Lydia . . . , or the wives of the chief men of the town. It is not possible to decide whether they were Jewesses or Gentiles. Women enjoyed a large measure of freedom in Macedonia."[5]

Paul was a Seventh-day Adventist! He worshiped on Sabbath and preached the second coming of Christ.

1. Ellen G. White, *The Acts of the Apostles* (Mountain View, CA: Pacific Press®, 1911), 221.
2. White, *Acts of the Apostles*, 229.
3. Francis D. Nichol, ed., *The Seventh-day Adventist Bible Commentary*, vol. 6 (Washington, DC: Review and Herald®, 1957), 341.
4. Nichol, *Seventh-day Adventist Bible Commentary*, vol. 6, 342.
5. Nichol, *Seventh-day Adventist Bible Commentary*, vol. 6, 342.

Turning the World Upside Down

"These who have turned the world upside down have come here too."

—Acts 17:6

A s in the places formerly entered, the apostles met with determined opposition. 'The Jews which believed not' were 'moved with envy.' These Jews were not then in favor with the Roman power, because, not long before, they had raised an insurrection in Rome. They were looked upon with suspicion, and their liberty was in a measure restricted. They now saw an opportunity to take advantage of circumstances to re-establish themselves in favor and at the same time to throw reproach upon the apostles and the converts to Christianity."[1] Raising a mob from the rascals lounging about in idleness in the marketplace, the unbelieving Jews started a riot. They immediately marched on the house of Jason. "That Paul had taken up residence with him would indicate that he was a Jew. His hospitable act now brought upon him the fanatical wrath of his unbelieving fellow countrymen."[2] Finding neither Paul nor Silas at the home, the crowd took Jason and hustled him away to the rulers of the city, saying, "These who have turned the world upside down have come here too. Jason has harbored them, and these are all acting contrary to the decrees of Caesar, saying there is another king—Jesus" (Acts 17:6, 7).

"In the present case the charge was doubtless exaggerated in the heat of the moment, but its import was serious. The Romans took pride in their Pax Romana ("Roman Peace"), and were ready to deal severely with those who disturbed it."[3] Roman emperors were notoriously nervous about retaining their jobs. The claim the apostles were promoting a new king or emperor was significant. "A more serious accusation could hardly be laid against any group (see Mark 12:14; . . . Luke 23:2), and although it was not true, it had enough basis to appear plausible. Christians everywhere taught the superiority of Christ's kingship . . . , and their words could readily be interpreted into seditious sentiments by hostile critics."[4] Stuck between an unsubstantiated accusation and a mob pushing a politically sensitive charge, the *politarchs* of Thessalonica compromised. As no apostles were handy to punish for sedition and treason, Jason had to post a bond guaranteeing he personally would keep the peace and see the apostles left town. Considering the charges, the sentence was very lenient but quelled the uproar.

These Christians have "turned the world upside down!" "Similar accusations will be brought against God's people in the last days."[5]

1. Ellen G. White, *The Acts of the Apostles* (Mountain View, CA: Pacific Press®, 1911), 229.

2. Francis D. Nichol, ed., *The Seventh-day Adventist Bible Commentary*, vol. 6 (Washington, DC: Review and Herald®, 1957), 342.

3. Nichol, *Seventh-day Adventist Bible Commentary*, vol. 6, 343.

4. Nichol, *Seventh-day Adventist Bible Commentary*, vol. 6, 343.

5. Nichol, *Seventh-day Adventist Bible Commentary*, vol. 6, 343.

Berea

Then the brethren immediately sent Paul and Silas away by night to Berea.
When they arrived, they went into the synagogue of the Jews.

—Acts 17:10

F earing further violence, the believers at Thessalonica spirited Paul and Silas out
of the city to safety. Paul found himself indebted to the believers in Thessalonica
for his safety. "Paul never forgot their kindness, and often longed to see them again.
On at least two other occasions he attempted to pay return visits to the church in
Thessalonica, but had to be content to send Timothy in his stead (. . . 1 Thess. 2:18; 3:1,
2)."[1] Now the apostles moved on to Berea.

Berea was "a small Macedonian city about 50 mi. southwest of Thessalonica. The
city was of far less commercial importance than Thessalonica. . . .

". . . The Jewish population was large enough to support its own place of worship.
It was Paul's custom to begin his gospel work in the synagogue. . . , but in this case,
immediately after the trouble in Thessalonica, such action called for unusual courage."[2]
The Berean Jews had open minds and were ready to put what Paul presented to the
test. "The Bereans used sanctified intelligence in the studying of the Scriptures, and
found that the inspired words told of a Messiah who would suffer and rise again. Having
examined the evidence, and having found what was true, they proved their sincerity
by accepting the new teaching."[3] Diligently searching Scripture on a daily basis still
brings conviction and conversion.

"The minds of the Bereans were not narrowed by prejudice. They were willing to
investigate the truthfulness of the doctrines preached by the apostles. They studied the
Bible, not from curiosity, but in order that they might learn what had been written
concerning the promised Messiah. Daily they searched the inspired records, and as they
compared scripture with scripture, heavenly angels were beside them, enlightening
their minds and impressing their hearts. . . .

"All will be judged according to the light that has been given. The Lord sends
forth His ambassadors with a message of salvation, and those who hear He will hold
responsible for the way in which they treat the words of His servants. Those who are
sincerely seeking for truth will make a careful investigation, in the light of God's word,
of the doctrines presented to them."[4]

Blindly accepting revered authority without personally checking Scripture for truth is dangerous.

---

1. Francis D. Nichol, ed., *The Seventh-day Adventist Bible Commentary*, vol. 6 (Washington, DC: Review and Herald®, 1957), 344.
2. Nichol, *Seventh-day Adventist Bible Commentary*, vol. 6, 344.
3. Nichol, *Seventh-day Adventist Bible Commentary*, vol. 6, 344.
4. Ellen G. White, *The Acts of the Apostles* (Mountain View, CA: Pacific Press®, 1911), 231, 232.

Followed!

But when the Jews from Thessalonica learned that the word of God was
preached by Paul at Berea, they came there also and stirred up the crowds.

—Acts 17:13

The unbelieving Jews of Thessalonica, filled with jealousy and hatred of the apostles, and not content with having driven them from their own city, followed them to Berea and aroused against them the excitable passions of the lower class. Fearing that violence would be done to Paul if he remained there, the brethren sent him to Athens, accompanied by some of the Bereans who had newly accepted the faith."[1] "This hasty retreat from Berea deprived Paul of the opportunity he had anticipated of again visiting the brethren at Thessalonica.

"Although the opposers of the doctrine of Christ could not hinder its actual advancement, they still succeeded in making the work of the apostles exceedingly hard. God, in his providence, permitted Satan to hinder Paul from returning to the Thessalonians. Yet the faithful apostle steadily pressed on through opposition, conflict, and persecution, to carry out the purpose of God as revealed to him in the vision at Jerusalem: 'I will send thee far hence unto the Gentiles.' "[2]

Repeatedly we see mainstream Jews rejecting the message of Jesus Christ as their Messiah. So vehement was their rejection that they not only went to great lengths to stop the preaching within their own synagogues and cities but also followed great distances to harass the apostles. The preachers of hate from Antioch in Pisidia had traveled ninety miles to Iconium and then twenty-four additional miles to Lystra to stop Paul and Barnabas. That pursuit had ended in the stoning of Paul. Falsely beaten and imprisoned in Philippi, run out of Thessalonica by a mob of idle marketplace Gentile hoodlums whipped to a frenzy of violence by Jews, followed fifty miles to Berea and again threatened by another mob of Gentiles stirred up by the same Jews from Thessalonica, Paul might be excused if he felt harassed and despondent. Such was not the case. He still praised God for the opportunity to suffer for His Lord and Savior, Jesus Christ.

In case you missed it, women took the lead in establishing and maintaining the new Christian churches at Philippi (Acts 16:13–15), Thessalonica (Acts 17:4), and Berea (Acts 17:12)! Without these strong and vital women, the message of the gospel would have been more greatly hindered.

---

1. Ellen G. White, *The Acts of the Apostles* (Mountain View, CA: Pacific Press®, 1911), 232, 233.
2. Ellen G. White, *Sketches From the Life of Paul* (Washington, DC: Review and Herald®, 1974), 88, 89.

Athens

So those who conducted Paul brought him to Athens.

—Acts 17:15

Leaving Silas and Timothy to strengthen the work in Thessalonica and Berea, Paul left town under the care of the Bereans. "From Berea Paul went to Athens. He was accompanied on his journey by some of the Bereans who had been newly brought into the faith, and who were desirous of learning more from him of the way of life. When the apostle arrived at Athens, he sent these men back with a message to Silas and Timothy to join him immediately in that city. Timothy had come to Berea previously to Paul's departure, and with Silas had remained to carry on the work so well begun there, and to instruct the new converts in the principles of their holy faith."[1] "There is reason to think that Paul could not easily travel or work alone because of his infirmities (cf. . . . [Acts] 9:18). He wanted the presence of his faithful companions that he might promptly set about his work. In 1 Thess. 3:1, 2 is an implication that Timothy, at least, came to Athens. Apparently soon afterward Paul sent him back to care for the Thessalonian converts. From Athens, Paul went to Corinth (Acts 18:1), where Silas and Timothy later joined him."[2]

"The city of Athens was the metropolis of heathendom. Paul did not here meet with an ignorant, credulous populace, as at Lystra; but he encountered a people famous for their intelligence and education. Statues of their gods and the deified heroes of history and poetry met the eye in every direction; while magnificent architecture and paintings also represented the national glory and the popular worship of heathen deities."[3] "According to one ancient report there were more than 3,000 statutes in the Athens of Paul's day. One of its streets was adorned with a bust of the messenger-god Hermes before every house. Temples, porticoes, colonnades, and courtyards were replete with exquisitely carved works of art that lavishly proclaimed the Greek love of beauty. Paul, with his Hellenistic background, could hardly have been indifferent to the aesthetic appeal of such artistic wealth, but any pleasure he may have felt would be overwhelmed by the spiritual implications of what he saw. The greater part of the statuary was linked with pagan worship, and could justifiably be described as 'idols.' To a Jew, such a display would glaringly flout the first and second commandments."[4]

Faced with such blatant disregard for God's commandments, what would you say and do?

---

1. Ellen G. White, *Sketches From the Life of Paul* (Washington, DC: Review and Herald®, 1974), 89.
2. Francis D. Nichol, ed., *The Seventh-day Adventist Bible Commentary*, vol. 6 (Washington, DC: Review and Herald®, 1957), 345.
3. White, *Sketches From the Life of Paul*, 89.
4. Nichol, *Seventh-day Adventist Bible Commentary*, vol. 6, 346.

The Center of Paganism

Now while Paul waited for them [Silas and Timothy] at Athens,
his spirit was provoked within him when he saw that the city was given over to idols.
—Acts 17:16

A thens was not a large city during the time of Paul, but it was considered "the university city of the Roman Empire. The population probably numbered 250,000 at that time."[1] "Because of its fame as the mother of Western culture, which included art, literature, architecture, and philosophy, it remained an important city in Roman times, although it had neither the economic nor the political importance of Corinth, the capital of the province. It was especially famous as a seat of learning, and its university was considered the best in the world. All the main schools of philosophy— Platonic, Stoic, Epicurean, and Peripatetic—were developed in Athens."[2]

"Josephus describes Athenians as being 'the most pious of the Greeks' (*Against Apion* ii. 12 [130]; Loeb ed., p. 345)."[3] Paul was distressed that the city was full of idols. Every Greco-Roman city had its share of idols, so this was not something new for Paul, but Athens had more concentrated in one place than any other city. They were present on every street corner and in front of every home. Sculptors displayed their work throughout the city, and no expense was spared in making these idols extravagant. As Paul entered the city coming from the port of Piraeus by a broad, walled arcade, he was faced with a heavy assemblage of statues in the northwest corner of the marketplace, or *agora*.

"While waiting for Silas and Timothy to meet him, Paul was not idle. 'He disputed in the synagogue with the Jews, and with the devout persons, and in the market daily with them that met with him.' "[4] Paul again sought out the local synagogue to start preaching the gospel of Jesus Christ. Perhaps he thought his fellow Jews would assist him in his fight against idolatry. We are not told of his reception. "The religion of the Athenians, of which they made great boast, was of no value, for it was destitute of the knowledge of the true God. It consisted, in great part, of art worship, and a round of dissipating amusement and festivities."[5] Paul was aghast at the idolatry that surrounded him, yet his first thought was to share the gospel with the Athenians.

The true Christian expresses love and concern for those ignorant of the True God.

1. Francis D. Nichol, ed., *The Seventh-day Adventist Bible Commentary*, vol. 6 (Washington, DC: Review and Herald®, 1957), 346.
2. Siegfried H. Horn, *Seventh-day Adventist Bible Dictionary*, ed. Don F. Neufeld, Commentary Reference Series, vol. 8 (Washington, DC: Review and Herald®, 1960), s.v. "Athens."
3. Nichol, *Seventh-day Adventist Bible Commentary*, vol. 6, 346.
4. Ellen G. White, *Sketches From the Life of Paul* (Washington, DC: Review and Herald®, 1974), 91.
5. White, *Sketches From the Life of Paul*, 91.

Paul's Philosophy of Life

Then certain Epicurean and Stoic philosophers encountered him.
—Acts 17:18

I n Athens there were two agorae [marketplaces], one being the commercial market place, whereas the other . . . was the social center of the city. In the time of Paul it was adorned with a host of statues, images of national heroes as well as of most of the gods in the Greek pantheon. This agora was the arena where most political and philosophical discussions were conducted in Athens. Here Paul would hear professional and amateur philosophers disputing with one another and with their hearers. The apostle would be free to participate in the discussions and to expound his own philosophy of life."[1] What an opportunity! Paul must have thought, *I am literally the right man in the right place at the right time with the right message!* Having grown up in Tarsus, the most celebrated city of philosophy in all Cilicia, Paul was familiar with both Stoic and Epicurean thought. Being one of the most learned Pharisees of his time and having been taught by Gamaliel I, the most revered Jewish teacher of the age, Paul was an accomplished public orator and debater who could hold his own in any public forum.

"The great men of Athens were not long in learning of the presence in their city of a singular teacher who was setting before the people doctrines new and strange. Some of these men sought Paul out and entered into conversation with him. Soon a crowd of listeners gathered about them. Some were prepared to ridicule the apostle as one who was far beneath them both socially and intellectually, and these said jeeringly among themselves, 'What will this babbler say?' Others, 'because he preached unto them Jesus, and the resurrection,' said, 'He seemeth to be a setter forth of strange gods.' "[2] Epicurean philosophers believed "man's goal was the attainment of happiness, and the first step toward it was emancipation from the idea of future punishment [no resurrection and no judgment]. The next step was to recognize that happiness consisted in pleasurable emotions."[3] Stoics "taught that true wisdom consists in being the master, and not the slave, of circumstances. . . . The seeker after wisdom was taught to be indifferent alike to pleasure or pain, and to maintain an intellectual neutrality."[4]

Self-indulgence versus self-restraint—which philosophy best describes our century?

---

1. Francis D. Nichol, ed., *The Seventh-day Adventist Bible Commentary*, vol. 6 (Washington, DC: Review and Herald®, 1957), 346, 347.
2. Ellen G. White, *The Acts of the Apostles* (Mountain View, CA: Pacific Press®, 1911), 235.
3. Nichol, *Seventh-day Adventist Bible Commentary*, vol. 6, 347.
4. Nichol, *Seventh-day Adventist Bible Commentary*, vol. 6, 348.

The Areopagus

And they took him and brought him to the Areopagus, saying,
"May we know what this new doctrine is of which you speak?"

—Acts 17:19

A mong those who encountered Paul in the market place were 'certain philosophers of the Epicureans, and of the Stoics;' but they, and all others who came in contact with him, soon saw that he had a store of knowledge even greater than their own. His intellectual power commanded the respect of the learned; while his earnest, logical reasoning and the power of his oratory held the attention of all in the audience. His hearers recognized the fact that he was no novice, but was able to meet all classes with convincing arguments in support of the doctrines he taught. Thus the apostle stood undaunted, meeting his opposers on their own ground, matching logic with logic, philosophy with philosophy, eloquence with eloquence."[1]

Paul was taken by the hand and led to the Areopagus, or "Hill of Ares,'" *Ares* being the Greek equivalent to the Latin *Mars*, the god of war; hence, *Areios Pagos* is translated 'Mars' hill.' "[2] "It was in this place that matters connected with religion were often carefully considered by men who acted as final judges on all the important moral as well as civil questions."[3] Here, before the most revered tribunal of Athens, the Athenian Council (similar to the Sanhedrin in Jerusalem), Paul was asked to state his doctrine. "Around him gathered poets, artists, and philosophers—the scholars and sages of Athens, who thus addressed him: 'May we know what this new doctrine, whereof thou speakest, is? For thou bringest certain strange things to our ears: we would know therefore what these things mean.'

"In that hour of solemn responsibility, the apostle was calm and self-possessed. His heart was burdened with an important message, and the words that fell from his lips convinced his hearers that he was no idle babbler."[4]

Paul told them about Jesus, our Creator and Redeemer. He explained that God lives in palaces not made by human hands. Artisans cannot craft the true God. God forbids the making and worshiping of idols (Exodus 20). Man is made in God's likeness, not the other way around. Unfortunately, Paul's audience was proud of their attainments; they saw no need for his God!

Selfish, indulgent behavior and rejection of intelligent design by the Creator are still accepted philosophies today.

---

1. Ellen G. White, *The Acts of the Apostles* (Mountain View, CA: Pacific Press®, 1911), 235, 236.
2. Francis D. Nichol, ed., *The Seventh-day Adventist Bible Commentary*, vol. 6 (Washington, DC: Review and Herald®, 1957), 349.
3. White, *Acts of the Apostles*, 236.
4. White, *Acts of the Apostles*, 236, 237.

The Unknown God

*"Men of Athens, I perceive that in all things you are very religious,
for as I was passing through and considering the objects of your worship,
I even found an altar with this inscription: TO THE UNKNOWN GOD."*
—Acts 17:22, 23

Paul was now brought face to face with [Epicurean philosophy]. In vs. 22–31 we learn how he dealt with it. He asserted the personality of the living God, as Creator, Ruler, Father; the binding force of a divine law written in the heart; the nobility of a life raised above a frantic search for pleasure, and spent, not for itself, but for others and for God. Finally, he pointed to man's moral accountability in the light of the resurrection and the judgment. Such teaching set the apostle apart from the pagan professors of higher philosophy."[1]

Paul started by saying that in passing through the city, he found an altar dedicated to the "Unknown God." (The Athenians had put up this altar to cover all bases just in case an unknown deity might have been missed and angered.) Paul now wished to acquaint them with that God, the One he served. Paul's God is the God of the universe, the Creator, One dwelling in temples not fashioned by hands (Isaiah 66:1, 2). No metal or stone idol could represent Jehovah. These images had no life. They depended upon men to be moved; thus, man was greater than they. "Men should think of God as the supreme giver, not requiring anything at their hands but justice, mercy, and humility (Micah 6:8)."[2] Now God was calling all men to repentance and in His mercy had provided a way for humanity to be forgiven. Paul argued that God was not far from any man. The Stoics could agree with that assessment but not the Epicureans.

When Paul mentioned the need for man to repent, he lost both Stoics and Epicureans—Stoics (Pharisees in Greek togas) because they felt they had attained ethical perfection and needed to repent of nothing, Epicureans because they saw nothing in their lifestyle to loathe. Neither group could accept a future judgment! And at the mention of the resurrection of Jesus, both groups scorned Paul for, like Sadducees, any belief in a resurrection was incredible to them.

"The world then, as now, was prepared to believe in the immortality of the soul, but was unwilling to accept the doctrine of the resurrection of the body."[3]

---

1. Francis D. Nichol, ed., *The Seventh-day Adventist Bible Commentary*, vol. 6 (Washington, DC: Review and Herald®, 1957), 347.
2. Nichol, *Seventh-day Adventist Bible Commentary*, vol. 6, 352.
3. Nichol, *Seventh-day Adventist Bible Commentary*, vol. 6, 356.

Dionysius and *Damaris*

However, some men joined him and believed, among them
Dionysius the Areopagite, a woman named Damaris, *and others with them.*

—Acts 17:34; emphasis added

The invitation extended to Paul to present his views on his "unknown God" was not without an element of danger. Socrates had been condemned to death because he had proposed strange new gods, and those escorting Paul to Mars Hill warned him that he might face a similar fate. Mars Hill was "the most sacred spot in all Athens, and its recollections and associations were such as to cause it to be regarded with superstitious awe and reverence, that with some amounted to dread. Here, the most solemn court of justice had long been held to determine upon criminal cases, and to decide difficult religious questions. The judges sat in the open air, upon seats hewn out in the rock, on a platform which was ascended by a flight of stone steps from the valley below. At a little distance was a temple of the gods; and the sanctuaries, statues, and altars of the city were in full view."[1]

As we have already seen, as soon as Paul spoke of a resurrection, his discourse was cut short. "Many who listened to the words of Paul were convinced of the truths presented, but they would not humble themselves to acknowledge God, and to accept the plan of salvation. . . .

"In their pride of intellect and human wisdom may be found the reason why the gospel message met with so little success among that people. . . . All worldly wise men who come to Christ as poor, lost sinners, will become wise unto salvation; but those who come as distinguished men, extolling their own wisdom, will fail to receive the light and knowledge which he alone can give."[2]

Dionysius, a prominent citizen of Athens, believed Paul's message. An Areopagite was required by the constitution of the council "to have filled a high magisterial function, such as that of archon, and to be above 60 years of age. Probably, therefore, this convert was a man of some note."[3] Little is known of the woman, Damaris, other than her bold stand for the truth. The results of Paul's work in Athens were somewhat disappointing. The record speaks of "some" joining him in contrast to "the 'great multitude' at Thessalonica ([Acts 17:]4) and the 'many' at Berea (v. 12). . . . No less striking is the lack of any mention of Athens in Paul's epistles."[4]

Proud, self-sufficient people find it difficult to believe they need a Savior.

---

1. Ellen G. White, *Sketches From the Life of Paul* (Washington, DC: Review and Herald®, 1974), 92, 93.
2. White, *Sketches From the Life of Paul*, 96.
3. Francis D. Nichol, ed., *The Seventh-day Adventist Bible Commentary*, vol. 6 (Washington, DC: Review and Herald®, 1957), 356.
4. Nichol, *Seventh-day Adventist Bible Commentary*, vol. 6, 356, 357.

Corinth

After these things Paul departed from Athens and went to Corinth.

—Acts 18:1

Paul did not wait at Athens for his brethren, Silas and Timothy, but leaving word for them to follow him, went at once to Corinth. Here he entered upon a different field of labor from that which he had left. Instead of the curious and critical disciples of schools of philosophy, he came in contact with the busy, changing population of a great center of commerce. Greeks, Jews, and Romans, with travelers from every land, mingled in its crowded streets, eagerly intent on business and pleasure, and having little thought of care beyond the affairs of the present life."[1] Corinth, synonymous with trade, was known for luxury, entertainment, and vice.

Located approximately forty miles southwest of Athens on a narrow isthmus of land separating southern Greece (the Peloponnesus) from the mainland; Corinth boasted two harbors. The eastern harbor of Cenchreae (on the Saronic Gulf of the Aegean) was but a short three-and-one-half mile portage from the western harbor of Lechaeum (on the Corinthian Gulf of the Adriatic). The voyage around Cape Malea at the southern tip of the Peloponnesus was hazardous. Corinth served as a safe shortcut between the two seas. "Since the canal (constructed from 1881 to 1893) through the 5-mile-wide isthmus did not exist in ancient times, small ships were often hauled overland on a track (called the *diolkos*); from the Saronic Gulf to the Corinthian Gulf and vice versa."[2]

Situated on a plateau two hundred feet above sea level, Corinth held strategic importance. When Paul visited the city, it had been rebuilt after being destroyed by the Roman general Mummius in 146 BC. "The earliest settlers of Corinth were non-Greeks. Later the Phoenicians settled colonists there who were engaged in the manufacture of purple dye from shellfish. They also introduced the manufacture of textiles, pottery, and armor."[3] While Corinth was the accepted political and commercial leader among all Greek cities, it also "was universally known for its immorality. The term 'Corinthian girl' was synonymous with 'prostitute,' and 'to Corinthianize' meant to lead an immoral life. In later Greek comedies 'Corinthian' is occasionally the designation for a drunkard."[4] Corinth was going to be a tough town from which to win converts to Christ.

Who will take the message of Jesus to those living in the corrupt crossroad cities of our world?

---

1. Ellen G. White, *Sketches From the Life of Paul* (Washington, DC: Review and Herald®, 1974), 98.
2. Siegfried H. Horn, *Seventh-day Adventist Bible Dictionary*, ed. Don F. Neufeld, Commentary Reference Series, vol. 8 (Washington, DC: Review and Herald®, 1960), s.v. "Corinth."
3. Horn, *Seventh-day Adventist Bible Dictionary*, s.v. "Corinth."
4. Horn, *Seventh-day Adventist Bible Dictionary*, s.v. "Corinth."

Aquila and *Priscilla*

*And he found a certain Jew named Aquila, born in Pontus, who had recently
come from Italy with his wife Priscilla (because Claudius had commanded
all the Jews to depart from Rome); and he came to them.*
                                        —Acts 18:2; emphasis added

After the ascension of Christ, the apostles went everywhere preaching the Word.
They bore witness to Christ's work as a teacher and healer. Their testimony in
Jerusalem, in Rome, and in other places was positive and powerful. The Jews, who
refused to receive the truth, could but acknowledge that a powerful influence attended
Christ's followers, because the Holy Spirit accompanied them. This created greater
opposition; but notwithstanding the opposition, twenty years after the crucifixion of
Christ there was a live, earnest church in Rome. This church was strong and zealous,
and the Lord worked for it.

"The envy and rage of the Jews against the Christians knew no bounds, and the
unbelieving residents were constantly stirred up. They made complaints that the
Christian Jews were disorderly, and dangerous to the public good. Constantly they were
setting in motion something that would stir up strife. This caused the Christians to be
banished from Rome. Among those banished, were Aquila and Priscilla, who went to
Corinth, and there established a business as manufacturers of tents."[1]

Aquila, the Latin for "eagle," or *Akulas* in the Greek, was born in Asia Minor
(Pontus). "The provinces of Asia Minor abounded with Jewish families of the Dispersion, as is seen throughout the book of Acts. . . . Some Jews from Pontus had been
in Jerusalem at Pentecost (Acts 2:9)."[2] Priscilla, in the form *Prisca*, of which it is the
diminutive, "probably reflects a connection with the *gens*, or clan, of the *Prisci*, which,
from earliest Roman times, provided the city-state with a long series of praetors and
consuls. The marriage of Aquila and Priscilla might be an example, therefore, of the
influence of educated Jews among the higher class of women at Rome. The placing
of Priscilla's name first (Acts 18:18; Rom. 16:3; 2 Tim. 4:19) would be explained if she
were a highborn Roman."[3]

*Paul knew sympathetic attitudes when he saw them, and he "unhesitatingly joined himself to
them . . . even before he had begun preaching in the synagogue."[4] Christians should be hospitable.*

---

1. Ellen G. White, "The Apostle Paul and Manual Labor," *Advent Review and Sabbath Herald*, March 6, 1900, 1.
2. Francis D. Nichol, ed., *The Seventh-day Adventist Bible Commentary*, vol. 6 (Washington, DC: Review and Herald®,
1957), 358.
3. Nichol, *Seventh-day Adventist Bible Commentary*, vol. 6, 358, 359.
4. Nichol, *Seventh-day Adventist Bible Commentary*, vol. 6, 359.

Tentmakers

So, because he was of the same trade, he stayed with them
and worked; for by occupation they were tentmakers.

—Acts 18:3

When Paul came to Corinth, he solicited work from Aquila. "The apostles counseled and prayed together, and decided that they would preach the gospel as it should be preached, in disinterested love for the souls who were perishing for lack of knowledge. Paul would work at tent-making, and teach his fellow laborers to work with their hands, so that in any emergency they could support themselves. Some of his ministering brethren presented such a course as inconsistent, saying that by so doing they would lose their influence as ministers of the gospel. The tenth chapter of Second Corinthians records the difficulties Paul had to contend with, and his vindication of his course. God had placed special honor upon Paul. He had given him his credentials, and had laid upon him weighty responsibility. And the apostle writes, 'I Paul myself beseech you by the meekness and gentleness of Christ, who' in presence am base among you—because he humbled himself to do mechanical work—'but being absent am bold toward you.' "[1]

"As Paul worked quickly and skillfully with his hands, he related to his fellow workers the specifications Christ had given Moses in regard to the building of the tabernacle. He showed them that the skill and wisdom and genius brought into that work were given by God to be used to his glory. He taught them that supreme honor is to be given to God."[2]

"Although feeble in health, he [Paul] labored during the day in serving the cause of Christ, and then toiled a large part of the night, and frequently all night, that he might provide for his own and others' necessities."[3] "Paul, the great apostle to the Gentiles, learned the trade of tent-making. There were higher and lower branches of tent-making. Paul learned the higher branches, and he could also work at the common branches when circumstances required. Tent-making did not bring returns so quickly as some other occupations, and at times it was only by the strictest economy that Paul could supply his necessities."[4] "Any labor that will benefit humanity or advance the cause of God, should be regarded as honorable."[5]

"He who does not teach his son a trade teaches him to be a thief."[6]—*Rabbinical proverb.*

---

1. Ellen G. White, "The Apostle Paul and Manual Labor," *Advent Review and Sabbath Herald*, March 6, 1900, 1; emphasis added.
2. White, "Paul and Manual Labor," 1.
3. Ellen G. White, "The Blessing of Labor," *Youth's Instructor*, February 27, 1902, 66.
4. White, "Paul and Manual Labor," 145.
5. Ellen G. White, *Sketches From the Life of Paul* (Washington, DC: Review and Herald®, 1974), 102.
6. Francis D. Nichol, ed., *The Seventh-day Adventist Bible Commentary*, vol. 6 (Washington, DC: Review and Herald®, 1957), 360.

Side-by-Side Sabbath Services

And many of the Corinthians, hearing, believed and were baptized.

—Acts 18:8

Paul started his Corinthian ministry among his Jewish brethren. And, as in previous cities, opposition to his message quickly arose. Every Sabbath would find Paul preaching in the synagogue, "reasoning from Moses and the prophets, showing what sins the Lord had most severely punished in olden times, and that murmuring and rebellion was the grievous crime that had brought God's displeasure upon the people of his choice."[1] Paul reviewed familiar types and shadows of the ceremonial law, revealing how Christ was the Antitype of all that preceded Him. "The apostle showed that according to the prophecies and the universal expectation of the Jews, the Messiah would be of the lineage of Abraham and David. He then traced his descent from the great patriarch Abraham, through the royal psalmist. He proved from Scripture what were to have been the character and works of the promised Messiah, and also his reception and treatment on earth, as testified by the holy prophets. He then showed that these predictions also had been fulfilled in the life, ministry, and death of Jesus, and hence that he was indeed the world's Redeemer."[2]

"The apostle then endeavored to bring home to their consciences the fact that repentance for their rejection of Christ could alone save the nation from impending ruin. He rebuked their ignorance concerning the meaning of those Scriptures which it was their chief boast and glory that they fully understood. He exposed their worldliness, their love of station, titles, and display, and their inordinate selfishness.

"But the Jews of Corinth closed their eyes to all the evidence so clearly presented by the apostle, and refused to listen to his appeals. The same spirit which had led them to reject Christ, filled them with wrath and fury against Paul. They would have put an end to his life, had not God guarded his servant, that he might do his work, and bear the gospel message to the Gentiles."[3] Yet some Jews believed. To make it easy for them to continue to come to hear his message, Paul moved next door to the synagogue, to the home of Justus. His continued proximity during Saturday services led to additional animosity among the Jews as synagogue attendance dropped and Paul's congregation grew.

Even Crispus (1 Corinthians 1:14), the chief ruler of the synagogue, believed Paul's message.

---

1. Ellen G. White, *Sketches From the Life of Paul* (Washington, DC: Review and Herald®, 1974), 103.
2. White, *Sketches From the Life of Paul*, 103, 104.
3. White, *Sketches From the Life of Paul*, 104.

Speak, Do *Not* Keep Silent

*Now the Lord spoke to Paul in the night by vision, "Do not be afraid,
but speak, and do not keep silent; for I am with you, and no one will
attack you to hurt you; for I have many people in this city."*

—Acts 18:9, 10

S ilas now arrived from Macedonia, and Timothy came from Thessalonica. Together the three-man evangelical team labored among the Corinthians. "Though Paul had a measure of success in Corinth, yet the wickedness that he saw and heard in that corrupt city almost disheartened him. The depravity that he witnessed among the Gentiles, and the contempt and insult that he received from the Jews, caused him great anguish of spirit. He doubted the wisdom of trying to build up a church from the material he found there."[1] Paul was certainly depressed, discouraged, and frightened (1 Corinthians 2:3). He "saw on every hand serious obstacles to the progress of his work. The city was almost wholly given up to idolatry. Venus was the favorite goddess, and with the worship of Venus were connected many demoralizing rites and ceremonies. The Corinthians had become conspicuous, even among the heathen, for their gross immorality. They seemed to have little thought or care beyond the pleasures and gaieties of the hour."[2]

"As he was planning to leave the city for a more promising field, and seeking earnestly to understand his duty, the Lord appeared to him in a vision and said, 'Be not afraid, but speak, and hold not thy peace: for I am with thee, and no man shall set on thee to hurt thee: for I have much people in this city.' Paul understood this to be a command to remain in Corinth and a guarantee that the Lord would give increase to the seed sown. Strengthened and encouraged, he continued to labor there with zeal and perseverance.

"The apostle's efforts were not confined to public speaking; there were many who could not have been reached in that way. He spent much time in house-to-house labor, thus availing himself of the familiar intercourse of the home circle."[3] At critical junctures during his lifetime, Paul had been given visions. His original commission (Acts 9:10–18) and the call to Macedonia (Acts 16:6–10) had given direction. Now he was being told to stay put and continue to magnify the name of Jesus. Humans often see failure and defeat where God sees opportunity and success!

Paul's vision, in some respects, mirrored Elijah's (1 Kings 19:18). Both men were discouraged.

---

1. Ellen G. White, *The Acts of the Apostles* (Mountain View, CA: Pacific Press®, 1911), 250.
2. White, *Acts of the Apostles*, 243, 244.
3. White, *Acts of the Apostles*, 250.

Gallio

When Gallio was proconsul of Achaia, the Jews with one
accord rose up against Paul and brought him to the judgment seat.

—Acts 18:12

T he hatred with which the Jews had always regarded the apostles was now inten-
sified. The conversion and baptism of Crispus had the effect of exasperating
instead of convincing these stubborn opposers. They could not bring arguments to
disprove Paul's preaching, and for lack of such evidence they resorted to deception and
malignant attack."[1] "Paul was an eloquent speaker. Before his conversion he had often
sought to impress his hearers by flights of oratory. But now he set all this aside. Instead
of indulging in poetic descriptions and fanciful representations, which might please
the senses and feed the imagination, but which would not touch the daily experience,
Paul sought by the use of simple language to bring home to the heart the truths that
are of vital importance."[2]

Suddenly one day, the Jews seized Paul and hustled him to the *bema*, or judgment seat,
of the proconsul Gallio. Gallio "was the brother of the Stoic philosopher Seneca, the
tutor of Nero. Seneca dedicated to his brother, the proconsul, two treatises, on 'Anger'
and the 'Blessed Life.' "[3] "It was customary for the Roman governors of provinces to
hold court in the agora, or forum, that is, the market place, on certain fixed days . . . ,
so that anyone might appeal to them to have his grievances satisfied."[4] The mob hoped
to get the Roman administrator to eject Paul from the city, for "this fellow persuades
men to worship God contrary to the law" (Acts 18:13). "Their line of thought would
be that though, as a matter of policy, Jews had been banished from Rome, Judaism was
still a *religio licita*, tolerated and recognized by the Roman state. Their charge would
therefore not have been about some point of the Jewish religion, but that Paul was
preaching a new religion, not recognized."[5]

Gallio, aware of the troubles over "Chrestus" in Rome, immediately recognized a
Jewish religious dispute when he saw one. "He did not intend to draw a definite line
between religions recognized by Rome, and those that were not."[6] Before Paul could
even open his mouth to undertake a formal defense, Gallio dismissed the crowd saying,
"I do not want to be a judge of such matters" (verse 15).

Sadly, intolerance and self-righteousness are attributes often found in "protectors of religion."

---

1. Ellen G. White, *The Acts of the Apostles* (Mountain View, CA: Pacific Press®, 1911), 249.
2. White, *Acts of the Apostles*, 251, 252.
3. Francis D. Nichol, ed., *The Seventh-day Adventist Bible Commentary*, vol. 6 (Washington, DC: Review and Herald®, 1957), 363.
4. Nichol, *Seventh-day Adventist Bible Commentary*, vol. 6, 363.
5. Nichol, *Seventh-day Adventist Bible Commentary*, vol. 6, 363.
6. Nichol, *Seventh-day Adventist Bible Commentary*, vol. 6, 363.

Sosthenes

Then all the Greeks took Sosthenes, the ruler of the synagogue,
and beat him before the judgment seat. But Gallio took no notice of these things.
—Acts 18:17

The Jewish religion was under the protection of the Roman power, and the accusers of Paul thought that if they could fasten upon him the charge of violating the laws of their religion, he would probably be delivered to them for trial and sentence. They hoped thus to compass his death."[1] If the Jews could get the proconsul to set a precedent, it would be easier to gain future convictions using the same logic. Gallio did not intend to set a precedent or put up with the Jewish rabble clogging his court. Complaints against Christians had nothing to do with Roman law and were an internal matter of Jewish religion. "Seated as he doubtless was in the agora, or forum, with his lictors and other officials about him, he now commanded the place to be cleared of the troublesome disputants."[2]

"Both Jews and Greeks had waited eagerly for Gallio's decision; and his immediate dismissal of the case, as one that had no bearing upon the public interest, was the signal for the Jews to retire, baffled and angry. The proconsul's decided course opened the eyes of the clamorous crowd who had been abetting the Jews. For the first time during Paul's labors in Europe, the mob turned to his side; under the very eye of the proconsul, and without interference from him, they violently beset the most prominent accusers of the apostle."[3]

"Sosthenes was apparently made the ruler of the synagogue after Crispus' conversion ([Acts 18:]8). He may have been eager to show his zeal against the Christians by laying charges immediately against Paul before the proconsul. As spokesman, he would catch the eye of the surrounding crowd, many of whom would be Greeks. They evidently caught Gallio's tone of contempt, and followed his adverse decision by a lesson of their own, and a rough one. Or it may be that the Jews turned on their new leader after his failure in the case. . . . Paul doubtless had not a few sympathizers among the Gentiles. In any case, the crowd singled out Sosthenes for their particular attention."[4] Gallio was so annoyed "he refused to become the dupe of the jealous, intriguing Jews."[5]

Writing 1 Corinthians 1, Paul lists a brother named "Sosthenes" as his secretary. Could this have been the same man? We are not told.

---

1. Ellen G. White, *The Acts of the Apostles* (Mountain View, CA: Pacific Press®, 1911), 253.
2. Francis D. Nichol, ed., *The Seventh-day Adventist Bible Commentary*, vol. 6 (Washington, DC: Review and Herald®, 1957), 364.
3. White, *Acts of the Apostles*, 253.
4. Nichol, *Seventh-day Adventist Bible Commentary*, vol. 6, 364.
5. White, *Acts of the Apostles*, 253.

Part 1: Reading Paul's Mail

Paul, Silvanus, and Timothy, to the church of the Thessalonians
in God the Father and the Lord Jesus Christ.

—1 Thessalonians 1:1

The arrival of Silas and Timothy from Macedonia, during Paul's sojourn in Corinth, had greatly cheered the apostle. They brought him 'good tidings' of the 'faith and charity' of those who had accepted the truth during the first visit of the gospel messengers to Thessalonica.[1] Paul's heart went out in tender sympathy toward these believers, who, in the midst of trial and adversity, had remained true to God. He longed to visit them in person, but as this was not then possible, he wrote to them."[2] We are not told why Paul could not return to Thessalonica. Perhaps the bond posted by Jason required Paul to remain away from the city for a certain length of time. Perhaps the mob that had rioted and sought the apostles was still active in persecuting the Gentile believers, and a return by Paul would put them in greater danger. Paul decided instead to write his friends a letter. "This epistle is generally considered to be the first of Paul's letters that has been preserved . . . , and, with the possible exception of the epistle of James, it was probably the first book of the New Testament to be written."[3]

That Paul loves the members in Thessalonica is evident from the language he uses in his letter. The term *brethren*, "used 19 times in its singular or plural form in this epistle, indicates Paul's intimate affection for the Christians in Thessalonica."[4] "The apostle is most thankful for Timothy's report of the faithfulness of the Thessalonians and of their tender regard for him. He hastens to commend them for their noble qualities of faith, love, and hope. . . .

"Certain problems, too, must have been reported by Timothy. Some at Thessalonica were grieving over loved ones who had died since receiving the gospel message, fearing that these loved ones could have no part in the glorious resurrection at the Lord's return. Some were fanatical in regard to the Second Advent, holding that they should not work, but await the Lord's coming in idle expectancy. Some were slipping back into the world, and were in danger of being lost in immorality. Others were inclined to independence, not willing to recognize the duly appointed leaders of the church."[5] Recognizing their individual needs, Paul stressed universal hope in Jesus, the hope of salvation in Him, the hope of His speedy return.

Hope is the anchor of every Christian soul (Hebrews 6:19).

---

1. For Paul's initial visit to Thessalonica, see the readings for April 27–29.
2. Ellen G. White, *The Acts of the Apostles* (Mountain View, CA: Pacific Press®, 1911), 255.
3. Francis D. Nichol, ed., *The Seventh-day Adventist Bible Commentary*, vol. 7 (Washington, DC: Review and Herald®, 1957), 225.
4. Nichol, *Seventh-day Adventist Bible Commentary*, vol. 7, 228.
5. Nichol, *Seventh-day Adventist Bible Commentary*, vol. 7, 225.

Part 2: Memories

You are our glory and joy.

—1 Thessalonians 2:20

The converts at Thessalonica knew better than any others what [the evangelizing visit of Paul and his company had] accomplished in their own lives."[1] The stripes on Paul and Silas's backs, inflicted by the Roman lash in Philippi, were still fresh. Such treatment had been a grave injustice and was extremely painful. Lesser men would have been reluctant to repeat the action that had brought public scourging. Paul was no coward! He not only had boldly proclaimed the gospel to the Thessalonians (1 Thessalonians 2:2) but also had practiced it.

"The holy life of a true Christian, his pious, reverent attitude toward his Maker, has a profound influence upon his attitude toward his fellow men, the children of God."[2] Paul did not preach smooth things or use flattering words to make the Thessalonians believe they had no need of a Savior. False prophets often used flattery to gain converts. Paul never did that. He and Silas "did not use their office for enriching themselves. On the contrary, they were most careful to give no occasion for such a charge … (Acts 20:33; cf. 2 Cor. 12:14)."[3] Paul toiled "night and day" so as not to burden anyone. "As a laborer in the gospel, Paul might have claimed support, instead of sustaining himself; but this right he was willing to forego. Although feeble in health, he labored during the day in serving the cause of Christ, and then toiled a large share of the night, and frequently all night, that he might make provision for his own and others' necessities. The apostle would also give an example to the Christian ministry, dignifying and honoring industry. While thus preaching and working, he presented the highest type of Christianity."[4] Paul felt he must be left free to preach the gospel with no strings attached (1 Corinthians 9:15–18).

Paul was worried about the infant church at Thessalonica. His desire was to return personally to strengthen their faith (1 Thessalonians 2:17), but Satan had hindered him (verse 18). Paul left Thessalonica rapidly because of the mob threat and whatever terms the politarchs had laid down with respect to the bond paid by Jason. These terms may very well have placed upon Paul a restriction mandating that he could not return to Thessalonica under pain of imprisonment. So Paul sent Timothy to be his eyes and ears.

Is it easier to preach a sermon confessing Christ or live a life that reveals Him to others?

---

1. Francis D. Nichol, ed., *The Seventh-day Adventist Bible Commentary*, vol. 7 (Washington, DC: Review and Herald®, 1957), 232.
2. Nichol, *Seventh-day Adventist Bible Commentary*, vol. 7, 234.
3. Nichol, *Seventh-day Adventist Bible Commentary*, vol. 7, 233.
4. Ellen G. White, *Sketches From the Life of Paul* (Washington, DC: Review and Herald®, 1974), 101.

Part 3: Timothy's Visit

Therefore, when we could no longer endure it, we thought it
good to be left in Athens alone, and sent Timothy.

—1 Thessalonians 3:1, 2

Paul was to be left alone in Athens. This decision must have been a most difficult one for him to make. The great sacrifice that the apostle was willing to make in depriving himself of Timothy's companionship and help, indicates the urgency of the needs of the Thessalonians. After his visit there, Timothy, accompanied by Silas, came to Paul at Corinth ([Acts] 18:5)."[1] Timothy reported persecution had not stopped in Thessalonica. "Paul's heart went out in tender sympathy toward these believers, who, in the midst of trial and adversity, had remained true to God. He longed to visit them in person, but as this was not then possible, he wrote to them."[2] Paul knew the Christian path was not perpetually smooth and easy. "The trials that our loving Father permits are the necessary means of salvation, and are directed and tempered toward that end (1 Cor. 10:13). Characters are perfected by trials, and Christians must not rebel at the refining process (. . . Mal. 3:3; Acts 14:22; 2 Tim. 3:12; 1 Peter 2:21; 4:12, 13)."[3] Timothy proudly reported that while the Thessalonians were experiencing persecution, their "faith had not been shaken, and their love had not waxed cold."[4] This must have been good news for Paul!

"Paul had feared that Jewish misrepresentations would have turned the Thessalonians against him when he was absent from them. The news that they still thought lovingly of him and were continually longing to see him, must have been very reassuring to the apostle. . . .

". . . Paul, who was so careful to encourage others, is himself comforted by those whom he is seeking to help. Even so may God's modern ministers be heartened by those for whom they labor. The best encouragement a convert can give to the one who has brought him to the Saviour, is to be steadfast in the Christian way."[5] Paul prayed "that Christ [would give his converts] an ever-deepening love, first, for their fellow believers, then for those without the church. He wanted the ardent love that he felt for them to be reproduced in their own hearts on others' behalf."[6]

"Fervent love for one another is a sign to the world of the genuineness of the Christian religion."[7]

---

1. Francis D. Nichol, ed., *The Seventh-day Adventist Bible Commentary*, vol. 7 (Washington, DC: Review and Herald®, 1957), 238.
2. Ellen G. White, *The Acts of the Apostles* (Mountain View, CA: Pacific Press®, 1911), 255.
3. Nichol, *Seventh-day Adventist Bible Commentary*, vol. 7, 239.
4. Nichol, *Seventh-day Adventist Bible Commentary*, vol. 7, 240.
5. Nichol, *Seventh-day Adventist Bible Commentary*, vol. 7, 240.
6. Nichol, *Seventh-day Adventist Bible Commentary*, vol. 7, 241.
7. Nichol, *Seventh-day Adventist Bible Commentary*, vol. 7, 241.

Part 4: Sexual Purity

For God did not call us to uncleanness, but in holiness.
—1 Thessalonians 4:7

Timothy reported that the Thessalonian church was in need of practical instruction on how to live a godly life. One is justified, or immediately made right before God, "when the repentant sinner accepts God's forgiveness."[1] Sanctification, however, is a continuous work of grace. It is "not the work of a moment, an hour, a day, but of a lifetime."[2] Idolatry, sexual impurity, and wickedness in all its forms accosted the new believers. The Thessalonians needed to be especially on guard against the lurid temptations of their wicked city.

The sin of fornication "needed emphatic denunciation among Gentile converts, for they had been reared in an atmosphere where moral laxity was accepted and vice consecrated as a religious rite. . . . The patron deity of Corinth, whence Paul was writing, was Aphrodite, the goddess of love and generation, and her worship was accompanied by the wildest orgies. It would be difficult for Christians in any pagan city to remain unaffected by such blatant immorality. But all that is contrary to chastity of heart, in speech and behavior, is contrary to the command of God in the Decalogue, and to that holiness which the gospel requires (cf. Matt. 5:27, 28; Acts 15:29; 1 Cor. 6:18; Gal. 5:19; Eph. 5:3). In our day, when standards of sexual conduct are lowered, when chastity is so commonly regarded as outmoded and divorces are so frequent, this injunction [1 Thessalonians 4:3] deserves the scrupulous attention of every professed follower of the Lord."[3]

Paul saw marriage as "a divinely appointed union that [would] aid Christian partners in avoiding sexual temptations (. . . 1 Cor. 7:1–5)."[4] When one honors one's marriage vows, one honors God, who ordained marriage between a man and a woman. Paul believed fornication "a form of robbery, since it takes that which rightfully belongs to another."[5] The Lord will judge all who violate their marriage relationship. "He who forms the tie that unites husband and wife, watches over it (see Matt. 19:5, 6). Relationships which are thought to be secret, which come before no earthly tribunal, are seen by the Lord (see Heb. 4:13). He judges. All will be judged. Sin will not go unpunished."[6]

Sanctification or "holiness should characterize every aspect of the Christian's life."[7]

1. Francis D. Nichol, ed., *The Seventh-day Adventist Bible Commentary*, vol. 7 (Washington, DC: Review and Herald®, 1957), 243.
2. Ellen G. White, *The Acts of the Apostles* (Mountain View, CA: Pacific Press®, 1911), 560.
3. Nichol, *Seventh-day Adventist Bible Commentary*, vol. 7, 243.
4. Nichol, *Seventh-day Adventist Bible Commentary*, vol. 7, 244.
5. Nichol, *Seventh-day Adventist Bible Commentary*, vol. 7, 244.
6. Nichol, *Seventh-day Adventist Bible Commentary*, vol. 7, 244.
7. Nichol, *Seventh-day Adventist Bible Commentary*, vol. 7, 245.

Part 5: A Quiet Life

But we urge you, brethren, that you increase more and more; that you also aspire to lead a quiet life, to mind your own business, and to work with your own hands, as we commanded you.
—1 Thessalonians 4:10, 11

The Christian path is one of continual progress."[1] "Holiness is within the reach of all who reach for it by faith, not because of their good works, but because of Christ's merits. Divine power is provided for every soul struggling for the victory over sin and Satan."[2]

Paul encouraged a "quiet life." "There may have been fanaticism among the Thessalonian believers. Fanciful ideas and doctrines were being promulgated by a few to the disquieting of the many (see 2 Thess. 3:11, 12)."[3] "The Thessalonian believers were greatly annoyed by men coming among them with fanatical ideas and doctrines. Some were 'disorderly, working not at all, but . . . busybodies.' The church had been properly organized, and officers had been appointed to act as ministers and deacons. But there were some, self-willed and impetuous, who refused to be subordinate to those who held positions of authority in the church. They claimed not only the right of private judgment, but that of publicly urging their views upon the church."[4] Some members had ceased to work, expecting the church to support them.

Paul urged the church to continue to be benevolent to those in need; however, he stressed that those who could, should be self-supporting. "One of the best safeguards against meddling is active pursuit of one's own work. But it seems that some were teaching that in view of the second advent it was too late to work at ordinary pursuits. As a result, some had stopped working for a livelihood and were depending for support upon the generosity of their brethren."[5] Probably the more affluent members of the church were behind the question asked of Paul. What exactly were the limits to "brotherly love," and when was it fair to make everyone shoulder a portion of the financial load? "It is a sin to support and indulge in idleness those who are able to labor. Some have been zealous to attend all the meetings, not to glorify God, but for the 'loaves and fishes.' Such would much better have been at home laboring with their hands, 'the thing that is good,' to supply the wants of their families, and to have something to give to sustain the precious cause."[6]

"The Christian should aim to be independent, not dependent on others for his support."[7]

1. Francis D. Nichol, ed., *The Seventh-day Adventist Bible Commentary*, vol. 7 (Washington, DC: Review and Herald®, 1957), 245.
2. Ellen G. White, MS 113, 1902.
3. Nichol, *Seventh-day Adventist Bible Commentary*, vol. 7, 246.
4. Ellen G. White, *The Acts of the Apostles* (Mountain View, CA: Pacific Press®, 1911), 261.
5. Nichol, *Seventh-day Adventist Bible Commentary*, vol. 7, 246.
6. Ellen G. White, *Early Writings* (Washington, DC: Review and Herald®, 1945), 95.
7. Nichol, *Seventh-day Adventist Bible Commentary*, vol. 7, 246.

Part 6: The Resurrection

But I do not want you to be ignorant, brethren, concerning those
who have fallen asleep, lest you sorrow as others who have no hope.
—1 Thessalonians 4:13

In his first epistle to the Thessalonian believers, Paul endeavored to instruct them regarding the true state of the dead. He spoke of those who die as being asleep—in a state of unconsciousness. [1 Thessalonians 4:13–17 quoted.] . . .

"The Thessalonians had eagerly grasped the idea that Christ was coming to change the faithful who were alive, and to take them to Himself. They had carefully guarded the lives of their friends, lest they should die and lose the blessing which they looked forward to receiving at the coming of their Lord. But one after another their loved ones had been taken from them, and with anguish the Thessalonians had looked for the last time upon the faces of their dead, hardly daring to hope to meet them in a future life.

"As Paul's epistle was opened and read, great joy and consolation was brought to the church by the words revealing the true state of the dead. Paul showed that those living when Christ should come would not go to meet their Lord in advance of those who had fallen asleep in Jesus. The voice of the Archangel and the trump of God would reach the sleeping ones, and the dead in Christ should rise first, before the touch of immortality should be given to the living. 'Then we which are alive and remain shall be caught up together *with them* in the clouds, to meet the Lord in the air: and so shall we ever be with the Lord. Wherefore comfort one another with these words.'

"The hope and joy that this assurance brought to the young church at Thessalonica can scarcely be appreciated by us. They believed and cherished the letter sent to them by their father in the gospel, and their hearts went out in love to him."[1]

" 'Even so them also which sleep in Jesus will God bring with Him,' Paul wrote. Many interpret this passage to mean that the sleeping ones will be brought with Christ from heaven; but Paul meant that as Christ was raised from the dead, so God will call the sleeping saints from their graves and take them with Him to heaven. Precious consolation! glorious hope! not only to the church of Thessalonica, but to all Christians wherever they may be."[2]

We all will enter the kingdom together (1 Thessalonians 4:17)! The saints at rest in the grave will not be forgotten (1 Thessalonians 5:10).

---

1. Ellen G. White, *The Acts of the Apostles* (Mountain View, CA: Pacific Press®, 1911), 257–259; emphasis added.
2. White, *Acts of the Apostles*, 259.

Part 7: Christ's Second Coming

For you yourselves know perfectly that the day of the Lord so comes as a thief in the night.
—1 Thessalonians 5:2

While laboring at Thessalonica, Paul had so fully covered the subject of the signs of the times, showing what events would occur prior to the revelation of the Son of man in the clouds of heaven, that he did not think it necessary to write at length regarding this subject."[1] But Paul did feel he needed to reemphasize the unexpectedness of Christ's second coming. In words echoing Christ's own, Paul restated that Christ's coming would be as a "thief in the night" (cf. Matthew 24:43; Luke 12:39, 40). "There are in the world today many who close their eyes to the evidences that Christ has given to warn men of His coming. They seek to quiet all apprehension, while at the same time the signs of the end are rapidly fulfilling, and the world is hastening to the time when the Son of man shall be revealed in the clouds of heaven. Paul teaches that it is sinful to be indifferent to the signs which are to precede the second coming of Christ. Those guilty of this neglect he calls children of the night and of darkness. He encourages the vigilant and watchful."[2]

"The watchful Christian is a working Christian, seeking zealously to do all in his power for the advancement of the gospel. As love for his Redeemer increases, so also does love for his fellow men. He has severe trials, as had his Master; but he does not allow affliction to sour his temper or destroy his peace of mind. He knows that trial, if well borne, will refine and purify him, and bring him into closer fellowship with Christ. Those who are partakers of Christ's sufferings will also be partakers of His consolation and at last sharers of His glory."[3]

Paul admonished the Thessalonians to take up a breastplate of faith and love and a helmet of hope for salvation. Timothy's report to Paul, as mentioned in 1 Thessalonians 3:6, praised the *faith* and *love* of the Thessalonian Christians. But what of the Christian's *hope*? Paul's helmet of salvation is crucial to the Christian experience. Hope in the soon appearing of our Lord and Savior is what keeps us focused on His sacrifice for us and our duty to work for others. "We have this hope. . . . Hope in the coming of the Lord."[4] Paul's triad of faith, hope, and love was finally complete.

Is your hope built on nothing less than Jesus and His righteousness?

---

1. Ellen G. White, *The Acts of the Apostles* (Mountain View, CA: Pacific Press®, 1911), 259, 260.
2. White, *Acts of the Apostles*, 260.
3. White, *Acts of the Apostles*, 261.
4. Wayne Hooper, "We Have This Hope" (1962).

Part 8: Community

Rejoice always, pray without ceasing, in everything give thanks;
for this is the will of God in Christ Jesus for you.
—1 Thessalonians 5:16–18

Paul had answered the questions the Thessalonians had asked Timothy to convey for them. He had received the report of Timothy's visit with great joy and had expressed his desire to return to them in person. He spoke of their responsibilities to each other as brothers. He spoke enthusiastically of the Second Coming and relieved their concerns regarding those of their loved ones who had died and now rested in the blessed hope of the soon coming of Christ. He reminded them that the Second Coming would come unexpectedly and that they needed to be ready always.

In closing, Paul cautioned them to respect the servants of the Lord, maintaining peace within the church, rejoicing in the Lord, praying without ceasing, giving thanks in everything, holding fast to messages from "true" prophets, and maintaining themselves free from every form of evil. These are still important lessons for twenty-first-century Christians to learn. Be at peace with all men. We have Jesus—rejoice! "Those professed Christians who are constantly complaining, and who seem to think cheerfulness and happiness a sin, have not genuine religion."[1] Pray! "There should be a constant spirit of prayer breathing through the Christian's life. Never must the connection with Heaven be broken (...Luke 18:1)."[2] Give thanks! "Thanksgiving should be the Christian's rule; health and joy are promoted by it."[3] Examine the prophets! "(1) The true prophet must confess Christ in life as well as in word (1 John 4:1–3). He will acknowledge and confess Christ's deity (1 John 2:22, 23). (2) His teachings must accord with the teachings of Scripture (see Acts 17:11; Gal. 1:8, 9). (3) The result or fruitage of his teaching must be good (Matt. 7:18–20)."[4] Hold fast to that which is good!

Paul "closed his letter with a prayer that God would sanctify them wholly, that in 'Spirit and soul and body' they might 'be preserved blameless unto the coming of our Lord Jesus Christ. Faithful is He that calleth you,' he added, 'who also will do it.' "[5] Paul admonished the Thessalonian believers to read his letter in public because some didn't wish it read, and others didn't want to listen. With love, Paul gave his letter to Timothy and sent him on his way.

"Be at peace among yourselves" (1 Thessalonians 5:13). There must be no rivalries, no divisions in the church!

1. Ellen G. White, *The Ministry of Healing* (Mountain View, CA: Pacific Press®, 1942), 251.
2. Francis D. Nichol, ed., *The Seventh-day Adventist Bible Commentary*, vol. 7 (Washington, DC: Review and Herald®, 1957), 255.
3. Nichol, *Seventh-day Adventist Bible Commentary*, vol. 7, 255.
4. Nichol, *Seventh-day Adventist Bible Commentary*, vol. 7, 256.
5. Ellen G. White, *The Acts of the Apostles* (Mountain View, CA: Pacific Press®, 1911), 263, 264.

Part 1: Stand Firm

*So that we ourselves boast of you among the churches of God for your patience
and faith in all your persecutions and tribulations that you endure.*

—2 Thessalonians 1:4

Paul was greatly relieved when Timothy returned from Thessalonica to report. Paul's first letter to them had been received with great rejoicing. Yet there were still some serious problems that needed to be addressed. "In his second letter Paul sought to correct their misunderstanding of his teaching [regarding the second coming of Christ] and to set before them his true position. He again expressed his confidence in their integrity, and his gratitude that their faith was strong, and that their love abounded for one another and for the cause of their Master. He told them that he presented them to other churches as an example of the patient, persevering faith that bravely withstands persecution and tribulation."[1]

Persecution was intensifying in Thessalonica, and Paul, no stranger to adversity himself, admonished the brethren to be steadfast in their faith. He applauded their courage and reminded them that "it is not the persecutions and tribulations that are proof of the righteous judgment of God, but rather the attitude of the believers toward such affliction. Patient endurance and courageous faith under persecution, being the result of God's grace, are evidence of His present interest and care for the sufferers, and thus proof that He will finally reverse the injustices of the world."[2] "Those who afflict the Thessalonians are not here [2 Thessalonians 1:6] identified, but from the narrative in Acts (ch. 17:5–9) it is clear that the Jews were the instigators of the persecution."[3]

Paul assured the Thessalonians their persecutors would not go unpunished. "Paul conceives those whom the Lord punishes as belonging to two classes, those who know not God and those who obey not the gospel. . . . The first are those who have had opportunity to know God but have spurned the privilege (see Ps. 19:1–3; Rom. 1:18–21). The second class are those who know the gospel message but have refused to obey it. Their reasons for rejecting the gospel are clearly shown by the Lord Himself to be their love of sin (see John 3:17–20)."[4]

Enduring suffering doesn't make a Christian worthy of God's kingdom. It is God's forgiving grace that makes one worthy! (Romans 6:23).

---

1. Ellen G. White, *The Acts of the Apostles* (Mountain View, CA: Pacific Press®, 1911), 264.
2. Francis D. Nichol, ed., *The Seventh-day Adventist Bible Commentary*, vol. 7 (Washington, DC: Review and Herald®, 1957), 265.
3. Nichol, *Seventh-day Adventist Bible Commentary*, vol. 7, 265.
4. Nichol, *Seventh-day Adventist Bible Commentary*, vol. 7, 266.

Part 2: Misconceptions

*Now, brethren, concerning the coming of our Lord Jesus Christ
and our gathering together to Him.*
—2 Thessalonians 2:1

It appears that erroneous ideas concerning Paul's teaching about the nearness of Christ's coming were being circulated in the church at Thessalonica. To correct these misconceptions Paul wrote the second epistle. He handles the matter with great tact, addressing his readers, not as inferiors, but as brethren, and begs them to heed the instruction he is about to give. He desires to encourage, not discourage, the faint-hearted."[1] "The instruction that Paul sent the Thessalonians in his first epistle regarding the second coming of Christ, was in perfect harmony with his former teaching. Yet his words were misapprehended by some of the Thessalonian brethren. They understood him to express the hope that he himself would live to witness the Saviour's advent. This belief served to increase their enthusiasm and excitement. Those who had previously neglected their responsibilities and duties, now became more persistent in urging their erroneous views."[2]

"Paul's words were not to be misinterpreted. It was not to be taught that he, by special revelation, had warned the Thessalonians of the immediate coming of Christ. Such a position would cause confusion of faith; for disappointment often leads to unbelief. The apostle therefore cautioned the brethren to receive no such message as coming from him."[3] The Thessalonians were not to be "carried about with every wind of doctrine" (Ephesians 4:14). "The thought that the coming of the Lord was imminent had been keeping the Thessalonians in a state of continuous alarm."[4]

So how should the Thessalonians react to the second coming of their Lord and Savior? "Paul had emphasized in his first epistle, as had the Lord in His teachings, that Christians should be living in a state of preparedness for the Lord's return (Matt. 24:42, 44; 1 Thess. 1:10; 5:23). They are to watch and be ready, but they are never to be so imbued with a sense of the second advent's immediacy as to be in a state of unreasonable agitation."[5] They are to be encouraged rather than discouraged.

"Watch therefore, for you do not know what hour your Lord is coming" (Matthew 24:42).

1. Francis D. Nichol, ed., *The Seventh-day Adventist Bible Commentary*, vol. 7 (Washington, DC: Review and Herald®, 1957), 269.
2. Ellen G. White, *The Acts of the Apostles* (Mountain View, CA: Pacific Press®, 1911), 264.
3. White, *Acts of the Apostles*, 265, 266.
4. Nichol, *Seventh-day Adventist Bible Commentary*, vol. 7, 269.
5. Nichol, *Seventh-day Adventist Bible Commentary*, vol. 7, 269.

Part 3: A Falling Away

*Let no one deceive you by any means; for that Day will not come unless
the falling away comes first, and the man of sin is revealed, the son of perdition.*
—2 Thessalonians 2:3

Paul foretold a religious "falling away" or an "apostasy" that would occur within the church before the Second Coming. It would not only "precede the second advent (2 Thess. 2:2), it would serve as a sign of the nearness of Christ's return."[1] Tradition would trump Scripture. Saints would be venerated. Christ's atonement would be misunderstood. The emblems of the Lord's Supper would be given magical power. Children would be baptized to save them from their father's sins. A human priesthood would usurp the heavenly priesthood of Jesus Christ. And a "man of sin" would arise to change the Sabbath day. "Thus Paul outlined the baleful work of that power of evil which was to continue through long centuries of darkness and persecution before the second coming of Christ."[2]

"There is one pointed out in prophecy as the man of sin. He is the representative of Satan. Taking the suggestions of Satan concerning the law of God, which is as unchangeable as his throne, this man of sin comes in and represents to the world that he has changed that law, and that the first day of the week instead of the seventh is now the Sabbath. Professing infallibility, he claims the right to change the law of God to suit his own purposes. By so doing, he exalts himself above God, and leaves the world to infer that God is fallible. If it were indeed true that God had made a rule of government that needed to be changed, it would certainly show fallibility.

"But Christ declared that not one jot or tittle of the law should fail until heaven and earth should pass away. The very work that He came to do was to exalt that law, and show to the created worlds and to heaven that God is just, and that His law need not be changed. But here is Satan's right-hand man ready to carry on the work that Satan commenced in heaven, that of trying to amend the law of God."[3] The man of sin has set up a common working day as "a rival sabbath, to be observed and honored. Thus the world has been turned against God; for the Lord declares that he has sanctified the day of his rest."[4]

Revelation 14:6–12 says worship the Creator. Keep the seventh day Sabbath, God's memorial to His creation.

1. Francis D. Nichol, ed., *The Seventh-day Adventist Bible Commentary*, vol. 7 (Washington, DC: Review and Herald®, 1957), 270.
2. Ellen G. White, *The Acts of the Apostles* (Mountain View, CA: Pacific Press®, 1911), 266.
3. Ellen G. White, "The Government of God," *Advent Review and Sabbath Herald*, March 9, 1886, 2.
4. Ellen G. White, "Go, Preach the Gospel—No. 2," *Advent Review and Sabbath Herald*, July 26, 1898, 1.

Part 4: The Mystery of Lawlessness

For the mystery of lawlessness is already at work; only He who now restrains will do so until He is taken out of the way.

—2 Thessalonians 2:7

D aniel had prophesied that a kingdom would arise whose leader "shall speak pompous words against the Most High, shall persecute the saints of the Most High, and *shall intend to change times and law*" (Daniel 7:25; emphasis added). Paul now echoed those words of Daniel as he warned the church about the developing "mystery of lawlessness" (2 Thessalonians 2:7). "In the last analysis, this description applies to Satan, the author of lawlessness . . . , but the devil has generally camouflaged his personality by working through agents. In the last days he will personally play a more direct role, culminating his deception by personally counterfeiting the coming of Christ."[1] "It will not be possible for Satan accurately and completely to counterfeit such a *parousia* [Second Coming]. . . . God's own people will, by diligent study of the Scriptures, and by reminding themselves of prophetic details concerning the genuine second advent, be able to escape the devil's deception (. . . Matt. 24:24)."[2]

"The Restrainer, God, who holds the evil in check [GC 589, 614], will continue to restrain, until the time comes for the mystery of iniquity to be 'revealed' [v. 8] and 'taken out of the way.' "[3] We are therefore assured that "in spite of the operation of the apostate power, it will not continue forever. God will, in His appointed time, bring its activities to an end."[4] Paul warned his friends in Thessalonica that there would be some who would not love the truth, and as such, they would be lost. There is danger in believing what one wishes to believe, especially when one's belief runs contrary to a plain "thus saith the Lord." The Scriptures alone define what is true and what is false doctrine. "Especially solemn is the apostle's statement regarding those who should refuse to receive 'the love of the truth.' . . . Men cannot with impunity reject the warnings that God in mercy sends them. From those who persist in turning from these warnings, God withdraws His Spirit, leaving them to the deceptions that they love."[5] Beware the strong delusion (lie)!

Is there a worse "lie" (2 Thessalonians 2:11) than Satan trying to impersonate the second coming of Christ?

---

1. Francis D. Nichol, ed., *The Seventh-day Adventist Bible Commentary*, vol. 7 (Washington, DC: Review and Herald®, 1957), 272.
2. Nichol, *Seventh-day Adventist Bible Commentary*, vol. 7, 274.
3. Nichol, *Seventh-day Adventist Bible Commentary*, vol. 7, 272, 273.
4. Nichol, *Seventh-day Adventist Bible Commentary*, vol. 7, 273.
5. Ellen G. White, *The Acts of the Apostles* (Mountain View, CA: Pacific Press®, 1911), 266.

Part 5: Lazy Busybodies

But we command you, brethren, in the name of our Lord Jesus Christ, that you withdraw from every brother who walks disorderly and not according to the tradition which he received from us.
—2 Thessalonians 3:6

Paul had admonished the Thessalonian church in his first letter to "warn those who are unruly" (1 Thessalonians 5:14). Now in 2 Thessalonians 3, he took a stronger stand and counseled the members to "withdraw from every brother who walks disorderly." "The disorderly behavior to which Paul was alluding (v. 6), seems to have been due to the fanatical idea that since the Lord was about to come, it was too late to continue worldly pursuits. Those who were imbued with this thought may have urged the principle of community of goods upon the church for selfish reasons, in order to profit from others' labor. Paul denounced these indolent agitators (v. 11), but first he reminded the brethren that his example had been a positive one. He was able boldly to appeal to his busy life among them."[1]

"The apostle in his day considered idleness a sin, and those who indulge this evil today disgrace their profession. They will criticize the faithful worker, and bring reproach upon the gospel of Christ. Those who would believe, they turn from the way of truth and righteousness. We should be warned not to associate with those who by their course of action lay a stumbling block in the way of others. . . .

"The custom of supporting men and women in idleness by private gifts or church money encourages them in sinful habits, and this course should be conscientiously avoided."[2] "The fact that there are slothful, improvident, undeserving ones who look to the church for its bounty, must not be allowed to dry up the springs of Christian generosity. The church needs the blessing that comes from helping its poor. It is a privilege to share our temporal blessings with those less fortunate, and thus be mutually helpful."[3] If they are able to work, they should work!

"Busybodies are busy in unimportant things, in those things which do not concern them, in everybody's business but their own. Honest toil is the best cure for such people; for those who are conscientious in the discharge of their own duties will not find time, nor have the inclination, to be meddling in the affairs of others."[4]

"The true Christian goes about his duties in a quiet, unostentatious way, being diligent in business, serving the Lord (see Rom. 12:11)."[5]

---

1. Francis D. Nichol, ed., *The Seventh-day Adventist Bible Commentary*, vol. 7 (Washington, DC: Review and Herald®, 1957), 280.
2. Ellen G. White, Ms. 93, 1899.
3. Nichol, *Seventh-day Adventist Bible Commentary*, vol. 7, 281.
4. Nichol, *Seventh-day Adventist Bible Commentary*, vol. 7, 280, 281.
5. Nichol, *Seventh-day Adventist Bible Commentary*, vol. 7, 281.

Part 6: Tired of Doing Good?

Moreover, brethren, we make known to you the grace of God bestowed on
the churches of Macedonia: that in a great trial of affliction the abundance
of their joy and their deep poverty abounded in the riches of their liberality.
—2 Corinthians 8:1, 2

If one correctly assumes 2 Corinthians 8:1, 2, speaking about the Macedonian churches, includes the Thessalonians, one may assume they were not a rich congregation. The zeal with which they embraced the gospel and the generosity that flowed from their limited means to support the ministry is worthy of note. Those with means shared what they had with their impoverished brethren. Christ, the supreme example of giving, was their selfless model. Christ became poor that through Him, we might all become rich (verse 9). He left heaven and the companionship of His Father to minister to a group of people who wanted Him silenced and dead. He was scorned, rejected, despised and hated for His message of love. He had no place to lay His head. He grew physically weary, yet He steadfastly continued His ministry, fully aware that upon His shoulders rested the great and awesome responsibility for mankind's salvation.

Paul exhorted the Thessalonian brethren to continue in good works. "But as for you brethren, *do not grow weary* of doing good" (2 Thessalonians 3:13; emphasis added). It is difficult to maintain one's integrity in the pollution of our secular world. It is hard to continually give of one's time and talents when no recognition or even appreciation is forthcoming. The human spirit craves positive comments. Christians need to recognize those who day in and day out serve the church. When did you last thank those who faithfully come early to set the church thermostat, cut the grass, clean the sanctuary, teach you and your children's Sabbath School lesson, sing in the choir, bring tasty potluck dishes, stay after potluck to clean up, visit shut-ins, greet visitors, prepare your bulletin?

Paul knew the dangers of "burnout." He also knew that God recognizes the faithful service of His believers. One day you may stand beside the Thessalonian believers and hear Jesus say, "Well done, good and faithful servant; you were faithful over a few things, I will make you ruler over many things. Enter into the joy of your Lord" (Matthew 25:21).

What other reward would you wish?

Ephesus

So Paul still remained a good while [in Corinth]. Then he took leave of the brethren and sailed for Syria [Ephesus], and Priscilla *and* Aquila *were with him.*
                                                    —Acts 18:18; emphasis added

Paul had lived and worked [at Corinth] in reasonable quiet for a year and six months ([Acts 18:]11). After this period, or perhaps during the latter part of it, he was haled before Gallio. Following this crisis, the apostle had another time of peace in which to labor."[1] For some time, Paul had been collecting gifts for the disciples in Jerusalem (Romans 15:25, 26; Galatians 2:10). He may have had several motives for finally leaving Corinth: "(1) . . . He doubtless wished to deliver the gifts collected for the disciples at Jerusalem, in person. . . . (2) His recent vow required a visit to the Temple. (3) He would wish to report the results of his labors among the Gentiles, especially in the yet distant regions of Macedonia and Achaia (cf. Acts 15:4)."[2] Paul embarked from the port of Cenchrea, the eastern harbor of Corinth on the Saronic Gulf. "Romans 16:1 implies that there was an organized church there. The gratitude with which Paul refers to *Phoebe*, and to her Christian service (Rom. 16:2) indicates that he had had intimate contact with that church. Probably he had founded it."[3] Paul sailed east across the Aegean to Ephesus. His traveling companions were now *Priscilla* and Aquila.

"Ephesus was a famous city, capital of the Greek district of Ionia and later of the Roman province of Asia. It became the scene of the apostle John's later labors. The city stood not far from the sea, on hilly ground at the mouth of the Cayster, between the larger rivers Hermus and Maeander. . . . From the first it had been a center for the worship of Artemis (the Roman Diana . . .) whose temple there was visited by pilgrims from all over the known world. For centuries East and West had come into close contact at Ephesus, and there the religion of Greece took on a more Oriental character and involved magic, mysteries, and charms. In Paul's day Ephesus was by far the busiest and most popular city in proconsular Asia. There were enough Jews for at least one synagogue."[4] As was his custom, Paul sought out the Jewish synagogue and continued to preach the gospel. "Nowhere, unless at Beroea, did Paul find a more receptive attitude toward the truth he was presenting."[5] Although entreated to remain, Paul's plans did not allow him to tarry. Instead, he left Aquila and Priscilla to carry on the work.

Paul continued to reach out to the largest cosmopolitan centers of his time. Big city evangelism!

---

1. Francis D. Nichol, ed., *The Seventh-day Adventist Bible Commentary*, vol. 6 (Washington, DC: Review and Herald®, 1957), 364, 365.
2. Nichol, *Seventh-day Adventist Bible Commentary*, vol. 6, 365.
3. Nichol, *Seventh-day Adventist Bible Commentary*, vol. 6, 365; emphasis added.
4. Nichol, *Seventh-day Adventist Bible Commentary*, vol. 6, 365.
5. Nichol, *Seventh-day Adventist Bible Commentary*, vol. 6, 367.

On to Jerusalem

When they asked him to stay a longer time with them, he did not consent, but took leave of them,
saying, "I must by all means keep this coming feast in Jerusalem."
—Acts 18:20, 21

P aul had taken a vow. "There can be little doubt that the 'vow' was a private vow, a modified form of the temporary Nazirite vow, described in Num. 6:1–21. . . .
"The chief impulse out of which vows have grown has often been a marked thankfulness for deliverance from danger following upon fear. The fear, the promise, and the deliverance have been noted in the record of Paul's work at Corinth, and a vow of consecration to the program of preaching the gospel would be a natural result. Paul neither despised nor condemned expressions of devout feeling, for he did not consider them legalistic, as he did certain other practices of the Jews.

"It is possible also that Paul was applying his principle of being 'all things to all men' (1 Cor. 9:22), and therefore as a Jew was acting in sympathy with Jews (v. 20). A Nazirite vow would demonstrate to all his Jewish brethren that he, himself, was not despising the law, nor teaching other Jews to despise it (. . . Acts 21:21–24)."[1] Once a Nazarite vow was completed, the individual would shave his head and burn the hair on the temple altar. "Persons at a distance from Jerusalem were apparently allowed to cut their hair short and bring the shorn locks with them to the Temple, to offer them up when the remainder of their hair was shaved from their heads. This is what Paul did at Cenchreae, before starting on his voyage to Syria."[2]

Paul could not remain in Ephesus but needed to hurry on his way to reach Jerusalem in time to place his shorn hair on the altar during the festival. From Ephesus, Paul set sail for the coast of Phoenicia, making landfall at Caesarea. "At Caesarea he doubtless renewed his contact with Philip the evangelist. He was a guest in Philip's home in Caesarea on a later occasion ([Acts] 21:8)."[3] From Caesarea, Paul climbed the hills to Jerusalem. This was his fourth visit to the city since his conversion. We have no information concerning his reception there or the fulfillment of his vow. All we know is "the apostle hastened on as soon as possible to what must have been the congenial society of the Christians at Antioch.

". . . Paul's return to Antioch marks the end of the Second Missionary Journey. It was about AD 52."[4]

Paul "was convinced that the learning of the world was powerless to move the hearts of men, but that the gospel was the power of God to salvation."[5]

---

1. Francis D. Nichol, ed., *The Seventh-day Adventist Bible Commentary*, vol. 6 (Washington, DC: Review and Herald®, 1957), 365.
2. Nichol, *Seventh-day Adventist Bible Commentary*, vol. 6, 365.
3. Nichol, *Seventh-day Adventist Bible Commentary*, vol. 6, 367.
4. Nichol, *Seventh-day Adventist Bible Commentary*, vol. 6, 367.
5. Ellen G. White, "Divine Wisdom," *Advent Review and Sabbath Herald*, August 3, 1911, 3.

Apollos

Now a certain Jew named Apollos, born at Alexandria,
an eloquent man and mighty in the Scriptures, came to Ephesus.

—Acts 18:24

It was at this time that Apollos, an Alexandrian Jew, visited Ephesus. He had received the highest Grecian culture, and was a scholar and an orator. He had heard the teachings of John the Baptist, had received the baptism of repentance, and was a living witness that the work of the prophet was not in vain. Apollos was a thorough student of the prophecies, and an able expounder of the Scriptures, publicly proclaiming his faith in Christ, as far as he himself had received the light.

"Aquila and *Priscilla* listened to him, and saw that his teachings were defective. He had not a thorough knowledge of the mission of Christ, his resurrection and ascension, and of the work of his Spirit, the Comforter which he sent down to remain with his people during his absence. They accordingly sent for Apollos, and the educated orator received instruction from them with grateful surprise and joy. Through their teachings he obtained a clearer understanding of the Scriptures, and became one of the ablest defenders of the Christian church. Thus a thorough scholar and brilliant orator learned the way of the Lord more perfectly from the teachings of a Christian man and woman whose humble employment was that of tent-making."[1]

Note that Priscilla "evidently took an active part in instructing Apollos, indicating that she was a woman of great power and zeal among the Christians. Aquila and Priscilla had apparently continued to attend the services of the synagogue. When Apollos appeared there in the character of a rabbi and delivered his message (cf. Acts 13:14, 15), they heard him and were attracted to him."[2] What did Aquila and Priscilla share with Apollos? They would have no doubt explained "the doctrines of salvation by grace, justification by faith, the gift of the Holy Spirit after conversion and baptism, and the meaning and necessity of the Lord's Supper. It would doubtless follow, as in the case of the twelve men discussed in [Acts] 19:1–7, that Apollos, who formerly knew only John's baptism, would be rebaptized into 'the name of the Lord Jesus.' "[3]

Established Christians need to mentor new believers, encouraging them to soar high on wings of eagles (Isaiah 40:31). Is it any wonder that the Latin name Aquila means "eagle"?

---

1. Ellen G. White, *Sketches From the Life of Paul* (Washington, DC: Review and Herald®, 1974), 11; emphasis added.

2. Francis D. Nichol, ed., *The Seventh-day Adventist Bible Commentary*, vol. 6 (Washington, DC: Review and Herald®, 1957), 369.

3. Nichol, *Seventh-day Adventist Bible Commentary*, vol. 6, 369.

Idolizing Ministers at Corinth

And when he desired to cross to Achaia, the brethren wrote, exhorting the disciples to receive him;
and when he arrived, he greatly helped those who had believed through grace.

—Acts 18:27

Apollos wished to go into Achaia to preach the gospel. The church at Ephesus wrote introductory letters of commendation to the church at Corinth on his behalf. "They were the 'credentials' of that time. The fact that the church at Ephesus was willing to give Apollos such a letter shows the excellent impression he had made while there."[1] "He went to Corinth, where, in public labor and from house to house, 'he mightily convinced the Jews, . . . showing by the Scriptures that Jesus was Christ.' Paul had planted the seed of truth; Apollos now watered it. The success that attended Apollos in preaching the gospel led some of the believers to exalt his labors above those of Paul. This comparison of man with man brought into the church a party spirit that threatened to hinder greatly the progress of the gospel."[2]

Paul "had purposely presented the gospel in its simplicity. . . .

"It had been Paul's work to instruct the Corinthian converts in the rudiments, the very alphabet, of the Christian faith. . . .

". . . He dwelt especially upon practical godliness and the holiness to which those must attain who shall be accounted worthy of a place in God's kingdom. . . . Therefore, the burden of his teaching among them was Christ and Him crucified. . . .

". . . Paul saw that the character of Christ must be understood before men could love Him or view the cross with the eye of faith. Here must begin that study which shall be the science and the song of the redeemed through all eternity. In the light of the cross alone can the true value of the human soul be estimated."[3]

Nevertheless, a division occurred within the Corinthian church. Apollos's preaching style was probably different from that of Paul. "His labors naturally attracted followers to the new preacher, and perhaps gave him a larger numerical success than had attended the efforts of Paul."[4] "He who sends forth gospel workers as His ambassadors is dishonored when there is manifested among the hearers so strong an attachment to some favorite minister that there is an unwillingness to accept the labors of some other teacher. The Lord sends help to His people, not always as they may choose, but as they need; for men are shortsighted and cannot discern what is for their highest good.[5]

"The truths that the servants of God bring are to be accepted and appreciated in the meekness of humility, but no minister is to be idolized." [6]

---

1. Francis D. Nichol, ed., *The Seventh-day Adventist Bible Commentary*, vol. 6 (Washington, DC: Review and Herald®, 1957), 369.
2. Ellen G. White, *The Acts of the Apostles* (Mountain View, CA: Pacific Press®, 1911), 270.
3. White, *Acts of the Apostles*, 270–273.
4. Nichol, *Seventh-day Adventist Bible Commentary*, vol. 6, 370.
5. White, *Acts of the Apostles*, 278.
6. White, *Acts of the Apostles*, 277, 278.

Paul's Third Missionary Journey

With Tychicus, Trophimus, Sopater, Aristarchus, Secundus, Gaius, Timotheus, and Luke to Galatia, Phrygia, Ephesus, Macedonia, Greece, Corinth, Troas, Miletus, Tyre, Caesarea, and Jerusalem

AD 53–58

Acts 18:23–21:17
The Acts of the Apostles, pp. 281–398
Sketches From the Life of Paul, pp. 128–207

Paul Returns to Ephesus

And it happened, while Apollos was at Corinth, that Paul,
having passed through the upper regions, came to Ephesus.

—Acts 19:1

While Apollos was preaching at Corinth, Paul fulfilled his promise to return to Ephesus. He had made a brief visit to Jerusalem and had spent some time at Antioch, the scene of his early labors. Thence he traveled through Asia Minor, 'over all the country of Galatia and Phrygia' (Acts 18:23), visiting the churches which he himself had established, and strengthening the faith of the believers.

"In the time of the apostles the western portion of Asia Minor was known as the Roman province of Asia. Ephesus, the capital, was a great commercial center. Its harbor was crowded with shipping, and its streets were thronged with people from every country. Like Corinth, it presented a promising field for missionary effort."[1] All roads might lead to Rome, but Ephesus straddled the main road from Rome to the Orient. All Roman milestones were calculated in miles from Ephesus and not Rome. "The city suffered much from an earthquake in A.D. 29, but was rebuilt by Tiberius. It was this new and modern city to which Paul and John came....

"... One of the most impressive ruins is the great theater.... Its semicircular auditorium was 495 ft. in diameter. ... The stage was 22 ft. wide. The theater contained 66 rows of seats accommodating 24,500 people. This was the scene of the riot against Paul and his teachings recorded in Acts 19:23–41.

"The main street connecting the theater with the harbor was called the Arkadiane. Its 1,735 ft. were paved with marble slabs, and it was lined with colonnaded shops. At night the street was lighted, something unusual in an ancient city."[2] Ephesus was the third-largest city of the empire, with an estimated population exceeding a quarter-million inhabitants.

Here in Ephesus, Paul left Aquila and Priscilla to continue the work when he journeyed on to Jerusalem. Paul would spend a major portion (two and a half to three years) of his third missionary tour laboring at Ephesus (Acts 20:31). Paul started his ministry in the Jewish synagogue. "He continued to labor there for three months, 'disputing and persuading the things concerning the kingdom of God.' At first he met with a favorable reception; but as in other fields, he was soon violently opposed."[3]

Prejudice and unbelief often cannot be overcome, even in the face of convincing evidence.

---

1. Ellen G. White, *The Acts of the Apostles* (Mountain View, CA: Pacific Press®, 1911), 281.

2. Siegfried H. Horn, *Seventh-day Adventist Bible Dictionary*, ed. Don F. Neufeld, Commentary Reference Series, vol. 8 (Washington, DC: Review and Herald®, 1960), s.v. "Ephesus."

3. White, *Acts of the Apostles*, 285.

The School of Tyrannus

But when some were hardened and did not believe, but spoke evil of the Way before the multitude,
he departed from them and withdrew the disciples, reasoning daily in the school of Tyrannus.
—Acts 19:9

O n his arrival at Ephesus, Paul found twelve brethren, who, like Apollos, had been disciples of John the Baptist, and like him had gained some knowledge of the mission of Christ. They had not the ability of Apollos, but with the same sincerity and faith they were seeking to spread abroad the knowledge they had received."[1] "Paul summarized what John taught—the baptism of repentance and faith on Him who should follow—but these Ephesian disciples knew nothing of the baptism of the Spirit and the gifts of the Spirit, and little of the doctrines of faith in Christ" (compare Luke 7:18–23).[2]

Paul's ministry to his fellow countrymen in the synagogue met with resistance. "The unbelieving Jews acted at Ephesus as their fellows had at Thessalonica. They probably displayed their hatred of Paul by attempting to turn the Gentiles against him. People of the lower classes were always ready to riot."[3] Paul, therefore, separated himself and his followers from those meeting on Sabbath at the Jewish synagogue. "This is the first recorded time when the entire group of Christian believers severed their connection with the Jewish synagogue."[4] Paul moved his congregation, "fearing that the faith of the believers would be endangered by continued association with these opposers of the truth."[5]

Paul took his Jewish followers to the school of Tyrannus. We know little of Tyrannus other than that he was "a teacher of some note."[6] He might even have been a Jew. "Some therefore think this was a Jewish school, a *Beth-Hammidrash*, in which Paul's Jewish hearers would be more likely to assemble."[7] One alternate reading for Acts 19:9 "reasoning daily" would suggest Paul's teaching took place between the fifth and the tenth hours. If this reading is regarded as the original text, it is of interest because "the period from the fifth to the tenth hour (about 11 AM to 4 PM) is the *siesta* [rest] hour in Eastern countries[; therefore] Paul would have used this building for his teaching during 'off-hours,' when Tyrannus' school would not have been in session."[8]

Paul taught daily at the school. Every Christian needs a humble and teachable spirit!

---

1. Ellen G. White, *The Acts of the Apostles* (Mountain View, CA: Pacific Press®, 1911), 282.

2. Francis D. Nichol, ed., *The Seventh-day Adventist Bible Commentary*, vol. 6 (Washington, DC: Review and Herald®, 1957), 372, 373.

3. Nichol, *Seventh-day Adventist Bible Commentary*, vol. 6, 373, 374.

4. Nichol, *Seventh-day Adventist Bible Commentary*, vol. 6, 374.

5. White, *Acts of the Apostles*, 286.

6. White, *Acts of the Apostles*, 286.

7. Nichol, *Seventh-day Adventist Bible Commentary*, vol. 6, 374.

8. Nichol, *Seventh-day Adventist Bible Commentary*, vol. 6, 374.

Jewish Occultists

*Then some of the itinerant Jewish exorcists took it upon themselves to
call the name of the Lord Jesus over those who had evil spirits.*

—Acts 19:13

T he apostle Paul, in his labors at Ephesus, was given special tokens of divine favor. The power of God accompanied his efforts, and many were healed of physical maladies. . . . These manifestations of supernatural power were far more potent than had ever before been witnessed in Ephesus, and were of such a character that they could not be imitated by the skill of the juggler or the enchantments of the sorcerer. As these miracles were wrought in the name of Jesus of Nazareth, the people had opportunity to see that the God of heaven was more powerful than the magicians who were worshipers of the goddess Diana."[1]

Certain itinerant Jewish exorcists decided they would seek "to benefit themselves by employing the names of Paul and Jesus. These Jews professed to cure diseases by charms and spells."[2] "Sorcery had been prohibited in the Mosaic law, on pain of death, yet from time to time it had been secretly practiced by apostate Jews."[3] Seven brothers, the sons of Sceva, a Jewish priest, had come to Ephesus and decided they would call upon the name Jesus to heal a man possessed of a demon. They addressed the demon. "We exorcise you by the Jesus whom Paul preaches" (Acts 19:13).

The demon replied, " 'Jesus, I know, and Paul I know; but who are you?'

"Then the man in whom the evil spirit was leaped on them, overpowered them, and prevailed against them, so that they fled out of the house naked and wounded" (verses 15, 16).

As a result of this event, "unmistakable proof had been given of the sacredness of that name, and the peril which they incurred who should invoke it while they had no faith in Christ's divine mission. Terror seized the minds of many, and the work of the gospel was regarded by all with awe and reverence.

"Facts which had previously been concealed were now brought to light."[4] Confessing their error to Paul, these men publicly burned their books on magic and sorcery before the people. The books were valued at approximately fifty thousand pieces of silver.

"The heathen oracles have their counterpart in the spiritualistic mediums, the clairvoyants, and fortune-tellers of today."[5]

---

1. Ellen G. White, *The Acts of the Apostles* (Mountain View, CA: Pacific Press®, 1911), 286, 287.
2. Francis D. Nichol, ed., *The Seventh-day Adventist Bible Commentary*, vol. 6 (Washington, DC: Review and Herald®, 1957), 375.
3. Ellen G. White, *Sketches From the Life of Paul* (Washington, DC: Review and Herald®, 1974), 136.
4. White, *Sketches From the Life of Paul*, 137.
5. White, *Sketches From the Life of Paul*, 139.

Diana of the Ephesians

*And when they heard this, they were full of wrath
and cried out, saying, "Great is Diana of the Ephesians!"*

—Acts 19:28

E phesus was not only the most magnificent, but the most corrupt, of the cities of Asia. . . .

"The city was famed for the worship of the goddess Diana and the practice of magic. Here was the great temple of Diana, which was regarded by the ancients as one of the wonders of the world. Its vast extent and surpassing magnificence made it the pride, not only of the city, but of the nation. Kings and princes had enriched it by their donations. The Ephesians vied with one another in adding to its splendor, and it was made the treasure-house for a large share of the wealth of Western Asia.

"The idol enshrined in this sumptuous edifice was a rude, uncouth image, declared by tradition to have fallen from the sky. Upon it were inscribed mystic characters and symbols, which were believed to possess great power. When pronounced, they were said to accomplish wonders. When written, they were treasured as a potent charm to guard their possessor from robbers, from disease, and even from death. Numerous and costly books were written by the Ephesians to explain the meaning and use of these symbols."[1]

Artemis, named Diana by the Romans, was the goddess of fertility. "She was depicted as a woman whose upper body was covered with many breasts. Ancient replicas of her image have been found, and she is also depicted on coins. However, silver models of her temple, such as those made by Demetrius the silversmith and his fellow craftsmen (Acts 19:24), have not yet been discovered in excavations. The cult statue that originally stood in the temple dedicated to the goddess Artemis in Ephesus was made either of black olivewood, as some sources seem to indicate, or of a meteoric iron, as the city clerk seems to have believed, who said that her image had fallen from heaven (v 35). This goddess must not be confused with the Artemis of Greek mythology, the goddess of hunting, and the symbol of chastity and virginity, the twin sister of Apollo."[2]

Charms, amulets, and good-luck medals are nothing new. They have their basis in idol worship.

---

1. Ellen G. White, *Sketches From the Life of Paul* (Washington, DC: Review and Herald®, 1974), 134, 135.
2. Siegfried H. Horn, *Seventh-day Adventist Bible Dictionary*, ed. Don F. Neufeld, Commentary Reference Series, vol. 8 (Washington, DC: Review and Herald®, 1960), s.v. "Artemis."

Demetrius

*For a certain man named Demetrius, a silversmith, who made
silver shrines of Diana, brought no small profit to the craftsmen.*

—Acts 19:24

For upwards of three years, Ephesus was the center of Paul's work....
"The apostle had for some time contemplated another missionary journey. He
desired again to visit the churches in Macedonia and Achaia, and after spending some
time at Corinth, to go to Jerusalem, after which he hoped to preach the gospel at Rome.
In pursuance of his plan, he sent Timothy and Erastus before him into Macedonia; but
feeling that the cause in Ephesus still demanded his presence, he decided to remain till
after Pentecost. An event soon occurred, however, which hastened his departure.

"The month of May was especially devoted to the worship of the goddess of Ephesus.
...The people gave themselves up to feasting, drunkenness, and the vilest debauchery....

"...The company of believers who met in the school of Tyrannus were an inhar-
monious note in the festive chorus. Ridicule, reproach, and insult were freely heaped
upon them. By the labors of Paul at Ephesus, the heathen worship had received a telling
blow. There was a perceptible falling-off in attendance at the national festival, and in
the enthusiasm of the worshipers."[1]

Sales of replicas of the goddess Diana and her temple were the economic mainstay
of those engaged in their manufacture. "The craftsmen at Ephesus created the uproar
because their profits were disappearing. Perhaps Demetrius himself, the fiercest of
all the rioters, did none of the actual work, but through employing many workmen
received a large share of the gains. All the imagery and symbolism of Artemis would
furnish an abundant opportunity for the craft of the silversmiths....

"...Every city had its temples and priests, its oracles and sanctuaries. Sacrifices and
feasts created a market for industry that would otherwise have been lacking. Thus
in early Christian times, when the gospel was placed in conflict with paganism, the
economic interference it presented not infrequently aroused the wrath of those whose
incomes were affected."[2]

Demetrius's financial pain would not elicit the response he needed from the general
populace. He needed to arouse a more general furor, so he hit on a more volatile
issue—civic pride. Paul was a direct threat to the reputation of their temple, their
goddess, and, therefore, their city.

Would you accept truth if it threatened your pet beliefs, employment, or source of income?

---

1. Ellen G. White, *Sketches From the Life of Paul* (Washington, DC: Review and Herald®, 1974), 140–142.
2. Francis D. Nichol, ed., *The Seventh-day Adventist Bible Commentary*, vol. 6 (Washington, DC: Review and Herald®, 1957), 379.

The City Clerk

For we are in danger of being called in question for today's uproar,
there being no reason which we may give to account for this disorderly gathering.
—Acts 19:40

D emetrius's speech circulated rapidly throughout the city, and soon, a mob was
searching for Paul. The brethren hid him. "Angels of God had been sent to guard
the apostle; his time to die a martyr's death had not yet come.

"Failing to find the object of their wrath, the mob seized 'Gaius and Aristarchus,
men of Macedonia, Paul's companions in travel,' and with these 'they rushed with
one accord into the theater.' "[1] Hearing his friends were in peril, Paul's first thought
was to go to the theater to address the rioters. This, his disciples would not let him
do. "Gaius and Aristarchus were not the prey the people sought; no serious harm to
them was apprehended. But should the apostle's pale, care-worn face be seen, it would
arouse at once the worst passions of the mob and there would not be the least human
possibility of saving his life."[2]

Attempting to distance themselves from the Christians, local Jews chose a Jew
named Alexander to speak for them. Their aim was to direct anger specifically at
Christians, not Jews in general. Seeing Alexander was Jewish, the mob refused to hear
him, rather, chanting "great is Diana of the Ephesians" for two hours. "At last, from
sheer exhaustion, they ceased, and there was a momentary silence. Then the recorder
of the city arrested the attention of the crowd, and by virtue of his office obtained a
hearing."[3] "Men of Ephesus, what man is there who does not know that the city of
Ephesus is temple guardian of the great goddess Diana, and of the image which fell
down from Zeus? Therefore, since these things cannot be denied, you ought to be quiet
and do nothing rashly. For you have brought these men here who are neither robbers
of temples nor blasphemers of your goddess. Therefore, if Demetrius and his fellow
craftsmen have a case against anyone, the courts are open and there are proconsuls. Let
them bring charges against one another. But if you have any other inquiry to make,
it shall be determined in the lawful assembly. For we are in danger of being called in
question for today's uproar, there being no reason which we may give to account for
this disorderly gathering" (Acts 19:35–40).

"God had raised up a great magistrate to vindicate His apostle and hold the tumultuous mob
in check."[4]

---

1. Ellen G. White, *The Acts of the Apostles* (Mountain View, CA: Pacific Press®, 1911), 293.
2. White, *Acts of the Apostles*, 293.
3. White, *Acts of the Apostles*, 294.
4. White, *Acts of the Apostles*, 295.

Part 1: Trouble in Corinth

Now I plead with you, brethren . . . , that you all speak the same thing,
and that there be no divisions among you, but that you be perfectly joined together.
—1 Corinthians 1:10

About this time there came to Ephesus members of the household of *Chloe*, a Christian family of high repute in Corinth.[1] Paul asked them regarding the condition of things, and they told him that the church was rent by divisions. . . . False teachers were leading the members to despise the instructions of Paul. The doctrines and ordinances of the gospel had been perverted. Pride, idolatry, and sensualism, were steadily increasing among those who had once been zealous in the Christian life.

"As this picture was presented before him, Paul saw that his worst fears were more than realized."[2] Divisions and splinter groups were tearing apart the Corinthian church.

Paul's Ephesus ministry "had been a season of incessant labor, of many trials, and of deep anguish. He had taught the people in public and from house to house, with many tears instructing and warning them. Continually he had been opposed by the Jews, who lost no opportunity to stir up the popular feeling against him. . . .

"News of apostasy in some of the churches of his planting caused him deep sorrow. He feared that his efforts for them might prove to be in vain. Many a sleepless night was spent in prayer and earnest thought as he learned of the methods employed to counteract his work. As he had opportunity and as their condition demanded, he wrote to the churches, giving reproof, counsel, admonition, and encouragement. In these letters the apostle does not dwell on his own trials, yet there are occasional glimpses of his labors and sufferings in the cause of Christ. Stripes and imprisonment, cold and hunger and thirst, perils by land and by sea, in the city and in the wilderness, from his own countrymen, from the heathen, and from false brethren—all this he endured for the sake of the gospel. He was 'defamed,' 'reviled,' made 'the offscouring of all things,' 'perplexed,' 'persecuted,' 'troubled on every side,' 'in jeopardy every hour,' 'always delivered unto death for Jesus' sake.'

"Amidst the constant storm of opposition, the clamor of enemies, and the desertion of friends the intrepid apostle almost lost heart. But he looked back to Calvary and with new ardor pressed on to spread the knowledge of the Crucified."[3] How could Paul get the church to unite under Christ?

Satan enjoys bringing petty divisions and doctrinal controversies into the church.

---

1. For Paul's initial visit to Corinth, see the readings for May 8–29.
2. Ellen G. White, *The Acts of the Apostles* (Mountain View, CA: Pacific Press®, 1911), 300; emphasis added.
3. White, *Acts of the Apostles*, 296, 297.

Part 2: The Christian Emphasis

For I determined not to know anything among you except Jesus Christ and Him crucified.
—1 Corinthians 2:2

Though Paul had sent both Timothy and Titus to the church at Corinth, he also dictated to Sosthenes "one of the richest, most instructive, and most powerful of all his letters,—the first extant Epistle to the Corinthians."[1] Paul spoke in a very forthright manner about the divisions that were shaking the church. Some were claiming to be followers of Paul, some of Apollos, some of Peter, and some of Christ. Each group had his or her own favorite preacher, and this was contrary to the Spirit of Christ. The Greeks were in danger of valuing the eloquence and skills of the particular orator they favored at the expense of the message. "The 'preaching of the cross' is the message of salvation through faith in the crucified Lord. Such a message appeared as the height of foolishness to the philosophy-loving Greek and to the ritualistic-minded Jew."[2]

"The preaching of the cross depends for its success, not upon the power of human reasoning and the charm of polished argumentation, but upon the impact of its simple truth attended by the power of the Holy Spirit."[3] "The Apostle Paul could meet eloquence with eloquence, logic with logic; he could intelligently enter into all controversies. But was he satisfied with this worldly knowledge? He writes: 'And I, brethren, when I came to you, came not with excellency of speech or of wisdom, declaring unto you the testimony of God. For I determined not to know any thing among you, save Jesus Christ, and him crucified.'

"Here is a very important lesson. . . .

". . . Paul was a very great teacher; yet he felt that without the Spirit of God working with him, all the education he might obtain would be of little account. We need to have this same experience. . . . All need individually to sit at the feet of Jesus, and listen to His words of instruction."[4]

Paul was entirely capable of debating theological minutia, but the Corinthians needed to hear about Jesus. Paul, therefore, stressed the most important part of the gospel. He stressed Jesus Christ and His sacrifice for humanity. The Cross is the centerpiece of the gospel.

The truth is—Jesus died for our sins. You can believe it and be saved—or not.

---

1. Ellen G. White, *Sketches From the Life of Paul* (Washington, DC: Review and Herald®, 1974), 151.
2. Francis D. Nichol, ed., *The Seventh-day Adventist Bible Commentary*, vol. 6 (Washington, DC: Review and Herald®, 1957), 665.
3. Nichol, *Seventh-day Adventist Bible Commentary*, vol. 6, 664.
4. Ellen G. White, MS 84, 1901.

Part 3: Educating the Imagination

But it is written: Eye has not seen, nor ear heard, nor have entered into the heart of man the things which God has prepared for those who love Him.

—1 Corinthians 2:9

The wisdom of God comes not from humans but from the Spirit of God. True education comes from the Bible and is not measured by college degrees and formal education. Paul told the Corinthians that their knowledge was immature because the yardstick they were using to measure it was inaccurate. "To those who relied on philosophy, logic, science, and intellectual discoveries, the idea that one who was put to death by the most humiliating form of punishment used by the Romans—crucifixion—could save them, was sheer nonsense."[1] Yet it is only through knowledge of Jesus Christ and His sacrifice that we are made wise unto salvation!

Paul told the Corinthians what Ellen White tells us today, "You need to dwell upon the assurances of God's Word, to hold them before the mind's eye. Point by point, day by day, repeat the lessons there given, over and over, until you learn the bearing and import of them. We see a little today, and by meditation and prayer, more tomorrow. Thus little by little, we take in the gracious promises until we can almost comprehend their full significance.

"Oh, how much we lose by not educating the imagination to dwell upon divine things, rather than upon the earthly. We may give fullest scope to the imagination, and yet, 'Eye hath not seen, nor ear heard, neither have entered into the heart of man, the things which God hath prepared for them that love him.' Fresh wonders will be revealed to the mind the more closely we apply it to divine things. We lose much by not talking more of Jesus and of heaven, the saints' inheritance. The more we contemplate heavenly things, the more new delights we shall see and the more will our hearts be brim full of thanks to our beneficent Creator."[2]

Our physical senses tell us of this world that surrounds us, but the "grand realities of the kingdoms of grace and glory cannot be fully understood either through the avenue of the senses or by the intellect."[3] "A continuous acquisition of knowledge is possible only for those who willingly submit to the guidance and illumination of the Holy Spirit (see Rom. 8:5, 14, 16)."[4]

Spiritual senses are needed to discern spiritual truths. "Blessed are the poor [humble] in spirit" (Matthew 5:3).

---

1. Francis D. Nichol, ed., *The Seventh-day Adventist Bible Commentary*, vol. 6 (Washington, DC: Review and Herald®, 1957), 666.
2. Ellen G. White, Letter 4, 1885.
3. Nichol, *Seventh-day Adventist Bible Commentary*, vol. 6, 671.
4. Nichol, *Seventh-day Adventist Bible Commentary*, vol. 6, 671.

Part 4: The Lord's Garden

Who then is Paul, and who is Apollos, but ministers through whom you believed, as the Lord gave to each one. I planted, Apollos watered, but God gave the increase.

—1 Corinthians 3:5, 6

P aul's method of preaching at Corinth had been simplistic. These were new Christians who could not yet understand the "meat" of the gospel. He, therefore, taught them the basics. Where Paul had given the members the "milk" of the elementary gospel, Apollos expanded upon these simple truths, carrying the members further along in their spiritual development. Paul, in his letter, uses metaphors of gardeners and builders to show why the workers are secondary. It is the project upon which they toil that is to be regarded as of primary importance! "For no other foundation can anyone lay than that which is laid, which is Jesus Christ" (1 Corinthians 3:11).

"He who plants and he who waters are not working at cross-purposes. They are united in their aims and objectives. It is ridiculous to set them up as rival leaders."[1] "There can be no stronger evidence in churches that the truths of the Bible have not sanctified the receivers than their attachment to some favorite minister, and their unwillingness to accept and be profited by the labors of some other teacher who is sent to them in the providence of God. The Lord sends help to His church as they need, not as they choose; for shortsighted mortals cannot discern what is for their best good. It is seldom that one minister has all the qualifications necessary to perfect any one church in all the requirements of Christianity; therefore God sends other ministers to follow him, one after another, each one possessing some qualifications in which the others were deficient.

"The church should gratefully accept these servants of Christ, even as they would accept their Master Himself. They should seek to derive all the benefit possible from the instruction which ministers may give them from the Word of God. But the ministers themselves are not to be idolized; there should be no religious pets and favorites among the people; it is the truths they bring which are to be accepted, and appreciated in the meekness of humility."[2] "Paul's warning [was] primarily directed toward those who by their schismatic policy were destroying the Corinthian church. . . . It is a fearful thing to bring injury to the church of God."[3]

Be warned—it is wrong to create divisions within the church! Severe punishment awaits those who do.

---

1. Francis D. Nichol, ed., *The Seventh-day Adventist Bible Commentary*, vol. 6 (Washington, DC: Review and Herald®, 1957), 675.

2. "Ellen G. White Comments—1 Corinthians," in *Seventh-day Adventist Bible Commentary*, ed. Francis D. Nichol, vol. 6, 1086.

3. Nichol, *Seventh-day Adventist Bible Commentary*, vol. 6, 678.

Part 5: God's Temple

Do you not know that you are the temple of God and that the Spirit of God dwells in you?
—1 Corinthians 3:16

The context of this verse makes plain that Paul is speaking to the Corinthian church as a whole. It is the responsibility of every church member to maintain unity and avoid dissension. "It is true, of course, that the individual Christian is also the dwelling place of the Holy Spirit, but this thought is given primary emphasis in [1 Corinthians] 6:19, 20."[1] Unfortunately, we cannot touch on every text written by Paul. Let's consider here the question, what is a Christian's responsibility to his or her body temple?

Paul speaks in 1 Corinthians 6 about the sin of immorality—"an evil to which the Corinthians were specially exposed. No doubt the believers were conscious of the wickedness of licentiousness, but they lived among people who not only practiced it but considered it a part of their normal living. . . . Man was created in the image of God (Gen. 1:27), for His glory (see 1 Cor. 6:20; Rev. 4:11), to reflect the divine image (Eph. 4:13 . . .), and to demonstrate God's power (see 1 Peter 2:9; 4:14); therefore the Christian is under obligation to preserve his body undefiled, that it may be a fitting offering to present to the Lord (see Rom. 12:1)."[2]

"God evaluates the human race highly, as shown by the fact that He paid an infinite price for man's redemption. This fact reveals the importance of each individual human being. Jesus would have come to the earth and given His life for one sinner (see Matt. 18:12–14 . . .). Being thus purchased by God, the redeemed sinner is morally obligated to live for God only, to obey all His commands, and to 'flee' from all forms of licentiousness. . . . Because men have been redeemed from eternal death, it is their duty to do all in their power to keep their bodies in the best condition, so that they may best glorify God by serving Him acceptably. . . . An understanding of physiology, anatomy, and the laws of health is necessary if the body is to be taken care of intelligently."[3]

"Christ's followers will not permit bodily appetites and desires to control them. Instead, they will make their bodies servants to regenerated minds that are constantly guided by divine wisdom. (see Rom. 6:13; 12:1; 1 Cor. 9:25, 27 . . .)."[4]

---

1. Francis D. Nichol, ed., *The Seventh-day Adventist Bible Commentary*, vol. 6 (Washington, DC: Review and Herald®, 1957), 677.

2. Nichol, *Seventh-day Adventist Bible Commentary*, vol. 6, 701.

3. Nichol, *Seventh-day Adventist Bible Commentary*, vol. 6, 703.

4. Nichol, *Seventh-day Adventist Bible Commentary*, vol. 6, 703.

Part 6: Boasting Factions

*Now these things, brethren, I have figuratively transferred to myself and Apollos
for your sakes, that you may learn in us not to think beyond what is written,
that none of you may be puffed up on behalf of one against the other.*

—1 Corinthians 4:6

Paul counsels the Corinthians to regard him and his fellow workers as ministers and stewards, not of men, but of God. Being called by God to their work in the ministry of the gospel, they were not to be considered as leaders of various factions in the church or as heads of conflicting parties."[1] The term *hupēretai*, "servants" or "ministers," comes from the term used to describe those who rowed the huge war galleys for the soldiers on the decks. These men served their commander in chief, and "those who are entrusted with the work of the gospel ministry are, in a special sense, the attendants of the great heavenly Commander in Chief, Jesus."[2]

"Paul makes it plain that it is wrong to entertain a harsh or unkind opinion regarding our fellow men. Being imperfect ourselves, we are not qualified to form correct estimates of the characters of others (see Matt. 7:1–3; Rom. 2:1–3; James 4:11, 12 . . .). It is particularly dangerous to indulge in destructive criticism of God's workers."[3] Congregations should also be careful of giving praise to God's servants, lest they become conceited and proud. God alone is to be exalted and praised. Paul in today's text applies these principles to himself and Apollos. Not all the religious leaders in Corinth who headed the various factions could call themselves servants of God and of the people. "Paul condemns the pride of those who exalted their party above others, or their party leader over other party leaders. Believers should consider themselves to be on a level with one another, and no Christian should regard any other as inferior to him or as deserving of contempt."[4]

"Since the entrance of sin into the world, it has been natural for men to indulge in pride, particularly in connection with their own accomplishments. In this tendency they are following the example of Satan, who fell from his high estate in heaven because of his insufferable pride (see Isa. 14:12–14; Eze. 28:15, 17)."[5]

"The Christian must guard against this fault at all times. Especially subtle is the temptation to yield to spiritual pride."[6]

1. Francis D. Nichol, ed., *The Seventh-day Adventist Bible Commentary*, vol. 6 (Washington, DC: Review and Herald®, 1957), 680.
2. Nichol, *Seventh-day Adventist Bible Commentary*, vol. 6, 680.
3. Nichol, *Seventh-day Adventist Bible Commentary*, vol. 6, 682.
4. Nichol, *Seventh-day Adventist Bible Commentary*, vol. 6, 682, 683.
5. Nichol, *Seventh-day Adventist Bible Commentary*, vol. 6, 683.
6. Nichol, *Seventh-day Adventist Bible Commentary*, vol. 6, 683.

Part 7: Immorality

It is actually reported that there is sexual immorality among you, and such sexual immorality as is not even named among the Gentiles—that a man has his father's wife!
—1 Corinthians 5:1

A mong the more serious of the evils that had developed among the Corinthian believers, was that of a return to many of the debasing customs of heathenism. One former convert had so far backslidden that his licentious course was a violation of even the low standard of morality held by the Gentile world. The apostle pleaded with the church to put away from among them 'that wicked person.' 'Know ye not,' he admonished them, 'that a little leaven leaveneth the whole lump? Purge out therefore the old leaven, that ye may be a new lump, as ye are unleavened.' "[1]

We know Paul was referring to a case of scandalous incest. First Corinthians 5:1 goes on to clarify the sin: "that a man has his father's wife!" "The Greek may mean that he had either married her or that he was simply maintaining her for immoral purposes. The father may earlier have died or his wife may have run away or have been divorced by him."[2] This was not the mother of the son but rather his stepmother. It made no difference in Jewish law (Leviticus 18:6–8), for the crime, in either case, was punishable by death (Leviticus 20:11). Add to this a congregation so puffed up and proud of their exclusivity that the offense was tolerated and not addressed. The Corinthians had problems!

"The presence of gross wickedness in the church is always a cause for sorrow to those members who have the best interests of their brethren at heart, and who are jealous for the good name of the church (see Jer. 13:17). The Lord makes it plain that those who truly mourn on account of the wrongs that prevail in the church will be spared in the time of test (see Eze. 9:4–6; 2 Peter 2:8, 9)....The Corinthian believers should have been much concerned over the evil in their midst and should have proceeded to remove the offender from the church. Such disciplinary measures should be conducted from proper motives. Never should anger, pride, revenge, party feelings, dislike, or any carnal sentiment of the natural heart prompt the church members to take action against an offending brother. On the contrary there should be compassionate love and tender pity manifested toward him, together with care lest anyone else fall into the same error."[3]

God cannot bless a church that knowingly allows open sin to exist within the membership.

---

1. Ellen G. White, *The Acts of the Apostles* (Mountain View, CA: Pacific Press®, 1911), 303, 304.
2. Francis D. Nichol, ed., *The Seventh-day Adventist Bible Commentary*, vol. 6 (Washington, DC: Review and Herald®, 1957), 689.
3. Nichol, *Seventh-day Adventist Bible Commentary*, vol. 6, 689.

Part 8: Lawsuits

Dare any of you, having a matter against another,
go to law before the unrighteous, and not before the saints?

—1 Corinthians 6:1

As if internal divisions, incest, and backsliding were not enough, members were suing each other before heathen judges instead of settling their differences within the church. Many of the courts were corrupt, and judges were easily bribed to render biased judgments. The good name of the church was being besmirched, and the lack of love between members was being highlighted on the community stage.

"Satan is constantly seeking to introduce distrust, alienation, and malice among God's people. We shall often be tempted to feel that our rights are invaded, even when there is no real cause for such feelings. Those whose love for self is stronger than their love for Christ and His cause will place their own interests first and will resort to almost any expedient to guard and maintain them. Even many who appear to be conscientious Christians are hindered by pride and self-esteem from going privately to those whom they think in error, that they may talk with them in the spirit of Christ and pray together for one another. When they think themselves injured by their brethren, some will even go to law instead of following the Saviour's rule [Matthew 18:15–18].

"Christians should not appeal to civil tribunals to settle differences that may arise among church members. Such differences should be settled among themselves, or by the church, in harmony with Christ's instruction. Even though injustice may have been done, the follower of the meek and lowly Jesus will suffer himself 'to be defrauded' rather than open before the world the sins of his brethren in the church.

"Lawsuits between brethren are a reproach to the cause of truth. Christians who go to law with one another expose the church to the ridicule of her enemies and cause the powers of darkness to triumph. They are wounding Christ afresh and putting Him to open shame. By ignoring the authority of the church, they show contempt for God, who gave to the church its authority."[1]

"The spirit of retaliation and self-justification is a direct denial of Christ."[2]

---

1. Ellen G. White, *The Acts of the Apostles* (Mountain View, CA: Pacific Press®, 1911), 305, 306.

2. Francis D. Nichol, ed., *The Seventh-day Adventist Bible Commentary*, vol. 6 (Washington, DC: Review and Herald®, 1957), 698.

Part 9: Marital Advice

*But I say to the unmarried and to the widows: It is good for them
if they remain even as I am; but if they cannot exercise self-control,
let them marry. For it is better to marry than to burn with passion.*

—1 Corinthians 7:8, 9

First Corinthians chapter seven answers questions the Corinthians had asked Paul to address. "It seems fitting that the topic of marriage should be dealt with first, in Paul's reply, in view of his earnest warning against fornication [found in chapters 5 and 6]. Then there were probably those in Corinth who wondered whether the rigid Jewish rules that made it obligatory for all, at least the men, to marry . . . , were applicable to Christians. Some in the church may have had no particular desire to marry, and may have asked Paul whether it would be acceptable for them to remain single. . . . Some Christians apparently believed that marriage was a sinful state, which ought to be avoided and if possible broken up. This would be an understandable reaction against the licentiousness that was so common in Corinth at the time. In their zeal to avoid anything in the nature of fornication they might swing over to the other extreme of complete abstention from the marriage relation."[1] Paul addresses several marriage-related questions in 1 Corinthians 7, including sexual expression in marriage, marriage between a Christian and a non-Christian, divorce, celibacy, advice to unmarried women, and advice to widows.

Was he married? "That Paul was previously married cannot be proved conclusively. According to Acts 26:10 Paul gave his voice against the saints, which has been interpreted to mean that he was a member of the Sanhedrin. . . .[2] Members of that body were required to be married. . . .[3] Furthermore, it is most natural to assume that Paul, as a strict Pharisee, would not have neglected what the Jews regarded as a sacred obligation, namely marriage. . . . His detailed counsel in this chapter suggests an intimate acquaintance with problems such as marriage would provide. There seems to be little doubt, therefore, that sometime prior to the writing of the First Epistle to the Corinthians, Paul had been married."[4]

Paul uses marriage as an example of the close relationship between Christ and His church (Ephesians 5:22–27). This shows Paul's high regard for the marital state as ordained by God.

---

1. Francis D. Nichol, ed., *The Seventh-day Adventist Bible Commentary*, vol. 6 (Washington, DC: Review and Herald®, 1957), 705, 706.
2. Compare Ellen G. White, *The Acts of the Apostles*, 112.
3. Compare Ellen G. White, *The Desire of Ages*, 133.
4. Nichol, *Seventh-day Adventist Bible Commentary*, vol. 6, 707.

Part 10: Relationships and Marriage Specifics

*Nevertheless, because of sexual immorality, let each man
have his own wife, and let each woman have her own husband.*

—1 Corinthians 7:2

The very nature of marriage implies that the granting or withholding of the marriage privilege should not be subject to the whim of either party. . . . ". . . Christians are told that they must not deprive one another of the intimate privileges of marriage, except for a limited time, under special circumstances and by mutual consent."[1] Paul's general advice for the unmarried bachelor or widow was that they should stay single unless they could not control their sex drive, in which case he urged that they marry. Christians already married should not divorce in accordance with the teachings of Jesus. "The Saviour declared that the marriage bond was sacred and unchangeable (see Matt. 5:31, 32; Mark 10:2–12; Luke 16:18). The command of Jesus leaves no room for the many excuses for legal separation that are accepted by the civil courts today, such as incompatibility, mental cruelty, and others of a more trivial nature."[2] Paul allowed one exception to his no-divorce rule. "A marriage to an unbeliever is to be regarded as binding on a believer so long as the unbeliever does not voluntarily separate himself [or herself] from his [or her] believing companion and enter into another marriage."[3]

Paul also spoke to one's station in life. Devotion to Christ should rank first in any decision regarding the future. Members were better off if they remained single, but they committed no sin in marrying should that become necessary. Time was short, and the world was passing away. Christians should not bind themselves to earthly possessions. "They will not allow anything, not even family relationships, to interfere with their determination to be ready for heaven."[4] Family responsibilities added another layer of stress during times of trouble. Single persons could better give their undivided attention and devotion to communion with God and preparation for His coming; therefore, verses 32–35 stress remaining single. Finally, Paul has a word for widows: remain single.

"God intended that nothing but death bring about a separation between husband and wife (. . . Matt. 19:5–9 . . .)."[5] Choose with care. Choose with prayer.

---

1. Francis D. Nichol, ed., *The Seventh-day Adventist Bible Commentary*, vol. 6 (Washington, DC: Review and Herald®, 1957), 707.
2. Nichol, *Seventh-day Adventist Bible Commentary*, vol. 6, 708.
3. Nichol, *Seventh-day Adventist Bible Commentary*, vol. 6, 709.
4. Nichol, *Seventh-day Adventist Bible Commentary*, vol. 6, 714.
5. Nichol, *Seventh-day Adventist Bible Commentary*, vol. 6, 718.

Part 11: Meat Offered to Idols

Therefore, if food makes my brother stumble,
I will never again eat meat, lest I make my brother stumble.
—1 Corinthians 8:13

In Corinth, it was next to impossible not to come into contact with meat that had been offered to pagan gods. Meals were offered within the temple, and not only had the meat being consumed been offered to gods but also the very eating of the meat constituted a form of worship. Social events were common on the temple grounds, and food consumed at these marriages and club meetings was presumed to have been blessed by the gods. The Corinthians wanted to know whether eating this meat was wrong now that they did not believe in idols. "There were some among the church members who could not regard food that had been sacrificed to idols as ordinary food, even though they no longer believed in the existence of idols. As a result of lifelong custom they could not completely dissociate themselves from the past. Partaking of such food placed them vividly in their former setting, a situation that was more than they could bear."[1]

Although there is only one true God, many Gentiles still believed in the heathen gods of the pagan world and worshiped them as well. They had once eaten the sacrificial meat and believed that by doing so, they were communing with the gods. These new Christians were in real danger of slipping back into pagan worship practices. If they saw fellow Christians eating in a pagan temple, they might feel it was justified for them to do so as well. There was a real danger for them because they might easily slip back into their old worship of pagan gods, and Jesus would become just another God among many.

Paul's advice on the matter came down to this: "The believer must always remember that he is his brother's keeper. It is his duty so to live that no word or deed of his shall in any way make it more difficult for someone else to live in harmony with the will of God. Personal convenience and inclination must not be the first consideration; one must give thought to the effect of his acts upon others."[2] How often do we stop and think about the example our actions have upon our church and its members? Too many times, little thought is given to how our acts reflect on our faith. Many go a step further and simply don't care to set any type of example. They feel they can do what they want, and no one can tell them otherwise. This attitude can poison a congregation and bring disrepute upon a church.

Followers of Jesus will deny self for the good of others. This is the essence of the spirit of Jesus.

1. Francis D. Nichol, ed., *The Seventh-day Adventist Bible Commentary*, vol. 6 (Washington, DC: Review and Herald®, 1957), 721.
2. Nichol, *Seventh-day Adventist Bible Commentary*, vol. 6, 722.

Part 12: Running the Race

*But I discipline my body and bring it into subjection, lest, when
I have preached to others, I myself should become disqualified.*

—1 Corinthians 9:27

Paul had taught the Corinthians that there was freedom in Christ. But there was a limit when it came to individual freedom. Paul had a right to expect to be supported by the congregations he ministered to, yet he chose not to exercise that right because it might be a stumbling block for some members. Paul consistently made himself subordinate to others so that he might win them to Jesus. He made himself "a servant to all, that I might win the more" (1 Corinthians 9:19). Such self-discipline is not an easy thing for even a strong Christian to exercise.

Paul closes his comparison of the freedom found in Christ and the self-denial needed to bring salvation to others by comparing the Christian life to an athlete training for a race. Paul knew the congregation paid special attention to the Isthmian games that took place regularly at Corinth. "The games consisted of contests in foot racing, boxing, wrestling, and throwing the discus. Paul alludes to two, foot racing (vs. 24, 25) and boxing (vs. 26, 27)....

"...The prize given to the victor consisted of a wreath of pine, laurel, olive, parsley, or apple leaves....

"...All who entered the Greek races put forth their best efforts to win the prize. They used all the skill and stamina they had acquired as a result of their intensive training. None of them was indifferent, lethargic, or careless. The crown of life eternal is offered to all, but only those who subject themselves to strict training will obtain the prize. This means that at all times the Christian will be guided in word, thought, and deed by the high standards found in the Bible, and will not be controlled by the desires and inclinations of his own heart....

"...Though eternal life is entirely the gift of God, it is given only to those who seek and strive for it with all their energy (see Rom. 2:7; Heb. 3:6, 14)."[1] Paul knew he must set both the training example and the race pace. "God will give eternal life only to those who use this present life as an opportunity to gain the victory over everything that would interfere with mental, physical, and spiritual health, thus demonstrating their true love for, and obedience to, the Saviour, who endured so much for them (see James 1:12; 1 Peter 5:4; Rev. 2:10; 3:10, 11; 7:14–17)."[2]

How hard are you training for the victor's heavenly crown?

---

1. Francis D. Nichol, ed., *The Seventh-day Adventist Bible Commentary*, vol. 6 (Washington, DC: Review and Herald®, 1957), 735, 736.
2. Nichol, *Seventh-day Adventist Bible Commentary*, vol. 6, 736, 737.

Part 13: God Is Faithful

No temptation has overtaken you except such as is common to man; but God is faithful, who will not allow you to be tempted beyond what you are able, but with the temptation will also make the way of escape, that you may be able to bear it.

—1 Corinthians 10:13

T he race is not to the swift, nor the battle to the strong. The weakest saint, as well as the strongest, may wear the crown of immortal glory. All may win who, through the power of divine grace, bring their lives into conformity to the will of Christ."[1] Those who fail will not be able to blame God for their failures. "God is true to His promises, true to the call He has extended to men to serve Him. If He permitted temptations to come to His people that were beyond their strength to overcome, then His promises would appear to be wholly unreliable (see Ps. 34:19; 1 Cor. 1:9; 2 Peter 2:9). The faithfulness of God is the Christian's source of security against the enemy. There is no security in depending on self, but if the believer relies entirely on the promises of our covenant-keeping God, he will be safe. However, he should remember that God will not deliver him if he deliberately places himself on the enemy's ground by going where he is likely to meet temptation (see Matt. 7:13, 14, 24, 25; 1 Cor. 9:25, 27; 10:14; Gal. 5:24; 2 Tim. 2:22 . . .)."[2]

Temptations develop character, yet "God does not tempt man (see James 1:13). Man has brought this condition of affairs upon himself by his disobedience (Gen. 1:27, 31; 3:15–19; Eccl. 7:29; Rom. 6:23). Since this is the case, God uses these experiences to develop human character according to His will (see 1 Peter 4:12, 13 . . .). When men are tempted, therefore, they should remember that the temptation comes, not because God sends it, but because He permits it. Moreover, if rightly met, in the strength God supplies, temptations may be the means of accelerating the Christian's growth in grace. Seeing that God has given assurance that temptations are never beyond the individual's strength to endure, man himself is entirely responsible for falling into sin.

". . . At the same time that God permits the trial or temptation to come, He will also have in readiness the means whereby we may gain the victory and escape from committing sin."[3]

Calling upon Jesus for deliverance, when troubles arise, is the right thing to do (Psalms 9:9; 27:5; 41:1; 91:15; 2 Peter 2:9; Revelation 3:10). He has promised deliverance.

---

1. Ellen G. White, *The Acts of the Apostles* (Mountain View, CA: Pacific Press®, 1911), 313.
2. Francis D. Nichol, ed., *The Seventh-day Adventist Bible Commentary*, vol. 6 (Washington, DC: Review and Herald®, 1957), 744.
3. Nichol, *Seventh-day Adventist Bible Commentary*, vol. 6, 744.

Part 14: It's Your Choice

Therefore, whether you eat or drink, or whatever you do, do all to the glory of God.
—1 Corinthians 10:31

In conclusion Paul sets forth a rule that is simple, easily understood, yet comprehensive, profound, and far reaching. Consciously and with unwavering determination the Christian must do everything, even the routine items of daily life, in such a way that God, not man, is honored. Such a course calls for constant dedication of all the powers of mind and body to Him, and daily surrender of all one's being to His Spirit (see Prov. 18:10; 1 Cor. 15:31; 2 Cor. 4:10; Col. 3:17)."[1] Concerning the question of eating foods offered as a part of idol worship, Paul concludes that the Christian must exercise his power of choice to do only those things that will bring glory to God. We are "to care for [our] bodies and to keep them fit to be temples of His Spirit (see 1 Cor. 6:19, 20). . . . The Christian ideal is the original diet provided by the Creator in Eden (Gen. 1:29)."[2]

Paul's "words of warning to the Corinthian church are applicable to all time and are especially adapted to our day. By idolatry he meant not only the worship of idols, but self-serving, love of ease, the gratification of appetite and passion. A mere profession of faith in Christ, a boastful knowledge of the truth, does not make a man a Christian. A religion that seeks only to gratify the eye, the ear, and the taste, or that sanctions self-indulgence, is not the religion of Christ."[3] "Christians are not at liberty to follow the promptings of the natural, unconverted heart and the impulses of the unregenerate body. They are under obligation to bring every thought, word, and deed into harmony with God's revealed will. . . .

". . . The Christian's first motive in living in harmony with the laws of God should be to promote the honor of God."[4] The second motive should be to see that one never acts in a manner that will adversely influence another by leading them to sin. "Paul had the all-absorbing purpose of saving men, and he was prepared to do whatever could be legitimately done in order to achieve this objective; therefore he was determined to make the interests of others superior to his own interests, in order that he might draw them to Christ."[5]

Christians should engage in only those physical, mental, spiritual, and moral acts that glorify God.

---

1. Francis D. Nichol, ed., *The Seventh-day Adventist Bible Commentary*, vol. 6 (Washington, DC: Review and Herald®, 1957), 750.
2. Nichol, *Seventh-day Adventist Bible Commentary*, vol. 6, 750.
3. Ellen G. White, *The Acts of the Apostles* (Mountain View, CA: Pacific Press®, 1911), 317.
4. Nichol, *Seventh-day Adventist Bible Commentary*, vol. 6, 750.
5. Nichol, *Seventh-day Adventist Bible Commentary*, vol. 6, 751.

Part 15: Worship Conflicts

Judge among yourselves. Is it proper for a woman *to pray to God with her head uncovered?*
—1 Corinthians 11:13; emphasis added

Paul next undertook to discuss proper worship decorum. It must be remembered that he wrote in the context of the worship customs and practices of his day. Paul was speaking of reverence in the house of the Lord. "In the time of Paul it was customary for Jewish, Greek, and Roman males to wear short hair. Among the Israelites it was looked upon as disgraceful for a man to have long hair, with the exception of one who had taken a vow as a Nazarite."[1] "Corinth was a Grecian city, and out of consideration for Grecian custom, Paul taught that in worshiping God in that city men should follow the usual manner of showing respect by removing the head covering in the presence of a superior. Men were not to act like women [and remain veiled during worship]."[2] "It is possible that the Corinthian women argued that in their discharge of spiritual functions such as prayer and prophesying they should appear uncovered as did the men (1 Cor. 11:4). Some may have also reasoned that the liberty of the gospel (see Gal. 3:28) set aside the obligation to observe various marks of distinction between the sexes. Paul exposed the falsity of their reasoning."[3]

"In view of the fact that anciently women did not go abroad with uncovered heads, it would be regarded as a disgrace to a woman and to her husband if she should appear publicly without a veil, especially in the capacity of a leader of worship. For a woman at Corinth to take public part in the services of the church with her head uncovered would give the impression that she acted shamelessly and immodestly, without the adorning of shamefacedness and sobriety (see 1 Tim. 2:9). Paul seems to reason that by thus discarding the veil, a recognized emblem of her sex and position, she shows a lack of respect for husband, father, the female sex in general, and Christ."[4] "The apostles neither taught nor followed the practice of sanctioning the appearance of women in public worship unveiled. The fact that in Christian churches elsewhere, in Judea particularly, the women did not take part in the services with uncovered heads should have decided the matter for the women of Corinth."[5]

One's behavior must not counter social conventions of the day nor disrupt worship services.

---

1. Francis D. Nichol, ed., *The Seventh-day Adventist Bible Commentary*, vol. 6 (Washington, DC: Review and Herald®, 1957), 758.
2. Nichol, *Seventh-day Adventist Bible Commentary*, vol. 6, 755.
3. Nichol, *Seventh-day Adventist Bible Commentary*, vol. 6, 755.
4. Nichol, *Seventh-day Adventist Bible Commentary*, vol. 6, 755, 756.
5. Nichol, *Seventh-day Adventist Bible Commentary*, vol. 6, 759.

Part 16: Spiritual Gifts

Now, concerning spiritual gifts, brethren, I do not want you to be ignorant.
—1 Corinthians 12:1

T he Corinthians had some concerns about spiritual gifts. The gifts of the Spirit were creating two major difficulties for the Corinthians believers. First, those who had not experienced the endowment were feeling left out, and second, those with the gifts were causing disruption in worship by their uncontrolled displays of the Spirit. Paul stressed that the gifts were diverse in nature (1 Corinthians 12:4–11), and he proceeded to give a listing of them moving from wisdom and knowledge to the more ecstatic gifts of speaking in tongues and interpretation of tongues. Despite this diversity, there must be unity within the church and the body of Christ (verses 12–26). Paul illustrates his point by using the various organs of the human body. Each member of the body has a job to do, and no part of the body can be dispensed with if the body is to function efficiently. Just so, the church needs all the gifts of the Spirit to make it whole. "Unity in diversity, and diversity in unity, is the arrangement that produces the best results."[1]

Paul wanted the Corinthians to realize that while they might have gifts, what they lacked was Christian love. "The lowliest member of the church is as much a member of the body of Christ as the most highly endowed (see Matt. 23:8–12; James 3:1; 1 Peter 5:3). All members are dear to Christ. He gave His life for all. He would have died for one soul (Luke 15:4–7 . . .)."[2] Spiritual gifts are "distributed by God; man [has] no part in apportioning them."[3] There is no need for pride in those who feel more highly gifted. Each member of the church has a position to fill just as each part of the human body has its function to perform for the good of the whole.

"Instead of pride and discontent, brethren should manifest love and sympathy for one another. Those who appear to be more generously gifted should cherish their less favored brethren and let them know that they appreciate what they are doing for the cause that is loved by all members of the body of Christ."[4] Paul also impressed upon the Corinthians that their current spiritual gifts were not necessarily their final gifts. "As in the parable of the Talents (. . . Matt. 25:14–30) faithfulness to duty may lead to increased endowments."[5]

Are you using the spiritual gifts God has bestowed upon you for the benefit of His church?

---

1. Francis D. Nichol, ed., *The Seventh-day Adventist Bible Commentary*, vol. 6 (Washington, DC: Review and Herald®, 1957), 774.
2. Nichol, *Seventh-day Adventist Bible Commentary*, vol. 6, 773.
3. Nichol, *Seventh-day Adventist Bible Commentary*, vol. 6, 773.
4. Nichol, *Seventh-day Adventist Bible Commentary*, vol. 6, 774.
5. Nichol, *Seventh-day Adventist Bible Commentary*, vol. 6, 777.

Part 17: The Body of Christ

Now you are the body of Christ, and members individually.
—1 Corinthians 12:27

The analogy Paul uses of the human body and its interrelated parts is perfect when one wishes to understand the distribution and use of spiritual gifts. Paul reminds us that the church is the body of Christ, one body with Christ as the head. Despite our diversity, there should be unity in Him. "There was apparently a spirit of discontent on the part of some in Corinth with the way God had distributed the gifts. Those who did not hold prominent offices in the church seemed to be disgruntled, feeling that if they were not ministers or teachers they were of no account. By an effective illustration from the human body Paul sought to dispel these false ideas, pointing to the absurdity that would result if all parts of the human body were fused into one particular member, such as the eye or the ear.

"... For the hands, feet, eyes, ears, etc., to perform their allotted service they must be united in the body; not one of them can function if that union is broken. If all the strength of the body were to be channeled into one particular member such as the eye, all other parts would suffer, and the eye itself would become useless. Thus Paul emphasizes that any interference with the Creator's plan for the orderly operation of the body is not beneficial, but harmful, in its results."[1] "The idea is that each individual member has his own responsibility to serve God in his own place and according to his own function."[2]

So whether you have been given wisdom, knowledge, faith, the ability to heal, to work miracles, discern spirits, speak in divers tongues, or interpret tongues, whatever your gift, you must use it to improve the church. Whether you fill the position of missionary, minister, prophet, teacher, miracle worker, healer, helper, administrator, or linguist, you are important to God's cause! "The vine has many branches, but though all the branches are different, they do not quarrel. In diversity there is unity. All the branches obtain their nourishment from one source. This is an illustration of the unity that is to exist among Christ's followers. In their different lines of work they all have but one Head. The same Spirit, in different ways, works through them. There is harmonious action, though the gifts differ. . . . The man [or woman] who is truly united with Christ will never act as though he [or she] were a complete whole in himself [or herself]."[3]

I am the vine, you are the branches. He who abides in Me, and I in him, bears much fruit. (John 15:5)

---

1. Francis D. Nichol, ed., *The Seventh-day Adventist Bible Commentary*, vol. 6 (Washington, DC: Review and Herald®, 1957), 773, 774.
2. Nichol, *Seventh-day Adventist Bible Commentary*, vol. 6, 776.
3. Ellen G. White, Letter 19, 1901.

Part 18: Christians Love!

Though I speak with the tongues of men and of angels, but have not love,
I have become sounding brass or a clanging cymbal.
—1 Corinthians 13:1

Ellen G. White writes, "The Lord desires me to call the attention of his people to the thirteenth chapter of First Corinthians. Read this chapter every day, and from it obtain comfort and strength. Learn from it the value that God places on sanctified, heaven-born love, and let the lesson that it teaches come home to your hearts. Learn that Christlike love is of heavenly birth, and that without it all other qualifications are worthless."[1] According to Paul, love is more precious than the gifts of the Spirit, and this is what the Corinthians should have been seeking.

"No matter how high the profession, he whose heart is not filled with love for God and his fellow men is not a true disciple of Christ. Though he should possess great faith and have power even to work miracles, yet without love his faith would be worthless. He might display great liberality; but should he, from some other motive than genuine love, bestow all his goods to feed the poor, the act would not commend him to the favor of God. In his zeal he might even meet a martyr's death, yet if not actuated by love, he would be regarded by God as a deluded enthusiast or an ambitious hypocrite."[2]

How great it would be if every member of the family of God always exhibited love for fellow believers. "Love is a plant of heavenly origin, and if we would have it flourish in our hearts, we must cultivate it daily. Mildness, gentleness, long-suffering, not being easily provoked, bearing all things, enduring all things,—these are the fruits upon the precious tree of love."[3] "A Christian is one who follows Christ. Therefore he is one who denies the clamors of the natural heart for devotion to self, and who is willing to sacrifice his own comfort, time, ease, wealth, and talents to advance the welfare of mankind."[4] "For the Christian, personal opinions, desires, and practices are supplanted by love in the interests of the comfort, convenience, and happiness of others."[5]

"Love puts the best possible construction on the behavior of others. One under the control of love is not censorious, disposed to find fault, or to impute wrong motives to others."[6]

---

1. Ellen G. White, "The Value of Christlike Love," *Advent Review and Sabbath Herald*, July 21, 1904, 7.
2. Ellen G. White, *The Acts of the Apostles* (Mountain View, CA: Pacific Press®, 1911), 318, 319.
3. Ellen G. White, "Love One Another," *Advent Review and Sabbath Herald*, June 5, 1888, 1.
4. Francis D. Nichol, ed., *The Seventh-day Adventist Bible Commentary*, vol. 6 (Washington, DC: Review and Herald®, 1957), 782.
5. Nichol, *Seventh-day Adventist Bible Commentary*, vol. 6, 781.
6. Nichol, *Seventh-day Adventist Bible Commentary*, vol. 6, 782.

Part 19: The Gift of Prophecy

Pursue love, and desire spiritual gifts, but especially that you may prophesy.
—1 Corinthians 14:1

A pparently, there was confusion and chaos going on in worship services at Corinth. The Corinthians wanted Paul to give them some guidance on how their worship services should be conducted. It must be remembered that early Christian worship services differed from those we have come to accept as "traditional." Christian worship in the first century AD was a cacophony of noise. Anyone who felt the urge could speak, and many did so simultaneously. Things rapidly could go downhill, resulting in chaos. Paul suggested those who spoke in tongues should be limited to three and that there must be a translator present (1 Corinthians 14:27). If no translator was present, the speaker should remain silent (verse 28). He applied the same formula to those who had a prophecy to relate. They should limit themselves to two or three and let there be no repetition if two had the same prophecy to relate (verses 29–32). Most of all, the gifts were for the edification of the whole church. "God is the author of peace in all places, and true believers in Him will seek to preserve peace in worshiping Him, by restraining any desire to exalt self by an untimely display of the endowments of the Spirit given to them."[1]

"The Corinthians exalted the gift of tongues above that of prophecy, doubtless because of its spectacular nature. Some may have despised prophecy, as appears to have been the case in Thessalonica (1 Thess. 5:20). The Corinthians were urged to pursue love, which leads men to seek gifts that can benefit others as well as themselves. Men should not seek for the gifts in order to exalt themselves in any way, but that they might serve God better and bring more help to His church."[2] Twenty-first-century Christians view prophets from a different perspective than did first-century Christians. We are more skeptical of one claiming to have a message from God. Our approach to someone claiming the gift of prophecy should be one of caution. We are not left without tests to apply to those calling themselves a prophet, and we are told to test them (1 John 4:1). Do you know the four tests of a prophet?

(1) By their fruits, you will know them (Matthew 7:18–20). (2) They will speak according to the law and the testimonies (Isaiah 8:20). (3) They will confess Jesus Christ has come in the flesh (1 John 4:1–3). (4) What they prophesy happens (Deuteronomy 18:21, 22).

---

1. Francis D. Nichol, ed., *The Seventh-day Adventist Bible Commentary*, vol. 6 (Washington, DC: Review and Herald®, 1957), 793.
2. Nichol, *Seventh-day Adventist Bible Commentary*, vol. 6, 787, 788.

Part 20: Speaking in Tongues

I thank my God I speak with tongues more than you all; yet in the church
I would rather speak five words with my understanding, that I may teach others also,
than ten thousand words in a tongue.

—1 Corinthians 14:18, 19

Lest he be accused of unduly belittling any gift of the Spirit, Paul expressed a desire that all the believers could speak with tongues. It was an important gift, and had a prominent part to play in the work of the church. However, this gift was not to overshadow the less spectacular but more important gift of prophecy."[1] So what was the "speaking in tongues" that Paul mentions in his letter to the Corinthians? The "gift of tongues" the Spirit bestowed at Pentecost was an ability to speak various languages or dialects (Acts 2). This gift greatly aided the church in its global mission outreach. Commentators hold two views regarding Paul's reference. The first, "the language spoken under the influence of the gift was a foreign language, one that could be easily understood by a foreigner of that tongue."[2] The second view is that "the language was not one spoken by men, and that thus no man could understand unless there was present an interpreter who possessed the gift of the Spirit to understand the language (1 Cor. 12:10)."[3]

"Because of certain obscurities with regard to the precise manner in which the gift of tongues was anciently manifested, Satan has found it easy to counterfeit the gift. Incoherent [outbursts] were well known and widely met with in pagan worship. Also in later times, under the guise of Christianity, various manifestations of so-called tongues have from time to time appeared. However, when these manifestations are compared with the scriptural specifications of the gift of tongues they are found to be something quite at variance with the gift anciently imparted by the Spirit. These manifestations must therefore be rejected as spurious. However, the presence of the counterfeit must not lead us to think meanly of the genuine. The proper manifestation of the gift with which Paul deals [in 1 Corinthians 14] performed a useful function. True, it was abused, but Paul attempted to correct the abuses and to assign the operation of the gift to its proper place and function."[4]

How would you respond to someone exercising this gift in your church? Would it seem odd? Consider: five words understood in worship are preferable to a torrent of incoherent phrases.

---

1. Francis D. Nichol, ed., *The Seventh-day Adventist Bible Commentary*, vol. 6 (Washington, DC: Review and Herald®, 1957), 788.
2. Nichol, *Seventh-day Adventist Bible Commentary*, vol. 6, 795.
3. Nichol, *Seventh-day Adventist Bible Commentary*, vol. 6, 795.
4. Nichol, *Seventh-day Adventist Bible Commentary*, vol. 6, 796.

Part 21: Order in Worship

For God is not the author of confusion but of peace, as in all the churches of the saints.
—1 Corinthians 14:33

Paul plainly states that the worship service should be orderly. "God is not a being who either has in Himself or produces disorder, disunion, discord, or confusion. The true worship of God will not result in disorder of any kind. This verse presents a general, governing principle of Christianity that is derived from the nature of God. He is the God of peace, and it is not to be taught that He could be pleased by a form of worship characterized by confusion of any kind (see Rom. 15:33; 16:20; 1 Thess. 5:23; Heb. 13:20). Christianity tends to promote order (see 1 Cor. 14:40). No one who is submissive to the leading of the Holy Spirit will be disposed to engage in scenes of disorder and confusion such as that which would result from several persons speaking at the same time in tongues or in prophecy. The worshiper will be ready to express his love and gratitude to God in prayer and testimony, but he will express it with seriousness, tenderness, and a genuine respect for the maintenance of order in the house of God, and not with a desire to interrupt and disturb the dignified worship of God.

". . . This principle of orderly procedure in the worship of God, Paul notes, prevails in all the churches, and should therefore be accepted in Corinth also."[1]

The worship service at Corinth must have been extremely raucous. The church was also experiencing divisions and schisms. Believers were segregating themselves based on their own hierarchy of spiritual gifts, their financial status, and their talent. This Paul condemned by stating they needed overarching love for each other rather than a spirit of competitiveness and exclusion.

Worship had become a showcase for talent and show. "The Christian must always guard against the evil of formality in public worship. God looks not for outward show and display of talent, but for sincere, loving devotion to Him expressed in prayer and praise (see John 4:24 . . .). Dignity and reverence are essential, but they will be inspired by a genuine sense of the majesty and greatness of God, and not by any response to the promptings of the natural heart for self-exaltation."[2]

Where does your church stand when it comes to applause for a performance?

---

1. Francis D. Nichol, ed., *The Seventh-day Adventist Bible Commentary*, vol. 6 (Washington, DC: Review and Herald®, 1957), 792, 793.
2. Nichol, *Seventh-day Adventist Bible Commentary*, vol. 6, 795.

Part 22: *Women* Be Silent

Let your women keep silent in the churches, for they are not permitted to speak;
but they are to be submissive, as the law also says.

—1 Corinthians 14:34

W hy would Paul write such a thing? "Some have found difficulty in understanding this prohibition in terms, not only of our modern ideas of the place of women in the church, but also of the place and service of *women* in Bible history (see Judges 4:4; 2 Kings 22:14; Luke 2:36, 37; Acts 21:9). Paul himself commended the *women* who labored with him in the gospel (Phil. 4:3). There is no doubt that women played a definite part in the life of the church. Why, then, should they be prevented from speaking in public? The answer is found in v. 35."[1] "And if they want to learn something, let them ask their own husbands at home; for it is shameful for women to speak in church" (1 Corinthians 14:35). "Greek and Jewish custom dictated that women should be kept in the background in public affairs. Violation of this custom would be looked upon as disgraceful and would bring reproach upon the church.

"...The church at Corinth was not the first, but one of the last, that Paul had founded. Hence that church was not in a position to prescribe rules of conduct for other churches, or to claim the right to differ from them. It was not alone in proclaiming the gospel; therefore it must give due consideration to generally accepted principles of behavior and procedure in worship. The Corinthian church had apparently adopted unusual customs, such as that of permitting women to appear in public services unveiled (...[1 Corinthians] 11:5, 16) and to speak in the church in a way unknown to other churches. They had allowed irregularity and confusion to exist in the church. But they had no right to differ from other churches in this way, nor had they any right to tell the other churches that they too should tolerate such confusion and disorder."[2]

Paul was very much aware that Corinth was home to *Chloe*, the freedwoman who aided in the establishment of the church. After all, members of her household had brought the report of church turmoil to Paul at Ephesus. Paul's advice to the women of Corinth sustained his belief that a Christian should rightly represent the gospel to others, giving offense to no one (1 Corinthians 10:32, 33).

Customs change. Requiring women to be silent in church today would deprive us of their wisdom!

---

1. Francis D. Nichol, ed., *The Seventh-day Adventist Bible Commentary*, vol. 6 (Washington, DC: Review and Herald®, 1957), 793; emphasis added.
2. Nichol, *Seventh-day Adventist Bible Commentary*, vol. 6, 793, 794.

Part 23: Christ Is Risen

Christ died for our sins according to the Scriptures, and . . . He was buried,
and . . . He rose again the third day according to the Scriptures.
—1 Corinthians 15:3, 4

In the lowering of the moral standard among the Corinthian believers, there were those who had given up some of the fundamental features of their faith. Some had gone so far as to deny the doctrine of the resurrection. Paul met this heresy with a very plain testimony regarding the unmistakable evidence of the resurrection of Christ. He declared that Christ, after His death, 'rose again the third day according to Scriptures,' after which 'He was seen of Cephas, then of the Twelve: after that, He was seen of above five hundred brethren at once; of whom the greater part remain unto this present, but some are fallen asleep. After that, He was seen of James; then of all the apostles. And last of all He was seen of me also.'

"With convincing power the apostle set forth the great truth of the resurrection. 'If there be no resurrection of the dead,' he argued, 'then is Christ not risen: and if Christ be not risen, then is our preaching vain, and your faith is also vain. Yea, and we are found false witnesses of God; because we have testified of God that He raised up Christ: whom He raised not up, if so be that the dead rise not. For if the dead rise not, then is not Christ raised: and if Christ be not raised, your faith is vain; ye are yet in your sins. Then they also which are fallen asleep in Christ are perished. If in this life only we have hope in Christ, we are of all men most miserable. But now is Christ risen from the dead, and become the first fruits of them that slept.' "[1]

"After His resurrection, Christ did not show Himself to any save His followers, but testimony in regard to His resurrection was not wanting. It came from various sources, from the five hundred who assembled in Galilee to see their risen Lord. This testimony could not be quenched. The sacred facts of Christ's resurrection were immortalized."[2] There is an "emptiness of faith without the resurrection of Christ; vs. 16, 17 reveal the hopelessly lost condition of man apart from the resurrection. Although it is true that 'Christ died for our sins' (v. 3), it is also true that He 'was raised again for our justification' (Rom. 4:25 . . .)."[3]

Praise God that He called Jesus from the dead. For by the Father's acceptance of His Son's sacrifice for our sins, we are saved by our belief in Him!

---

1. Ellen G. White, *The Acts of the Apostles* (Mountain View, CA: Pacific Press®, 1911), 319, 320.
2. Ellen G. White, MS 115, 1897.
3. Francis D. Nichol, ed., *The Seventh-day Adventist Bible Commentary*, vol. 6 (Washington, DC: Review and Herald®, 1957), 803.

Part 24: What, No Resurrection?

Now if Christ is preached that He has been raised from the dead,
how do some among you say that there is no resurrection of the dead?
—1 Corinthians 15:12

Paul has already dealt with the historical facts surrounding the resurrection of Jesus. Now, he wonders aloud how the Corinthians can continue to deny that there will be a general resurrection of the saints. Paul develops his argument for the resurrection in the next eight verses. "If a resurrection of the dead is considered to be impossible, and belief in it to be absurd, then it must follow that Christ did not rise from the grave, for the general objection to the resurrection of the dead would apply in His case also. Therefore it is not possible to deny the general resurrection without denying the well-established resurrection of Jesus. This, says Paul, is the inevitable result of denying the resurrection, and involves a denial of Christianity, the removal of the Christian's hope of eternal life."[1]

Without the resurrection of Jesus, baptism would also lose its significance. "Baptism, which is a type of the death, burial, and resurrection of Christ, would lose its significance if there were no resurrection, for the exhortation is given, to rise and 'walk in newness of life,' even as Christ was raised from the dead (see Rom. 6:3, 4)."[2]

There were those among the Corinthians who taught that at the end of life on earth, humans became spirits. Paul was concerned "over the insidious teaching that had turned some of the Corinthian believers away from the truth about the resurrection. Satan tries to undermine faith in the resurrection in order to make it easier for men to accept the first great lie, with which he denied God's sentence of death for disobedience (see Gen. 2:17; 3:4). If man does not really die when this earthly life comes to an end, then there is no need for a resurrection. If, on the other hand, death is a cessation of existence, then further life would be dependent upon the resurrection (. . . Ps. 146:4; Eccl. 9:5, 6, 10)."[3] "If there be no resurrection, then those who have died remain dead, the prospects held out by Christianity are a cruel delusion, and all the righteous dead are doomed to remain asleep in their graves. No Christian could accept such hope-destroying conclusions. Thus Paul's reasoning again stresses the vital position of the resurrection in Christian doctrine."[4]

We have hope—hope in the coming of the Lord!

---

1. Francis D. Nichol, ed., *The Seventh-day Adventist Bible Commentary*, vol. 6 (Washington, DC: Review and Herald®, 1957), 802.
2. Nichol, *Seventh-day Adventist Bible Commentary*, vol. 6, 803.
3. Nichol, *Seventh-day Adventist Bible Commentary*, vol. 6, 803.
4. Nichol, *Seventh-day Adventist Bible Commentary*, vol. 6, 803.

Part 25: A Mysterious New Body

*Behold, I tell you a mystery: We shall not all sleep, but we shall
all be changed—in a moment, in the twinkling of an eye, at the last trumpet.*
—1 Corinthians 15:51, 52

Paul wanted the Corinthians to embrace the future resurrection of the saints. He, therefore, painted a picture of that glorious day when Jesus returns a second time to claim His church. "There are some who will not die, but who will be translated from the imperfect physical state to the perfect heavenly state. This instantaneous change will make them like the resurrected saints."[1] "The time when this glorious transformation will take place is . . . at the second coming of Christ, for it is then that the 'trump of God' will sound, and faithful believers who have died will be raised in bodies that are entirely free from all effects of sin (Col. 3:4; . . . 1 Thess. 4:16). Then Christians who are alive and looking eagerly for the coming of their Lord will undergo a marvelous change, whereby all traces of corruption and imperfection will be removed from their bodies, which will be made like unto Christ's glorious body (see Phil. 3:20, 21; 1 John 3:2)."[2]

"The resurrection of Jesus was a sample of the final resurrection of all who sleep in him. The risen body of the Saviour, his deportment, the accents of his speech, were all familiar to his followers. In like manner will those who sleep in Jesus rise again. We shall know our friends even as the disciples knew Jesus. Though they may have been deformed, diseased, or disfigured in this mortal life, yet in their resurrected and glorified body their individual identity will be perfectly preserved, and we shall recognize, in the face radiant with the light shining from the face of Jesus, the lineaments of those we love."[3] At the Second Coming, death, the result of sin, will be forever destroyed. "When, at Christ's coming, the amazing transformation from mortal to immortal has taken place, both of the righteous dead and the righteous living, then man's great enemy will no longer trouble the redeemed. The last thought that occupied their minds as the shadow of death overtook the saints was that of approaching sleep, their last feeling was that of the pain of death. As they see that Christ has come and conferred on them the gift of immortality, their first sensation will be one of great rejoicing that never again will they succumb to the power of death."[4]

What a glorious day that will be!

---

1. Francis D. Nichol, ed., *The Seventh-day Adventist Bible Commentary*, vol. 6 (Washington, DC: Review and Herald®, 1957), 812.
2. Nichol, *Seventh-day Adventist Bible Commentary*, vol. 6, 812.
3. Ellen G. White, *The Spirit of Prophecy*, vol. 3 (Oakland, CA: Pacific Press®, 1878), 219.
4. Nichol, *Seventh-day Adventist Bible Commentary*, vol. 6, 813.

Part 26: Your Character Is Preserved

For this corruptible must put on incorruption, and this mortal must put on immortality.
—1 Corinthians 15:53

Paul continues to put forth his belief in the resurrection and how it will occur. He writes, "But someone will say, 'How are the dead raised up? And with what body do they come?' " (1 Corinthians 15:35). He uses the example of a kernel of grain that is planted, decays, and then comes forth as a new kernel producing wheat. "Our personal identity is preserved in the resurrection, though not the same particles of matter or material substance as went into the grave. The wondrous works of God are a mystery to man. The spirit, the character of man, is returned to God there to be preserved. In the resurrection every man will have his own character. God in His own time will call forth the dead, giving again the breath of life, and bidding the dry bones live. The same form will come forth, but it will be free from disease and every defect. It lives again bearing the same individuality of features, so that friend will recognize friend. There is no law of God in nature which shows that God gives back the same identical particles of matter which composed the body before death. God shall give the righteous dead a body that will please Him.

"Paul illustrates this subject by the kernel of grain sown in the field. The planted kernel decays, but there comes forth a new kernel. The natural substance in the grain that decays is never raised as before, but God giveth it a body as it hath pleased Him. A much finer material will compose the human body, for it is a new creation, a new birth. It is sown a natural body, it is raised a spiritual body."[1]

"We have a living, risen Saviour. He burst the fetters of the tomb after He had lain there three days, and in triumph. He proclaimed over the rent sepulcher of Joseph, 'I am the resurrection and the life.'

"And He is coming. Are we getting ready for Him? Are we ready so that if we shall fall asleep, we can do so with hope in Jesus Christ? Are you laboring for the salvation of your brothers and sisters?"[2]

Our resurrected bodies will be "flesh and blood," for we will be like Christ (Luke 24:39).

---

1. Ellen G. White, MS 76, 1900.
2. Ellen G. White, MS 18, 1894.

Part 27: The Collection

On the first day of the week let each one of you lay something aside,
storing up as he may prosper, that there be no collections when I come.
—1 Corinthians 16:2

Paul now concludes his letter to the believers in Corinth. "This verse is often cited in support of Sunday observance. However, when it is examined with the apostle's project for the poor believers in Jerusalem, it is seen to be an exhortation to systematic planning on the part of the Corinthian church members for their part in the offering. There is nothing in the verse that even remotely suggests that there is any sacredness attached to the first day of the week. . . . If all believers today were to adopt this principle of systematic benevolence, there would be an abundance of means for speedily carrying the message of salvation to all the world."[1]

Throughout his ministry to the Gentiles, Paul always held the Jewish believers and their poverty close to his heart. He longed to see Jew and Gentile united together in bonds of love and mutual support. "The economic conditions and burdens in Palestine were oppressive upon both Jew and Christian. It has been estimated that the combined taxes, both civil and religious, reached the staggering total of almost 40 per cent of a person's income. For the common people there was no hope of escaping poverty. In addition, the church in Jerusalem suffered much persecution. The majority of the believers there were poor, some of them as a result of becoming Christians. . . . They needed help from their more fortunately situated brethren in other places. . . . Paul had undertaken the responsibility of soliciting help for them from other churches that he visited, and he appealed to the Corinthians to do their share by setting before them the example of their sister churches in Achaia and Macedonia (see Rom. 15:25, 26; 2 Cor. 8:1–7)."[2]

Paul concludes by mentioning Fortunatus, Achaicus, and Stephanas. They probably brought the Corinthian concerns to Paul, and he may have entrusted his answer to them. Signing his letter "with [his] own hand," he sought to frustrate the designs of those who would forge letters from him.

We need to support our brethren in Christ as well as give liberally to spread the gospel. How tight are your purse strings? "The coming of Jesus should be the theme of every Christian's life."[3]

---

1. Francis D. Nichol, ed., *The Seventh-day Adventist Bible Commentary*, vol. 6 (Washington, DC: Review and Herald®, 1957), 815.
2. Nichol, *Seventh-day Adventist Bible Commentary*, vol. 6, 815.
3. Nichol, *Seventh-day Adventist Bible Commentary*, vol. 6, 818.

Times of Concern

After the uproar [with the silversmiths over Diana] had ceased, Paul called the disciples to himself, embraced them, and departed to go to Macedonia.

—Acts 20:1

Paul had spent a total of three years at Ephesus (AD 54–57), and now it was time to leave. He wanted to revisit the churches he had formed during his second missionary tour, especially those at Thessalonica and Berea. Always in the back of his mind, however, was the controversy swirling through the congregation at Corinth. Aquila and *Priscilla* were no longer at Corinth, for they had accompanied Paul to Ephesus at the close of his second missionary tour. The Corinthians were in trouble, and Paul wasn't entirely persuaded that rushing to their aid might not be the worst thing he could do.

"Tarrying for a time at Troas, 'to preach Christ's gospel,' he found some who were ready to listen to his message. 'A door was opened unto me of the Lord,' he afterward declared of his labors in this place. But successful as were his efforts at Troas, he could not remain there long. 'The care of all the churches,' and particularly of the church at Corinth, rested heavily on his heart. He had hoped to meet Titus at Troas and to learn from him how the words of counsel and reproof sent to the Corinthian brethren had been received, but in this he was disappointed. 'I had no rest in my spirit,' he wrote concerning this experience, 'because I found not Titus my brother.' . . .

"During this time of anxiety concerning the church at Corinth, Paul hoped for the best; yet at times feelings of deep sadness would sweep over his soul, lest his counsels and admonitions might be misunderstood. 'Our flesh had no rest,' he afterward wrote, 'but we were troubled on every side; without were fightings, within were fears.' "[1]

"After the letter [1 Corinthians] had been dispatched, Paul feared lest that which he had written might wound too deeply those whom he desired to benefit. He keenly dreaded a further alienation and sometimes longed to recall his words. Those who, like the apostle, have felt a responsibility for beloved churches or institutions, can best appreciate his depression of spirit and self-accusing."[2]

"The servants of God who bear the burden of His work for this time know something of the same experience of labor, conflict, and anxious care that fell to the lot of the great apostle."[3]

---

1. Ellen G. White, *The Acts of the Apostles* (Mountain View, CA: Pacific Press®, 1911), 323, 324.
2. White, *Acts of the Apostles*, 321, 322
3. White, *Acts of the Apostles*, 322.

Paul's Second Greatest Heartache

For out of much affliction and anguish of heart I wrote to you, with many tears, not that you should be grieved, but that you might know the love which I have so abundantly for you.
—2 Corinthians 2:4

Paul's first and greatest heartache was the rejection of Jesus Christ as Messiah by the majority of his fellow Jews; his second was administering stern reproofs and discipline. "Christ wept as He yearned for His people (Matt. 23:37, 38). Reproof intended to win back the erring must never be done in harshness or with an overbearing attitude, but with great tenderness and compassion. Paul possessed boundless courage in the face of danger, persecution, and death, but he wept when compelled to censure his brethren in Christ (see Acts 20:31; Phil. 3:18).

"Successful dealing with sinners is not achieved by bitter denunciation, by ridicule or sarcasm, by making public their sins. What these harsh weapons cannot accomplish may be done by affectionate concern, with 'many tears.' . . .

". . . It is never a demonstration of love to pass by sin. Sometimes love must needs be severe. Love in the church does not mean the display of pity and long-suffering toward obdurate members at the expense of the integrity of the church or the safety of other members. To consider love as something always necessarily flaccid is to identify it with weakness, lack of initiative, forcefulness, and courage. The minister's love for his people means more than a feeling of tender emotion for them, it means also a continuous attitude of concern for their well-being, joy in their spiritual growth, sadness over their sins, strong leadership, and firm, unyielding courage when the enemy of souls seeks to scatter the flock. Paul, as a minister of the everlasting gospel, was prepared to go through any amount of suffering, even to the sacrifice of life itself, for the salvation of others."[1] For a year and a half, Paul had labored for the Corinthians. Now Satan was active in Paul's absence, trying to cause these new converts to slip back into old lifestyles.

Satan's goal in bringing temptations is to confuse our consciences. Rationalizing sinful behavior is the first step on a long, slippery slope to apostasy. Any soul still cherishing sin, refusing to surrender the entire will to God, is in danger!

---

1. Francis D. Nichol, ed., *The Seventh-day Adventist Bible Commentary*, vol. 6 (Washington, DC: Review and Herald®, 1957), 836, 837.

Paul's Unrecorded "Painful" Visit to Corinth

Moreover I call God as witness against my soul, that to spare you I came no more to Corinth.
—2 Corinthians 1:23

Following the establishment of the church at Corinth, Paul left for Jerusalem by way of Ephesus in AD 52, taking with him Aquila and *Priscilla*. Upon his return to Ephesus in AD 54, he learned Apollos had been working in Corinth. Soon thereafter, things seemed to go off track. Paul sent Timothy as his personal envoy to Corinth (1 Corinthians 4:17). Sometime during the three years that Paul labored in Ephesus (AD 54–57), he made an unrecorded trip back to Corinth. Apparently, Timothy had brought disconcerting news from Corinth. Paul decided he needed to visit in person. The visit is not mentioned in Acts but is implied in 2 Corinthians. Paul's founding visit (Acts 18:1–18) could hardly have been "painful." He did make a visit mentioned in Acts 20:1–3, but that came much later. We know he made this unscheduled second visit to Corinth because 2 Corinthians 12:14 speaks of his coming there a "third time," which would logically imply he had already made a "second," unrecorded, visit.

Paul was concerned with the backsliding of the Corinthian church. Christians were resorting to secular courts to settle quarrels. The Lord's Supper had become an excuse for feasting after the pagan patterns. "Questions had also arisen regarding marriage and related social problems (ch. 7), the eating of foods sacrificed to idols (ch. 8), the proper conduct of women in public worship (ch. 11:2–16). There was misunderstanding also regarding the proper function of spiritual gifts (chs. 12–14). Some were skeptical regarding the fact and manner of the resurrection (ch. 15)."[1] Furthermore, the Judaizing faction was undermining Paul's authority.

Paul's "painful visit" seems to have included a direct and public confrontation with a church member (2 Corinthians 2:1–11) during which the church did not immediately support Paul! "Probably following such a visit and the receipt of further disconcerting news from Corinth (1 Cor. 1:11), he dispatched a letter of reprimand and counsel (1 Corinthians), and sent Titus to prepare the way for a further visit he planned to make (2 Cor. 8:6; 13:1, 2 . . .)."[2]

Scholars think Paul's status as an ordained minister was challenged. Having one's credentials questioned hurts. Losing the support of one's congregation is painful!

---

1. Francis D. Nichol, ed., *The Seventh-day Adventist Bible Commentary*, vol. 6 (Washington, DC: Review and Herald®, 1957), 656.
2. Nichol, *Seventh-day Adventist Bible Commentary*, vol. 6, 822.

Titus Brings Wonderful Tidings

Therefore we have been comforted in your comfort. And we rejoiced exceedingly more for the joy of Titus, because his spirit has been refreshed by you all.

—2 Corinthians 7:13

As we have seen, Paul wrote 1 Corinthians from Ephesus. Few but Bible scholars are aware Paul sent an earlier letter "in which he had admonished his readers to have no company with fornicators (1 Cor. 5:9). Hence, the so-called first epistle to the Corinthians is really the second letter addressed to that church."[1] Paul was now in Macedonia (Europe—Northern Greece), having left Troas (Asia) by crossing the Aegean Sea. "Happy as Paul was at the factual report of the spiritual condition now prevailing in the church at Corinth, he was infinitely more pleased by the enthusiasm of Titus, who had been there in person. Paul had dispatched Titus under a cloud of apprehension and overwhelming anxiety. . . . But the Corinthians had received Titus with such obvious affection as to convince him of the genuineness of their repentance and of their firm loyalty to Paul."[2] Paul would write, " 'Nevertheless God, that comforteth those that are cast down, comforted us by the coming of Titus.'

"This faithful messenger brought the cheering news that a wonderful change had taken place among the Corinthian believers. Many had accepted the instruction contained in Paul's letter and had repented of their sins. Their lives were no longer a reproach to Christianity, but exerted a powerful influence in favor of practical godliness."[3]

"When Paul learned that Titus' tactful work had been successful above expectations, he requested the young man to return to Corinth and continue the good work already begun (ch. 8:16–18, 22–24), while Paul spent more time among the churches of Macedonia. Paul gave Titus another letter, our 2 Corinthians, in which he eloquently expressed his joy over the good reports he had received concerning the church of Corinth. He also announced to them his plan to come to Corinth after a short stay in Macedonia (chs. 12:14; 13:1)."[4] Titus, as a peacemaker, was reliable (2 Corinthians 7:7) and hardworking (2 Corinthians 8:17). He dearly loved the brethren (2 Corinthians 7:13–15).

Are you a peacemaker? "Blessed are the peacemakers: for they shall be called the children of God" (Matthew 5:9, KJV).

---

1. Francis D. Nichol, ed., *The Seventh-day Adventist Bible Commentary*, vol. 6 (Washington, DC: Review and Herald®, 1957), 103.

2. Nichol, *Seventh-day Adventist Bible Commentary*, vol. 6, 885.

3. Ellen G. White, *The Acts of the Apostles* (Mountain View, CA: Pacific Press®, 1911), 324.

4. Nichol, *Seventh-day Adventist Bible Commentary*, vol. 6, 104.

Part 1: Be Comforted

Blessed be the God and Father of our Lord Jesus Christ, the Father of mercies and God of all comfort, who comforts us in all our tribulation, that we may be able to comfort those who are in any trouble, with the comfort with which we ourselves are comforted by God.
—2 Corinthians 1:3, 4

Paul now writes an interesting letter. "The first nine chapters of 2 Corinthians are characterized by gratitude and appreciation; the last four, by marked severity and self-defense. It has been suggested that the former chapters were addressed to the majority, who had accepted Paul's counsel and reproof, and the latter to a minority who persisted in opposing his efforts to restore the church to a spirit of harmony. At length, and in various ways, Paul essays to prove his authority and vindicate his conduct among them. For proof of his apostleship he appeals to his visions and revelations from the Lord, to his unparalleled sufferings for the Lord Jesus, and to the seal of divine approval evident in the fruitfulness of his labors. The severity of Paul's words, addressed to the Corinthian church concerning certain false apostles and possibly a minority of its members still under their influence, is without parallel in his epistles to other churches."[1]

But Paul begins his letter with praises to the Father. "Men sometimes experience difficulty comprehending the omnipresence, the omnipotence, and the omniscience of the Infinite God. But all men can understand and appreciate Him as the loving Father, who gave His only Son to live and die for a race of sinners (John 3:16)."[2] When the Christian experiences trials and sorrow, he learns to lean upon his Heavenly Father. "It is much more difficult to believe in God in the midst of luxury, worldly comfort, and ease. In the providence of God, tribulation and sorrow can lead us closer to Him."[3] "The value of suffering depends, however, not so much upon the circumstances that occasion it, as upon the attitude of the sufferer toward it (cf. 1 Cor. 13:3, RSV). Willingness to suffer is not of itself an evidence of Christianity. Countless thousands who have uncomplainingly experienced trials and sufferings were not children of God. It is fellowship with Christ that ennobles and sanctifies suffering (see 1 Peter 2:20, 21)."[4]

Trusting in Jesus, we gain strength through enduring trials. We learn to empathize with fellow sufferers. Many who are now discouraged and faint-hearted need your support.

---

1. Francis D. Nichol, ed., *The Seventh-day Adventist Bible Commentary*, vol. 6 (Washington, DC: Review and Herald®, 1957), 823, 824.
2. Nichol, *Seventh-day Adventist Bible Commentary*, vol. 6, 827.
3. Nichol, *Seventh-day Adventist Bible Commentary*, vol. 6, 828.
4. Nichol, *Seventh-day Adventist Bible Commentary*, vol. 6, 828.

Part 2: Walk in the Spirit

Now the Lord is the Spirit; and where the Spirit of the Lord is, there is liberty.
—2 Corinthians 3:17

Having spoken at length concerning his apostolic credentials in 2 Corinthians 3:1–6, Paul now sought to explain the Christian experience. Ancient Israel was given the law. Yet their religion had become formal and rigid, lacking feeling and spirit. "There was nothing wrong about having the law of God inscribed upon tables of stone, but so long as it was written only there, and was not transferred to the tables of men's hearts, it remained, for all practical purposes, a dead letter."[1] Paul "had been educated according to the rigid letter of the law (Acts 22:3; Phil. 3:4–6), but the spirit of life in Christ Jesus had set him free from that rigid system (Rom. 8:2)."[2] "Under the old covenant, Jewish reverence for the simple 'letter' of the law practically became idolatry. It stifled the 'spirit.' The Jews chose to live under the dominion of the 'letter' of the law. Their obedience to the law, to ritual, and to the prescribed ceremonies was formal and external. A Christian's devotion and obedience will not be characterized by any mechanical method, by elaborate rules and requirements, but by the presence and power of the Spirit of God."[3]

Jesus explained during His sermon on the mount that the "spirit" of the law transcends the "letter" of the law. Being angry with your neighbor violates the sixth commandment just as much as killing him (Matthew 5:17–22). "Obedience to the 'letter' of the law without the 'spirit' of obedience falls short of meeting His [Christ's] standard of righteousness."[4] The "spirit" of the law never abolishes the "letter" of the law. Jesus came not to destroy the Law and the Prophets but to fulfill them (Matthew 5:17). We cannot, of ourselves, keep God's law. Only Jesus can truly make us free (John 8:36). When a man is born again, his desire is to follow God's will. The Christian does not do what is right because the law tells him he is forbidden to do wrong but because he loves his Redeemer enough to want to gladden Him.

"Liberty in Christ does not mean license to do as one pleases, unless one pleases to obey Christ in all things."[5]

1. Francis D. Nichol, ed., *The Seventh-day Adventist Bible Commentary*, vol. 6 (Washington, DC: Review and Herald®, 1957), 844.
2. Nichol, *Seventh-day Adventist Bible Commentary*, vol. 6, 845.
3. Nichol, *Seventh-day Adventist Bible Commentary*, vol. 6, 845.
4. Nichol, *Seventh-day Adventist Bible Commentary*, vol. 6, 846.
5. Nichol, *Seventh-day Adventist Bible Commentary*, vol. 6, 851.

Part 3: Clay Jars

But we have this treasure in earthen vessels, that the excellence of the power may be of God and not of us. We are hard-pressed on every side, yet not crushed; we are perplexed, but not in despair; persecuted, but not forsaken; struck down, but not destroyed.

—2 Corinthians 4:7–9

Paul believed "the knowledge of the glory of God in the face of Jesus Christ" (verse 6) was treasure indeed! And who was entrusted with this knowledge? "God could have proclaimed His truth through sinless angels, but this is not His plan. He chooses human beings, men compassed with infirmity, as instruments in the working out of His designs. The priceless treasure is placed in earthen vessels. Through men His blessings are to be conveyed to the world. Through them His glory is to shine forth into the darkness of sin. In loving ministry they are to meet the sinful and the needy, and lead them to the cross. And in all their work they are to ascribe glory, honor, and praise to Him who is above all and over all."[1]

In using his "clay jars" example, perhaps Paul was "thinking of the ancient practice of storing treasure in great earthen jars for safekeeping."[2] "Men would be inclined to use valuable containers for storing their treasures. But in the working out of His plan God often chooses the humblest of men, lest they take credit to themselves (1 Cor. 1:28, 29). It is not for man's good that he should receive credit for saving himself or his fellow man. There is no greater hindrance to the life of the minister or the believer than pride. It is not the containers, but their contents, that are important; thus with the minister and his message. God might have commissioned angels to do the work He has committed to frail men, but in doing so He works in such a way as to make it evident that the work of redemption is of God and not of man. The vessel or instrument has no value of itself (cf. 2 Tim. 2:19, 20); His presence and power alone determine its value."[3] Paul believed no man should glory save "in the cross of our Lord Jesus Christ" (Galatians 6:14).

It is important to remember we are but clay jars entrusted with the treasure of the gospel. Remembering that will keep us from becoming sanctimonious.

---

1. Ellen G. White, *The Acts of the Apostles* (Mountain View, CA: Pacific Press®, 1911), 330.
2. Francis D. Nichol, ed., *The Seventh-day Adventist Bible Commentary*, vol. 6 (Washington, DC: Review and Herald®, 1957), 856.
3. Nichol, *Seventh-day Adventist Bible Commentary*, vol. 6, 856.

Part 4: Headed for Eternity

For we walk by faith, not by sight.

—2 Corinthians 5:7

Paul may have been experiencing difficulties, but he kept his eyes fixed on the prize of heaven. Christians live in the hope of the resurrection and being united with their Lord and Savior Jesus Christ. "We believe in the Lord without having seen Him. Until the time when we do see Him face to face our manner of life as Christians rests on our belief in the unseen. There are two worlds, the visible and the invisible, which would be one except for the entrance of sin. A person walks by sight when he is under the influence of the material things of time, but he walks by faith when he is under the influence of things eternal. The decisions of the unregenerate man are made, his conduct determined, by external appearances. But the Christian has so firm a conviction regarding the realities of the eternal world that he thinks and acts by faith, in the light of things visible only to the eye of faith (...Matt. 6:24–34; 2 Cor. 4:18). Those who walk by sight instead of by faith thereby express doubt concerning the invisible realities and the promises of God. By faith the kingdom of God becomes a living reality, here and now. Faith comes by 'hearing,' and 'hearing by the word of God' (...Rom. 10:17)."[1]

Some are confused with what Paul goes on to say in 2 Corinthians 5:8: "We are confident, yes, well pleased rather to be absent from the body and to be present with the Lord." They conclude Paul is saying that at death, the soul of the Christian immediately goes "to be present with the Lord." Paul is not saying that at all. What he is saying is that he would welcome even death if it would hasten being with his Lord (verse 2). In verses 3 and 4, "Paul describes death as a state of being 'naked,' or 'unclothed.' He hopes, if at all possible, to avoid this intermediate state, and ardently desires to be 'clothed' with his 'house . . . from heaven.' In other words, he hopes to be translated without seeing death. . . . Elsewhere (...1 Cor. 15:51–54; 1 Thess. 4:15–17; 2 Tim. 4:6–8; etc.) Paul makes it certain that men are not 'clothed' with immortality individually at death, but simultaneously at the resurrection of the just."[2] The dead in Christ are waiting to be awakened at His coming.

The Bible says the dead are asleep! (John 11:11–14, 25, 26; 1 Corinthians 15:20, 51–54; 1 Thessalonians 4:14–17; 5:9, 10). To believe otherwise is to listen to the human teachings.

---

1. Francis D. Nichol, ed., *The Seventh-day Adventist Bible Commentary*, vol. 6 (Washington, DC: Review and Herald®, 1957), 863.
2. Nichol, *Seventh-day Adventist Bible Commentary*, vol. 6, 863.

Part 5: The New Birth

Therefore, if anyone is in Christ, he is a new creation;
old things have passed away; behold, all things have become new.
—2 Corinthians 5:17

Paul loves to use the phrase "in Christ." This is what he believes a Christian to be, one who is united to Christ in all things. When Paul "became a Christian he was baptized 'into Jesus Christ' (Rom. 6:3), and the new life he lives henceforth is centered in Christ (John 15:3–7). He is joined to Christ and wholly subject to His life, power, influence, and word. Paul's whole life moves in a new, spiritual sphere. Nothing is exempted.

"Only 'in Christ' can a sinner find acceptance with God (Phil. 3:9) and sustenance for living the new life (John 15:4, 5; Gal. 2:20). The joys and sorrows, triumphs and sufferings, of life are all 'in Christ' (Rom. 14:17; Phil. 3:9, 10). Even death is robbed of its sting, for those who 'die in the Lord' are blessed (Rev. 14:13). Christianity elevates every human experience and obligation into a new relationship, designated by the term 'in Christ.' "[1]

Man becomes a new being when he aligns himself with God. His "new nature is not the product of moral virtue presumed by some to be inherent in man, and requiring only growth and expression. There are thousands of so-called moral men who make no profession of being Christians, and who are not 'new' creatures. The new nature is not merely the product of a desire, or even a resolution, to do right (Rom. 7:15–18), of mental assent to certain doctrines, of an exchange of one set of opinions or feelings for another, or even of sorrow from sin. It is the result of the presence of a supernatural element introduced into a man, which results in his dying to sin and being born again. Thus are we created anew in the likeness of Christ, adopted as sons and daughters of God, and set on a new path. . . . Thus we are made partakers of the divine nature and are granted possession of eternal life. . . . The new believer is not born a full-grown, mature Christian; he first has the spiritual inexperience and immaturity of infancy. But as a son of God he does have the privilege and opportunity to grow up into the fall stature of Christ."[2]

"To be a Christian is to be Christlike."[3] Growing daily to be more like Jesus is sanctification.

---

1. Francis D. Nichol, ed., *The Seventh-day Adventist Bible Commentary*, vol. 6 (Washington, DC: Review and Herald®, 1957), 868.
2. Nichol, *Seventh-day Adventist Bible Commentary*, vol. 6, 868, 869.
3. Ellen G. White, "The True Missionary Spirit," *Advent Review and Sabbath Herald*, July 10, 1883, 1.

Part 6: Sticks and Stones

Behold, now is the accepted time; behold, now is the day of salvation.
—2 Corinthians 6:2

In 2 Corinthians 6:2, Paul references the Septuagint, quoting Isaiah. When Isaiah penned these words, he was looking forward to the time of the Messiah. "Paul here recognizes that the prophecy has been fulfilled in Christ. The first advent of Christ ushered in an era that is favorable to salvation. . . . So long as Christ intercedes for sinners the 'day of salvation' will continue."[1] The time is coming; however, when probation for sinners will close. "Eventually the day of mercy will close, and when it does there will be no second chance for those who have spurned God's grace. Men often procrastinate because they think the day of salvation will continue indefinitely, that temporal matters require first consideration, that pleasure must be pursued, that it will be easier to repent and believe tomorrow than it is today. They forget that the only time man has for salvation and for victory over sin is the present moment, and that victory postponed becomes defeat. Delay is both foolish and dangerous. Life may be cut short; deterioration of mind and body may make attention to spiritual things difficult or impossible. The heart may be fatally hardened and the desire for salvation lost; the Holy Spirit may cease to strive. Procrastination is ultimately equivalent to rejection."[2]

While Paul wanted the Corinthians to confirm their salvation through Jesus Christ, he also wanted them to endorse his own ministry. "The false apostles at Corinth had spoken evil of him. There were still some who held Paul's preaching and ministry in contempt and spoke of him as an impostor (2 Cor. 2:17; 4:2 . . .). For Paul, this only provided an opportunity for fellowship with Christ in His sufferings (Phil. 3:10; cf. Matt. 5:11; 1 Peter 4:14)."[3] He, therefore, listed his sufferings for Christ as proof of his devotion to the gospel. While his earthen jar was shattered, the treasure he held within was untouched! Despite his enemies' slander, Paul had reason to rejoice. He had been saved by the gospel of Jesus Christ!

Have you ever felt surrounded by critics? Remember— "No Christian has ever encountered more enemies than Christ."[4]

---

1. Francis D. Nichol, ed., *The Seventh-day Adventist Bible Commentary*, vol. 6 (Washington, DC: Review and Herald®, 1957), 872.
2. Nichol, *Seventh-day Adventist Bible Commentary*, vol. 6, 872.
3. Nichol, *Seventh-day Adventist Bible Commentary*, vol. 6, 874, 875.
4. Nichol, *Seventh-day Adventist Bible Commentary*, vol. 6, 873.

Part 7: Be Separate

Do not be unequally yoked together with unbelievers. For what fellowship has righteousness with lawlessness? And what communion has light with darkness?
—2 Corinthians 6:14

Paul had just told the Corinthians they should not be exclusive and narrow in their gospel outreach (1 Corinthians 6:12, 13). Now he was concerned that perhaps in their zeal to win others for Christ, they would enter into relationships with unbelievers that would cause them to be in danger of losing their own souls. Here he sets forth a principle for Christians to follow in dealing with non-Christian friends. "So great is the difference in ideals and conduct between Christians and non-Christians, believers and unbelievers, that to enter into any binding relationship with them, whether in marriage, in business, or otherwise, inevitably confronts the Christian with the alternatives of abandoning principle or enduring difficulties occasioned by differences in belief and conduct. To enter into such a union is to disobey God and to bargain with the devil. Separateness from sin and sinners is explicitly set forth throughout the Scriptures (Lev. 20:24; Num. 6:3; Heb. 7:26; etc.). No other principle has been more strictly enjoined by God. Throughout the history of God's people the violation of this principle has inevitably resulted in spiritual disaster.

". . . To those who do not accept Christ as their Saviour, and His teachings as their standard of belief and conduct, the ideals, principles, and practice of Christianity are foolishness (1 Cor. 1:18). By reason of their outlook on life, unbelievers often find it most difficult to tolerate a pattern of conduct that tends to restrict their own ways of living, or implies that their concepts and practices are evil or inferior. Paul does not forbid all association with unbelievers, but only such association as would tend to diminish the Christian's love for God, to adulterate the purity of his outlook on life, or to lead him to deviate from a strict pattern of conduct. Christians are not to shun their relatives and friends, but to associate with them as living examples of applied Christianity and so win them to Christ (1 Cor. 5:9, 10; 7:12; 10:27)."[1]

The critical question then is, "Whose influence is likely to prevail, that of Christ or that of the evil one?"[2]

---

1. Francis D. Nichol, ed., *The Seventh-day Adventist Bible Commentary*, vol. 6 (Washington, DC: Review and Herald®, 1957), 876, 877.
2. Nichol, *Seventh-day Adventist Bible Commentary*, vol. 6, 877.

Part 8: You Bring Me Joy

Now I rejoice, not that you were made sorry, but that your sorrow led to repentance.
For you were made sorry in a godly manner, that you might suffer loss from us in nothing.
—2 Corinthians 7:9

No church that Paul had founded gave him so much cause for anxiety and suffering as that at Corinth. Much of this was due to the false apostles ..., who had followed Paul to Corinth and deliberately set about to destroy his work, to discredit his apostleship, to ridicule his gospel and his person ..., to assail his character, and to charge him with mishandling money, with cowardice and insincerity, with usurpation of authority. They may also have sought to impose certain ritual requirements on the Gentile converts, contrary to the decision of the church (cf. Acts 15:1–5, 19–24; Gal. 2:1–8).

"Furthermore, the membership at Corinth was divided into four factions (1 Cor. 1:10–12). In addition, one of the members was guilty of the most despicable immorality (1 Cor. 5:1–5), and the church had failed to deal with him. Some were guilty of going to law with their brethren in pagan courts (1 Cor. 6:1–8). Some had debased the Lord's Supper, and were guilty of desecrating this sacred service (1 Cor. 11:20–30). Some had manifested a false zeal for spiritual gifts (1 Cor. 14:1, 2, 39, 40).

"In spite of all this, Paul did not wish to relinquish his claim to being their spiritual father."[1]

The Corinthians responded favorably to Paul's letter and repented. They rallied to his side. This was critical, for "an open break between Paul and the Corinthians appeared almost inevitable. There was the possibility that they might repudiate his apostolic authority and spiritual leadership altogether. The effect upon other churches of such a course of action on the part of so important a church as that at Corinth, would be disastrous. The cause of God among the Gentiles was at stake."[2] Paul now exulted. Not that he had distressed the Corinthians but rather that his forthright manner had led to genuine repentance on their part. "Hesitancy to impose even the least distress upon others, except where there is absolute need, is one mark of a true minister."[3] Paul rejoiced that the Corinthians had come through his rebuke victorious.

"True repentance makes the angels sing with joy (Luke 15:7)."[4]

---

1. Francis D. Nichol, ed., *The Seventh-day Adventist Bible Commentary*, vol. 6 (Washington, DC: Review and Herald®, 1957), 882.
2. Nichol, *Seventh-day Adventist Bible Commentary*, vol. 6, 883.
3. Nichol, *Seventh-day Adventist Bible Commentary*, vol. 6, 883.
4. Nichol, *Seventh-day Adventist Bible Commentary*, vol. 6, 883.

Part 9: The Example of Christ

For you know the grace of our Lord Jesus Christ, that though He was rich,
yet for your sakes He became poor, that you through His poverty might become rich.
—2 Corinthians 8:9

When the plan of redemption was laid, it was decided that Christ should not appear in accordance with His divine character; for then He could not associate with the distressed and the suffering. He must come as a poor man. He could have appeared in accordance with His exalted station in the heavenly courts; but no, He must reach to the very lowest depths of human suffering and poverty, that His voice might be heard by the burdened and disappointed, that to the weary, sin-sick soul He might reveal Himself as the Restorer, the desire of all nations, the Rest-giver. And to those who are longing for rest and peace today just as truly as to those who listened to His words in Judea, He is saying, 'Come unto me, all ye that labor and are heavy laden, and I will give you rest.' "[1]

"The Son of God had left His heavenly home, with its riches and honor and glory, and clothed His divinity with humanity—not to live in the palaces of kings, without care or labor, and to be supplied with all the conveniences which human nature naturally craves.

"In the councils of heaven He had chosen to stand in the ranks of the poor and oppressed, to take His part with the humble workers, and learn the trade of His earthly parent, which was that of a carpenter, a builder. He came to the world to be a reconstructor of character, and He brought into all His work of building the perfection which He desired to bring into the characters He was transforming by His divine power.

"Paul presents his pattern, his ideal. Christ had given Himself to a life of poverty that they might become rich in heavenly treasure. He would refresh their memories in regard to the sacrifice made in their behalf. Christ was Commander in the heavenly courts, yet He took the lowest place in this world. He was rich, yet for our sakes He became poor. It was not spiritual riches that He left behind; He was always abounding in the gifts of the Spirit. But He was of poor parentage."[2]

"The world never saw its Lord wealthy."[3]

---

1. Ellen G. White, MS 14, 1897.
2. Ellen G. White, MS 98, 1899
3. Ellen G. White, MS 98, 1899.

Part 10: Why Do You Give?

*But this I say: He who sows sparingly will also reap sparingly, and he who
sows bountifully will also reap bountifully. So let each one give as he purposes
in his heart, not grudgingly or of necessity; for God loves a cheerful giver.*
—2 Corinthians 9:6, 7

As his third mission trip came to a close, it became obvious Paul was preoccupied with taking up a collection for the Christians at Jerusalem. Every epistle he wrote during this time period (Galatians, 1 and 2 Corinthians, and Romans) dealt with that collection. Paul stressed the importance of having the collection ready before his arrival. "It is not simply money that is at stake, or the needs of the poor. It is the spirit and character of the Corinthians, their Christian maturity. True giving is an act of the soul."[1] "Nearly all of the Macedonian believers were poor in this world's goods, but their hearts were overflowing with love for God and His truth, and they gladly gave for the support of the gospel. When general collections were taken up in the Gentile churches for the relief of the Jewish believers, the liberality of the converts in Macedonia was held up as an example to other churches."[2] Paul called the attention of the Corinthians to the example of their brethren in Philippi and Thessalonica and Berea. Through Titus, he encouraged them to be liberal in their giving.

"The spirit of liberality is the spirit of heaven. This spirit finds its highest manifestation in Christ's sacrifice on the cross. In our behalf the Father gave His only-begotten Son; and Christ, having given up all that He had, then gave Himself, that man might be saved. The cross of Calvary should appeal to the benevolence of every follower of the Saviour. . . .

"On the other hand, the spirit of selfishness is the spirit of Satan. The principle illustrated in the lives of worldlings is to get, get. Thus they hope to secure happiness and ease, but the fruit of their sowing is misery and death."[3] "It were better not to give at all than to give grudgingly; for if we impart of our means when we have not the spirit to give freely, we mock God. Let us bear in mind that we are dealing with One upon whom we depend for every blessing. One who reads every thought of the heart, every purpose of the mind."[4]

"Spiritual prosperity is closely bound up with Christian liberality."[5] *Giving of one's time and talents is just as important as giving money!*

1. Francis D. Nichol, ed., *The Seventh-day Adventist Bible Commentary*, vol. 6 (Washington, DC: Review and Herald®, 1957), 895.
2. Ellen G. White, *The Acts of the Apostles* (Mountain View, CA: Pacific Press®, 1911), 343.
3. White, *Acts of the Apostles*, 339.
4. Ellen G. White, "God Loveth a Cheerful Giver," *Advent Review and Sabbath Herald*, May 15, 1900, 1.
5. White, *Acts of the Apostles*, 344.

Part 11: Paul Defends His Honor

*But "he who glories, let him glory in the Lord." For not he who
commends himself is approved, but whom the Lord commends.*
—2 Corinthians 10:17, 18

In the first nine chapters [of 2 Corinthians] Paul addresses the cooperative majority, and there is only passing reference to the false leaders and any who may have been influenced by them (chs. 2:17; 3:1; 5:12)."[1] Now in chapter ten, he speaks out against the false apostles who are telling the congregation Paul is weak. "Paul's opponents were arrogant, willful, and self-conceited. They misconstrued his meekness for weakness, his gentleness for cowardice. Accordingly they were beyond the reach of conciliatory appeals and kind exhortation."[2] "What these few rebels have interpreted as cowardice and timidity on his part was simply patience, which he [Paul] exercised in the hope that others might be won over."[3]

Paul's ordination to the gospel should never have been in doubt. His authority was "equal to that of the Twelve. . . . He was called and commissioned directly by the Lord (Acts 9:3–9; 22:17–21 . . .). He had experienced fellowship with Christ in His sufferings ([2 Corinthians] 11:23–33). He had received visions and revelations directly from Christ ([2 Corinthians] 12:1–6)."[4] His detractors ridiculed his physical appearance.

"Writers before the 4th century stated that Paul was short of stature, stooped—probably from repeated beatings (2 Cor. 11:24, 25)—bald, and had crooked thighs, but was full of grace, and had eyes burning with love, nobility, and zeal for Christ. . . . Paul apparently confirms the idea that in personal appearance he was anything but impressive. But that his opponents at Corinth should stoop to ridicule his physical weaknesses, and perhaps slight deformity, reveals their despicable character."[5] To say Paul's speech was "contemptible" (2 Corinthians 10:10) was slanderous. "Paul was a superior speaker (Acts 14:12),"[6] and yet he never sought to glorify himself by using high oratory or rhetoric to impress others. "The self-commendation of the false apostles at Corinth, who in reality had no success of their own to boast of, conclusively proved them to be wholly without approval from God."[7]

Any success Paul achieved in winning souls for Christ, he attributed directly to God.

1. Francis D. Nichol, ed., *The Seventh-day Adventist Bible Commentary*, vol. 6 (Washington, DC: Review and Herald®, 1957), 899.
2. Nichol, *Seventh-day Adventist Bible Commentary*, vol. 6, 900.
3. Nichol, *Seventh-day Adventist Bible Commentary*, vol. 6, 902.
4. Nichol, *Seventh-day Adventist Bible Commentary*, vol. 6, 903.
5. Nichol, *Seventh-day Adventist Bible Commentary*, vol. 6, 904.
6. Nichol, *Seventh-day Adventist Bible Commentary*, vol. 6, 904.
7. Nichol, *Seventh-day Adventist Bible Commentary*, vol. 6, 906.

Part 12: Paul Defends His Apostleship

For I consider that I am not at all inferior to the most eminent apostles.
—2 Corinthians 11:5

Paul "is not a man to avoid acknowledging his limitations. He puts on no false front to hide his weaknesses. Boasting is not natural to him. But if his patience is to be construed as weakness, he will show that he can be 'bold also.' "[1] He writes, "Are they Hebrews? So am I. Are they Israelites? So am I. Are they the seed of Abraham? So am I" (2 Corinthians 11:22). "This verse definitely identifies Paul's opponents in the church at Corinth as Jews. Throughout their history the Jews had come to believe in their superiority as a race and as the chosen people of God (Deut. 7:6; Amos 3:2; John 8:33–39)....

"...Though born abroad, Paul had learned Aramaic, and this reflected his respect for, and adherence to, Hebrew traditions. The Hellenistic Jews of the Dispersion commonly spoke Greek and used the Greek translation of the [Old Testament], the LXX [Septuagint]. Because Paul was born outside of Palestine, in Tarsus, the capital of Cilicia, and because he spoke Greek, his opponents—Palestinian Jews—doubtless classed him as a Hellenist, and thus less loyal to Judaism than they supposed themselves to be....

"... Generally speaking, the nucleus of the Christian believers in each community came from the Jewish synagogue, for Paul began his preaching of the gospel in the local synagogue. The Jews naturally felt entitled to special consideration and privileges in the Christian church, and considered themselves better fitted for leadership. Their comparative religious maturity would obviously give them an advantage over the religious immaturity of the Gentiles. But their attitude and their abuse of authority, in various instances, had resulted in a religion of self-righteousness, which was abhorrent both to God and to man (Luke 18:10–14)."[2]

"To be a true son of Abraham meant to be taken into covenant relationship with God (Gen. 17:7; Gal. 4:22–26), to experience righteousness by faith (Rom. 4; Gal. 3:6–9, 14–16), to belong to the race through which the Messiah was to come (Gal. 3:16), and to inherit the exalted promises given to him as father of the Hebrew race (Gal. 3:14–18)."[3]

Paul understood that it took more than a pedigree to make one a true son of Abraham!

---

1. Francis D. Nichol, ed., *The Seventh-day Adventist Bible Commentary*, vol. 6 (Washington, DC: Review and Herald®, 1957), 914.
2. Nichol, *Seventh-day Adventist Bible Commentary*, vol. 6, 914, 915.
3. Nichol, *Seventh-day Adventist Bible Commentary*, vol. 6, 915.

Part 13: Paul's Testimonial

Three times I was beaten with rods; once I was stoned; three times I was shipwrecked; a night and a day I have been in the deep; in journeys often, in perils of waters, in perils of robbers, in perils of my own countrymen, in perils of the Gentiles, in perils in the city, in perils in the wilderness, in perils in the sea, in perils among false brethren; in weariness and toil, in sleeplessness often, in hunger and thirst, in fastings often, in cold and nakedness.

—2 Corinthians 11:25–27

Could the Judaizers claim as much devotion to duty as Paul's devotion? We don't know how many times Paul was cast into prison. "Clement of Rome observes that Paul was imprisoned seven times."[1] Often he came face to face with what must have seemed to be certain death. In 2 Corinthians 11:24, he mentions that he received the Jewish punishment of forty lashes minus one five times. His back must have been badly scarred! Three times Roman lictors beat him with rods. We know of the one recorded time in Philippi (Acts 16:22, 23). He had been stoned at Lystra (Acts 14:19, 20). "Five sea voyages are recorded in Acts, but nothing is said of shipwreck prior to that of Acts 27. The shipwreck en route to Rome came long after the writing of this epistle."[2]

"There would be few bridges along most of the highways and byways Paul traveled. He would have to ford the rivers. Most of what we know as Asia Minor, Greece, and Macedonia is mountainous, and many an unbridged mountain torrent would constitute a dangerous obstacle.

". . . Every road, except perhaps the great Roman highways, was infested with robbers."[3] While Paul's worst opposition came from fellow Jews, the Gentiles at Philippi and Ephesus had made his life miserable.

Extreme weariness made sleep difficult. "Perhaps by 'hunger' Paul refers to an inadequate diet, and by 'fastings' to occasions when he had nothing whatever to eat.

". . . Perhaps Paul had, at times, lacked sufficient clothing in the mountainous regions of central Asia Minor, or perhaps he had suffered robbery."[4] "Gain courage from the experience of the apostle Paul. He had many trials. He was an unwearied worker and traveled constantly, sometimes through inhospitable regions, sometimes on the water, in storm and tempest. Far harder than ours was his lot; for traveling then had not the conveniences that it has now."[5]

"Paul allowed nothing to hinder him from his work."[6]

---

1. Francis D. Nichol, ed., *The Seventh-day Adventist Bible Commentary*, vol. 6 (Washington, DC: Review and Herald®, 1957), 916.
2. Nichol, *Seventh-day Adventist Bible Commentary*, vol. 6, 916.
3. Nichol, *Seventh-day Adventist Bible Commentary*, vol. 6, 916.
4. Nichol, *Seventh-day Adventist Bible Commentary*, vol. 6, 917.
5. Ellen G. White, Letter 107, 1904.
6. Ellen G. White, Letter 107, 1904.

Part 14: A Thorn in the Flesh

And lest I should be exalted above measure by the abundance of the revelations, a thorn in the flesh was given to me, a messenger of Satan to buffet me, lest I be exalted above measure.
—2 Corinthians 12:7

Commentators have tried for years to identify the "thorn" in Paul's flesh. Some, facetiously, think the "thorn" was a wife who refused to accept his conversion. Others think he might have suffered from relapses of malaria contracted while in Asia Minor. Still others believe his eyesight constantly plagued him since "seeing the light" on the Damascus Road. We know "the infirmity was bodily, not spiritual or mental. It was apparently something prominent, which caused him considerable embarrassment as well as discomfort and inconvenience."[1] Ellen White says, "Paul had a bodily affliction; his eyesight was bad. He thought that by earnest prayer the difficulty might be removed. But the Lord had His own purpose, and He said to Paul, Speak to Me no more of this matter. My grace is sufficient. It will enable you to bear the infirmity."[2]

Depression was involved. "A deep sadness still rested upon the mind and heart of Paul because of his apprehensions concerning the Corinthian church. While at Philippi he commenced his second epistle to them; for they hung as a heavy weight upon his soul. The depression of spirits from which the apostle suffered was, however, attributable in a great degree to bodily infirmities, which made him very restless when not engaged in active service. But when working for the salvation of souls, he rose superior to physical debility. He felt that the disease under which he suffered was a terrible impediment to him in his great work, and repeatedly besought the Lord to relieve him."[3]

Three times Paul asked the Lord to remove the affliction. "And He said to me, 'My grace is sufficient for you, for My strength is made perfect in weakness' " (2 Corinthians 12:8, 9). "When the answer was clear he accepted it as the will of God for him."[4] Consider, "a man strong in his own strength tends to be self-reliant instead of relying on God, and often does not realize his need of divine grace. The great heroes of the Bible learned the same lesson, men such as Noah, Abraham, Moses, Elijah, Daniel."[5]

"Only those whose weakness and insecurity have been completely submerged in the blessed will of God know what it is to possess true power."[6]

---

1. Francis D. Nichol, ed., *The Seventh-day Adventist Bible Commentary*, vol. 6 (Washington, DC: Review and Herald®, 1957), 920.
2. Ellen G. White, Letter 207, 1899.
3. Ellen G. White, *Sketches From the Life of Paul* (Washington, DC: Review and Herald®, 1974), 175, 176.
4. Nichol, *Seventh-day Adventist Bible Commentary*, vol. 6, 921.
5. Nichol, *Seventh-day Adventist Bible Commentary*, vol. 6, 921
6. Nichol, *Seventh-day Adventist Bible Commentary*, vol. 6, 921.

Part 15: Satan's Little Wedges

Examine yourselves as to whether you are in the faith. Test yourselves. Do you not know
yourselves, that Jesus Christ is in you?—unless indeed you are disqualified.

—2 Corinthians 13:5

God has never promised to alter circumstances or release men from trouble. To Him, bodily infirmities and untoward circumstances are matters of secondary concern. Inward strength to endure is a far higher manifestation of the divine grace than mastery of the outward difficulties of life. Outwardly a man may be torn, worn, wearied, and almost broken, yet inwardly it is his privilege—in Christ—to enjoy perfect peace (. . . Isa. 26:3, 4)."[1] Though suffering, Paul still needed to deal with the rebels at Corinth. "A serious state of spiritual declension still prevailed in one section of the church. . . . Paul now warns the members regarding this wayward group. . . . Only one alternative remains—to deal with them firmly and unsparingly in the power and authority of Christ. . . .

". . . Punishment would doubtless include expulsion. . . .

". . . Paul's foes had dared the apostle to carry out what they chose to consider threats. When members of this worldly-minded group looked at Paul they saw nothing more than what they took to be a weak, contemptible human being."[2] However, they were contesting the power of God, not the physical appearance of Paul.

Paul called upon the congregation to test self before testing others. How is your personal relationship with God? "Many nominal Christians think it sufficient to test themselves on points of secondary importance such as church membership, church attendance, tithes and offerings, and Sabbath observance. To be sure, these are not to be neglected. But there are even weightier matters that demand consideration (see . . . Micah 6:8; Matt. 19:16–22; 23:23). Things that are of major importance include personal experience with the saving, transforming grace of Christ, absolute loyalty to all the revealed will of God, sincerity of motives, and a selfless interest in, and service for, one's fellow men."[3] "Those who have no time to give attention to their own souls, to examine themselves daily whether they be in the love of God and place themselves in the channel of light, will have time to give to the suggestions of Satan and the working out of his plans.

"Satan will insinuate himself by little wedges, that widen as they make a place for themselves."[4]

God will judge the character traits of justice, mercy, faith, and humility.

---

1. Francis D. Nichol, ed., *The Seventh-day Adventist Bible Commentary*, vol. 6 (Washington, DC: Review and Herald®, 1957), 921.
2. Nichol, *Seventh-day Adventist Bible Commentary*, vol. 6, 925.
3. Nichol, *Seventh-day Adventist Bible Commentary*, vol. 6, 926.
4. Ellen G. White, MS 16, 1890.

Corinth at Last!

*Now when he had gone over that region and encouraged
them with many words, he came to Greece and stayed three months.*

—Acts 20:2, 3

I t was autumn when Paul again visited Corinth. As he beheld the Corinthian towers and lofty citadel in the distance, the clouds that enshrouded the mountains and cast a shadow upon the city beneath, seemed a fitting emblem of the error and immorality which threatened the prosperity of the Christian church in that place. The mind of Paul was agitated by conflicting thoughts. He was to meet his children in the faith of the gospel. Some of them had been guilty of grievous sins. Some of his former friends had forgotten his love and the sweet fellowship and confidence of earlier days. They had become his enemies, and questioned and disputed whether he was a true apostle of Christ, intrusted with the gospel. Though the majority of the church had turned from their sins and submitted to the commands of Paul, yet it could not be with them entirely as it was before their immorality. There could not exist that union, love, and confidence between teacher and people, as upon the occasion of his former visit."[1]

"Paul was accompanied to Corinth by a little band of fellow-laborers, some of whom had been his companions during the months spent in Macedonia, and his assistants in gathering funds for the church at Jerusalem. He could rely upon these brethren for sympathy and support in the present crisis. And though the condition of the Corinthian church was in some respects painful and discouraging, there were also reasons for joy and gratitude. . . . Not a few still regarded the apostle with warm affection, as the one who had first borne to them the precious light of the gospel. As he once more greeted these disciples, and saw the proof of their fidelity and zeal, he felt that his labor had not been in vain. In the society of his beloved companions and these faithful converts, his worn and troubled spirit found rest and encouragement.

"For three months Paul stayed at Corinth."[2] While at Corinth, Paul formulated plans to carry the gospel to Rome and Spain. Difficulties were a challenge and not a hindrance to him.

Trials "are God's workmen, ordained for the perfection of character."[3]

---

1. Ellen G. White, *Sketches From the Life of Paul* (Washington, DC: Review and Herald®, 1974), 183, 184.
2. White, *Sketches From the Life of Paul*, 186.
3. "Ellen G. White Comments—2 Corinthians," in *The Seventh-day Adventist Bible Commentary*, ed. Francis D. Nichol, vol. 6 (Washington, DC: Review and Herald®, 1957), 1099.

Part 1: Greetings, Romans

*Now I do not want you to be unaware, brethren, that I often
planned to come to you (but was hindered until now).*

—Romans 1:13

While at Corinth, Paul's "thoughts were still occupied with his contemplated journey from Jerusalem to Rome. To see the Christian faith firmly established at the great center of the known world was one of his dearest hopes and most cherished plans. A church had already been raised up at Rome, and the apostle desired to secure their cooperation in the work which he hoped to accomplish. To prepare the way for his labors among these brethren, as yet strangers, he addressed them by letter, announcing his purpose to visit Rome and also, by their aid, to plant the standard of the cross in Spain.

"In his Epistle to the Romans, Paul set forth the great principles of the gospel which he hoped to present in person. He stated his position on the questions which were agitating the Jewish and Gentile churches, and showed that the hopes and promises which once belonged especially to the Jews were now offered to the Gentiles. With great clearness and power he presented the doctrine of justification by faith in Christ. While addressing the Roman Christians, Paul designed to instruct other churches also; but how little could he foresee the far-reaching influence of his words! The great truth of justification by faith, as set forth in this epistle, has stood through all the ages as a mighty beacon to guide the repentant sinner into the way of life. This light scattered the darkness which enveloped Luther's mind, and revealed to him the power of the blood of Christ to cleanse from sin. It has guided thousands of sin-burdened souls to the same source of pardon and peace. Every Christian has reason to thank God for that epistle to the church at Rome."[1]

When Paul wrote Romans, he was still occupied with the issues raised in his controversies with the Judaizers. He, therefore, takes up the "problem of sin and God's plan to meet the emergency. . . . Only God Himself can provide a remedy. And this He has done—by the sacrifice of His Son."[2]

"All that is asked of fallen man is that he exercise faith, faith to accept the provisions made to cover his sinful past, and faith to accept the power offered to lead him into a life of righteousness."[3]

---

1. Ellen G. White, *Sketches From the Life of Paul* (Washington, DC: Review and Herald®, 1974), 187, 188.
2. Francis D. Nichol, ed., *The Seventh-day Adventist Bible Commentary*, vol. 6 (Washington, DC: Review and Herald®, 1957), 468.
3. Nichol, *Seventh-day Adventist Bible Commentary*, vol. 6, 468.

Part 2: The Gospel Is Powerful

For I am not ashamed of the gospel of Christ, for it is the power of God to salvation for everyone who believes, for the Jew first and also for the Greek.

—Romans 1:16

Notwithstanding the opposition, twenty years after the crucifixion of Christ there was a live, earnest church in Rome. This church was strong and zealous, and the Lord worked for it."[1] "The epistle to the Romans and that addressed to the Galatians deal with the same general subject—righteousness by faith in Christ. But whereas the latter was composed at a time of crisis, when the churches in Galatia were confronted by the teachings of the Judaizing party in the early church . . . , and was thus designed to meet a particular threat, the former deals with the subject in a more systematic, reasoned, and complete way. There is no evidence of any crisis in the city of Rome comparable to that in Galatia. . . . The epistle to the Galatians has been called the Magna Carta of Christianity, and the epistle to the Romans, its constitution. Under any circumstances it is obvious that the apostle's mind was full of the issues that had arisen in his many controversies with the Judaizers, since he takes up the basic questions and deals with them against the background of the whole problem of sin and of God's plan to meet the emergency sin created."[2] In Romans, Paul speaks to almost every Christian doctrine.

"The Jews considered Paul an apostate. He had been despised and persecuted among the Gentiles. He had been driven from city to city and had been regarded as the 'filth of the world' and 'the offscouring of all things' (1 Cor. 4:13). He was well aware that the preaching of the cross was 'foolishness' to the Greeks and a 'stumbling block' to the Jews (1 Cor. 1:23). But because Paul was so thoroughly convinced of the truth of the gospel, and because he himself had so fully experienced its blessing and power, he not only was not ashamed of any part of it but even gloried in that which was most offensive to many, the cross of Christ (Gal. 6:14). . . .

". . . The gospel is the way in which God exerts His power for the salvation of men. Wherever the gospel finds believing hearts it is a divine power by which all the obstacles to man's redemption are removed. Paul is stating a fact that he knows to be true from his own experience. He has felt this 'power of God' in his own life and has witnessed its effect upon others (1 Cor. 1:18, 24; 2:1–5)."[3]

The gospel changes lives! Whatever your difficulty, there is power in the blood of Jesus.

---

1. Ellen G. White, "The Apostle Paul and Manual Labor," *Advent Review and Sabbath Herald*, March 6, 1900, 1.
2. Siegfried H. Horn, *Seventh-day Adventist Bible Dictionary*, ed. Don F. Neufeld, Commentary Reference Series, vol. 8 (Washington, DC: Review and Herald®, 1960), s.v. "Romans, Epistle to the."
3. Francis D. Nichol, ed., *The Seventh-day Adventist Bible Commentary*, vol. 6 (Washington, DC: Review and Herald®, 1957), 476.

Part 3: Justification by Faith

For in it the righteousness of God is revealed from faith to faith;
as it is written, "The just shall live by faith."

—Romans 1:17

For many years I read today's text and attributed the idea to Paul. I must have read it dozens of times without catching that Paul was quoting someone else. He tells us, "it is written" and takes no credit for himself. "The quotation is from Hab. 2:4. During the Chaldean invasion, Habakkuk was comforted by the assurance that the righteous person is kept safe by his trust and confidence in God."[1] Paul uses this text to show that "the just man will not live by reliance on his own works and merit but by confidence and faith in God."[2]

In no more powerful way was the righteousness of God revealed to humanity than in the death of His Son. Yet every believer must come to accept God on his or her own. "The revelation is repeated in the continuous proclamation of the gospel and in the spiritual experience of each person who hears and believes the gospel (Gal. 1:16). Man could never conceive or attain to this divine righteousness by his own unaided reason and philosophy. The righteousness of God is a revelation from God. . . .

"[It] is received by faith, and when received, results in ever-increasing faith. As faith is exercised we are able to receive more and still more of the righteousness of God until faith becomes a permanent attitude toward Him."[3]

"The righteousness of Christ is revealed from faith to faith; that is, from your present faith to an increased understanding of that faith which works by love and purifies the soul."[4] Justification is the process by which a man is brought into a proper relationship with God. God exonerates the guilty of wrongdoing. He cancels all charges standing against the believer in the heavenly court. "If you give yourself to Him [Jesus], and accept Him as your Saviour, then, sinful as your life may have been, for His sake you are accounted righteous."[5] Most of us don't appreciate the gift of God as much as we should.

God loves us (John 3:16). He gave His Son to die for us. He offers us salvation. All we must do is accept His gift.

1. Francis D. Nichol, ed., *The Seventh-day Adventist Bible Commentary*, vol. 6 (Washington, DC: Review and Herald®, 1957), 477.
2. Nichol, *Seventh-day Adventist Bible Commentary*, vol. 6, 477.
3. Nichol, *Seventh-day Adventist Bible Commentary*, vol. 6, 476, 477.
4. Ellen G. White, "Lamps Without Oil," *Advent Review and Sabbath Herald*, September 17, 1908, 7.
5. Ellen G. White, *Steps to Christ* (Washington, DC: Review and Herald®, 1956), 62.

Part 4: Societal Ills

*And even as they did not like to retain God in their knowledge, God gave
them over to a debased mind, to do those things which are not fitting.*
—Romans 1:28

Paul minces no words when he talks about the human condition. The list of societal woes reads like the front page of any modern newspaper. People of the first century could easily be mistaken for those of the twenty-first. They were "filled with all unrighteousness, fornication, wickedness, covetousness, maliciousness; full of envy, murder, debate, deceit, malignity; whisperers, backbiters, haters of God, despiteful, proud, boasters, inventors of evil things, disobedient to parents, without understanding, covenantbreakers, without natural affection, implacable, unmerciful" (Romans 1:29–31, KJV).

Paul takes on the tough calls. Some churches were busy seeking to accommodate the sins of humanity, saying certain behaviors weren't really sin at all. Paul pulled no punches. He stated that sodomy, homosexuality (Romans 1:27), fornication (verse 29), and immorality dishonor the body (1 Corinthians 6:15–19; 1 Thessalonians 4:3, 4) and are sins. While heathens may incorporate these acts into their worship, acceptance of this behavior has no place in any Christian church. Paul's treatment of the man practicing gross immorality (incest) at Corinth (1 Corinthians 5:1–13) is an example of how he expects such behavior to be treated by church members. Churches must purge out the old leaven (1 Corinthians 5:7)! Once the man confessed and repented of his sin, then the way was clear to accept him into fellowship again (2 Corinthians 2:5–11). While it is proper to hate sin, we must love the sinner for whom Christ died.

"If we are defective in character, we could not pass the gates that mercy has opened to the obedient; for justice stands at the entrance and demands holiness, purity, in all who would see God.

"Were justice extinct, and were it possible for divine mercy to open the gates to the whole race, irrespective of character, there would be a worse condition of disaffection and rebellion in heaven than before Satan was expelled. The peace, happiness, and harmony of heaven would be broken up. The change from earth to heaven will not change men's characters; the happiness of the redeemed in heaven results from the characters formed in this life, after the image of Christ. The saints in heaven will first have been saints on earth."[1]

Character counts!

---

1. Ellen G. White, Letter 1f, 1890.

Part 5: God Loves Sinners? Thank God!

But God demonstrates His own love toward us,
in that while we were still sinners, Christ died for us.

—Romans 5:8

It is God who, in His great love, initiates the reconciliation: 'God was in Christ, reconciling the world unto himself' (2 Cor. 5:19; cf. Eph. 2:16; Col. 1:20). Though God strongly hates sin, His love for sinners is even stronger, and He has spared nothing, however dear, to bring about a reconciliation. . . . Christ did not die to win God's love for man, but to win man back to God. . . . In fact, God's plan and provision for man's reconciliation was conceived back in eternity, even before man sinned (Rev. 13:8 . . .). Thus, in anticipation of the atoning sacrifice, it was possible for Abraham's faith to be reckoned for righteousness (Rom. 4:3) and for the patriarch to be regarded as the friend of God (James 2:23) long before Christ actually died on the cross."[1]

"There was nothing in man to deserve God's love. . . . But the love that God exercised toward us was not a response to any love we had for Him, for we were His enemies. 'Herein is love, not that we loved God, but that he loved us' (1 John 4:10)."[2] While a man might surrender his life for a truly good man, he might think twice about sacrificing his own life for a scoundrel. Paul goes one step further. He says, "Though one would hardly be willing to die for the merely upright or strictly just person, who may command respect, one might possibly be willing to give his life for the noble, kindly person who inspires love and affection.

"'Greater love hath no man than this, that a man lay down his life for his friends' (John 15:13). But Paul is emphasizing that this is the utmost that can be expected of human love. It is remotely possible that someone would be willing to sacrifice himself for a dear friend who is sufficiently good and lovable. But so great is the love of God for His erring creatures that Jesus died for us when we were godless and rebellious enemies."[3]

"If Christ died for us when we were sinners, it is certain that He will save us now that we are justified. If His love was so great that He was willing to give His life for His enemies, surely He will save His friends from wrath."[4]

---

1. Francis D. Nichol, ed., *The Seventh-day Adventist Bible Commentary*, vol. 6 (Washington, DC: Review and Herald®, 1957), 528.
2. Nichol, *Seventh-day Adventist Bible Commentary*, vol. 6, 527.
3. Nichol, *Seventh-day Adventist Bible Commentary*, vol. 6, 527.
4. Nichol, *Seventh-day Adventist Bible Commentary*, vol. 6, 528.

Part 6: Salvation Is a Gift

For the wages of sin is death, but the gift of God is eternal life in Christ Jesus our Lord.
—Romans 6:23

C an you earn a gift? By its very nature, a gift is given, and the recipient is not charged. Why is it that so many Christians have difficulty accepting that they are saved? Perhaps it is a matter of too little faith. "Faith is not the ground of our salvation, but it is the great blessing—the eye that sees, the ear that hears, the feet that run, the hand that grasps. It is the means, not the end. If Christ gave His life to save sinners, why shall I not take that blessing? My faith grasps it, and thus my faith is the substance of things hoped for, the evidence of things unseen. Thus resting and believing, I have peace with God through the Lord Jesus Christ."[1]

"In the final destruction, sinners will be treated as they deserve. They have rejected God's offer of grace and eternal life and will receive the results of their own deliberate choice."[2] Final destruction is what we have "earned" as sinners. It is our just wage. It is the payment for our lives of sin. We are told, "The soul that sinneth, it shall die" (Ezekiel 18:4, KJV). Consider, however, that God has prepared a way out for all who believe. Rather than what we have earned, we receive that which we do not expect, a gift. Even a born-again Christian cannot claim his or her conversion and subsequent behavior is his or her own doing. "None of us can earn salvation. None of us deserves redemption. We are saved by grace through faith as 'the gift of God' (Eph. 2:8). . . .

". . . The gift of everlasting life, which Adam and Eve forfeited by their transgression . . . , will be restored to all those who are willing to receive it and prepare themselves for it by devoting their lives to God's service (Rom. 2:7; 6:22; cf. Rev. 21:4; 22:2, 3)."[3]

"Christ is the 'resurrection, and the life' (John 11:25). He is the author of life, who gives everlasting life to all who have faith in Him (John 6:40). God's gift of eternal life is not only bestowed through Christ, but it is in Christ, its abiding source, and can be received only through union with Him, who is 'our life' (Col. 3:4 . . .)."[4]

"For by grace you have been saved through faith, and that not of yourselves; it is the gift of God"
(Ephesians 2:8).

---

1. Ellen G. White, Letter 329a, 1905
2. Francis D. Nichol, ed., *The Seventh-day Adventist Bible Commentary*, vol. 6 (Washington, DC: Review and Herald®, 1957), 544.
3. Nichol, *Seventh-day Adventist Bible Commentary*, vol. 6, 544.
4. Nichol, *Seventh-day Adventist Bible Commentary*, vol. 6, 544, 545.

Part 7: Inner Turmoil

For the good that I will to do, I do not do; but the evil I will not to do, that I practice.
—Romans 7:19

Paul certainly knew what it meant to try to live a blameless and righteous life by keeping the law. As a Pharisee, he was meticulous and scrupulous in the observance of tradition and custom. "Paul says that 'as touching the law,'—as far as outward acts were concerned,—he was 'blameless,' but when the spiritual character of the law was discerned, when he looked into the holy mirror, he saw himself a sinner. Judged by a human standard, he had abstained from sin, but when he looked into the depths of God's law, and saw himself as God saw him, he bowed in humiliation, and confessed his guilt. . . .

". . . He became humble. He no longer ascribed goodness and merit to himself. He ceased to think more highly of himself than he ought, and he ascribed all the glory to God. He was no longer ambitious for greatness. He ceased to want to avenge himself, and was no longer sensitive to reproach, neglect, or contempt. He no longer sought earthly alliance, station, or honor. He did not pull others down to uplift himself. He became gentle, condescending, meek and lowly of heart, because he had learned his lesson in the school of Christ. He talked of Jesus and His matchless love, and grew more and more into His image. He bent his whole energy to win souls to Christ."[1]

But the struggle to overcome his sinful human nature was not easy, nor was it ever over. "Martin Luther had evidently learned the meaning of this experience when he said, 'I am more afraid of my own heart than of the Pope and all his cardinals.' "[2] Even a converted Christian is faced with constant warfare against self and sin. Paul wrote that he was "engaged in a life-and-death struggle to escape from the captivating power of his evil inclinations."[3] In Romans 7:24, Paul asks, "Who will deliver me?" "The question provides Paul with an opportunity to express the good news that is the theme of his whole epistle. Does deliverance come through law? Can a man win release and freedom by the strength of his own will and intellect? In vain have these methods been tried, and the disastrous results have been clearly seen. There is only one way, 'through Jesus Christ our Lord' (v. 25)."[4]

Jesus is our only hope for deliverance from the bondage of sin.

---

1. Ellen G. White "Go and Tell Him His Fault Between Thee and Him Alone," *Advent Review and Sabbath Herald*, July 22, 1890, 2.

2. Francis D. Nichol, ed., *The Seventh-day Adventist Bible Commentary*, vol. 6 (Washington, DC: Review and Herald®, 1957), 556.

3. Nichol, *Seventh-day Adventist Bible Commentary*, vol. 6, 557.

4. Nichol, *Seventh-day Adventist Bible Commentary*, vol. 6, 537.

Part 8: The Spirit-Filled Life

For as many as are led by the Spirit of God, these are sons of God.
—Romans 8:14

Romans 8:14 is interesting because of the little word *led* found in the middle. That little word is loaded with meaning. "The present tense indicates continuous action. The leading of the Spirit does not mean a momentary impulse but a steady, habitual influence. It is not those whose hearts are occasionally touched by the Spirit, or those who now and then yield to His power, who are the sons of God. God recognizes as His sons only those who are continually led by His Spirit.

"It is important to notice that the guiding and transforming power of the Holy Spirit is described as leading, not forcing. There is no coercion in the plan of salvation. The Spirit dwells only in the hearts of those who accept Him in faith. And faith implies a loving and willing submission to the will of God and the directing influence of the Holy Spirit."[1]

The Christian does not look at obedience to God's law as a duty but rather as a privilege. It is the Christian's pleasure to do those things that are pleasing to God. We obey Him because we love Him. In Paul's day, adoption was commonplace among Greeks and Romans but not Jews. "Adoption is the taking and treating of a stranger as one's own child, and Paul applies the term to Christians because God treats them as His own sons, even though by nature they were strangers and enemies (Rom. 5:10; Col. 1:21). . . . [Thus,] as adopted sons, we are now under His protection and care. . . . In loving gratitude, we ought to manifest the spirit of children in willingly obeying Him in all things (. . . Rom. 8:12)."[2] "All things work together for good to those who love God, to those who are the called according to His purpose" (verse 28).

How do you know you are a child of God? "God recognizes as His sons [and daughters] only those who are continually led by His Spirit."[3] "That He is dwelling in us may be known by the presence of the fruit of the Spirit in our lives (Gal. 5:22). If there is love in our hearts toward God and toward our fellow men, we may know that we have passed from death unto life (1 John 3:14) and have become the children of our heavenly Father (Matt. 5:44, 45), adopted into the heavenly family."[4]

Love for God and our neighbors is sure evidence of the Holy Spirit's work within us.

---

1. Francis D. Nichol, ed., *The Seventh-day Adventist Bible Commentary*, vol. 6 (Washington, DC: Review and Herald®, 1957), 566.

2. Nichol, *Seventh-day Adventist Bible Commentary*, vol. 6, 567.

3. Nichol, *Seventh-day Adventist Bible Commentary*, vol. 6, 566.

4. Nichol, *Seventh-day Adventist Bible Commentary*, vol. 6, 568.

Part 9: God Loves Believers

What then shall we say to these things? If God is for us, who can be against us?
He who did not spare His own Son, but delivered Him up for us all,
how shall He not with Him also freely give us all things?

—Romans 8:31, 32

Can Christ support us during difficulties? David certainly thought so. "The LORD is my light and my salvation; whom shall I fear? The LORD is the strength of my life; of whom shall I be afraid?" (Psalm 27:1, KJV). "The LORD is on my side; I will not fear: what can man do unto me?" (Psalm 118:6, KJV). Here, in the middle verse of the Bible, David shows his reliance and confidence in God. Paul likewise asserts that if God would give up His own Son, is there anything of lesser value He would withhold from us? "When God gave His Son, He also gave Himself (2 Cor. 5:19 . . .), and thereby revealed to the universe how far He was willing to go to save repentant sinners. Surely, then, no matter what trials may come, we should never doubt that God is ever working for us and that He will give us all that is necessary for our present and future good."[1]

While persecution may come and trials assail us on every side, there is no cause to feel that God has abandoned us. From the beginning of time, those who would live a righteous life have faced persecution. Paul himself was instrumental in putting to death many Christians. While Paul believed a Christian could distance himself from Jesus, he also believed Jesus would not surrender us unless it was our decision to leave Him. "For I am persuaded, that neither death, nor life, nor angels, nor principalities, nor powers, nor things present, nor things to come, nor height, nor depth, nor any other creature, shall be able to separate us from the love of God, which is in Christ Jesus our Lord" (Romans 8:38, 39, KJV). "Paul lists ten items that cannot separate us from the love of God. The tenth is broad enough to include anything that may have been omitted. . . .

"With this expression of unlimited confidence in the saving love of God . . . , Paul reaches the climax of his explanation of God's plan for the restoration of man."[2]

"Righteousness and salvation come by faith. And this faith is to be placed in a person whose love is so great and whose purpose to save is so strong that He has made every conceivable provision for our salvation."[3]

---

1. Francis D. Nichol, ed., *The Seventh-day Adventist Bible Commentary*, vol. 6 (Washington, DC: Review and Herald®, 1957), 577.
2. Nichol, *Seventh-day Adventist Bible Commentary*, vol. 6, 580.
3. Nichol, *Seventh-day Adventist Bible Commentary*, vol. 6, 580.

Part 10: The Election of Israel

Brethren, my heart's desire and prayer to God for Israel is that they may be saved.
—Romans 10:1

E ven though Paul just finished speaking in Romans 9 of the rejection of Jesus by the Jews, "it is significant that [in chapter 10] . . . Paul should pray for their salvation. This shows that he did not regard their case as hopeless, despite their sinful conduct. Moreover, if Paul had considered their rejection as the predetermined will of God for their destruction, as some have understood the doctrine of predestination, he would not have prayed that they might yet be saved. The gospel teaches that 'whosoever shall call upon the name of the Lord shall be saved' ([Romans 10:]13). The gospel is for all men, including the Jews."[1]

Paul firmly believed there would come out of Israel a remnant that would accept Jesus as the Messiah. "Even so then, at this present time there is a remnant according to the election of grace" (Romans 11:5). "As in Elijah's time the apostasy of Israel was not so universal as it seemed to be, and as the prophet in his despondency believed it to be, so now the rejection of Christ by the Jews was not so complete in extent as some might suppose. There was now, as there was then, a faithful remnant. God was still dealing with His people upon the same principles. . . .

". . . If salvation is by grace, then it is no longer on the basis of what men have done. Otherwise grace would no longer be grace. . . . If the gift of God's grace could be earned or deserved, then grace would lose its specific character and meaning. However, all but the remnant of Israel have failed to understand this."[2] Have Christians done better in trying to merit salvation by doing penance?

There will be a Christian remnant saved. "If we comply with the conditions the Lord has made, we shall secure our election to salvation. Perfect obedience to His commandments is the evidence that we love God, and are not hardened in sin.

"Christ has a church in every age. There are in the church those who are not made any better by their connection with it. They themselves break the terms of their election. Obedience to the commandments of God gives us a right to the privileges of His church."[3]

Thank God, for it is His grace that saves us and not our works!

1. Francis D. Nichol, ed., *The Seventh-day Adventist Bible Commentary*, vol. 6 (Washington, DC: Review and Herald®, 1957), 594.
2. Nichol, *Seventh-day Adventist Bible Commentary*, vol. 6, 604, 605.
3. Ellen G. White, MS 166, 1898.

Part 11: A Christian's Relationship to Self

I beseech you therefore, brethren, by the mercies of God, that you present your bodies a living sacrifice, holy, acceptable to God, which is your reasonable service.
—Romans 12:1

A study of the twelfth chapter of Romans would be of profit to us. It is a sermon by the apostle Paul, written for our instruction."[1] It is important to understand that Paul believes a follower of Christ will exemplify the One he professes to follow. "The doctrine of righteousness by faith and salvation by grace does not encourage or permit lawlessness or a careless disregard of God's commandments. On the contrary, the believer who has been justified and is being sanctified becomes ever more willing to obey as 'the righteousness of the law' is being fulfilled in him. . . . In love and gratitude he seeks ever more earnestly to know, to understand, and to perform the 'good, and acceptable, and perfect, will of God' ([Romans] 12:2)."[2] "True sanctification is the dedication of the entire being—body, mind, and soul (1 Thess. 5:23); the harmonious development of the physical, mental, and spiritual powers, until the image of God, in which man was originally created, is perfectly restored (Col. 3:10).

". . . Any harmful practice or selfish indulgence that lessens physical strength makes it more difficult for us to develop mentally and spiritually."[3]

"The Christian's dedication of himself to a life of purity and holiness is an act of spiritual worship. He no longer offers animals in sacrifice but rather himself as an act of religious service that pertains to his reason. Thus Peter describes believers as 'an holy priesthood, to offer up spiritual sacrifices, acceptable to God by Jesus Christ' (1 Peter 2:5 . . .).

"This verse [Romans 12:2] attaches profound significance to the principles of healthful living. The believer performs an act of spiritual worship by offering God a holy and healthy body, along with a consecrated mind and heart, because by so doing he submits all there is of him to God's will, and opens the way for the full restoration in him of the divine image. It is an act of religious service to preserve the physical powers in the best possible condition."[4]

"The Christian glorifies God in his body."[5]

---

1. Ellen G. White, MS 50, 1903.
2. Francis D. Nichol, ed., *The Seventh-day Adventist Bible Commentary*, vol. 6 (Washington, DC: Review and Herald®, 1957), 615.
3. Nichol, *Seventh-day Adventist Bible Commentary*, vol. 6, 615.
4. Nichol, *Seventh-day Adventist Bible Commentary*, vol. 6, 616
5. Nichol, *Seventh-day Adventist Bible Commentary*, vol. 6, 616.

Part 12: Christians' Relations to Their Neighbors

If it is possible, as much as depends on you, live peaceably with all men. Beloved, do not avenge yourselves, but rather give place to wrath; for it is written, "Vengeance is Mine, I will repay," says the Lord. Therefore "if your enemy is hungry, feed him; if he is thirsty, give him drink; for in so doing you will heap coals of fire on his head."

—Romans 12:18–20

Relations in Rome between Christians and the populace were not always good. Christians had already been banished once from the city by the emperor, Claudius. "Followers of an unpopular cause who wish to persuade others of the truth and excellence of their message, must see to it that their behavior is consistently above reproach. They must never give occasion for suspicion or offense. The Christian who wishes his light to shine before men so that they may see his good works and glorify his Father who is in heaven (Matt. 5:16) will never engage in activities or enterprises of a doubtful character that might bring not only himself but also the whole Christian body into disrepute.

"Paul was never afraid to incur opposition when duty and conscience so required. Nevertheless, he is here advising and exhorting Christians to exercise caution and foresight, so as not to offend unnecessarily and thereby stir up the hostility of others. This is the course dictated not only by love but also by good, practical sense. It is impossible to persuade and antagonize people at the same time."[1]

"So far as the Christian is concerned, he is to do everything he can to maintain peace. But there are times when fidelity to principle may necessitate his incurring the antagonism of others. Therefore Paul adds the qualification, 'if it be possible.' The record of Paul's own life, which was one of almost constant conflict, shows that it is not always possible to be at peace."[2]

"Christians are never to attempt to seek revenge upon those who treat them unjustly. They should leave the matter with God. Only a perfect, all-knowing, all-loving God can rightly judge and justly punish evildoers. . . .

"Kindness is the best vengeance that a Christian can take against an enemy."[3]

"The infliction of vengeance is a sign, not of strength, but of weakness."[4]

---

1. Francis D. Nichol, ed., *The Seventh-day Adventist Bible Commentary*, vol. 6 (Washington, DC: Review and Herald®, 1957), 624.
2. Nichol, *Seventh-day Adventist Bible Commentary*, vol. 6, 624.
3. Nichol, *Seventh-day Adventist Bible Commentary*, vol. 6, 624, 625.
4. Nichol, *Seventh-day Adventist Bible Commentary*, vol. 6, 625.

Part 13: A Christian's Relation to the State

Let every soul be subject to the governing authorities. For there is no authority except from God, and the authorities that exist are appointed by God.
—Romans 13:1

N o human authority exists except by God's permission and under His control. . . . "Paul does not imply in these verses [Romans 13:1, 2] that God always approves the conduct of civil governments. Nor does Paul mean that it is the Christian's duty always to submit to them. The requirements of government may at times be contrary to the law of God, and under such circumstances the Christian is 'to obey God rather than men' (Acts 4:19; 5:29). Paul's point is that the ruling power of human governments is entrusted to men by God, according to His own purposes for man's welfare. Their continuance in power, or their fall from authority, is in His hands. Therefore, the Christian will support the authority of the existing state. He will not presume to take it into his own hands to resist or to depose 'the powers that be.'

"Such instruction was especially needful in Paul's day, for at that time the Jews were in a turbulent mood and had already stirred up rebellion in various parts of the Roman Empire."[1]

Paul counseled Christians to pay their taxes. "In Paul's time the agents of the Roman government who were empowered to collect taxes and customs were, to the Jews at least, the object of popular hatred and contempt. Therefore, Paul's counsel to the believers in Rome that they should not only submit to taxation but also give due honor and respect to their rulers was in striking contrast with the growing sentiment of rebellion that was being stirred up by fanatical Jews and that was soon to bring destruction upon their nation."[2] When the Pharisees tried to entrap Jesus by asking Him whether it was lawful to pay tribute to Rome, Jesus counseled that one must "render therefore to Caesar the things that are Caesar's, and to God the things that are God's" (Matthew 22:21). Peter also encouraged Christians to "submit yourselves to every ordinance of man for the Lord's sake" (1 Peter 2:13).

Christians should obey the laws of the land and those appointed over them unless those laws conflict with God's Ten Commandments.

---

1. Francis D. Nichol, ed., *The Seventh-day Adventist Bible Commentary*, vol. 6 (Washington, DC: Review and Herald®, 1957), 626.
2. Nichol, *Seventh-day Adventist Bible Commentary*, vol. 6, 628.

Part 14: Nearness of the Second Coming

The night is far spent, the day is at hand.

—Romans 13:12

P aul frequently spoke in his letters of the nearness of the Second Coming. He mentioned it in speaking with the Corinthians (1 Corinthians 15:51, 52) and the Thessalonians (1 Thessalonians 4:15, 17). Now he brings it up again in his letter to the Romans. "Some would hasten to conclude that the Bible writers were hopelessly mistaken men, or at least, that nothing can be known regarding the time of Christ's coming."[1] However, the writers of the New Testament firmly believed the Second Coming would occur: "But the day of the Lord *will* come" (2 Peter 3:10; emphasis added). It was fact. Jesus would keep His promise (John 14:1–3). "The Bible writers emphasized that the day of the Lord would come suddenly, unexpectedly. Christ's statements are the best exhibit of this. Said He: 'Watch therefore: for ye know not what hour your Lord doth come' (Matt. 24:42). . . .

"Paul echoes the words of our Lord: 'The day of the Lord so cometh as a thief in the night' (1 Thess. 5:2). Peter writes similarly: 'The day of the Lord will come as a thief in the night' (2 Peter 3:10).

"Now in view of the fact that the Lord did not see fit to reveal the 'day and hour' (Matt. 24:36) of His coming, and urged constant watchfulness upon His followers lest that day come upon them as a 'thief,' what else should we expect but that the NT [New Testament] writers would write of the advent with the overtone of imminency?"[2]

"However, there is certain evidence in the NT that God did give a measure of light to His penmen regarding the time that would elapse before Christ's coming."[3] Paul spoke of those things that needed to be fulfilled before the coming of the Lord (2 Thessalonians 2:3–12). He told Timothy to train faithful ministers to carry on once he passed from the scene (2 Timothy 2:2). Paul understood that Christians should live in constant expectancy with an eye to the signs of the times, but "we need not wait till we are translated to follow Christ. God's people may do this here below."[4]

"We shall follow the Lamb of God in the courts above only if we follow Him here. Following Him in heaven depends on our keeping His commandments now."[5]

---

1. Francis D. Nichol, ed., *The Seventh-day Adventist Bible Commentary*, vol. 6 (Washington, DC: Review and Herald®, 1957), 630.
2. Nichol, *Seventh-day Adventist Bible Commentary*, vol. 6, 631.
3. Nichol, *Seventh-day Adventist Bible Commentary*, vol. 6, 632.
4. Ellen G. White, "Waiting and Working for Christ," *Advent Review and Sabbath Herald*, April 12, 1898, 1.
5. White, "Waiting and Working for Christ," 1.

Part 15: Did Paul Abolish the Sabbath?

One person esteems one day above another; another esteems every day alike. Let each be fully convinced in his own mind.

—Romans 14:5

Romans 14 has "been used by some: (1) to disparage a vegetarian diet, (2) to abolish the distinction between clean and unclean meats, and (3) to remove all distinction between days, thus abolishing the seventh-day Sabbath. That Paul is doing none of these three becomes evident when this chapter is studied in light of certain religious and related problems that troubled some of the 1st-century Christians."[1] When Paul wrote 1 Corinthians 8, he was dealing with the issue of foods that had been offered to pagan gods. Strong Christians realized these gods were "nothing," and they could, with a free conscience, eat these foods. But Paul advised them to always be aware that their example might create a stumbling block for those not as strong in the faith. Novice Christians were looking to the more "seasoned" Christians for guidance.

"Paul now discusses the observance of special days, another cause of dissension and confusion among believers . . . [Galatians 4:10, 11; Colossians 2:16, 17].

"Those believers whose faith enables them immediately to leave behind all ceremonial holy days should not despise others whose faith is less strong. Nor, in turn, may the latter criticize those who seem to them lax. Each believer is responsible to God (Rom. 14:10–12)."[2]

Many early Christians still observed Jewish feast days and scrupulously kept the ceremonial law. But should these Christians be keeping Jewish holy days? "Paul himself attended a number of the feasts after his conversion (Acts 18:21; etc.). . . . Under the circumstances it appeared best to allow the various elements of the Jewish ceremonial law gradually to disappear as the mind and conscience became enlightened."[3] Paul was not advocating the abolition of the seventh-day Sabbath found in God's Decalogue. The Sabbath had existed from Eden, even before there were "special" Jewish ceremonial Sabbaths.

Jesus Himself said, "Do not think that I came to destroy the Law or the Prophets. I did not come to destroy but to fulfill" (Matthew 5:17). Paul would agree!

---

1. Francis D. Nichol, ed., *The Seventh-day Adventist Bible Commentary*, vol. 6 (Washington, DC: Review and Herald®, 1957), 634.
2. Nichol, *Seventh-day Adventist Bible Commentary*, vol. 6, 637.
3. Nichol, *Seventh-day Adventist Bible Commentary*, vol. 6, 635.

Part 16: Be Compassionate

*Now may the God of patience and comfort grant you to be
like-minded toward one another, according to Christ Jesus.*

—Romans 15:5

A mong today's Christians, just as in the early Christian church, we find diversity. Christians aren't stamped out with a cookie cutter from the same batch of dough. We each bring to the church not only our unique spiritual gifts but also our racial, cultural, and ethnic baggage. Just so, some Jewish converts brought with them inherent feelings of superiority over their Gentile brethren. Likewise, Gentiles brought prejudices against the Jews and most "foolish" Jewish traditions. Mix in pagans, who came from a place neither good Jew nor good Gentile would even dare approach for depravity and debasement, and you have the church of the first century. Bringing unity in Christ from such cultural diversity was hard!

Yet Paul urged unity. He believed all could gather around the cross of Jesus, and there find common ground. He further believed all should be willing to concede some perceived rights to others. "Paul does not mean that the strong should please the weak by agreeing with their opinions and practices or by feebly complying with what they may mistakenly think is good.

"... Paul illustrates and enforces the duty of sacrificing our own pleasure for the good of our brethren by referring to the one supreme example of self-sacrificing love. Christ was willing to give up even His heavenly glory for the sake of fallen man, and He expects corresponding self-denial and sacrifice on the part of those whom He came to save and bless. . . . Surely His servants . . . should not deem themselves too exalted to condescend as their Master has done."[1]

It is important to remember, however, that "Paul is not praying for identity of opinion on inconsequential matters, but for a spirit of unity and harmony, in spite of differences of opinion."[2]

"Believers are to acknowledge one another as Christians and to treat one another as such, even though they may have different opinions about minor matters."[3] When Paul told church members to, "as far as possible, be at peace with all men" (Romans 12:18), he did not mean that we should put on one face for outsiders and treat fellow believers with contempt.

"To be a Christian is to be Christlike."[4]

1. Francis D. Nichol, ed., *The Seventh-day Adventist Bible Commentary*, vol. 6 (Washington, DC: Review and Herald®, 1957), 643.
2. Nichol, *Seventh-day Adventist Bible Commentary*, vol. 6, 643.
3. Nichol, *Seventh-day Adventist Bible Commentary*, vol. 6, 644.
4. Ellen G. White, "The Spirit of a Christian," *Advent Review and Sabbath Herald*, February 24, 1891, 1.

Part 17: *Phoebe's* Letter of Recommendation

I commend to you Phoebe our sister, who is a servant of the church in Cenchrea, that you may receive her in the Lord in a manner worthy of the saints, and assist her in whatever business she has need of you, for indeed she has been a helper of many and of myself also.

—Romans 16:1, 2

Paul closes his letter to the Romans by commending *Phoebe* to them. "The name means 'radiant,' or 'bright.' . . . She may have been the bearer of Paul's epistle. . . .

" . . . She was a fellow Christian. . . .

" . . . Phoebe was in some sense a servant or minister in the congregation at Cenchreae [the eastern seaport for Corinth]."[1] Have you noticed women often played principal roles in Paul's churches? *Lois* and *Eunice* of Lystra, *Lydia* of Philippi, *Chloe* and *Priscilla* of Corinth, *Phoebe* of Cenchreae; all were devout, strong women! Though often overlooked in a man's world, they were key to the planting of new churches in new territories.

Paul also asked the Romans to greet *Priscilla* (mentioned first!) and Aquila. When last we saw these two, they were helping to establish the work in Ephesus. Now it would appear they had returned to Rome (see Romans 12:3). Paul mentions Epaenetus and *Mary*, as well as fellow prisoners Andronicus and Junia. At some time in the past, these two must have shared one of Paul's many incarcerations. He sends greetings to Amplias, Urbanus, Stachys, Apelles, Aristobulus (possibly the grandson of Herod the Great), Herodion, Narcissus, *Persis*, and the two sisters—*Tryphena* and *Tryphosa*. He wishes to be remembered to Rufus and his *mother*, whom Paul called a "mother" to himself also. He mentions Asyncritus, Phlegon, and Hermas, Patrobas, Hermes, Philologus, *Julia*, Nereus and his *sister*, and *Olympas*. Note how many women are mentioned in Paul's list!

Why are we spending a devotional day on these individuals? Other than Priscilla and Aquila, are these names familiar to you? That's the point. While we may not be as well known in church circles as a Paul, Timothy, Peter, or Luke, our support and friendship are critical to those who minister on the front lines. "Those who are sons [and daughters] of God will represent Christ in character. Their works will be perfumed by the infinite tenderness, compassion, love, and purity of the Son of God."[2] These women were integral to the early Christian churches. Women still show forth Christ's character in our churches today.

Paul never forgot his church family. Jesus remembers each of us to His Father as well!

---

1. Francis D. Nichol, ed., *The Seventh-day Adventist Bible Commentary*, vol. 6 (Washington, DC: Review and Herald®, 1957), 649.

2. Ellen G. White, "The Right Use of God's Gifts," *Advent Review and Sabbath Herald*, November 24, 1896, 2.

Apostasy in Galatia

I marvel that you are turning away so soon from Him who called you in the grace of Christ, to a different gospel.

—Galatians 1:6

A s if Paul didn't have enough to worry about with the church at Corinth, now he heard disturbing news from the churches in Galatia.[1] "Tidings had been received at Corinth from the churches in Galatia, revealing a state of great confusion, and even of absolute apostasy. Judaizing teachers were opposing the work of the apostle, and seeking to destroy the fruit of his labors.

"In almost every church there were some members who were Jews by birth. To these converts the Jewish teachers found ready access, and through them gained a foot-hold in the churches. It was impossible, by scriptural arguments, to overthrow the doctrines taught by Paul; hence they resorted to the most unscrupulous measures to counteract his influence and weaken his authority. They declared that he had not been a disciple of Jesus, and had received no commission from him; yet he had presumed to teach doctrines directly opposed to those held by Peter, James, and the other apostles. Thus the emissaries of Judaism succeeded in alienating many of the Christian converts from their teacher in the gospel. Having gained this point, they induced them to return to the observance of the ceremonial law as essential to salvation. Faith in Christ, and obedience to the law of ten commandments, were regarded as of minor importance. Division, heresy, and sensualism were rapidly gaining ground among the believers in Galatia."[2]

The Jerusalem Council had dealt with the question of whether Gentile converts were to be required to follow Jewish customs. These Judaizers had bided their time, and now they struck at Paul behind his back. They knew the council's decision. They set themselves in direct opposition to the stated position of the church. Paul was outraged. Perhaps these were the very men who had sought to destroy him at the council itself. They knew they were lying when they discredited Paul's ordination and the commission he received from Jesus Christ Himself. Further, their position that righteousness is attained through compliance with the works of the Jewish legal system went contrary to righteousness by faith in Jesus. They didn't care!

Christians build up; they don't destroy.

---

1. For Paul's initial visit to Galatia, see the readings for April 17–19.
2. Ellen G. White, *Sketches From the Life of Paul* (Washington, DC: Review and Herald®, 1974), 188.

Part 1: Jewish Christians

I have been crucified with Christ; it is no longer I who live, but Christ lives in me; and the life which I now live in the flesh I live by faith in the Son of God, who loved me and gave Himself for me.

—Galatians 2:20

So what was the position of the Judaizers? They believed "a man could save himself by meticulously keeping ... 'the law,' which consisted of moral, ceremonial, and civil precepts. ... The Jews erred in: (1) considering that salvation could be attained by one's own efforts, through compliance with the requirements of 'the law,' and by virtue of a meritorious life in which a surplus of good deeds would cancel out evil deeds, (2) adding to the law, as given by God, a mass of man-made requirements, commonly called 'tradition' ..., and (3) extending, and attempting to enforce, certain features of the ritual and ceremonial provisions of 'the law' beyond the cross, when they expired by limitation. ...

"... Justification comes as a free gift of God through Jesus Christ (... John 3:16). Works have no part in this transaction. On God's part it is a gift made possible through Jesus Christ. On man's part it requires complete faith and trust in God that He is able and willing to justify a sinner. Faith is the means by which man receives justification."[1]

If the Galatians accepted the argument of the Judaizers, then they would be back under the rigorous requirements of the ceremonial law to gain salvation. Why then did Jesus die? The law condemns them as sinners, and they cannot possibly gain their own salvation. The Judaizers would, therefore, put the Galatians in a hopeless position. We are speaking here of the ceremonial law, not the Decalogue. Remember, "the Christian keeps the Decalogue, not to gain salvation, but because he is saved. Indeed only a saved man can keep it, for Christ dwells within him."[2]

Paul knew what was involved in trying to gain salvation by keeping the law. He had been a zealous Pharisee. Here then was the crux of the matter—the Jews had to accept Christ, and to do that meant they would have to admit that "Judaism could not save a man."[3] Abandoning national pride, religious heritage, and the quest for perfection were sacrifices they would not make.

If Adventists truly believe salvation is gained only through faith in Jesus Christ and His sacrifice, why do so many also clutch an "I must do this to be saved" checklist?

---

1. Francis D. Nichol, ed., *The Seventh-day Adventist Bible Commentary*, vol. 6 (Washington, DC: Review and Herald®, 1957), 949.

2. Nichol, *Seventh-day Adventist Bible Commentary*, vol. 6, 934.

3. Nichol, *Seventh-day Adventist Bible Commentary*, vol. 6, 950.

Part 2: Foolish Galatians!

What purpose then does the law serve?

—Galatians 3:19

Paul met the Judaizers on their own ground. "Paul's opponents had made it appear that Paul had no regard for the writings of Moses, to which they had attached an exaggerated importance."[1] Paul argued from Old Testament Scripture that Abraham's standing with God was not due to his circumcision but rather his faith. Again, Paul used Habakkuk 2:4 to put forth the truth, "the just shall live by his faith." Many mistakenly believe Paul was saying *all* Old Testament laws were nailed to the cross. "Growing out of this interpretation is the view that in the pre-Christian era men were saved by the keeping of the law, and in the Christian Era by grace through faith. But such a view is contrary to the whole body of Scripture. God has had only one means of saving man, from Adam onward; that is, by faith in the sacrifice of our Lord. The good news of that salvation has been proclaimed to man in all ages (see Heb. 4:2)."[2] Paul himself writes, "Do we then make void the law through faith? Certainly not! On the contrary, we establish the law" (Romans 3:31).

Paul wanted the Galatians to understand something of Jewish history. "It was at Sinai that God most literally called them [Israel] out for His own and made them His peculiar people, His holy nation. The distinctive mark of that initial experience at Sinai was the announcing to Israel of the great moral code that was ever to be the standard of their lives, plus (a) civil statutes that were an interpretation and application of the moral code to the Jewish State and (b) certain statutes that were to govern the symbolic ritual of sacrifices and offerings pointing forward to the great sacrifice of Christ."[3] The Jews thought that doing all these things would make them acceptable to God. True, Abraham kept the law, but it was his faith that commended him to God (Hebrews 11:8–19)!

The Ten Commandments delineate sin. They are the yardsticks by which righteousness is measured. Paul wrote the Romans, "I had not known sin, but by the law" (Romans 7:7).

How foolish of the Galatians to reject salvation by faith in Christ's atonement. To believe a man's works save him brings only frustration and grief.

---

1. Francis D. Nichol, ed., *The Seventh-day Adventist Bible Commentary*, vol. 6 (Washington, DC: Review and Herald®, 1957), 954.
2. Nichol, *Seventh-day Adventist Bible Commentary*, vol. 6, 958.
3. Nichol, *Seventh-day Adventist Bible Commentary*, vol. 6, 958.

Part 3: Faith Versus Legalism

Therefore the law was our tutor to bring us to Christ, that we might be justified by faith.
—Galatians 3:24

To which law, ceremonial or moral, was Paul referring in this text? "In this scripture, the Holy Spirit through the apostle is speaking especially of the moral law. The law reveals sin to us, and causes us to feel our need of Christ, and to flee unto Him for pardon and peace by exercising repentance toward God and faith toward our Lord Jesus Christ. . . .

"The law of Ten Commandments is not to be looked upon as much from the prohibitory side as from the mercy side. Its prohibitions are the sure guarantee of happiness in obedience. As received in Christ, it works in us the purity of character that will bring joy to us through eternal ages. To the obedient it is a wall of protection. We behold in it the goodness of God, who by revealing to men the immutable principles of righteousness, seeks to shield them from the evils that result from transgression.

"We are not to regard God as waiting to punish the sinner for his sin. The sinner brings the punishment upon himself. His own actions start a train of circumstances that bring the sure result. . . . By choosing to sin, men separate themselves from God, cut themselves off from the channel of blessing, and the sure result is ruin and death.

"The law is an expression of God's idea. When we receive it in Christ, it becomes our idea. It lifts us above the power of natural desires and tendencies, above temptations that lead to sin."[1]

Paul uses the Greek word *paidagōgos* to explain the *function* of the law. In Greek families, the *pedagogue*, or tutor, "was a supervisor of, and companion to, boys. He accompanied them to school, protected them from harm, kept them from mischief, and had the right to discipline them. . . .

". . . 'The law' served as the guardian, supervisor, or custodian of the chosen people in [Old Testament] times, and like the *paidagōgos*, was charged with their moral training."[2] "The law has no power to pardon the transgressor, but it points him to Christ Jesus, who says to him, I will take your sin and bear it myself, if you will accept me as your substitute and surety. Return to your allegiance, and I will impute to you my righteousness."[3]

The Ten Commandments are God's guardians keeping us from mischief.

---

1. Ellen G. White, Letter 96, 1896.
2. Francis D. Nichol, ed., *The Seventh-day Adventist Bible Commentary*, vol. 6 (Washington, DC: Review and Herald®, 1957), 961.
3. Ellen G. White, "The Great Standard of Righteousness," *Advent Review and Sabbath Herald*, May 7, 1901, 1.

Part 4: All One in Christ

*There is neither Jew nor Greek, there is neither slave nor free,
there is neither male nor female; for you are all one in Christ Jesus.*
—Galatians 3:28

We are all children of God. Paul takes this idea one step further. He says, "For you are all sons of God through faith in Christ Jesus. For as many of you as were baptized into Christ have put on Christ" (Galatians 3:26, 27). Paul wanted the Galatians to understand that ethnicity, social status, gender—all had no place within the church. "Christianity subordinates the role of race and nationality to the principle of the brotherhood of all men (Acts 17:26). . . . In Christ's kingdom all are covered with the same garment of Christ's righteousness, which they receive by faith in Jesus Christ. But to the Judaizing Christians of Paul's day such an idea was rank heresy. They maintained that the only way into the Christian church was through Judaism, that a Gentile must first be circumcised—become a Jew, as it were—before being accepted into the Christian communion."[1]

Paul wanted everyone to know the playing field was level for all when it came to the sinner's need of salvation. This was a radical idea for his time. To equate a slave with a master or a woman with a man was unheard of in first-century Roman society. "Christianity alone eliminates distinctions based on race, nationality, and social standing."[2] "In the ancient world women were commonly considered as little more than chattels, and thus infinitely inferior to men. Pagan philosophers sometimes argued as to whether a woman even had a soul. In some pagan societies a father or husband had authority over the women of his household to the point of ordering their execution. The elevation of women to equality with men is the direct result of Christian teaching and practice. Here, however, Paul is thinking of the status of women before God as sinners in need of salvation."[3] "As the divine precepts of love for God and for one's fellow men are made operative, men's hearts are united in a close bond of fellowship, each with others, under their heavenly Father."[4]

A truly "Christian" church is not clannish, rank conscious, prejudiced, or gender biased.

---

1. Francis D. Nichol, ed., *The Seventh-day Adventist Bible Commentary*, vol. 6 (Washington, DC: Review and Herald®, 1957), 962.
2. Nichol, *Seventh-day Adventist Bible Commentary*, vol. 6, 962.
3. Nichol, *Seventh-day Adventist Bible Commentary*, vol. 6, 962.
4. Nichol, *Seventh-day Adventist Bible Commentary*, vol. 6, 962.

Part 5: No Longer Slaves

But now after you have known God, or rather are known by God, how is it that you turn again to the weak and beggarly elements, to which you desire again to be in bondage?
—Galatians 4:9

The epistle to the Galatians was written to meet a specific situation in the apostolic church, but the principle therein set forth—that men are saved, not by supposed works of merit, but by faith alone—is as true today as it was then. Legalism of any kind—the seeking of merit with God by the performance of certain acts—is worthless, since 'man is not justified by works of the law, but by the faith of Jesus Christ' (Gal 2:16)."[1] Paul was worried for the Galatians. Where they had once been slaves to false gods, they now were falling back into slavery to the law. He was personally distressed for them. "I am afraid for you, lest I have labored for you in vain" (Galatians 4:11).

"For practical purposes Judaism had degenerated into a system of external observances, in some respects hardly distinguishable from those of the heathen religions.... 'The law' . . . was 'weak' in that it had no power to save even the most ardent devotees, and it was 'beggarly,' or poor, in that it lacked the vital spark of life. Furthermore, the Jews had added so many traditions to 'the law' that its original purpose had been obscured, and it had become a burden to those who sought to meet its requirements as a means of earning salvation.... The Galatians were giving up all the benefits of the gospel and receiving nothing in return."[2]

Paul argued that he "had once been a Jew, zealously devoted to the legal system as only a dyed-in-the-wool, bigoted Pharisee could be (Acts 26:5). But he had given up the legal system, once so dear to him, and had, for practical purposes, become a Gentile so that he might win the Gentiles to Christ (1 Cor. 9:20–23; 10:32, 33). Why should Gentile Galatians now adopt Judaism? If he had given it up for their sakes, could they not give it up for him?"[3]

It is a joyless religion that enslaves its members with endless rules without preaching the freedom found in salvation through Jesus Christ, our Lord.

---

1. Siegfried H. Horn, *Seventh-day Adventist Bible Dictionary*, ed. Don F. Neufeld, Commentary Reference Series, vol. 8 (Washington, DC: Review and Herald®, 1960), s.v. "Galatians, Epistle to."
2. Francis D. Nichol, ed. *The Seventh-day Adventist Bible Commentary*, vol. 6 (Washington, DC: Review and Herald®, 1957), 967.
3. Nichol, *Seventh-day Adventist Bible Commentary*, vol. 6, 968.

Part 6: Two Sons—An Allegory

For it is written that Abraham had two sons: the one by a bondwoman, the other by a freewoman.
—Galatians 4:22

P aul now turns to 'the law' . . . itself for an illustration of the difference between bondage to 'the law' and freedom in Christ. Inasmuch as portions of the Pentateuch were read every Sabbath in the synagogues . . . , the books of Moses were well known to all Jews and to Gentiles who had been attending the synagogue services. The story related was a simple fact of Jewish history, but Paul uses it in an allegorical sense ([Galatians 4:]24) to show the difference between being in bondage to the ceremonial law and enjoying the freedom that comes from faith in Jesus Christ."[1] It is possible he used this very example of Abraham's two sons because the Judaizers were making their case using the same text from Genesis. Their argument would have required the Galatians to join the true heirs of Abraham by submitting to the ceremonial law and being circumcised before they could join the church. Paul used an analogy to show that the Judaizers were really making the Galatians slaves to the ceremonial law.

Hagar, as a "bondwoman," represented slavery. Paul equated Hagar with Jews who were enslaved to the Torah, Jews who believed only Israelites were God's chosen people; Jews enslaved to the ceremonial law. The children of Sarah represented the free children. These were the true descendants of Abraham, the children of the promise, the children of the Christian church. Whereas the children in slavery focused on their earthly Jerusalem, the children of freedom focused on the promise of a heavenly New Jerusalem. His contrast between the two was clear. The Galatians were free sons of the promise God made to Abraham. Why would they want to submit to being slaves to the Torah? Paul's quotation of Genesis 21:10 in verse Galatians 4:30 sums up what he wanted the Galatians to do to the Judaizers and their enslaving message: "Cast out this bondwoman and her son, for the son of the bondwoman shall not be heir with my son."

"The solution of the problem that faced the church in Galatia and elsewhere was not to blend Judaism with Christianity, but to 'cast out' the principle of Judaizing, together with all who prompted it."[2]

"Salvation by works is altogether incompatible with salvation by faith (. . . Rom. 11:6; Eph. 2:8, 9). A blend of the two is impossible, for once faith is diluted by works it ceases to be pure faith."[3]

---

1. Francis D. Nichol, ed., *The Seventh-day Adventist Bible Commentary*, vol. 6 (Washington, DC: Review and Herald®, 1957), 971.
2. Nichol, *Seventh-day Adventist Bible Commentary*, vol. 6, 973
3. Nichol, *Seventh-day Adventist Bible Commentary*, vol. 6, 973.

Part 7: Circumcision and Liberty

Stand fast therefore in the liberty by which Christ has made us free,
and do not be entangled again with a yoke of bondage.

—Galatians 5:1

H ere is an illustration taken straight from the battlefield. When faced by an onslaught of enemy attacks, the commander rallies the troops and orders all to "stand fast; hold your ground." "For the Christian, this ground is truth as set forth in Holy Writ. The diligent Christian will persevere in his examination of the Scriptures (2 Tim. 3:16, 17 . . .), and then examine himself to discover whether he stands fast in the faith (2 Cor. 13:5)."[1]

The Galatians needed to regroup and realize that the Judaizers were dividing them by claiming those who observed the ceremonial law were better Christians and closer to God than those who did not. Circumcision was the dividing line. "Paul's indignation was stirred. His voice was raised in stern rebuke: 'If ye be circumcised, Christ shall profit you nothing.' The party maintaining that Christianity was valueless without circumcision arrayed themselves against the apostle, and he had to meet them in every church which he founded or visited; in Jerusalem, Antioch, Galatia, Corinth, Ephesus, and Rome. God urged him out to the great work of preaching Christ, and him crucified; circumcision or uncircumcision was nothing. . . .

"These divisions in regard to the ceremonial law, and the relative merits of the different ministers teaching the doctrine of Christ, caused the apostle much anxiety and hard labor."[2] Paul was saying Judaizers were no better than the heathen because they also emphasized religious rites and ceremonies.

Paul charged straight at the Judaizers. He accused them of obstructing the Galatians' advance toward truth (see Galatians 5:7). He likened them to leaven, which, like yeast, would start small and eventually change the whole congregation (see verse 9). He was confident their character and motives would eventually be revealed, and they would pay the price for their treachery (see verse 10). Paul ends by suggesting the Judaizers, who advocated circumcision as a measure of virtue, should go one step further and really gain virtue by castrating themselves. Heathen followers of Cybele became eunuchs in the service of the nature goddess of ancient Anatolia.

"For in Christ Jesus neither circumcision nor uncircumcision avails anything, but a new creation"
(Galatians 6:15).

---

1. Francis D. Nichol, ed., *The Seventh-day Adventist Bible Commentary*, vol. 6 (Washington, DC: Review and Herald®, 1957), 975.
2. Ellen G. White, *Sketches From the Life of Paul* (Washington, DC: Review and Herald®, 1974), 122.

Part 8: Inner Conflict

I say then: Walk in the Spirit, and you shall not fulfill the lust of the flesh.
—Galatians 5:16

The life of the Christian is not all smooth. He has stern conflicts to meet. Severe temptations assail him. 'The flesh warreth against the Spirit, and the Spirit against the flesh.' The nearer we come to the close of this earth's history, the more delusive and ensnaring will be the attacks of the enemy. His attacks will grow fiercer and more frequent. Those who resist light and truth will become more hardened and unimpressible, and more bitter against those who love God and keep His commandments."[1]

"Genuine faith always works by love. When you look to Calvary, it is not to quiet your soul in the non-performance of duty, not to compose yourself to sleep, but to create faith in Jesus, faith that will work, purifying the soul from the slime of selfishness. When we lay hold of Christ by faith, our work has just begun. Every man has corrupt and sinful habits that must be overcome by vigorous warfare. Every soul is required to fight the fight of faith. If one is a follower of Christ, he cannot be sharp in deal, he cannot be hardhearted, devoid of sympathy. He cannot be coarse in speech, he cannot be full of pomposity and self-esteem. He cannot be overbearing, nor can he use harsh words, and censure and condemn.

"The labor of love springs from the work of faith. Bible religion means constant work. 'Let your light so shine before men, that they may see your good works, and glorify your Father which is in heaven.' 'Work out your own salvation with fear and trembling, for it is God that worketh in you, both to will and to do of his good pleasure.' We are to be zealous of good works; be careful to maintain good works. And the true Witness says, 'I know thy works.'

"While it is true that our busy activities will not in themselves insure salvation, it is also true that faith which unites us to Christ will stir the soul to activity."[2]

While character is formed by the unending warfare between right and wrong tendencies, Paul stressed victory over sin is possible only through Jesus Christ.

1. Ellen G. White, MS 31, 1889.
2. Ellen G. White, MS 16, 1890.

Part 9: Fruit of the Spirit

But the fruit of the Spirit is love, joy, peace, longsuffering, kindness,
goodness, faithfulness, gentleness, self-control. Against such there is no law.

—Galatians 5:22, 23

Paul set out a list of vices and virtues for the Galatians to ponder. This was typical ethical training of the time. Obviously, the Galatians were having conflicts between one another. Paul speaks to these social ills directly. In the matter of sexuality, they should avoid adultery, fornication, uncleanness, and lasciviousness. Regarding false worship, they should avoid idolatry and witchcraft. When dealing with each other, they should avoid hatred, variance (contention), emulations (jealousy), wrath (anger), strife (selfish ambition), seditions (dissensions), and heresies. Dealing with fellow church members was then, and sometimes still is today, difficult for those who are not truly converted.

Paul next listed the virtues to be sought by a true Christian. He called these "*fruit* of the Spirit" (note the singular, not "fruits"), fruit that grows out of a relationship with the Spirit and not something attained by works. Every one of the traits listed will be seen in the life of the Christian. The attributes grow as we develop into mature Christians. Paul's list gives no greater importance to one fruit over another, but he heads his list with "love." Perhaps this is so there is no mistake that love is the soil from which all others spring. "It is the privilege of every Christian not only to look for but to hasten the coming of our Lord Jesus Christ (2 Peter 3:12 . . .). Were all who profess His name bearing fruit to His glory, how quickly the world would be sown with the seed of the gospel. Quickly the last great harvest would be ripened, and Christ would come to gather the precious grain."[1]

"The influence of the Holy Spirit is the life of Christ in the soul. We do not see Christ and speak to Him, but His Holy Spirit is just as near us in one place as in another. It works in and through every one who receives Christ. Those who know the indwelling of the spirit reveal the fruit of the spirit—love, joy, peace, long-suffering, gentleness, goodness, faith."[2] "It takes *all* the Christian graces to make a man a true follower of Christ, but *only one* of the 'works of the flesh' to make a man a follower of the evil one."[3] Paul wants us to compare and contrast our character traits with those exhibited by sinners and those held by Spirit-filled Christians.

Which list best defines you?

---

1. Ellen G. White, *Christ's Object Lessons* (Washington, DC: Review and Herald®, 1941), 69.
2. Ellen G. White, MS 41, 1897.
3. Francis D. Nichol, ed., *The Seventh-day Adventist Bible Commentary*, vol. 6 (Washington, DC: Review and Herald®, 1957), 982; emphasis added.

Part 10: Help Each Other

Bear one another's burdens, and so fulfill the law of Christ.

—Galatians 6:2

What is the law of Christ? "The law, or principle, that motivated Christ's life was that of bearing others' burdens. Christ came to earth as man's great burden bearer.... The only formal 'commandment' our Lord gave His disciples while on earth was to 'love one another' (see John 13:34).... Christ declared also that 'all the law and the prophets'— all of God's revealed will ... are based on love, love for God and one's fellow men. To the Romans, Paul wrote that love fulfills the law (ch. 13:10). Thus, 'the law of Christ' is the epitome of the Ten Commandments, for when we live out those laws, we truly love both God and man."[1] Each of us is to look to our own character development while assisting others. "Every soldier is expected to carry his own kit; it is his responsibility to do so."[2] Jesus stands ever ready to assist each of us by allowing us to lean on Him.

Paul, as he neared the end of his letter, wrote the following: "See with what large letters I have written to you with my own hand!" (Galatians 6:11). There could have been several reasons for Paul adding this comment to his letter. "Some years prior to this time he began the practice of adding a brief section in his own handwriting, as a guarantee of the genuineness of his letters.... Apparently, letters had been forged in his name (see 2 Thess. 2:2; 3:17)."[3] It is now accepted that Paul dictated most of his letters. "Paul's writing in 'large letters' suggests that, at the time he wrote Galatians at least, his penmanship was faulty. Paul's great learning precludes the possibility that the apostle did not know how to write acceptably. Some have suggested that his poor penmanship was the result of defective vision (... 2 Cor. 12:7–9; Gal. 4:15), others, that his hands had suffered more or less permanent injury from the treatment of his persecutors (cf. 2 Cor. 11:24–27)."[4]

Paul closes with perhaps the most humble of all statements he ever wrote: "But God forbid that I should glory, save in the cross of our Lord Jesus Christ, by whom the world is crucified unto me, and I unto the world" (Galatians 6:14, KJV). Paul refused to boast of his outstanding Jewish heritage and status, for they were as nothing compared to the sacrifice of Jesus!

"The fact that nothing further is heard of trouble in Galatia over the subject of Judaizing is silent testimony to the success of his present appeal to them."[5]

---

1. Francis D. Nichol, ed., *The Seventh-day Adventist Bible Commentary*, vol. 6 (Washington, DC: Review and Herald®, 1957), 985.
2. Nichol, *Seventh-day Adventist Bible Commentary*, vol. 6, 986.
3. Nichol, *Seventh-day Adventist Bible Commentary*, vol. 6, 987.
4. Nichol, *Seventh-day Adventist Bible Commentary*, vol. 6, 987.
5. Nichol, *Seventh-day Adventist Bible Commentary*, vol. 6, 989.

A Jewish Plot

*And when the Jews plotted against him as he was
about to sail to Syria, he decided to return through Macedonia.*

—Acts 20:3

P aul spent three months in Corinth, but his focus was ever westward. His greatest desire was to preach the gospel in Rome and Spain, but first, he needed to make a quick trip to Jerusalem to deliver the collection for the Jewish believers and gain acceptance for his proposed undertaking. "Having completed his work at Corinth, he determined to sail directly for one of the ports on the coast of Palestine. All the arrangements had been made, and he was about to step on board the ship, when he was told of a plot laid by the Jews to take his life. In the past these opposers of the faith had been foiled in all their efforts to put an end to the apostle's work.

"The success attending the preaching of the gospel aroused the anger of the Jews anew. From every quarter were coming accounts of the spread of the new doctrine by which Jews were released from the observance of the rites of the ceremonial law and Gentiles were admitted to equal privileges with the Jews as children of Abraham. His [Paul's] . . . emphatic statement, 'There is neither Greek nor Jew, circumcision nor uncircumcision' (Colossians 3:11), was regarded by his enemies as daring blasphemy, and they determined that his voice should be silenced."[1] This they intended to do once the ship was upon the high seas and outside the protection of Roman law.

Paul learned of the plot and decided to travel north through Macedonia rather than board the ship. He did not travel alone. With him went a party of eight for protection and as representatives of the various churches, accompanying their respective church contributions. "Accompanying Paul and Luke were 'Sopater of Berea; and of the Thessalonians, Aristarchus and Secundus; and Gaius of Derbe, and Timotheus; and of Asia, Tychius and Trophimus.' . . .

"At Philippi Paul tarried to keep the Passover. Only Luke remained with him, the other members of the company passing on to Troas to await him there. The Philippians were the most loving and truehearted of the apostle's converts, and during the eight days of the feast he enjoyed peaceful and happy communion with them."[2]

Our churches should be islands of safety midst seas of danger.

---

1. Ellen G. White, *The Acts of the Apostles* (Mountain View, CA: Pacific Press®, 1911), 389, 390.
2. White, *Acts of the Apostles*, 390.

A Man Called "Lucky"

*And in a window sat a certain young man named Eutychus, who was
sinking into a deep sleep. He was overcome by sleep; and as Paul continued
speaking, he fell down from the third story and was taken up dead.*

—Acts 20:9

Sailing from Philippi, Paul and Luke reached their companions at Troas five days later, and remained for seven days with the believers in that place.

"Upon the last evening of his stay the brethren 'came together to break bread.' The fact that their beloved teacher was about to depart, had called together a larger company than usual. They assembled in an 'upper chamber' on the third story. There, in the fervency of his love and solicitude for them, the apostle preached until midnight."[1] Paul planned to leave early Sunday morning on foot for Assos. The rest of his party was to travel there by ship.

The interesting thing about this farewell meeting is the story of Eutychus. This young man's Greek name meant "good fortune." We today might call him "Lucky." The company gathers in a crowded upper room to hear Paul speak. Lamps are lit. Heat and smoke add to the drowsy nature of the room. There is little circulation of air, and it becomes stifling. Eutychus, while perched on a window ledge, nods off into a sound sleep and slowly tumbles backward to the courtyard, three stories below. The alarm is raised. People rush from the room. Paul hastens down the outer staircase and pushes through the frightened crowd surrounding the victim. Luke, ever the physician, says the lad "was taken up dead." Paul embraces the boy, calls for calm, and offers an earnest prayer to the Lord for the life of the young man. His prayer is answered. Paul says to those around him, "Trouble not yourselves; for his life is in him" (Acts 20:10, KJV). Immediately Paul climbs the stairs, breaks bread with them, and preaches until daybreak. I would imagine Lucky was given a seat closer to the front of the company and did not resume his perilous perch on the windowsill.

The eight days of Passover had just been celebrated by Paul at Philippi. The resurrection of Eutychus occurred twelve days later. No doubt, many of the Christians in Troas remembered Jesus had risen from the dead during Passover season. Jesus had said, "I am the resurrection and the life. He who believes in Me, though he may die, he shall live" (John 11:25).

It doesn't take "luck or good fortune" to be raised at the second coming of Christ. Only believe!

1. Ellen G. White, *The Acts of the Apostles* (Mountain View, CA: Pacific Press®, 1911), 391.

By Sea and Land

*Then we went ahead to the ship and sailed to Assos, there intending to
take Paul on board; for so he had given orders, intending himself to go on foot.*
—Acts 20:13

Considering the recent plot to kill him, it seems strange Paul would separate from
his traveling companions at this point. Why do it? Fortunately, Ellen G. White
answers the question. "The ship on which Paul and his companions were to continue
their journey, was about to sail, and the brethren hastened on board. The apostle himself,
however, chose to take the nearer route by land between Troas and Assos, meeting his
companions at the latter city. This gave him a short season for meditation and prayer.
The difficulties and dangers connected with his coming visit to Jerusalem, the attitude
of the church there toward him and his work, as well as the condition of the churches
and the interests of the gospel work in other fields, were subjects of earnest, anxious
thought, and he took advantage of this special opportunity to seek God for strength
and guidance."[1]

I have no trouble visualizing Paul, alone, deep in thought, walking the thirty-five
miles from Troas to Assos on the paved Roman road, holding communion with Jesus,
and perhaps praying and singing aloud. The distance by ship was twice that which
Paul had to travel, and he easily rejoined his party. Paul rejoined the ship at Assos, and
the ship put out for Mitylene, the capital city on the island of Lesbos. Hopscotching
along the coast from Mitylene to Chios to Samos to Trogyllium, putting in to port
each evening when the winds died down, it took five days to reach Miletus. Miletus
was about forty miles from Ephesus, and the ship had bypassed it as it would have
meant more time being spent than Paul wanted. His priority was to reach Jerusalem
by Pentecost. Paul called for the leaders of the church at Ephesus to come to Miletus
to talk over problems with their church.

"In answer to his call they came, and he spoke to them strong, touching words of
admonition and farewell."[2] " 'And now, behold, I know that ye all, among whom I
have gone preaching the kingdom of God, shall see my face no more' [Acts 20:25].

"Paul had not designed to bear this testimony; but, while he was speaking, the Spirit
of Inspiration came upon him, confirming his fears that this would be his last meeting
with his Ephesian brethren."[3]

Exceptional Christians hunger and thirst for private time with their Savior!

---

1. Ellen G. White, *The Acts of the Apostles* (Mountain View, CA: Pacific Press®, 1911), 391, 392.
2. White, *Acts of the Apostles*, 392.
3. White, *Acts of the Apostles*, 393.

250

Do Not Go to Jerusalem!

Thus says the Holy Spirit, "So shall the Jews at Jerusalem bind the man who owns this belt, and deliver him into the hands of the Gentiles."

—Acts 21:11

The elders of Ephesus stayed with Paul until the very last minute, accompanying him to his ship. "From Miletus the travelers sailed in a 'straight course unto Coos, and the day following unto Rhodes, and from thence unto Patara,' on the southwest shore of Asia Minor, where, 'finding a ship sailing over unto Phoenicia,' they 'went aboard, and set forth.' At Tyre, where the ship was unloaded, they found a few disciples, with whom they were permitted to tarry seven days. Through the Holy Spirit these disciples were warned of the perils awaiting Paul at Jerusalem, and they urged him 'that he should *not* go up to Jerusalem' [Acts 21:4.]. But the apostle allowed not the fear of affliction and imprisonment to turn him from his purpose.

"At the close of the week spent in Tyre, all the brethren, with their wives and children, went with Paul to the ship, and before he stepped on board, they knelt upon the shore and prayed, he for them, and they for him."[1] The ship traveled south and made port at Caesarea, where the travelers "entered the house of Philip the evangelist, who was one of the seven, and stayed with him" (verse 8).

While lodging with Philip, "a certain prophet named Agabus came down from Judea. When he had come to us, he took Paul's belt, bound his own hands and feet, and said, 'Thus says the Holy Spirit, "So shall the Jews at Jerusalem bind the man who owns this belt, and deliver him into the hands of the Gentiles" ' " (verses 10, 11). Paul had been twice warned that his trip to Jerusalem would end badly. Even though his companions urged him to stay in Caesarea, "Paul would not swerve from the path of duty. He would follow Christ if need be to prison and to death."[2]

Why was he so headstrong in refusing the advice of those who heard the warning? Simply put, the Holy Spirit was not telling Paul he should *not* go to Jerusalem but rather what to expect once he arrived. His friends were the ones telling him not to go. "Paul and his company set out for Jerusalem, their hearts deeply shadowed by the presentiment of coming evil."[3]

Is your trust in God strong enough to stay the course in the face of possible physical suffering or death?

---

1. Ellen G. White, *The Acts of the Apostles* (Mountain View, CA: Pacific Press®, 1911), 396.
2. White, *Acts of the Apostles*, 397.
3. White, *Acts of the Apostles*, 397.

Paul's Arrest and Trials

Before the Sanhedrin, Felix, Festus, and Herod Agrippa II

AD 58–60

Acts 21:18–26:32
The Acts of the Apostles, pp. 399–438
Sketches From the Life of Paul, pp. 207–261

Back in Jerusalem

And when we had come to Jerusalem, the brethren received us gladly.

—Acts 21:17

Before moving on in the narrative, we should consider Philip of Caesarea and his four *daughters* who were prophetesses (Acts 21:9). Did they warn Paul not to go up to Jerusalem? Women played important roles in the early church.

Philip, one of the seven deacons—the man who evangelized Samaria, baptized the Ethiopian eunuch, and preached up and down the coasts of Phoenicia and Palestine—is last mentioned in Acts as being surrounded by his exceptional family in Caesarea.

Meanwhile, Paul was accompanied from Caesarea by many of the believers. "The 64-mi. distance from Caesarea to Jerusalem was too far for one day's journey, but could be covered in two or three days. . . . [Rather than go all the way to Jerusalem], it is far more likely that they [the Caesareans] escorted him one day's journey, to the home of their friend Mnason in a village on the way, where Paul and his company lodged that one night."[1] "Never before had the apostle approached Jerusalem with so sad a heart. He knew that he would find few friends and many enemies. He was nearing the city which had rejected and slain the Son of God and over which now hung the threatenings of divine wrath. . . .

"And he could not count upon the sympathy and support of even his own brethren in the faith. The unconverted Jews who had followed so closely upon his track, had not been slow to circulate the most unfavorable reports at Jerusalem, both personally and by letter, concerning him and his work; and some, even of the apostles and elders, had received these reports as truth, making no attempt to contradict them, and manifesting no desire to harmonize with him."[2]

As soon as possible, Paul presented himself to James, the brother of Jesus and chair of the Council of Jerusalem. Paul delivered the contributions of the Gentile churches for the support of the Jewish poor. "The sum, which far exceeded the expectations of the elders at Jerusalem, represented many sacrifices and even severe privations on the part of the Gentile believers."[3] Paul was greeted warmly by James and the elders, but the greeting by the entire council on the morrow was to be of a different sort. Here ends Paul's third missionary journey.

The unconverted are still causing trouble!

---

1. Francis D. Nichol, ed., *The Seventh-day Adventist Bible Commentary*, vol. 6 (Washington, DC: Review and Herald®, 1957), 401.

2. Ellen G. White, *The Acts of the Apostles* (Mountain View, CA: Pacific Press®, 1911), 397, 398.

3. White, *Acts of the Apostles*, 399.

A Target

Now when the seven days were almost ended, the Jews from Asia,
seeing him in the temple, stirred up the whole crowd and laid hands on him.

—Acts 21:27

C onverts among the Gentiles were multiplying rapidly, and many Jews saw this as a threat to their own ideas regarding Christianity. "Paul's Judaizing opponents had not only been 'zealous of the law' (v. 20), but apparently had also been zealous in spreading exaggerated and damaging reports concerning his theological teachings. No wonder Paul admonishes so earnestly against judging one another concerning performance of ceremonies in religion (Rom. 14:1–10; Col. 2:16). He himself suffered severely at the hands of zealous legalistic critics."[1] The charge leveled against Paul was this—"you teach all the Jews who are among the Gentiles to forsake Moses, saying that they ought not to circumcise their children nor to walk according to the customs" (Acts 21:21).

"There was no basis for the charge that Paul taught the Jewish Christians 'not to circumcise their children.' The charge was a fabrication of his enemies."[2] The council, "instead of uniting in an effort to do justice to the one who had been injured, . . . gave him counsel which showed that they still cherished a feeling that Paul should be held largely responsible for the existing prejudice."[3] Their suggestion was that he should financially sponsor four members of the Jewish Christian community who were in the last week of their thirty-day Nazarite vows. A Nazarite was "a person who took certain special or voluntary and temporary vows dedicating himself to God (see Num 6:2)."[4] Paul's participation would show his constancy to Judaism.

The next day Paul took the men into the temple as the council had advised. "Those who advised Paul to take this step had not fully considered the great peril to which he would thus be exposed. At this season, Jerusalem was filled with worshipers from many lands. . . . Among these were men whose hearts were filled with bitter hatred for Paul, and for him to enter the temple on a public occasion was to risk his life."[5] Paul's "efforts for conciliation only precipitated the crisis."[6]

Paul's concern for the weak, reverence for the leadership, and desire to be all things to all men caused him to listen to bad advice.

1. Francis D. Nichol, ed., *The Seventh-day Adventist Bible Commentary*, vol. 6 (Washington, DC: Review and Herald®, 1957), 403.

2. Nichol, *Seventh-day Adventist Bible Commentary*, vol. 6, 403.

3. Ellen G. White, *The Acts of the Apostles* (Mountain View, CA: Pacific Press®, 1911), 403.

4. Siegfried H. Horn, *Seventh-day Adventist Bible Dictionary*, ed. Don F. Neufeld, Commentary Reference Series, vol. 8 (Washington, DC: Review and Herald®, 1960), s.v. "Nazirite."

5. White, *Acts of the Apostles*, 406.

6. White, *Acts of the Apostles*, 405.

Arrested

*Then the commander came near and took him, and commanded him
to be bound with two chains; and he asked who he was and what he had done.*
—Acts 21:33

F or several days he [Paul] passed in and out among the worshipers, apparently unnoticed; but before the close of the specified period, as he was talking with a priest concerning the sacrifices to be offered, he was recognized by some of the Jews from Asia.

"With the fury of demons they rushed upon him, crying, 'Men of Israel, help: This is the man, that teacheth all men everywhere against the people, and the law, and this place.' And as the people responded to the call for help, another accusation was added—'and further brought Greeks also into the temple, and hath polluted this holy place.'

"By the Jewish law it was a crime punishable by death for an uncircumcised person to enter the inner courts of the sacred edifice. Paul had been seen in the city in company with Trophimus, an Ephesian, and it was conjectured that he had brought him into the temple. This he had not done; and being himself a Jew, his act in entering the temple was no violation of the law. But though the charge was wholly false, it served to arouse the popular prejudice. As the cry was taken up and borne through the temple courts, the throngs gathered there were thrown into wild excitement. The news quickly spread through Jerusalem, 'and all the city was moved, and the people ran together.' "[1]

Things were rapidly deteriorating. The crowd was ready to kill Paul on the spot! " 'As they went about to kill him, tidings came unto the chief captain of the band, that all Jerusalem was in an uproar.' Claudius Lysias well knew the turbulent elements with which he had to deal, and he 'immediately took soldiers and centurions, and ran down unto them: and when they saw the chief captain and the soldiers, they left beating of Paul.' Ignorant of the cause of the tumult, but seeing that the rage of the multitude was directed against Paul, the Roman captain concluded that he must be a certain Egyptian rebel of whom he had heard, who had thus far escaped capture."[2]

Jerusalem was a powder keg of nationalistic emotion, ready to explode. As Paul represented a potential flash point, the Romans arrested him "for his own good."

1. Ellen G. White, *The Acts of the Apostles* (Mountain View, CA: Pacific Press®, 1911), 406, 407.
2. White, *Acts of the Apostles*, 407, 408.

Hear My Defense

Men, brethren, and fathers, hear ye my defence which I make now unto you.
—Acts 22:1, KJV

Reports of the Temple desecration [spread] like wildfire and the Jews [were] ready to act on what was to them a genuine provocation. The year was about AD 58. About eight years later the revolt of the Jews against Rome would begin. The city was already restive. . . .

". . . The Levite gatekeepers shut the gates [of the Temple] promptly, not only to guard against further desecration, but to prevent the Temple from becoming the setting of the riot itself, as it sometimes was."[1] The crowd started beating Paul mercilessly. "The chiliarch, or tribune, took down into the disturbed crowd several hundred soldiers, with a centurion, somewhat like a sergeant, heading each platoon.

". . . The presence of the Roman soldiers cowed Paul's Jewish captors. The incident was not worth a revolt, as even the excited Jews realized."[2]

Agabus's prediction (Acts 21:11) had come true as prophesied. "The soldiers took him [Paul] as far as one of the stairways leading up from the Temple to the Tower of Antonia. . . .

"The idea was not to rescue Paul, but to learn what the trouble was, and to prevent a chief actor in it from being killed before the affair could be properly investigated. But for Paul it was a rescue, as at Corinth ([Acts] 18:14–17).

". . . In keeping with Roman practice, a chain was doubtless fastened to each of his arms, with the two ends of the chain held by soldiers guarding Paul. . . . Thus held, Paul was brought before the tribune Lysias . . . for a preliminary examination."[3]

Paul identified himself to Lysias as a Greek-speaking Jew from Tarsus, in Cilicia, and asked to be allowed to address the people. Standing above the crowd on the staircase, Paul waved his hand for silence. "The gesture attracted their attention, while his bearing commanded respect. The scene changed as suddenly as when Christ drove the traffickers from the temple courts."[4] His address, found in Acts 22:1–21, makes for interesting reading. He spoke of his training at the feet of elders present in the crowd.

"Although perhaps 23 years had intervened since Paul's conversion, some of 'the elders' then living probably had joined in sanctioning Paul's persecution of the Christians."[5]

---

1. Francis D. Nichol, ed., *The Seventh-day Adventist Bible Commentary*, vol. 6 (Washington, DC: Review and Herald®, 1957), 406.
2. Nichol, *Seventh-day Adventist Bible Commentary*, vol. 6, 406.
3. Nichol, *Seventh-day Adventist Bible Commentary*, vol. 6, 406.
4. Ellen G. White, *Sketches From the Life of Paul* (Washington, DC: Review and Herald®, 1974), 218.
5. Nichol, *Seventh-day Adventist Bible Commentary*, vol. 6, 409.

Defense Cut Short

And they listened to him until this word, and then they raised their voices and said,
"Away with such a fellow from the earth, for he is not fit to live!"
—Acts 22:22

When Paul started speaking in Hebrew, the crowd became silent and listened intently. " 'I am verily a man which am a Jew, born in Tarsus, a city in Cilicia, yet brought up in this city at the feet of Gamaliel, and taught according to the perfect manner of the law of the fathers, and was zealous toward God, as ye all are this day.' None could deny the apostle's statements, as the facts that he referred to were well known to many who were still living in Jerusalem. He then spoke of his former zeal in persecuting the disciples of Christ, even unto death; and he narrated the circumstances of his conversion, telling his hearers how his own proud heart had been led to bow to the crucified Nazarene. Had he attempted to enter into argument with his opponents, they would have stubbornly refused to listen to his words; but the relation of his experience was attended with a convincing power that for the time seemed to soften and subdue their hearts.

"He then endeavored to show that his work among the Gentiles had not been entered upon from choice. He had desired to labor for his own nation; but in that very temple the voice of God had spoken to him in holy vision, directing his course, 'far hence unto the Gentiles.'

"Hitherto the people had listened with close attention, but when Paul reached the point in his history where he was appointed Christ's ambassador to the Gentiles, their fury broke forth anew. Accustomed to look upon themselves as the only people favored by God, they were unwilling to permit the despised Gentiles to share the privileges which had hitherto been regarded as exclusively their own. Lifting their voices above the voice of the speaker, they cried, 'Away with such a fellow from the earth: for it is not fit that he should live.' "[1] Many Jewish Christians were not ready to abandon cherished ceremonies for the sake of their new religion. They were intolerant of those who differed. After all, they were in the "right."

When should a Christian defy accepted doctrine? When, if ever, is compromise acceptable? Preach Jesus!

---

1. Ellen G. White, *The Acts of the Apostles* (Mountain View, CA: Pacific Press®, 1911), 409, 410.

A Born Citizen

Then the commander came and said to him, "Tell me, are you a Roman?"
He said, "Yes."

—Acts 22:27

The crowd went wild when they heard Paul say he had been sent to offer salvation to Gentiles. "As they cried out, and cast off their clothes, and threw dust into the air, the chief captain commanded him to be brought into the castle, and bade that he should be examined by scourging; that he might know wherefore they cried so against him. And as they bound him with thongs, Paul said unto the centurion that stood by, Is it lawful for you to scourge a man that is a Roman, and uncondemned? When the centurion heard that, he went and told the chief captain, saying, Take heed what thou doest: for this man is a Roman. Then the chief captain came, and said unto him, Tell me, art thou a Roman? He said, Yea. And the chief captain answered, With a great sum obtained I this freedom. And Paul said, But I was free born. Then straightway they departed from him which should have examined him: and the chief captain also was afraid, after he knew that he was a Roman, and because he had bound him" (Acts 22:23–29, KJV).

Unlike the treatment Paul received at the hands of the Romans in Philippi (Acts 16:19–40), here he immediately brought his citizenship to the attention of his "protectors." Paul had been stripped and bound for the standard practice of eliciting the truth from a suspected criminal. "The Romans would beat the prisoner with a flagellum to obtain a confession. The flagellum was a leather whip with metal balls or bits of metal attached to its ends, designed to tear into the flesh of the victim. It was usually effective in getting to the truth but was not to be applied to Roman citizens, particularly one who had not yet been formally charged."[1] Paul was well aware of his rights under Roman law.

Claudius Lysias, the chief captain, had bought his citizenship. "In former times, one could not purchase citizenship. It had to be conferred or secured through special services to the state. But in the time of Claudius, it evidently became possible to purchase Roman citizenship. Lysias probably derived his name of Claudius from the emperor from whom he had purchased his citizen rights. Paul did not receive his citizenship in such a mundane fashion. He was born a Roman citizen (v. 28). This gave Paul considerably more status in the tribune's eyes, and he was literally terrified at the prospect of having almost scourged a Roman."[2] He had bound a Roman citizen with thongs for a flogging. A Roman citizen might be placed in chains and bound, but never with thongs!

Do you readily identify yourself as a Seventh-day Adventist Christian, or hide the fact?

---

1. John B. Polhill, *Paul and His Letters* (Nashville, TN: Broadman & Holman, 1999), 321.
2. Polhill, *Paul and His Letters*, 321.

Back Among Friends?

The next day, because he wanted to know for certain why he was accused by the Jews, he released him from his bonds, and commanded the chief priests and all their council to appear, and brought Paul down and set him before them.

—Acts 22:30

All Lysias knew about Paul was that the Jews were somehow offended by his actions. That this was a religious dispute seemed to be sensible. Therefore it seemed reasonable to hear what the top Jewish judicial body had to say about actual charges against Paul. Taking Paul to the chamber of the Sanhedrin the next day, he sought the advice of the chief priests and all their counsel. Paul's bonds were removed, and he was set at liberty to address the group. The Roman guards stood nearby just in case things got out of hand (Acts 23:10). *The Seventh-day Adventist Bible Commentary* says, "The presence of the Roman guard guaranteed Paul's personal safety."[1] Paul was obviously "escorted" from the Castle of Antonia to the Sanhedrin chamber in the temple.

Consider the drama of the scene. Paul was to be heard "by the same tribunal of which he himself had been a member before his conversion. As he stood before the Jewish rulers, his bearing was calm, and his countenance revealed the peace of Christ."[2] "The apostle gazes intently upon the highest Jewish assembly for the first time in a quarter of a century. There had no doubt been many changes in personnel during the years, but some faces Paul may have recognized."[3]

Paul did not mince words. He immediately called the august body a group of hypocrites. He swore his conscience was clean before God concerning his conduct, implying, of course, that as they opposed him, theirs could not be. For this statement, Ananias, the high priest, commanded Paul to be struck across his "blasphemous" lips. Paul's response was to exclaim, "God will strike you [Ananias], you whitewashed wall! For you sit to judge me according to the law, and do you command me to be struck contrary to the law?" (Acts 23:3). Paul, as a lawyer, "knew the law and proper judicial procedure, and asserted his right to enjoy due process"[4] without intimidation.

Paul's prediction came true. "Ananias was assassinated when the Roman war began . . . , probably in A.D. 66."[5]

1. Francis D. Nichol, ed., *The Seventh-day Adventist Bible Commentary*, vol. 6 (Washington, DC: Review and Herald®, 1957), 412.

2. Ellen G. White, *The Acts of the Apostles* (Mountain View, CA: Pacific Press®, 1911), 410, 411.

3. Nichol, *Seventh-day Adventist Bible Commentary*, vol. 6, 414.

4. Nichol, *Seventh-day Adventist Bible Commentary*, vol. 6, 414.

5. Siegfried H. Horn, *Seventh-day Adventist Bible Dictionary*, ed. Don F. Neufeld, Commentary Reference Series, vol. 8 (Washington, DC: Review and Herald®, 1960), s.v. "Ananias."

Under House Arrest

Now when there arose a great dissension, the commander, fearing lest Paul might be pulled to pieces by them, commanded the soldiers to go down and take him by force from among them, and bring him into the barracks.

—Acts 23:10

T hose surrounding Paul asked him why he was insulting God's high priest. Paul immediately apologized for his words. It seems curious that Paul did not realize the high priest had given the order to have him struck across the mouth. Several reasons for this failure have been presented, the most logical being that Paul's defective eyesight was such that he really could not see well enough to know who had given the order to have him struck without cause.

Paul quoted Exodus 22:28: "You shall not revile God, nor curse a ruler of your people," showing he knew Israel's law mandated respect for its leaders. Paul was a great lawyer! He hid the reason he was in the chamber in the first place. Before he could be examined and indicted, he cried out, " 'Men and brethren, I am a Pharisee, the son of a Pharisee; concerning the hope and resurrection of the dead I am being judged!'

"And when he said this, a dissension arose between the Pharisees and Sadducees; and the assembly was divided. For Sadducees say that there is no resurrection—and no angel or spirit; but the Pharisees confess both. Then there arose a loud outcry. And the scribes of the Pharisees' party arose and protested saying, 'We find no evil in this man; but if a spirit or an angel has spoken to him, let us not fight against God' " (Acts 23:6–9). Suddenly, Paul found himself the object of a physical struggle with Sadducees trying to kill him and Pharisees seeking to protect him. Rome intervened.

"It is significant that Paul should have made this declaration so early in the hearing. He knew that he had no hope of a fair hearing before the Sanhedrin, and no doubt intended to reveal its incompetence to pass judgment on him. Therefore he brought the trial to a close by setting his judges against one another (v. 7). The subject chosen—the resurrection—was basic to Christianity (see 1 Cor. 15:12–23) and almost certain to produce the desired result."[1] "The sedate and learned members of the Sanhedrin proved to be as excitable and irrational as the fickle and illiterate mob."[2]

Paul touched on the real difference between himself and the Sanhedrin when he brought up the resurrection of Jesus. It is still the difference between Christians and atheists.

---

1. Francis D. Nichol, ed., *The Seventh-day Adventist Bible Commentary*, vol. 6 (Washington, DC: Review and Herald®, 1957), 415.
2. Nichol, *Seventh-day Adventist Bible Commentary*, vol. 6, 415.

Assassins

And when it was day, some of the Jews banded together and bound themselves under an oath,
saying that they would neither eat nor drink till they had killed Paul.

—Acts 23:12

From the safety of prison, Paul had time to reflect on his actions. Perhaps he had been rash in coming to Jerusalem. Perhaps he should have heeded the warnings of others. Was this to be the end of his labors for the Gentile churches he had founded? "In distress and discouragement he wept and prayed.

"In this dark hour the Lord was not unmindful of His servant. He had guarded him from the murderous throng in the temple courts; He had been with him before the Sanhedrin council; He was with him in the fortress; and He revealed Himself to His faithful witness in response to the earnest prayers of the apostle for guidance. 'The night following the Lord stood by him, and said, Be of good cheer, Paul: for as thou hast testified of Me in Jerusalem, so must thou bear witness also at Rome.' "[1]

But Paul's enemies were not idle. According to Acts 23:12, 13, there were about forty zealous Jews who took a solemn oath to kill Paul. An *anathematizo* invited severe divine penalties should they fail in their task. They additionally swore to neither eat nor drink until the task was accomplished. Because of the size of the group, Paul's life was in real danger. The plotters enlisted the Sanhedrin into their plan. The chief priests were to request Paul's presence the next day in the council chambers so they might resume their interrogation. Despite the Roman guard provided by Lysias during the short trip from the barracks (i.e., Tower of Antonia) to the temple, they would see Paul never reached that meeting alive.

Paul had a sister living in Jerusalem at the time. "So when Paul's sister's son heard of their ambush, he went and entered the barracks and told Paul" (verse 16). Paul immediately called over a centurion and had his nephew taken to the commander, Lysias. Claudius Lysias heard the boy out and cautioned him to tell no one that he had warned Paul and the Romans. "Lysias at once decided to transfer Paul from his jurisdiction to that of Felix the procurator"[2] in Caesarea. God once again "interposed to save the life of His servant."[3]

When we reach heaven, we will learn how many times God intervened to ensure our safety while we rested in His care!

---

1. Ellen G. White, *The Acts of the Apostles* (Mountain View, CA: Pacific Press®, 1911), 413.
2. White, *Acts of the Apostles*, 415.
3. White, *Acts of the Apostles*, 414.

A Crafty Letter

This man was seized by the Jews and was about to be killed by them. Coming with the troops I rescued him, having learned that he was a Roman.

—Acts 23:27

L ysias gladly improved this opportunity to get Paul off his hands. . . . A short time previous, a Roman knight of far higher rank than Lysias himself, had been violently taken and dragged by the maddened Jews around the walls of Jerusalem, and finally beheaded, because he received a bribe from the Samaritans. Upon the suspicion of similar crimes, other high officials had been imprisoned and disgraced. Should Paul be murdered, the chief captain might be charged with having been bribed to connive at his death. There was now sufficient reason to send him away secretly, and thus get rid of an embarrassing responsibility."[1]

Lysias wrote Procurator Felix an artful letter.

"To the most excellent governor Felix: [As a freedman Felix should not have been addressed as "Excellency."]

"Greetings.

"This man was seized by the Jews and was about to be killed by them. Coming with the troops I rescued him, having learned that he was a Roman. [Well, not exactly. Lysias only learned he was a citizen *after* he ordered him arrested and flogged.] And when I wanted to know the reason they accused him, I brought him before their council. I found out that he was accused concerning questions of their law, but had nothing charged against him deserving of death or chains. [Yet Lysias placed him in chains before he knew him to be a citizen.] And when it was told me that the Jews lay in wait for the man, I sent him immediately to you [to protect Lysias's own position and neck], and also commanded his accusers to state before you the charges against him.

"Farewell" (Acts 23:26–30).

Lysias put a positive spin on his actions when he sent his letter to Felix. He claimed he had intervened to protect a Roman citizen who was in danger (Acts 23:27). The truth of the matter was that he almost scourged Paul and that only Paul's announcement of citizenship had stopped that fate. The key point in the letter was Lysias's vouching for Paul's innocence. He was only guilty of raising theological questions that might disturb the peace. "The lenient treatment Paul enjoyed in Caesarea and later at Rome was no doubt due in part to Lysias' favorable report."[2]

"For You alone, O Lord, make me dwell in safety" (Psalm 4:8).

---

1. Ellen G. White, *Sketches From the Life of Paul* (Washington, DC: Review and Herald®, 1974), 227.
2. Francis D. Nichol, ed., *The Seventh-day Adventist Bible Commentary*, vol. 6 (Washington, DC: Review and Herald®, 1957), 419.

Lawyer Versus Lawyer

Now after five days Ananias the high priest came down with the elders and a certain orator named Tertullus. These gave evidence to the governor against Paul.

—Acts 24:1

Because forty Jewish zealots was no small group, Lysias sent a huge force to convey Paul to the governor in Caesarea. The troop would leave immediately because it was just more than sixty miles from Jerusalem to Caesarea. It was between nine o'clock and ten o'clock P.M. when the force was drawn up and ready to move. Darkness hid the identity of Paul as he was placed upon a horse. This was no small contingent of Roman soldiers. There were two centurions with one hundred men each or two hundred footmen, seventy cavalrymen, and two hundred spearmen. "The safety of a prisoner who claimed Roman citizenship, the lives of the centurions and the soldiers, and the ability of Roman arms to keep order were all at stake in this transfer of Paul from Jerusalem to Caesarea."[1] "The officer in charge of the detachment delivered his prisoner to Felix, also presenting [the] letter with which he had been entrusted by the chief captain. . . .

"After reading the communication, Felix inquired to what province the prisoner belonged, and being informed that he was of Cilicia, said: 'I will hear thee . . . when thine accusers are also come. And he commanded him to be kept in Herod's judgment hall.' "[2]

So things stood for five days until Paul's accusers appeared with an orator they hired as counsel. Tertullus opened by praising the corrupt and brutal rule of Felix. "Felix was known to deal harshly with insurrectionists . . . , and if Tertullus could convince him of this allegation, Paul's fate would be settled."[3] Tertullus accused Paul of being "a creator of dissension among all the Jews throughout the world, and a ringleader of the sect of the Nazarenes" (Acts 24:5). Tertullus was suggesting Christians were political revolutionaries. As to these first two charges, Felix was not fooled, and he deferred them (verse 22). Additionally, Tertullus stated, Paul had profaned the temple by bringing "Gentiles across the boundary of the Temple courtyard beyond which only Jews were permitted."[4] This was a serious charge. The Romans had given the Jews jurisdiction within the temple grounds for all desecration offenses, and they were allowed to execute the violator even if he were a Roman. If this charge were validated, Paul would have to be handed over to the Jews and to certain death.

"Blessed are you when they revile and persecute you, and say all kinds of evil against you falsely for My sake" (Matthew 5:11).

1. Francis D. Nichol, ed., *The Seventh-day Adventist Bible Commentary*, vol. 6 (Washington, DC: Review and Herald®, 1957), 418.
2. Ellen G. White, *The Acts of the Apostles* (Mountain View, CA: Pacific Press®, 1911), 415, 416.
3. Nichol, *Seventh-day Adventist Bible Commentary*, vol. 6, 422.
4. Nichol, *Seventh-day Adventist Bible Commentary*, vol. 6, 422.

Paul's Defense

"And they neither found me in the temple disputing with anyone nor inciting the crowd, either in the synagogues or in the city. Nor can they prove the things of which they now accuse me."
—Acts 24:12, 13

P aul's defense in Acts 24 is a direct denial of the four charges leveled against him. One by one, in order, he refutes the charges. "He makes four points: (1) He had come to Jerusalem to worship, and to bring 'alms' and 'offerings' ([Acts 24:]11, 17). (2) He had made no disturbance (vs. 12, 18). (3) He challenges his accusers to prove their accusations by producing witnesses (vs. 13, 19). (4) He insists that his only offense was obeying God and His law, and believing in the resurrection (vs. 14, 15, 21). The first half of his defense is evidently a general statement (vs. 11–16); and the last half a detailed repetition of the points made in that statement (vs. 16–21). The proceedings were probably conducted in Greek. If Paul had spoken in Latin, Luke would doubtless have noted it, as he did when Paul used Hebrew ([Acts] 21:40)."[1]

Paul accepted the charge that he was a Christian, yet he pointed out he had come to the temple to worship as a Jew who believed the Scriptures, kept the Torah, and believed in the resurrection as did the Pharisees and many other Jews. There was no law in existence, either Roman or Jewish, that prohibited a person from being a Nazarene or a Christian. He related that he had even taken a Nazarite vow and had been in the process of arranging for sacrifices for the four men with him when he was apprehended. He had not engaged in anything seditious. He had not been in Jerusalem long enough to foment dissension among the populace, and he certainly had no fight with Rome. Paul pointed out that the Jewish Council was divided as to his guilt or innocence.

His most telling argument in favor of dismissing all charges was the Roman law stating an accused could face his accusers in court. Where were these witnesses? The prosecution had prepared the case poorly. "The testimony of Paul ... made it obvious that his accusers had no case against him, and Felix therefore dismissed court."[2] Felix knew a setup when he saw one. Lysias's letter had commended Paul. Yet fear of offending the Jews held him back from releasing an innocent man. He ruled Paul be held until Lysias should appear in court.

God controls events in our lives.

---

1. Francis D. Nichol, ed., *The Seventh-day Adventist Bible Commentary*, vol. 6 (Washington, DC: Review and Herald®, 1957), 423.
2. Nichol, *Seventh-day Adventist Bible Commentary*, vol. 6, 426.

The Corrupt Governor and His Jewish Spouse

And after some days, when Felix came with his wife Drusilla, who was Jewish,
he sent for Paul and heard him concerning the faith in Christ.

—Acts 24:24

Marcus Antonius Felix was no saint. "The character of Felix was base and contemptible. It was said that he 'practiced all kinds of lust and cruelty with the power of a king and the temper of a slave.' "[1] He had faced Christians in Caesarea and knew more about them than the Jerusalem delegation suspected. Yet two other reasons delayed Felix's judgment. First, Felix was hoping Paul would pay a bribe to free himself. If Paul was important enough to get the Jewish leaders agitated, then maybe he was also a person of substance. He had brought money to the Christian Jews of Jerusalem. Maybe he had connections with wealthy friends who would come to his aid and bail him out (Acts 24:26). Second, by leaving Paul in prison, the Jews might be appeased and stop their constant complaining to Rome about Felix's rule.

Paul was given more freedom than most prisoners merited. He was allowed to have visitors and receive food from them. He could send and receive messages. Most of these privileges were designed to make it easy for Paul's friends to raise a ransom. Paul also was brought before the procurator and his wife, Drusilla, for additional conversations. Paul's message of the gospel probably struck too close to home.

Drusilla "was a daughter of Herod Agrippa I, grandson of Herod the Great and Mariamne, of the former Jewish royal house, the Hasmonaeans. . . . Herod Agrippa II was therefore her brother, and Berenice her sister. She had left her first husband, King Azizus of Emesa, a proselyte to Judaism, to marry Felix."[2] Felix trembled when he heard Paul preach that temperance and self-control were required of a person and that all must one day stand before the judgment bar of God. He postponed Paul's release and let him languish in prison for two years until Nero replaced Felix.

"The governor appointed in the place of Felix, was Porcius Festus, a far more honorable ruler. He had a higher sense of the responsibility of his position, and, refusing to accept bribes, he endeavored to administer justice. Three days after his arrival at Caesarea, Festus went up to Jerusalem. Here he was speedily importuned by the Jews, who lost no time in presenting their accusations against Paul."[3]

God intervenes for us too.

---

1. Ellen G. White, *Sketches From the Life of Paul* (Washington, DC: Review and Herald®, 1974), 235.
2. Francis D. Nichol, ed., *The Seventh-day Adventist Bible Commentary*, vol. 6 (Washington, DC: Review and Herald®, 1957), 426.
3. White, *Sketches From the Life of Paul*, 246, 247.

What Happened
to Felix and Drusilla?

But after two years Porcius Festus succeeded Felix; and Felix,
wanting to do the Jews a favor, left Paul bound.

—Acts 24:27

After two years under house arrest, it became clear Paul was too poor to pay a ransom, and he would not ask the Christians of Caesarea to take up a collection to free him. Felix and Paul had reached an impasse. "Toward the close of this time there arose a fearful strife among the population of Caesarea. There had been frequent disputes, which had become a settled feud, between the Jews and the Greeks, concerning their respective rights and privileges in the city. . . . The Jewish inhabitants were numerous and wealthy, and they claimed the city as theirs, because their king had done so much for it. The Greeks, with equal persistency, maintained their right to the precedence.

"Near the close of the two years, these dissensions led to a fierce combat in the market-place, resulting in the defeat of the Greeks. Felix, who sided with the Gentile faction, came with his troops and ordered the Jews to disperse. The command was not instantly obeyed by the victorious party, and he ordered his soldiers to fall upon them. Glad of an opportunity to indulge their hatred of the Jews, they executed the order in the most merciless manner, and many were put to death. As if this were not enough, Felix, whose animosity toward the Jews had increased every year, now gave his soldiers liberty to rob the houses of the wealthy.

"These daring acts of injustice and cruelty could not pass unnoticed. The Jews made a formal complaint against Felix, and he was summoned to Rome [by Nero] to answer their charges. He well knew that his course of extortion and oppression had given them abundant ground for complaint, but he still hoped to conciliate them. Hence, though he had a sincere respect for Paul, he decided to gratify their malice by leaving him a prisoner. But all his efforts were in vain; though he escaped banishment or death, he was removed from office, and deprived of the greater part of his ill-gotten wealth. Drusilla, the partner of his guilt, afterward perished, with their only son, in the eruption of Vesuvius. His own days were ended in disgrace and obscurity."[1]

Politics and politicians never change.

---

1. Ellen G. White, *Sketches From the Life of Paul* (Washington, DC: Review and Herald®, 1974), 245, 246.

A Change of Venue?

But Festus, wanting to do the Jews a favor, answered Paul and said, "Are you willing to go up to Jerusalem and there be judged before me concerning these things?"

—Acts 25:9

At Caesarea, Festus had already met the popular clamor against Paul, but at Jerusalem the demand for his death was not merely the cry of the mob. A deputation of the most honorable personages of the city, headed by the high priest, formally presented the request concerning Paul, not doubting that this new and inexperienced official could be molded at pleasure, and that to gain their favor he would readily grant all that they desired.

"...With keen insight he penetrated the motive that prompted their request, and courteously declined to send for Paul. He stated, however, that he himself would soon return to Caesarea, and that he would there give them a fair opportunity to prefer their charges against him.

"This was not what they wanted. Their former defeat was not forgotten."[1] They wanted Paul transferred to Jerusalem, where he could be tried before the Sanhedrin. Underlying their request was the knowledge that Paul would never live to see Jerusalem. Once he was out of protective custody in Caesarea, he would be murdered along the road, thus saving the Sanhedrin the trouble.

"God in his providence controlled the decision of Festus, that the life of the apostle might be preserved....

"...After a stay of eight or ten days in Jerusalem, Festus returned to Caesarea, and the next day took his seat at the tribunal to hear the case. The Jews, on this occasion being without a lawyer, preferred their charges themselves. The trial was a scene of passionate, unreasoning clamor on the part of the accusers, while Paul with perfect calmness and candor clearly showed the falsity of their statements."[2] Festus understood the charges against Paul dealt with Jewish religious doctrine. Even if guilty as charged, Paul's behavior did not warrant a decree of death. Yet Festus also understood that to release Paul would create a storm of rage. He asked Paul if he was willing to go to Jerusalem under his protection to face the Sanhedrin. Paul knew he could expect no justice in a Jewish court. As a Roman citizen, he, therefore, asserted his right to appeal to Caesar for justice. "Then Festus, when he had conferred with the council, answered, 'You have appealed to Caesar? To Caesar you shall go!' " (Acts 25:12).

God expects us to use common sense.

---

1. Ellen G. White, *Sketches From the Life of Paul* (Washington, DC: Review and Herald®, 1974), 247, 248.
2. White, *Sketches From the Life of Paul*, 248.

Almost a Christian

And after some days King Agrippa and Bernice came to Caesarea to greet Festus.
—Acts 25:13

K nowing that Agrippa was well versed in the laws and customs of the Jews, Festus during this visit called his attention to the case of Paul, as a prisoner left in bonds by Felix. Agrippa's interest was aroused by the account which Festus gave of the case, and he expressed a desire to see and hear Paul for himself. Accordingly the next day was fixed upon as the time for such an interview."[1] Here we see the fulfillment of God's words to Ananias about Paul in Acts 9:15. God said His apostle would appear before Gentiles, kings, and the sons of Israel. In Acts 22–26, we see Paul appearing before Roman governors Felix and Festus, before the Jewish king Agrippa, and before the Sanhedrin.

Paul was not in a court situation but rather being interviewed to satisfy the curiosity of the king. "At his command, Paul, still manacled as a prisoner, was led in, and the king gazed with cold curiosity upon him, now bowed and pale from sickness, long imprisonment, and continual anxiety."[2] "Then Agrippa said to Paul, 'You are permitted to speak for yourself' " (Acts 26:1). Paul passionately described his conversion and the faith he had in Jesus Christ as the Messiah. Acts 26 gives his eloquent testimony before Agrippa. "In the all-absorbing interest of his subject, he lost sight of kings and governors and chief captains, of wealth, rank, and titles. He was bearing the testimony which was the object of his life, and he could speak with the assurance of long familiarity and the fire of intense conviction. None who heard him could doubt his sincerity. . . . The whole audience had listened spell-bound."[3] Agrippa was so impressed he said to Paul, "You almost persuade me to become a Christian" (verse 28). "With solemn earnestness, the apostle made answer: 'I would to God that not only thou, but also all that hear me this day, were both almost and altogether such as I am,' adding, as he raised his fettered hands, 'except these bonds.' "[4] Agrippa was convinced of Paul's innocence. Cutting short the interview, he remarked to Festus that Paul should be released immediately had he not appealed to Caesar.

Do your words promote Christianity?

---

1. Ellen G. White, *Sketches From the Life of Paul* (Washington, DC: Review and Herald®, 1974), 253.
2. White, *Sketches From the Life of Paul*, 253, 254.
3. White, *Sketches From the Life of Paul*, 258.
4. White, *Sketches From the Life of Paul*, 259.

A Contrast in Characters

So the next day, when Agrippa and Bernice had come
with great pomp . . . at Festus' command Paul was brought in.

—Acts 25:23

W as King Agrippa serious when he said he was "almost" convinced to become a Christian? We cannot tell whether Agrippa's response, "You almost persuade me to become a Christian" (Acts 26:28), was spoken in sincerity or irony. Paul chose to believe it was the former. Most commentators believe Agrippa was being ironic.

Agrippa had grown up in Rome following the death of his father Agrippa I in AD 44 (Acts 12:20–23). He became a favorite of both Claudius and Nero, who bestowed upon him the title "king of the Jews" and certain territories and cities. This title carried with it no power, but the holder could name the Jewish high priest. "This last scion of a decayed line of Jewish kings, the Maccabees, and of the house of Herod, Agrippa professed to be a Jew but was at heart a Roman. His reign marked the end of a dynasty and of an era. From the first the Herodian dynasty had been captive to Rome, and had certainly made no brilliant record. Before him stands Paul, old now, but strong in his convictions, and confident despite the circumstances. Agrippa is cynical, indifferent to real values; Paul is ardent for truth, no matter what the cost to himself."[1] Accompanying Agrippa to Caesarea was his sister Bernice. Bernice was one year younger than her brother. She was married at the age of thirteen to her uncle, the king of Chalcis. At his death, Agrippa took over that kingdom and Bernice with it. Bernice became Agrippa's constant companion from that point forward. Gossip had it theirs was an incestuous relationship.

What a contrast between the characters of Agrippa and Bernice and that of Paul! Yet the day favored Paul, for "two years afterward, the result of that day's proceedings saved the life so precious to the cause of God. Festus, finding that his own judgment of the case, on grounds of Roman justice, was sustained from a Jewish stand-point by the protector of the temple [Agrippa], sent a letter to the emperor, stating that no legal charge could be found against the prisoner. And Nero, cruel and unscrupulous as he was, dared not put to death a man whom Lysias, Felix, Festus, and Agrippa pronounced guiltless, and whom even the Sanhedrin could not condemn."[2]

"God would have his people prepared for the soon-coming crisis."[3]

1. Francis D. Nichol, ed., *The Seventh-day Adventist Bible Commentary*, vol. 6 (Washington, DC: Review and Herald®, 1957), 436.
2. Ellen G. White, *Sketches From the Life of Paul* (Washington, DC: Review and Herald®, 1974), 261.
3. White, *Sketches From the Life of Paul*, 252.

Journey to Rome and Imprisonment

AD 60–63

Acts 27:1–28:31
Ephesians, Philippians, Colossians, Philemon, Hebrews
The Acts of the Apostles, pp. 439–487
Sketches From the Life of Paul, pp. 261–302

Paul's Sea Voyage

And when it was decided that we should sail to Italy, they delivered Paul and some other prisoners to one named Julius, a centurion of the Augustan Regiment. So, entering a ship of Adramyttium, we put to sea, meaning to sail along the coasts of Asia.

—Acts 27:1, 2

Aristarchus was traveling with Paul, as was Luke. "Roman law provided that Roman citizens traveling as prisoners might be accompanied by a slave and a personal physician. Perhaps Aristarchus served as Paul's servant and Luke as his physician."[1] Paul was no stranger to sea travel. His three missionary journeys had involved thousands of sea miles, and many times, he had been faced with contrary winds and rough seas. "In the first century of the Christian era, traveling by sea as well as by land was attended with far greater difficulty than at the present time. The arts of ship-building and navigation were not then matured as now. Mariners directed their course by the sun and stars; and when these did not appear, and there were indications of storm, they were fearful of trusting their vessels to the open sea.

"The season for safe navigation was already far advanced, before the apostle's ship left Caesarea, and the time was fast approaching when travel by sea would be closed for the year. Every day's delay increased the peril of the voyage. But the journey which would be difficult and dangerous to the ordinary traveler, would be doubly trying to the apostle as a prisoner. Roman soldiers were held responsible with their own lives for the security of their prisoners, and this had led to the custom of chaining prisoners by the right wrist to the left wrist of soldiers, who relieved each other in turn. Thus not only could the apostle have no movement free, but he was placed in close and constant connection with men of the most uncongenial and absolutely repulsive character; men who were not only uneducated and unrefined, but who, from the demoralizing influence of their surroundings, had become brutal and degraded."[2] This would be a sea voyage like no other Paul had ever taken.

Consider: Because of Aristarchus's affection for Paul, he chose to share his bondage and trials. Would you do as much for your pastor?

---

1. Francis D. Nichol, ed., *The Seventh-day Adventist Bible Commentary*, vol. 6 (Washington, DC: Review and Herald®, 1957), 443.
2. Ellen G. White, *Sketches From the Life of Paul* (Washington, DC: Review and Herald®, 1974), 261, 262.

A Storm Brewing

But not long after, a tempestuous head wind arose, called Euroclydon.

—Acts 27:14

Because the prisoner transfer ship was a coastal freighter, it hugged the coast of Syria after leaving Caesarea, putting in at the port of Sidon. "Here Julius, the centurion who had listened to the apostle's address before Agrippa, and had thus been favorably disposed toward him, 'courteously entreated Paul,' and being informed that there were Christians in the place, he 'gave him liberty to go unto his friends to refresh himself.' The favor was highly appreciated by the apostle, who was in feeble health, and but scantily provided with comforts for the long journey."[1] The stay in Sidon was brief. Late summer winds were tending from the west, so the ship hugged the leeward, or landward, side between Cyprus and the Palestine mainland (Acts 27:4). Finally, off the coast of Lycia, they made port in Myra (modern-day Turkey; verse 5). Myra was a transit port for wheat transports coming from Egypt to Rome. "This was not a usual port of call for ships sailing from Palestine to Rome. An ancient inscription names Myra as a storage place for grain."[2] The Mediterranean turned treacherous late in the season. "It was now probably the latter part of October, and severe storms were to be expected."[3]

Because of strong headwinds, the ship passed through the straits of Rhodes and arrived at Cnidus on the southwestern tip of Asia. Now they were forced to make a choice. Should they strike out directly across the Aegean to Greece or sail south by southwest to reach the leeward side of Crete and hug its southern coastline? The latter would give them protection and bring them closer to Greece. "The winds apparently forced the ship close to the coast. Now, out in the Aegean, it felt the full force of the gale and headed toward Crete."[4] Finally, the ship made port at a small settlement called Fair Havens. Here the captain waited for a favorable wind, and much critical time was lost. Paul had been shipwrecked before, and experience told him the party should stay put. "Paul advised them, saying, 'Men, I perceive that this voyage will end with disaster and much loss, not only of the cargo and ship, but also our lives.' Nevertheless the centurion was more persuaded by the helmsman and the owner of the ship than by the things spoken by Paul" (Acts 27:9-11). A fair wind finally arose, and the master of the vessel, as well as the owner, who was on board, recommended they set sail. "The centurion naturally preferred the judgment of an expert navigator to that of an itinerant Jewish rabbi."[5]

He should have listened to Paul! Storm clouds were gathering just over the horizon to the east.

1. Ellen G. White, *Sketches From the Life of Paul* (Washington, DC: Review and Herald®, 1974), 263.
2. Francis D. Nichol, ed., *The Seventh-day Adventist Bible Commentary*, vol. 6 (Washington, DC: Review and Herald®, 1957), 445.
3. Nichol, *Seventh-day Adventist Bible Commentary*, vol. 6, 445.
4. Nichol, *Seventh-day Adventist Bible Commentary*, vol. 6, 445.
5. Nichol, *Seventh-day Adventist Bible Commentary*, vol. 6, 446.

No Loss of Life

*"And now I urge you to take heart, for there will be no loss of life among you,
but only of the ship."*

—Acts 27:22

Attempting to hug the coast, the ship moved west toward Phenice, about forty miles away. Suddenly caught in open water south of Crete, "there was another abrupt change, from the gentle south wind to a strong north wind, and this forced the ship southward toward the island of Clauda."[1] The shift in the wind was a sign of a typhoon, a major tropical storm. The ancients called this wind pattern *Euroclydon*, from two "words meaning 'east wind' and 'great wave,' or 'rough water.' *Eurokludōn* would thus designate an east wind that raises great waves."[2]

The storm caused the ship to run before the wind because trying to tack would have ripped the sails to shreds. The ship was blown forty-five miles southwest of Cape Matala. Here, in the lee of the little island, the crew attempted to save the ship. First, they hoisted aboard the towed lifeboat that was filling with water (Acts 27:16). Next, they frapped (bound) the hull by passing heavy ropes under the keel to keep the leaking hull timbers together (verse 17). Last, they lowered all sails to cut the profile of the ship to the wind (verse 17). "The crew brought down everything from aloft that they could spare, particularly the heavy mainsail and its gear. They evidently left enough sail and gear to keep the ship under control, and so avoid the Syrtis, with its much feared shoals."[3] The North African coast has been known as the graveyard for ships since the dawn of navigation. Paul's ship was being drawn inexorably toward those quicksand, shoals, and certain doom.

Things looked bleak. The men were hungry and seasick. But Paul's prayers had received an answer. "In the midst of that terrible scene, the apostle retained his calmness and courage. Notwithstanding he was physically the greatest sufferer of them all, he had words of hope for the darkest hour, a helping hand in every emergency."[4] "Paul stood in the midst of them and said, 'Men, you should have listened to me, and not have sailed from Crete and incurred this disaster and loss. And now I urge you to take heart, for there will be no loss of life among you, but only of the ship' " (verses 21, 22).

Notice—Paul prayed for everyone on board, even his guards and the nonbelievers around him.

---

1. Francis D. Nichol, ed., *The Seventh-day Adventist Bible Commentary*, vol. 6 (Washington, DC: Review and Herald®, 1957), 446.
2. Nichol, *Seventh-day Adventist Bible Commentary*, vol. 6, 446.
3. Nichol, *Seventh-day Adventist Bible Commentary*, vol. 6, 447.
4. Ellen G. White, *Sketches From the Life of Paul* (Washington, DC: Review and Herald®, 1974), 266.

Abandon Ship!

*And as the sailors were seeking to escape from the ship . . . , Paul said to the centurion
and the soldiers, "Unless these men stay in the ship, you cannot be saved."*

—Acts 27:30, 31

Paul could have decided not to get involved. He could have remained silent with the knowledge of salvation he had been promised. But a Christian shows concern for those around him, always seeking to relieve their anxieties and burdens. Paul told the men the ship would eventually run aground on an island. Even though no sun or stars were available to fix a position, and the ship appeared to be doomed, the crew took heart. With the ship rigged for heavy weather, all the men could do was ride out the storm. With "the bow of the ship pointed nearly north and the northeaster striking the ship on its starboard beam, it would be driven, largely sideways, in a west-northwest direction. The distance from Clauda to Malta is about 475 mi."[1]

"It was the fourteenth night that they had been tossed up and down on the black, heaving billows, when, amid the sound of the storm, the sailors distinguished the roar of breakers, and reported that they were near some land. They 'sounded, and found it twenty fathoms [120 feet]; and when they had gone a little further, they sounded again, and found it fifteen fathoms [90 feet].' They were now threatened by a new danger, of having their ship driven upon some rock-bound coast. They immediately cast out four anchors, which was the only thing that could be done. . . .

"At last through rain and tempest the gray light fell upon their haggard and ghastly faces. The outlines of the stormy coast could be dimly seen, but not a single familiar landmark was visible. The selfish heathen sailors determined to abandon the ship and crew, and save themselves in the boat which they had with so much difficulty hoisted on board. Pretending that they could do something more to secure the safety of the ship, they unloosed the boat, and began to lower it into the sea. Had they succeeded, they would have been dashed in pieces upon the rocks, while all on board would have perished from their inability to handle the sinking vessel."[2] God's promise of safety had been conditional upon all performing their duties. "The soldiers, on hearing Paul's words, immediately cut off the ropes of the boat, letting her fall off into the sea."[3]

"God helps those only who help themselves."[4]

1. Francis D. Nichol, ed., *The Seventh-day Adventist Bible Commentary*, vol. 6 (Washington, DC: Review and Herald®, 1957), 447.
2. Ellen G. White, *Sketches From the Life of Paul* (Washington, DC: Review and Herald®, 1974), 267, 268.
3. White, *Sketches From the Life of Paul*, 268.
4. White, *Sketches From the Life of Paul*, 267.

Taking Nourishment

*"Therefore I urge you to take nourishment, for this is for your survival,
since not a hair will fall from the head of any of you."*

—Acts 27:34

T he most critical hour was still before them, when the skill, courage, and presence of mind of all on board would be tested. Again the apostle spoke words of encouragement, and entreated all, both sailors and passengers to take some food, saying, 'This day is the fourteenth day that ye have tarried and continued fasting, having taken nothing. Wherefore, I pray you to take some meat; for this is for your health; for there shall not an hair fall from the head of any of you.'

"Paul himself set the example. 'When he had thus spoken, he took bread, and gave thanks to God in presence of them all; and when he had broken it, he began to eat. Then were they all of good cheer, and they also took some meat.' That worn, drenched, discouraged throng of two hundred and seventy-six souls, who but for Paul would have become despairing and desperate, now took fresh courage, and joined with the apostle in their first meal for fourteen days. After this, knowing that it would be impossible to save their cargo, they righted up the ship by throwing overboard the wheat with which she was laden."[1]

"The ship must have been of considerable size. Ships more than 200 ft. in length are known to have plied the Mediterranean in Paul's day. It has been estimated that this ship was of about 1,200 tons' weight. . . . The fact that the ship had four anchors at the stern (v. 29) and others at the bow (v. 30) suggests a large ship."[2] Things must have been truly desperate for the ship's master to authorize the dumping of cargo. "The people of Italy, and especially of Rome, were dependent upon shipments of Egyptian wheat."[3]

Notice the interaction between Paul and the crew, the sailors, the centurion, and the master of the ship. He has gone from someone no one heeded to the one giving orders and being obeyed. Ellen White tells us Paul "had won the respect of both sailors and soldiers."[4] In times of crisis, it is reassuring to have someone in your midst who is calm, courageous, and steady. Paul's example was a beacon of hope for a crew realizing that a dangerous rocky coastline was close. "In this time of trial, he grasped by faith the arm of infinite power, his heart was stayed upon God, and amid the surrounding gloom his courage and nobility of soul shone forth with the brightest luster."[5]

Trust is built during trials, not during comfort.

---

1. Ellen G. White, *Sketches From the Life of Paul* (Washington, DC: Review and Herald®, 1974), 268, 269.
2. Francis D. Nichol, ed., *The Seventh-day Adventist Bible Commentary*, vol. 6 (Washington, DC: Review and Herald®, 1957), 449.
3. Nichol, *Seventh-day Adventist Bible Commentary*, vol. 6, 450.
4. White, *Sketches From the Life of Paul*, 264.
5. White, *Sketches From the Life of Paul*, 266.

Aground!

But the centurion, wanting to save Paul, kept them from their purpose,
and commanded that those who could swim should jump overboard first
and get to land, and the rest, some on boards and some on parts of the ship.
—Acts 27:43, 44

Day dawned, and the sailors spied a bay through a break in the rocks. If they could guide the ship into the bay, they might beach her with relative safety. "And when they had taken up the anchors, they committed themselves unto the sea, and loosed the rudder bands, and hoisted up the mainsail to the wind, and made toward shore. And falling into a place where two seas met, they ran the ship aground; and the forepart struck fast, and remained unmovable, but the hinder part was broken with the violence of the waves.

"Paul and the other prisoners were now threatened by a fate more terrible than shipwreck. The soldiers saw that in this crisis, it would be impossible for them to keep charge of their prisoners. Every man would have all that he could do to save himself. Yet if any of the prisoners were missing, the lives of those who had them in charge would be forfeited. Hence the soldiers desired to put all the prisoners to death. The Roman law sanctioned this cruel policy, and the proposal would have been executed at once, but for him to whom soldiers and prisoners alike owed their preservation. Julius the centurion knew that Paul had been instrumental in saving the lives of all on board, and he felt that it would be the basest ingratitude to allow him to be put to death; and more, he felt convinced that the Lord was with Paul, and he feared to do him harm. He, therefore, gave orders to spare the lives of the prisoners, and directed that all who could swim should cast themselves into the sea and get to land. The rest seized hold of planks and other fragments of the wreck, and were carried landward by the waves.

"When the roll was called, not one was missing. Nearly three hundred souls, sailors, soldiers, passengers, and prisoners, stood that stormy November morning upon the shore of the island of Melita [Malta]. And there were some that joined with Paul and his brethren in giving thanks to God who had preserved their lives, and brought them safe to land through the perils of the great deep."[1]

I, for one, would rather have sailed through a storm with Paul than with Jonah (see Jonah 1:3–16).

---

1. Ellen G. White, *Sketches From the Life of Paul* (Washington, DC: Review and Herald®, 1974), 269, 270.

The Viper

But when Paul had gathered a bundle of sticks and laid them on the fire,
a viper came out because of the heat, and fastened on his hand.

—Acts 28:3

Extensive examination in 1918 and 1919 by Lieutenant Edwin Smith, a naval officer who served in the Mediterranean, has proven with navigational charts and depth measurements that Luke's account of the shipwreck is highly accurate. Although unknown to the crew, their ship had come aground on the island of Malta to the southwest of Sicily and within easy reach of Italy. "The shipwrecked crew was kindly received by the barbarous people of Melita [Malta]. A rain having come on, the whole company were drenched and shivering, and the islanders kindled an immense fire of brushwood, and welcomed them all to its grateful warmth."[1]

Greeks and Romans, to define anyone whose speech was foreign, used the term *barbarous.* "The natives of Malta may have been related to the Phoenicians, or, as a result of contact with the Phoenicians, spoke a dialect of the Phoenician language, which was related, in turn, to the Hebrew. The island of Malta had been ruled by the Romans ever since the Second Punic War . . . when they took it from the Carthaginians."[2]

"Paul was among the most active in collecting fuel. As he was placing a bundle of sticks upon the fire, a viper that had been suddenly revived from its torpor by the heat, darted from the fagots and fastened upon his hand. The bystanders were horror-struck, and seeing by his chain that Paul was a prisoner, they said to one another, 'No doubt this man is a murderer, whom, though he hath escaped the sea, yet vengeance suffereth not to live.' But Paul shook off the creature into the fire, and suffered no harm. Knowing its venomous nature, they watched him closely for some time, expecting every moment to see him fall down, writhing in terrible agony. But as no unpleasant results followed, they changed their minds, and, like the people of Lystra, said that he was a god. By this circumstance Paul gained a strong influence over the islanders, and he sought faithfully to employ it in leading them to accept the truths of the gospel."[3] "Paul remained calm and composed in the presence of this new danger. Had God not promised that he would appear before Caesar?"[4] Paul's faith seemed strongest when facing disaster.

Shipwreck—now this! How calm would you be, having just been injected with certain death?

---

1. Ellen G. White, *Sketches From the Life of Paul* (Washington, DC: Review and Herald®, 1974), 270.
2. Francis D. Nichol, ed., *The Seventh-day Adventist Bible Commentary*, vol. 6 (Washington, DC: Review and Herald®, 1957), 459.
3. White, *Sketches From the Life of Paul*, 270, 271.
4. Nichol, *Seventh-day Adventist Bible Commentary*, vol. 6, 459.

Publius's Father

And it happened that the father of Publius lay sick of a fever and dysentery.
Paul went in to him and prayed, and he laid his hands on him and healed him.

—Acts 28:8

For three months the ship's company remained at Melita. During this time Paul and his fellow-laborers improved every opportunity to preach the gospel. The Lord wrought through them in a remarkable manner, and for Paul's sake the entire company were treated with great kindness; all their wants were supplied."[1]

It was during their stay on the island that Publius, the *protos*, meaning "first" or "primate," invited Julius, the centurion, to lodge with him. Paul was also extended an invitation to lodge with the ruler "until more permanent arrangements could be made."[2] "Probably the primate received the centurion, out of consideration for his rank, and with him Paul."[3] It was sometime during that winter that the father of Publius became ill with bloody dysentery. Paul prayed for the man, laid his hands upon him, and healed him. This was not the first time Paul had used the gift of healing he possessed. "Paul had exhibited the same power of the Spirit at Lystra ([Acts] 14:8–10), at Philippi ([Acts] 16:18), at Ephesus ([Acts] 19:11, 12), and at Troas ([Acts] 20:9, 10)."[4]

Soon others from all over the island began to bring their sick to Paul to be healed. This is reminiscent of the events after Jesus' healing of Peter's mother-in-law (Mark 1:32–34): "At evening, when the sun had set, they brought to Him all who were sick and those who were demon-possessed. And the whole city was gathered together at the door. Then He healed many who were sick with various diseases, and cast out many demons; and He did not allow the demons to speak, because they knew Him." The grateful islanders gave the crew honors, probably in the form of food and clothing for their journey ahead. Tradition holds that Paul preached the gospel on Malta and thus brought Christianity to the small island. This would not be hard to imagine as the crew wintered on the island for three months before continuing their journey to Rome (Acts 28:11).

Paul "had a living, abiding faith, for he cultivated a sense of the presence of Christ in all his works. He received strength in prayer, and as a faithful soldier of Christ he ever looked to his Captain for orders. No amount of obstacles piled up before him, could cause him to regard the work as an impossibility, for he realized 'all things are possible to them that believe.' "[5]

"Lord, I believe; help my unbelief!" (Mark 9:24).

---

1. Ellen G. White, *Sketches From the Life of Paul* (Washington, DC: Review and Herald®, 1974), 271.
2. Francis D. Nichol, ed., *The Seventh-day Adventist Bible Commentary*, vol. 6 (Washington, DC: Review and Herald®, 1957), 459.
3. Nichol, *Seventh-day Adventist Bible Commentary*, vol. 6, 459.
4. Nichol, *Seventh-day Adventist Bible Commentary*, vol. 6, 459.
5. Ellen G. White, MS 114, 1897.

The Castor and Pollux

After three months we sailed in an Alexandrian ship whose figurehead
was the Twin Brothers, which had wintered at the island.

—Acts 28:11

The million-plus Romans who inhabited the city of Rome were not self-supporting. The city imported nearly everything necessary to sustain life. Food, wine, leather, cloth, lumber, and stone were brought in from different areas in Italy and from overseas. North Africa, Sicily, and Egypt sent nearly twenty million bushels of grain each year to feed the capital. Paul took passage on an Egyptian grain ship headed for Rome. These ships were on regular schedules and could be counted on for reliability. Twenty-five 2,500-bushel grain barges, towed by slow oxen, came upriver from the Port of Puteoli daily. Free grain was dispensed to one-fifth of the population's poor, and grain cost to the middle and upper classes was subsidized. Free or subsidized grain, free water from the many municipal aqueducts, free entry to the Roman Circus, and the Colosseum games kept residents peaceful.[1]

It was probably the month of February when the shipwrecked crew set sail for Sicily on the Alexandrian grain vessel the *Castor and Pollux*, which had wintered on Malta as well. Castor and Pollux were a carved figurehead seen on ships probably even into the nineteenth century. These images were on the prow of the ship beneath the bowsprit and were often women or gods who were thought to bring good luck to all who sailed with them. Castor and Pollux were the patron saints of sailors and, therefore, a good omen for the superstitious. Luke doesn't give us the name of the ship that was lost, but he is quick to point out this ship's name. Perhaps he thought it appropriate that these twins were believed to be the enforcers of justice on the seas. "*Dioskouroi*, literally, the 'Twins,' [were] the legendary sons of Jupiter, borne him by Leda. The Latin names of the two boys were Castor and Pollux, who were called the Gemini."[2]

The ship sailed northeast to the port of Syracuse on the island of Sicily. Several days were spent here waiting for favorable winds. Tacking to gain headway, they moved up to the Straits of Messina at the tip of the Italian boot and stopped at Rhegium for three additional days awaiting a southerly wind. It took only twenty-four hours with a southern wind to reach Puteoli, 210 miles north. This must have been a difficult voyage for the apostle.[3]

"When every other trust fails, then it will be seen who have an abiding trust in God."[4]

1. See Howard F. Vos, *Nelson's New Illustrated Bible Manners and Customs—How People of the Bible Really Lived* (Nashville, TN: Thomas Nelson, 1999).
2. Francis D. Nichol, ed., *The Seventh-day Adventist Bible Commentary*, vol. 6 (Washington, DC: Review and Herald®, 1957), 460.
3. For itinerary, see Nichol, *Seventh-day Adventist Bible Commentary*, vol. 6, 460.
4. Ellen G. White, *Sketches From the Life of Paul* (Washington, DC: Review and Herald®, 1974), 252.

Puteoli

And the next day we came to Puteoli, where we found brethren,
and were invited to stay with them seven days. And so we went toward Rome.
—Acts 28:13, 14

P uteoli, "the modern Pozzuoli, [is] near Naples, Italy. Though it was about 140 mi. south of the capital, it was then a principal port for Rome, especially for the wheat ships from Egypt. Ostia, at the mouth of the Tiber, later replaced it.

"... It is encouraging to know that only about 30 years after the crucifixion a group of Christian believers was to be found in faraway Puteoli, a major port for the city of Rome."[1]

Ellen White relates the following account of Paul's visit to Puteoli. "Though somewhat delayed by contrary winds, the voyage was safely accomplished, and the ship cast anchor in the beautiful harbor of Puteoli, on the coast of Italy.

"There were a few Christians in this place, who entreated the apostle to remain with them seven days, and the privilege was kindly granted by the centurion. Since receiving Paul's Epistle to the Romans, the Christians of Italy had eagerly looked forward to a visit from the apostle. They had little expected to see him in chains as a prisoner, but his sufferings only endeared him to them the more. The distance from Puteoli to Rome being but a hundred and forty miles, and the seaport being in constant communication with the metropolis, the Roman Christians were informed of Paul's approach, and some of them started to meet and welcome him.

"On the eighth day after landing, the centurion and his prisoners set out for Rome. Julius willingly granted the apostle every favor which it was in his power to bestow; but he could not change his condition as a prisoner, or release him from the chain that bound him to his soldier guard. It was with a heavy heart that Paul went forward to his long-expected visit to the world's metropolis. How different the circumstances from what he had anticipated! How was he, fettered and stigmatized as a criminal, to proclaim the gospel? His hopes of winning many souls to the truth at Rome, seemed destined to be disappointed."[2]

What a blessing it must have been for Paul to spend the Sabbath with Christian believers at Puteoli.

---

1. Francis D. Nichol, ed., *The Seventh-day Adventist Bible Commentary*, vol. 6 (Washington, DC: Review and Herald®, 1957), 460.
2. Ellen G. White, *Sketches From the Life of Paul* (Washington, DC: Review and Herald®, 1974), 272, 273.

The Appii Forum

And from there, when the brethren heard about us, they came to meet us as far as Appii Forum and Three Inns. When Paul saw them, he thanked God and took courage.

—Acts 28:15

T he travelers reach Appii Forum, forty miles from Rome. As they make their way through the crowds that throng the great thoroughfare, the gray-haired old man, chained with a group of hardened-looking criminals, receives many a glance of scorn, and is made the subject of many a rude, mocking jest. Not one of all he meets bestows upon him a look of pity or sympathy. He meekly wears his chain, and silently, slowly pursues his way.

"Suddenly a cry of joy is heard, and a man springs out from the passing throng and falls upon the prisoner's neck, embracing him with tears and rejoicing, as a son would welcome a long-absent father. Again and again is the scene repeated. With eyes made keen by loving expectation, many discern in the chained captive the one who spoke to them the words of life at Corinth, at Philippi, or at Ephesus.

"The whole company is brought to a standstill, as warm-hearted disciples eagerly flock around their father in the gospel. The soldiers are impatient of delay, yet they have not the heart to interrupt this happy meeting; for they too have learned to respect and esteem their prisoner. In that worn, pain-stricken face, the disciples see the image of Christ reflected. They assure Paul that they have not forgotten him nor ceased to love him; that they are indebted to him for the joyful hope which animates their lives, and gives them peace toward God. In the ardor of their love they would bear him upon their shoulders the whole way to the city, could they but have the privilege.

"Few realize the significance of those words of Luke, that when Paul saw his brethren, 'he thanked God, and took courage.' The apostle praised God aloud in the midst of that weeping, sympathizing throng, who were not ashamed of his bonds. The cloud of sadness that had rested upon his spirit had been swept away. He felt that his labors had not been in vain."[1]

"Although his Christian life had been a succession of trials, sufferings, and disappointments, he felt in that hour abundantly repaid."[2]

---

1. Ellen G. White, *Sketches From the Life of Paul* (Washington, DC: Review and Herald®, 1974), 273, 274.
2. White, *Sketches From the Life of Paul,* 273, 274.

Rome!

Now when we came to Rome, the centurion delivered the prisoners to the captain of the guard;
but Paul was permitted to dwell by himself with the soldier who guarded him.
—Acts 28:16

Not only had Paul been met by a delegation of Christians at Appii Forum, a place noted "as abounding in tavernkeepers of bad reputation and frequented by sailors,"[1] but another group of Christians awaited him at Three Taverns. "The Latin *taberna* meant more than a 'saloon' or 'public house'; it included shops of any sort. The location of this village is not certain, but it is said to have been approximately 30 mi. south of Rome. . . . Here another group of Christians met Paul, probably having left Rome later than those who met him at Appii Forum."[2] Paul probably never expected to receive such a warm welcome. His prayers were answered, and he could truly thank God for his watch care and deliverance.

"The reader of the closing chapter of the book of Acts fervently wishes that a more complete account of Paul's experiences in Rome might have been given. Perhaps Luke intended to add further details, or to begin another volume with Paul's arrival there."[3] We will never know. Some things did end. "At Rome the charge of the centurion Julius ended. Here he delivered up his prisoners to the captain of the emperor's guard. The good account which he gave of Paul, however, together with the letter of Festus, the procurator of Judea, caused the apostle to be favorably regarded by the chief captain, and instead of being thrown into prison, he was permitted to live in his own hired house. The trial of having constantly to be chained to a soldier was continued; but he was at liberty to receive his friends, and to labor for the advancement of the cause of Christ."[4] "What must have been the effect upon a heathen soldier of being chained hour after hour to the apostle Paul?"[5]

"For years Paul had longed to visit Rome and preach the gospel there (Rom. 1:11–13). He must have reflected on the sharp contrast between that eager expectation and the realities of his arrival. But out of the shocking contrast Paul found reason to take courage, and fresh assurance of God's leading."[6]

"Paul was skilled at finding reasons for great hope in what appeared to be the most discouraging circumstances (see 2 Cor. 4:7–10 . . .). He was a confirmed and incurable Christian optimist."[7]

---

1. Francis D. Nichol, ed., *The Seventh-day Adventist Bible Commentary*, vol. 6 (Washington, DC: Review and Herald®, 1957), 460.
2. Nichol, *Seventh-day Adventist Bible Commentary*, vol. 6, 460.
3. Nichol, *Seventh-day Adventist Bible Commentary*, vol. 6, 461.
4. Ellen G. White, *Sketches From the Life of Paul* (Washington, DC: Review and Herald®, 1974), 274.
5. Nichol, *Seventh-day Adventist Bible Commentary*, vol. 6, 461.
6. Nichol, *Seventh-day Adventist Bible Commentary*, vol. 6, 461.
7. Nichol, *Seventh-day Adventist Bible Commentary*, vol. 6, 461.

The Best Defense
Is a Strong Offense

And it came to pass after three days that Paul called the leaders of the Jews together.
—Acts 28:17

The Jews who had been banished from Rome some years previous, had been tacitly permitted to return, so that large numbers were now to be found there. To these, first of all, Paul determined to present the facts concerning himself and his work, before his enemies should have opportunity to embitter them against him. Three days after his arrival at Rome, therefore, he called together their leading men, and in a simple, direct manner stated the reasons why he had come to Rome as a prisoner."[1]

Paul "said nothing of the abuse which he had suffered at the hands of the Jews, or of their repeated plots to assassinate him. His words were marked with caution and kindness. He was not seeking to win personal attention or sympathy, but to defend the truth and to maintain the honor of the gospel.

"In reply, his hearers stated that they had received no charges against him by letters public or private, and that none of the Jews who had come to Rome had accused him of any crime. They also expressed a strong desire to hear for themselves the reasons of his faith in Christ. . . .

"Since they themselves desired it, Paul bade them set a day when he could present to them the truths of the gospel. At the time appointed, many came together, 'to whom he expounded and testified the kingdom of God, persuading them concerning Jesus, both out of the law of Moses, and out of the prophets, from morning till evening.' He related his own experience, and presented arguments from the Old Testament scriptures with simplicity, sincerity, and power. Upon some minds, at least, his words made an impression which would never be effaced. All who were honestly seeking for truth were convinced, as Paul spoke of what he knew, and testified of what he had seen."[2]

"We should not be disheartened because those who have no love for truth refuse to be convinced by the clearest evidence. We need not flatter ourselves that the formal and world-loving churches of this age are more ready to receive the teachings of God's word than were those of ages past. Paul's worst enemies were among the Jews, who made the highest claims to godliness."[3]

"The most bitter opposers of truth today are found among those who profess to be its defenders."[4]

---

1. Ellen G. White, *Sketches From the Life of Paul* (Washington, DC: Review and Herald®, 1974), 275.
2. White, *Sketches From the Life of Paul*, 275, 276.
3. White, *Sketches From the Life of Paul*, 278, 279.
4. White, *Sketches From the Life of Paul*, 279.

A Rented House

Then Paul dwelt two whole years in his own rented house, and received all who came to him.
—Acts 28:30

The story of Paul, as recounted by Luke in the book of Acts, comes to an abrupt ending with Acts 28:30, 31. Luke tells us Paul lived two whole years in a hired house and that he preached the gospel of Jesus Christ to all who came to see him. "Our only information for these two years is from the four so-called prison epistles, generally thought to have been written from Rome during this period: Ephesians, Philippians, Colossians, and Philemon. We know that Paul felt the burden of imprisonment, both psychologically and physically (Eph. 3:1; 4:1; Phil. 1:16; Col. 4:18; Philemon 1, 9, 10)."[1] Luke probably meant to end his narrative with Paul finally preaching the gospel freely to both Jew and Gentile in Rome. "For the years following Paul's release and for his second imprisonment and death we have only hints in the so-called pastoral epistles, 1 Timothy, 2 Timothy, and Titus, and in early Christian tradition."[2]

"According to Roman law, the trial of Paul could not take place until his accusers should be present in person to state their charges against him. They had not yet come from Palestine, nor was it known at Rome whether they had even started on the long journey. Therefore the trial might be postponed indefinitely. . . .

"The Jews of Jerusalem were in no haste to present their accusations against Paul. They had been repeatedly thwarted in their designs, and had no desire to risk another defeat. . . . Delay would further their object, as it would afford them time to perfect and execute their plans.

"In the providence of God, all this delay resulted in the furtherance of the gospel. Paul was not condemned to a life of inactivity."[3]

Paul sent emissaries to the churches he had raised. He was kept informed of conditions within the churches and wrote messages entrusted to faithful messengers to deliver. "Thus while apparently cut off from active labor, Paul exerted a wider and more lasting influence than he could have exerted had he been free to travel among the churches as in former years."[4]

These two years of imprisonment gave the Christian church some of Paul's most powerful writings—epistles to the Ephesians, Philippians, Colossians, and Philemon.

1. Francis D. Nichol, ed., *The Seventh-day Adventist Bible Commentary*, vol. 6 (Washington, DC: Review and Herald®, 1957), 464.
2. Nichol, *Seventh-day Adventist Bible Commentary*, vol. 6, 464.
3. Ellen G. White, *Sketches From the Life of Paul* (Washington, DC: Review and Herald®, 1974), 280, 281.
4. White, *Sketches From the Life of Paul*, 281.

Former Companions and Fellow Workers

Then Paul dwelt two whole years in his own rented house, and received all who came to him, preaching the kingdom of God and teaching the things which concern the Lord Jesus Christ with all confidence, no one forbidding him.
—Acts 28:30, 31

During this time the churches that he had established in many lands were not forgotten. Realizing the dangers that threatened the converts to the new faith, the apostle sought so far as possible to meet their needs by letters of warning and practical instruction."[1] "Among the assistants of Paul in his labors were many of his former companions and fellow-workers. Luke, 'the beloved physician,' who had attended him in the journey to Jerusalem, through the two years' imprisonment at Caesarea, and upon his last perilous voyage, was with him still. Timothy also ministered to his comfort. Tychicus was his mail-bearer, taking his messages to the different churches which they had visited together. Demas and Mark also were with him.

"Mark had once been refused by Paul as unworthy to accompany him, because, when his help was much needed, he had left the apostle and returned to his home. He saw that, as Paul's companion, his life must be one of constant toil, anxiety, and self-denial; and he desired an easier path. This led the apostle to feel that he could not be trusted, and that decision caused the unhappy dissension between Paul and Barnabas.

"Mark had since learned the lesson which all must learn, that God's claims are above every other. He saw that there is no release in the Christian warfare. He had obtained a closer and more perfect view of his Pattern, and had seen upon his hands the scars of his conflict to save the lost and perishing. He was willing to follow his Master's example of earnestness and self-sacrifice. . . . And now, while sharing the lot of Paul the prisoner, Mark understood better than ever before, that it is infinite gain to win Christ at whatever cost, and infinite loss to win the world and lose the soul for whose redemption the blood of Christ was shed. Mark was now a useful and beloved helper of the apostle, and he continued faithful even unto the end."[2]

"In order to be happy, we must learn self-denial at the foot of the cross. We want no earthly hope so firmly rooted that we cannot transplant it to paradise."[3]

1. Ellen G. White, *The Acts of the Apostles* (Mountain View, CA: Pacific Press®, 1911), 453.
2. Ellen G. White, *Sketches From the Life of Paul* (Washington, DC: Review and Herald®, 1974), 282, 283.
3. White, *Sketches From the Life of Paul*, 284.

285

Part 1: Salvation Through Christ

For by grace you have been saved through faith, and that not of yourselves;
it is the gift of God, not of works, lest anyone should boast.

—Ephesians 2:8, 9

Paul's letter to the Ephesians[1] "has been called 'the Alps of the New Testament,' and stands in the midst of peaks—Paul's nine epistles written to seven churches. "...The subject of Ephesians is unity in Christ. He was writing to a church (or churches) consisting of Jews and Gentiles, Asiatics and Europeans, slaves and freemen—all symbols of a disrupted world that was to be restored to unity in Christ. This would necessitate unity of person, family, church, and race....

"There is no more urgent need today than that of a unity that preserves the freedom of the individual, unity without rigid uniformity."[2]

"It may be asserted that what the books of Galatians and Romans were to the 16th century and the Protestant Reformation, Ephesians is to the church of today. What does Christianity have to say regarding the relations of the individual to the family, of the family to the nation, of the nation to the race, and of all to the church and to God? Paul answers by presenting Christ as the center and end of all things, working out His purposes through the church, gathering 'together in one all things in Christ' ([Ephesians] 1:10)."[3] Paul stresses unity from the widest possible extent—the universe down to that of the individual believer. All things in the universe are gathered in Christ (Ephesians 1:10). Chapter 2 narrows the scope of unity further. God unites all people, Jew and Gentile alike, together in Christ (verse 15). Chapter 3 explains how Paul was chosen to preach this gospel, drawing both Jews and Gentiles together within the church. Chapter 4 moves to the need for unity within the church. With Christ as the head, the members are the whole body that should function as one (verse 16). Ephesians 5 examines families within the church. Ephesians 5:22–6:4 shows "the family is too fundamental a unit of society to be tampered with."[4] The family is composed of individuals who must strive to be strong in battle against spiritual wickedness (Ephesians 6:10–18).

In Ephesians we see the focus of unity in descending order from (1) the immense universe to (2) all of humanity to (3) different races represented by Jew and Gentile to (4) the Christian church to (5) families within the church to (6) individuals.

"God purposes to save all who choose to place their faith in Christ as their Redeemer."[5]

---

1. For Paul's initial visit to Ephesus, see the readings for May 29 and 30.
2. Francis D. Nichol, ed., *The Seventh-day Adventist Bible Commentary*, vol. 6 (Washington, DC: Review and Herald®, 1957), 995.
3. Nichol, *Seventh-day Adventist Bible Commentary*, vol. 6, 995.
4. Nichol, *Seventh-day Adventist Bible Commentary*, vol. 6, 1038.
5. Nichol, *Seventh-day Adventist Bible Commentary*, vol. 6, 998.

Part 2: The Mystery

To me, who am less than the least of all the saints, this grace was given,
that I should preach among the Gentiles the unsearchable riches of Christ.
—Ephesians 3:8

A mong the pagans *mustērion*, usually in the plural *mustēria*, was used for secrets or secret doctrines, to be made known only to those who had been specially initiated. It was the technical term for their secret rites and celebrations, and also for the mystic implements and ornaments they used in their ceremonies. . . .

"In the [New Testament], *mustērion* refers to something that God wills to make known to those who are willing to receive His revelation, rather than to something that He desires to keep secret. Throughout Paul's writings, the word carries the meaning of something which, though incapable of being fully understood by unassisted human reason, has now been made known by divine revelation. . . .

"Paul regarded it as his mission to make known the mystery 'which was kept secret since the world began' (Rom. 16:25; 1 Cor. 2:7; Eph. 3:3, 4). God's eternal purpose to redeem man in Christ has now been declared in Christianity. Thus Paul describes the whole Christian revelation as a mystery (Rom. 16:25; 1 Cor. 2:7–10; Eph. 1:9; 6:19; Col. 1:26; 2:2; 1 Tim. 3:9). He applies the term to the incarnation of Christ (1 Tim. 3:16), to the union of Christ and His church as typified by marriage (Eph. 5:32), to the transformation of the saints at the second coming (1 Cor. 15:51), to the opposition of Antichrist (2 Thess. 2:7), and especially [as in today's chapter] to the admission of the Gentiles to the kingdom of Christ (Rom. 16:25, 26; Eph. 3:1–6; Col. 1:26, 27)."[1] "None of the blessings of salvation were to be withheld from the Gentiles; thus would be fulfilled the promise to Abraham that in him all families of the earth would be blessed (Gen. 12:2, 3)."[2] Paul, as the apostle to the Gentiles, felt humbled to have been chosen to share the message of salvation with them. These letters contain the basic outline of the plan of salvation.

"The gospel brings to light the mysteries that were hidden ([Eph. 3:]3–5). Through the gospel the whole human family, Gentiles and Jews, was to see the purposes of God. Any church or any preaching that does not accomplish this is failing in its mission."[3]

---

1. Francis D. Nichol, ed., *The Seventh-day Adventist Bible Commentary*, vol. 6 (Washington, DC: Review and Herald®, 1957), 610.
2. Nichol, *Seventh-day Adventist Bible Commentary*, vol. 6, 1014.
3. Nichol, *Seventh-day Adventist Bible Commentary*, vol. 6, 1015.

Part 3: Unity of Life

There is one body and one Spirit, just as you were called in one hope of your calling; one Lord, one faith, one baptism; one God and Father of all, who is above all, and through all, and in you all.
—Ephesians 4:4–6

I n the fourth chapter of Ephesians the plan of God is so plainly and simply revealed, that all His children may lay hold upon the truth. Here the means which He has appointed to keep unity in His church, that its members may reveal to the world a healthy religious experience, is plainly declared."[1]

We see in Ephesians 4 the effective use of triads. Triads were used by the Greeks as an aid in memorization. Paul uses three sets of three in these verses, a near-perfect example of this device used to impress. It is easy to miss this rhetorical formula until it is brought to one's attention. The first set of three finds Paul listing one body, one Spirit, one hope (verse 4). The second grouping lists one Lord, one faith, one baptism (verse 5). This second group is perhaps the most perfect because it uses all three genders as well: one Lord (*heis* kurios—masculine), one faith (*mia* pistis—feminine), and one baptism *(hen* baptisma—neuter). The third group consists of three descriptions of God. He is above all, through all, and in all (verse 6). Thus a three-by-three pyramid, with emphasis on the middle set of three, is also broken into three verses.

"There is a sevenfold repetition of the word 'one' in chapter 4:4–6. Unity is the apostle's theme in these verses. . . . The Christian is not a solitary pilgrim; he belongs to a vital organism [the body], the family of God. . . .

". . . The Spirit dispels the divisions within a man's own life, the inner disharmonies that make of so many lives veritable battlefields. Disunity is a certain sign that the Holy Spirit is absent.

". . . Hope sprang up with God's appeal to men's hearts—the hope of salvation and the appearance of the Lord (Titus 2:13). . . . The Spirit validates this hope . . . , which, in turn, unifies believers and becomes, indeed, a 'lively hope' (1 Peter 1:3). Such a hope necessarily leads to the transformed life, for 'every man that hath this hope in him purifieth himself' (1 John 3:3)."[2]

"The common Father is the source of all unity. The greatest fact that the human heart can discover is that God is a father who can be trusted, one who is a friend to man. Through the ages men have yearned for someone to whom they might turn in what appeared to be an unfriendly world."[3]

"This whole chapter is a lesson that God desires us to learn and practice."[4]

---

1. Ellen G. White, MS 67, 1907.
2. Francis D. Nichol, ed., *The Seventh-day Adventist Bible Commentary*, vol. 6 (Washington, DC: Review and Herald®, 1957), 1021.
3. Nichol, *Seventh-day Adventist Bible Commentary*, vol. 6, 1022.
4. Ellen G. White, MS 55, 1903.

Part 4: Spiritual Gifts Differ

And He Himself gave some to be apostles, some prophets, some evangelists, and some pastors and teachers, for the equipping of the saints for the work of ministry, for the edifying of the body of Christ, till we all come to the unity of faith and of the knowledge of the Son of God, to a perfect man, to the measure of the stature of the fullness of Christ.
—Ephesians 4:11–13

The members of the church have been given a diversity of gifts. The gifts Paul lists in Ephesians 4 are more limited than those listed in 1 Corinthians 12. These gifts reflect those given to the church as ministries: apostles, prophets, evangelists, pastors, and teachers. Apostles enter new territory and plant churches where none have been before. It takes a courageous person to break new ground. Pioneering efforts given to planting the seed of truth often face hostile environments much as Paul did in his missionary efforts to win souls for Christ. Prophets, under the inspiration of the Holy Spirit, are able to expound and explain the will of God to the church. Prophets were especially active in the early Christian church. Agabus (Acts 11:28; Acts 21:10, 11) and the daughters of Philip (verses 8, 9) come to mind as some who had this gift.

Pastors are "shepherds" of the flock. Teachers have the gift of explaining difficult ideas. "The structure of this phrase [pastors and teachers], in the Greek, suggests that Paul intends to speak of two phases of one office. Any effective ministry is a teaching ministry. The pastoral function of the ministry is presented in John 21:16; Acts 20:28, 29; 1 Peter 5:2, 3; etc., and the teaching aspect in Acts 13:1; Rom. 12:7; 1 Tim. 3:2, and many other passages. The Master Himself was the great pastor-teacher, shepherding the flock and teaching them."[1]

The purpose of these gifts is to prepare God's people for works of service within the church. All have a job to do within the church. When all work together, the church matures. Likeness to Christ is our goal (Romans 8:29). Paul's example of the church as a human body with Christ as its head makes growing in stature understandable. As the human body grows to maturity, so too must the church grow into a full knowledge of Christ. "The refusal to grow is a greater sin than immaturity itself, and is the outcome of self-satisfaction and low ideals."[2]

"Christ must be all in all to us, He must dwell in the heart, His life must circulate through us as the blood circulates through the veins. His spirit must be a vitalizing power that will cause us to influence others to become Christlike and holy."[3]

1. Francis D. Nichol, ed., *The Seventh-day Adventist Bible Commentary*, vol. 6 (Washington, DC: Review and Herald®, 1957), 1023.
2. Nichol, *Seventh-day Adventist Bible Commentary*, vol. 6, 1024.
3. Ellen G. White, Letter 43, 1895.

Part 5: Spiritual Darkness Versus Light

And do not grieve the Holy Spirit of God, by whom you were sealed for the day of redemption.
—Ephesians 4:30

Paul had spent three years in Ephesus in fruitful ministry, and no doubt had made many intimate friends, . . . [but] there are no personal greetings or salutations in this epistle. Rather, it deals with doctrines applicable to the universal church."[1] Paul wanted his friends to press together and shun the evil practices of those around them. The practices of lying, anger, personal resentment, vindictiveness, loss of self-control, stealing, dishonest business practices, idleness, profanity, obscene jokes, frivolous conversations (Ephesians 4:25–29)—all could destroy the fellowship that should characterize the Christian church.

Verse 30 is pivotal to Paul's argument in favor of unity. How does one grieve the Spirit and thus destroy unity? "Blasphemy against the Holy Spirit, or the unpardonable sin, consists of progressive resistance to truth that culminates in a final and irrevocable decision against it, deliberately made in the full knowledge that by so doing one is choosing to pursue his own course of action in opposition to the divine will."[2] Such a choice pains the Spirit. The Spirit has a personality; only a person can grieve.

"The mighty power of the Holy Spirit works an entire transformation in the character of the human agent, making him a new creature in Christ Jesus. When a man is filled with the Spirit, the more severely he is tested and tried, the more clearly he proves that he is a representative of Christ. The peace that dwells in the soul is seen on the countenance. The words and actions express the love of the Saviour. There is no striving for the highest place. Self is renounced. The name of Jesus is written on all that is said and done.

"We may talk of the blessings of the Holy Spirit, but unless we prepare ourselves for its reception, of what avail are our works? Are we striving with all our power to attain to the stature of men and women in Christ? Are we seeking for his fullness, ever pressing toward the mark set before us,—the perfection of his character? When the Lord's people reach this mark, they will be sealed in their foreheads. Filled with the Spirit, they will be complete in Christ, and the recording angel will declare, 'It is finished.' "[3]

To be sealed, one must persevere! "Hold fast the confidence [in Christ] and the rejoicing of the hope [of salvation] firm to the end" (Hebrews 3:6).

---

1. Francis D. Nichol, ed., *The Seventh-day Adventist Bible Commentary*, vol. 6 (Washington, DC: Review and Herald®, 1957), 993.
2. Francis D. Nichol, ed., *The Seventh-day Adventist Bible Commentary*, vol. 5 (Washington, DC: Review and Herald®, 1956), 395.
3. Ellen G. White, "The Promise of the Spirit," *Advent Review and Sabbath Herald*, June 10, 1902, 9.

Part 6: Imitate God!

Therefore be imitators of God as dear children. And walk in love,
as Christ also has loved us and given Himself for us.

—Ephesians 5:1, 2

In Ephesians 5, Paul continues to describe how Christian behavior influences church unity. Small disagreements often lead to schisms in the church. The character that is not transformed by the Holy Spirit has not given up self and is quick to perceive personal affronts. Continual antagonism leads inevitably to a lack of unity and bitterness. All too often, members separate from the body of Christ because they cannot accept reproach. "Clamor soon becomes slander in an effort to ruin the reputation of others. All the evils mentioned in this passage [Ephesians 4:31] tend to disturb the unity of the body of believers, raising barriers between those who should be drawn together by virtue of their common citizenship in heaven."[1]

"In the life of the Christian there is no place for taking advantage of another in a business transaction, for the coloring of stories told, for the conveying of false impressions by innuendo, for the making of promises without the intention of keeping them, for the relaying of rumors and gossip."[2] "Speaking the truth is a confirmed habit with the Christian.

". . . Lying tends to breakdown the unity of brotherhood; deceit sets one member against another (cf. 1 Cor. 12:15)."[3] We either build up our church or destroy it.

Paul wrote, " 'Be angry, and do not sin': do not let the sun go down on your wrath, nor give place to the devil" (Ephesians 4:26, 27). What did he mean? The best explanation is that he was speaking of righteous indignation. "A Christian who is not aroused to the point of indignation by manifest wrongs and injustices may be insensitive to some things that ought to concern him. . . . Jesus was not angered by any personal affront, but by hypocritical challenges to God and injustices done to others (see Mark 3:5). Justifiable anger is directed against the wrong act without animosity toward the wrongdoer. To be able to separate the two is a supremely great Christian achievement."[4] "The anger referred to in v. 26 gives opportunity for the devil to set the members of the body of Christ one against the other—hence the counsel to give the devil no scope for his activities."[5] Paul was urging the Ephesians to forgive!

"Surely the earnest believer, by God's own grace, can learn to forgive even as God forgave."[6]

---

1. Francis D. Nichol, ed., *The Seventh-day Adventist Bible Commentary*, vol. 6 (Washington, DC: Review and Herald®, 1957), 1029.
2. Nichol, *Seventh-day Adventist Bible Commentary*, vol. 6, 1027.
3. Nichol, *Seventh-day Adventist Bible Commentary*, vol. 6, 1027.
4. Nichol, *Seventh-day Adventist Bible Commentary*, vol. 6, 1027.
5. Nichol, *Seventh-day Adventist Bible Commentary*, vol. 6, 1028.
6. Nichol, *Seventh-day Adventist Bible Commentary*, vol. 6, 1031.

Part 7: Husbands and Wives

Wives, submit to your own husbands, as to the Lord. . . . Husbands,
love your wives, just as Christ also loved the church and gave Himself for her.
—Ephesians 5:22, 25

Paul now turns to marriage as an example of Christ's marriage to and His love for His church. Paul systematically details the principle of submission concerning spouses, parents and children, masters and servants, pointing out that as Christ gave Himself for the church, church members must likewise submit to Christ as Head of the church. "Paul ascribes to women a position of subordination in relation to their husbands. . . . The ethics of Christian relationships within the family are clear when once it is seen that difference and subordination do not in any sense imply inferiority. The submission enjoined upon the wife is of the kind that can be given only between equals, not a servile obedience, but a voluntary submission in the respects in which the man was qualified by his Maker to be head (cf. Gen. 3:16). . . .

". . . The wife should see in her relation to her husband a reflection, or illustration, of her relation to Christ."[1]

"The response of the husband to the wife's submission is not to give a command, but to love. That immediately makes a partnership out of what otherwise would be a dictatorship. . . . The husband will properly provide for the wife's temporal support (1 Tim. 5:8); he will do everything possible to assure her happiness (1 Cor. 7:33); he will give her every honor (1 Peter 3:7). . . .

". . . The supreme test of love is whether it is prepared to forgo happiness in order that the other might have it. In this respect the husband is to imitate Christ, giving up personal pleasures and comforts to obtain his wife's happiness, standing by her side in the hour of sickness. Christ gave Himself for the church because she was in desperate need; He did it to save her. Likewise the husband will give himself for the salvation of his wife, ministering to her spiritual needs, and she to his, in a spirit of mutual love."[2] "Where there is mutual love and respect, questions of domination or alienation will not arise."[3]

"All heaven took a deep and joyful interest in the creation of the world and of man. Human beings were a new and distinct order. They were made in the 'image of God,' and it was the Creator's design that they should populate the earth."[4]

Those who exhibit the unfailing self-sacrificing love of Christ will one day inherit the new earth.

---

1. Francis D. Nichol, ed., *The Seventh-day Adventist Bible Commentary*, vol. 6 (Washington, DC: Review and Herald®, 1957), 1036.
2. Nichol, *Seventh-day Adventist Bible Commentary*, vol. 6, 1036.
3. Nichol, *Seventh-day Adventist Bible Commentary*, vol. 6, 1038.
4. Ellen G. White, "Purpose of Man's Creation," *Advent Review and Sabbath Herald*, February 11, 1902, 1.

Part 8: Children and Parents

Children, obey your parents in the Lord, for this is right. ....And you, fathers, do not provoke
your children to wrath, but bring them up in the training and admonition of the Lord.
—Ephesians 6:1, 4

Parents, God desires you to make your family a sample of the family in heaven. Guard your children. Be kind and tender with them. Father, mother, and children are to be joined together with the golden links of love. One well-ordered, well-disciplined family is a greater power in demonstrating the efficiency of Christianity than all the sermons in the world. When fathers and mothers realize how their children copy them, they will watch carefully every word and gesture."[1]

"Throughout Scripture, disobedience to parents is treated as one of the greatest evils (cf. Rom. 1:30; 2 Tim. 3:2). Obedience on the part of children is reasonable and just. Of all creatures that are born, a human babe is the most helpless, and for years it is entirely dependent on the kindness and love of parents. There can be no ordered family life without the obedience of the children, for the child is not competent to judge the reason for certain courses of action. But even more important, a child who is disobedient to parents will surely be disobedient to God, for he will know nothing of those disciplines and restraints that are absolutely essential to Christian growth. . . .

"In the very nature of things obedience is fitting, for God commands it, parents are entitled to it, and it is for the good of the children."[2]

While children don't come with owner's manuals, and each is an individual, parents have a responsibility before God to raise their children in the Lord. This does not mean they are to "lord it over" the child. "The present low ebb of parental authority sometimes springs from unjust, irritating, or even brutal demands made by parents on children, particularly the unwanted ones. . . . Another prolific cause of resentment among children is the capricious, inconsistent demands of some parents. Even if outward obedience is gained by violent means, it is at the expense of honor and respect."[3] But there is a reward for getting it right!

"The angels of God immortalize the names of the mothers whose efforts have won their children to Jesus Christ."[4]

---

1. Ellen G. White, MS 31, 1901.
2. Francis D. Nichol, ed., *The Seventh-day Adventist Bible Commentary*, vol. 6 (Washington, DC: Review and Herald®, 1957), 1039, 1040.
3. Nichol, *Seventh-day Adventist Bible Commentary*, vol. 6, 1041.
4. Ellen G. White, *Child Guidance* (Nashville, TN: Southern Publishing, 1954), 568.

Part 9: Slaves and Masters

Bondservants, be obedient to those who are your masters. . . . And you, masters,
do the same things to them, giving up threatening, knowing that your own
Master also is in heaven, and there is no partiality with Him.
—Ephesians 6:5, 9

S lavery was anciently practiced, not only by pagans, but also by Christians in the early Christian church. Nowhere in the Scriptures is this unnatural practice specifically condemned, but in both the [Old Testament] and the [New Testament] principles are enunciated that would tend in time to eradicate it (. . . Deut. 14:26; 1 Cor. 7:20–24; Philemon)."[1]

Roman slaves were found everywhere during the period when Paul lived. Their fate was not as difficult as that experienced by many slaves in other slaveholding countries. In most cases, they were indistinguishable from citizens other than not being allowed to wear the toga. Most citizens didn't wear a toga on the street anyway. For the most part, there was no color differentiation either. Almost all were Caucasians. Slaves were allowed to marry and raise families. Those families were hardly ever torn apart and sold off to other owners. While slaves could not own property, many were allowed to accept gratuities and fees earned from outside labor. It was not uncommon for a slave to be able to thus save up and purchase their freedom. Slaves were treated very much as human beings with intrinsic value who might one day become citizens. This was such a common occurrence that it has been estimated that one quarter of the population of Rome in the first century were freedmen or descendants of freedmen. Being a slave, one had the definite potential for upward mobility.

Paul encouraged slaves to be obedient. Their "one aim should be to please Christ in the discharge of duty to the slave master. . . .

" . . . Servants were to look on the service to their masters as part of their service to Christ."[2] Paul expected masters "to have the same spirit toward servants. . . . The apostle has insisted that servants act conscientiously and with fidelity, knowing that the eye of God was upon them; masters should do the same. . . . Although Paul is dealing primarily with slavery, all that he has to say may be applied also to employer-employee relations in our modern society. . . .

" . . . It is a tremendous challenge to any administrator to exercise his authority in love rather than through power and force."[3]

"Respect for the personalities of others is one of the first evidences of the converted life."[4]

1. Francis D. Nichol, ed., *The Seventh-day Adventist Bible Commentary*, vol. 6 (Washington, DC: Review and Herald®, 1957), 1041.
2. Nichol, *Seventh-day Adventist Bible Commentary*, vol. 6, 1042.
3. Nichol, *Seventh-day Adventist Bible Commentary*, vol. 6, 1043.
4. Nichol, *Seventh-day Adventist Bible Commentary*, vol. 6, 1043.

Part 10: The Armor of God

Therefore take up the whole armor of God, that you may be able
to withstand in the evil day, and having done all, to stand.

—Ephesians 6:13

I love Ephesians 6:13–18. Paul "is about to picture vast armies of evil gathered together to overwhelm the church. The contest is desperately uneven, with all the advantages on the side of the enemy, except as the church makes an alliance, through faith, with the resources of Omnipotence."[1] "The armor of Christ is available for all Christians, but theirs is the responsibility for putting it on. . . . God is with the one who fights 'the good fight of faith,' and will bring him victory (1 Tim. 6:12; . . . Rom. 8:37)."[2] Paul probably understood his "armor of God" analogy better than most, being chained to a Roman soldier for years. Christians are to "gird" themselves with God's truth and personal integrity. Next, we cover our hearts with the breastplate of righteousness (Romans 1:17). The breastplate is "the righteousness of Christ that covers the child of God . . . [and] the Christian's personal loyalty to principle. Both are essential for successful warfare."[3]

"The legs of the Roman soldier were covered by greaves, with sandals on the feet,"[4] giving solid footing on uneven ground. Christian warriors should be steadfast and solid having found "peace with God (Rom. 5:1). . . . The gospel is the good news that men need not die. . . . He stands firm on the knowledge of Christ incarnate, crucified, risen, ascended—the heart of the gospel, and the reason for peace."[5] Take shelter behind the shield of your faith (1 John 5:4). "This faith is active, like the shield that is raised to catch the fiery darts; it is also passive in that it trusts in God for deliverance. . . .

". . . Faith stops the arrows of temptation before they become sin in the soul."[6]

"The head needs special protection as being a most vital part, the seat of the will and the intelligence. . . .

"In 1 Thess. 5:8 the helmet is called the hope of salvation. Salvation is past, present, and future."[7] Embrace that hope with your whole mind. Last, take up the sword of the Spirit, which is the Word of God, using it as both a defensive and offensive blade. Constantly praying, and thus armed, expect to win the battle!

"If we have on the heavenly armor, we shall find that the assaults of the enemy will not have power over us. Angels of God will be round about us to protect us."[8]

1. Francis D. Nichol, ed., *The Seventh-day Adventist Bible Commentary*, vol. 6 (Washington, DC: Review and Herald®, 1957), 1043.

2. Nichol, *Seventh-day Adventist Bible Commentary*, vol. 6, 880.

3. Nichol, *Seventh-day Adventist Bible Commentary*, vol. 6, 1045.

4. Nichol, *Seventh-day Adventist Bible Commentary*, vol. 6, 1045.

5. Nichol, *Seventh-day Adventist Bible Commentary*, vol. 6, 1045.

6. Nichol, *Seventh-day Adventist Bible Commentary*, vol. 6, 1045.

7. Nichol, *Seventh-day Adventist Bible Commentary*, vol. 6, 1045.

8. Ellen G. White, "The Work for This Time," *Advent Review and Sabbath Herald*, May 25, 1905, 17.

Part 1: Gnosticism, Docetism, and Paganism

To the saints and faithful brethren in Christ who are in Colosse: Grace to you and peace from God our Father and the Lord Jesus Christ.

—Colossians 1:2

B efore dispatching Tychicus to Ephesus with his letter for the Ephesians, Paul wrote a letter for the church at Collosae.[1] "Although Paul himself may not have founded the Colossian church ... it is clear that he held himself responsible for the spiritual condition of the Colossian Christians, and that he knew well their needs and the dangers in which they stood. This information was brought to him in Rome, apparently by Epaphras (see Col. 1:8; cf. Philemon 23), and afforded the immediate reason for his writing the epistle to them. The danger confronting the Colossian believers arose from false teachings that were spreading among them. . . .

"In Galatians and elsewhere he rebuts Judaism solely, but here his target is hybrid. Not only is Paul concerned to refute Judaizing legalism, he also must contend with certain pagan elements that sought to degrade or eclipse the office of Christ."[2]

"Gnosticism was little more than a blend of various pagan philosophies masquerading under the guise of Christian terminology. . . .

". . . Gnostics, generally speaking, denied that He [Jesus] was a human being at all. They conceived of Christ as a phantom, or 'aeon,' that temporarily took possession of Jesus, an ordinary human being."[3] "The Docetists ... were a group of Gnostics who held that the first coming of Christ to earth must be explained only as an 'appearance.' ... Docetists denied the humanity of Christ entirely, regarding what was seen as a mere vision."[4]

"The false teachers at Colossae were teaching the existence of angelic beings arranged in different orders, intermediate between God and the world, who acted as mediators for men, brought them salvation, and merited worship. At the same time these teachers insisted on an extremely legalistic ceremonialism, following the Jewish pattern, and emphasizing circumcision, taboos in matters of food and drink, and observance of festivals. Against such teachings, Paul wrote the Colossian epistle."[5]

Some Christians still accept the Gnostic belief that saints should be worshiped as intermediaries mediating salvation rather than Christ alone.

---

1. Paul did not visit Colossae.

2. Francis D. Nichol, ed., *The Seventh-day Adventist Bible Commentary*, vol. 7 (Washington, DC: Review and Herald®, 1957), 183, 184.

3. Francis D. Nichol, ed., *The Seventh-day Adventist Bible Commentary*, vol. 5 (Washington, DC: Review and Herald®, 1956), 912, 913.

4. Francis D. Nichol, ed., *The Seventh-day Adventist Bible Commentary*, vol. 6 (Washington, DC: Review and Herald®, 1957), 58.

5. Nichol, *Seventh-day Adventist Bible Commentary*, vol. 7, 184.

Part 2: Christ the Creator

He is the image of the invisible God, the firstborn over all creation. For by Him all things were created that are in heaven and that are on earth, visible and invisible.
—Colossians 1:15, 16

P aul launches into the major theme of his letter to the Colossians in Colossians 1:15. Paul refers to Jesus as *prōtotokos*, or firstborn. While some debate has occurred regarding what Paul meant by the term *prōtotokos*, it is accepted "as a figurative expression describing Jesus Christ as first in rank, the figure being drawn from the dignity and office held by the first-born in a human family, or, more precisely, the first-born in a royal family. Christ's position is unique, authoritative, and absolute. He has been entrusted with all prerogatives and authority in heaven and earth. Paul emphasizes the position of Christ because he is seeking to meet the arguments of the false teachers, who declared that Christ was created, and who denied His supremacy."[1]

"If Christ made all things, he existed before all things. The words spoken in regard to this are so decisive that no one need be left in doubt [John 1:1–3]. Christ was God essentially, and in the highest sense. He was with God from all eternity, God over all, blessed forevermore.

"The Lord Jesus Christ, the divine Son of God, existed from eternity, a distinct person, yet one with the Father. He was the surpassing glory of heaven. He was the commander of the heavenly intelligences, and the adoring homage of the angels was received by him as his right. This was no robbery of God. . . . [Proverbs 8:22–27 quoted].

"There are light and glory in the truth that Christ was one with the Father before the foundation of the world was laid. This is the light shining in a dark place, making it resplendent with divine, original glory. This truth, infinitely mysterious in itself, explains other mysterious and otherwise unexplainable truths, while it is enshrined in light, unapproachable and incomprehensible."[2]

"Christ is the center, the source, the sphere, in which creation originated."[3] Paul met the "angelic orders argument" of the false teachers directly. He argues here that "whether there were such orders or not, Christ created them all, and consequently was far above them in rank."[4]

"We have only one perfect photograph of God, and this is Jesus Christ."[5]

---

1. Francis D. Nichol, ed., *The Seventh-day Adventist Bible Commentary*, vol. 7 (Washington, DC: Review and Herald®, 1957), 191.
2. Ellen G. White, "The Word Made Flesh," *Advent Review and Sabbath Herald*, April 5, 1906, 8.
3. Nichol, *Seventh-day Adventist Bible Commentary*, vol. 7, 191.
4. Nichol, *Seventh-day Adventist Bible Commentary*, vol. 7, 191.
5. Ellen G. White, MS 70, 1899.

Part 3: Paul's Concern

For I want you to know what a great conflict I have for you and those
in Laodicea, and for as many as have not seen my face in the flesh.

—Colossians 2:1

C olossae was "a town in Phrygia about 110 mi. east of the seaport Ephesus. . . .
Colossae was situated on the banks of the river Lycus [in the Lycus Valley] not far
from Hierapolis and Laodicea, about 13 mi. from the former and 10 mi. from the latter.
In previous centuries Colossae had occupied a position of considerable importance.
. . . But by [New Testament] times the population had shrunk to small proportions."[1]

"Surrounded by the practices and influences of heathenism, the Colossian believers
were in danger of being drawn away from the simplicity of the gospel, and Paul, in
warning them against this, pointed them to Christ as the only safe guide. 'I would that
ye knew,' he wrote, 'what great conflict I have for you, and for them at Laodicea, and
for as many as have not seen my face in the flesh; that their hearts might be comforted,
being knit together in love, and unto all riches of the full assurance of understanding,
to the acknowledgment of the mystery of God, and of the Father, and of Christ; in
whom are hid all the treasures of wisdom and knowledge.

" 'And this I say, lest any man should beguile you with enticing words. . . . As ye
have therefore received Christ Jesus the Lord, so walk ye in Him: rooted and built up
in Him, and stablished in the faith, as ye have been taught, abounding therein with
thanksgiving. Beware lest any man spoil you through philosophy and vain deceit, after
the tradition of men, after the rudiments of the world, and not after Christ. For in Him
dwelleth all the fullness of the Godhead bodily. And ye are complete in Him, which
is the head of all principality and power.' "[2]

The church has always stood in more danger from those within than from those
without. False teachers bring in errors that gradually become accepted as truth. "The
work of higher criticism, in dissecting, conjecturing, reconstructing, is destroying faith
in the Bible as a divine revelation."[3]

The true believer makes the Word of God "the subject for his contemplation and meditation. He
is to regard the Bible as the voice of God speaking directly to him. Thus he will find the wisdom
which is divine."[4]

---

1. Francis D. Nichol, ed., *The Seventh-day Adventist Bible Commentary*, vol. 7 (Washington, DC: Review and Herald®, 1957), 187.
2. Ellen G. White, *The Acts of the Apostles* (Mountain View, CA: Pacific Press®, 1911), 473.
3. White, *Acts of the Apostles*, 474.
4. White, *Acts of the Apostles*, 475.

Part 4: Avoid Speculation

Beware lest anyone cheat you through philosophy and empty deceit, according to the tradition of men, according to the basic principles of the world, and not according to Christ. For in Him dwells all the fullness of the Godhead bodily.

—Colossians 2:8, 9

The warnings of the word of God regarding the perils surrounding the Christian church belong to us today. As in the days of the apostles men tried by tradition and philosophy to destroy faith in the Scriptures, so today, by the pleasing sentiments of higher criticism, evolution, spiritualism, theosophy, and pantheism, the enemy of righteousness is seeking to lead souls into forbidden paths. To many the Bible is as a lamp without oil, because they have turned their minds into channels of speculative belief that bring misunderstanding and confusion."[1]

"As we near the end of time, falsehood will be so mingled with truth, that only those who have the guidance of the Holy Spirit will be able to distinguish truth from error.

"We need to make every effort to keep the way of the Lord. We must in no case turn from His guidance to put our trust in man. The Lord's angels are appointed to keep strict watch over those who put their faith in the Lord, and these angels are to be our special help in every time of need. Every day we are to come to the Lord with full assurance of faith, and to look to Him for wisdom. . . . Those who are guided by the Word of the Lord will discern with certainty between falsehood and truth, between sin and righteousness."[2]

"Traditions are the habitual patterns of human beliefs and behavior, transmitted from one generation to the next. Traditions may be good or bad. Paul warns against those that are heretical, having a human instead of a divine source. . . .

". . . The norm must always be what Christ would have. Christ is placed in opposition to all deceitful philosophy. The wares of false teachers should be compared with the doctrines of the Master Teacher. Christ, the Creator and Sustainer, is the measuring rod of all true knowledge."[3]

We would do well to consider: "The Majesty of heaven was made to suffer at the hands of religious zealots, who claimed to be the most enlightened people upon the face of the earth."[4] Religious zealots are usually blind to reason and truth.

1. Ellen G. White, *The Acts of the Apostles* (Mountain View, CA: Pacific Press®, 1911), 474.
2. Ellen G. White, MS 43, 1907.
3. Francis D. Nichol, ed., *The Seventh-day Adventist Bible Commentary*, vol. 7 (Washington, DC: Review and Herald®, 1957), 202.
4. Ellen G. White, MS 153, 1898.

Part 5: Worship Only God

*Let no one cheat you of your reward, taking delight in false humility
and worship of angels, intruding into those things which he has not seen.*
—Colossians 2:18

P aul warned the Colossians against accepting the idea that man could not approach God (Christ) without an intermediary. This philosophy went a step further when the worshiper transferred adoration and worship to the intermediary. This idea "runs contrary to the teaching of Christ. Jesus, citing Deut. 6:13, declared, 'Thou shalt worship the Lord thy God, and him only shalt thou serve' (Matt. 4:10). Heavenly angels prohibit adoration of themselves (Rev. 22:9)."[1]

"No man can ever truly excel in knowledge and influence unless he is connected with the God of wisdom and power.

". . . All the philosophies of human nature have led to confusion and shame when God has not been recognized as all in all. . . .

"The most profound intellects of the world, when not enlightened by God's Word, become bewildered and lost while trying to investigate the matters of science and revelation. The Creator and His works are beyond finite comprehension, and men conclude that because they cannot explain the works and ways of God from natural causes, the Bible history is not reliable. Many are so intent upon excluding God from the exercise of sovereign will and power in the established order of the universe that they demean man, the noblest of His creatures. The theories and speculations of philosophy would make us believe that man has come by slow degrees, not merely from a savage state, but from the very lowest form of the brute creation. They destroy man's dignity because they will not admit God's miraculous power.

"God has illuminated human intellects, and poured a flood of light on the world through discoveries in art and science. But those who view these from a merely human standpoint will most assuredly come to wrong conclusions. The thorns of error, skepticism, and infidelity are disguised by being covered with the garments of philosophy and science.[2]

Satan has devised this ingenious manner of winning souls away from the living God, away from the truth and religion. He exalts nature above nature's Creator."[3]

---

1. Francis D. Nichol, ed., *The Seventh-day Adventist Bible Commentary*, vol. 7 (Washington, DC: Review and Herald®, 1957), 206
2. Ellen G. White, MS 4, 1882
3. Ellen G. White, MS 4, 1882.

Part 6: Off and On

But now you yourselves are to put off all these: anger, wrath, malice, blasphemy, filthy language out of your mouth. Do not lie to one another.

—Colossians 3:8, 9

At the time of their conversion and baptism the Colossian believers pledged themselves to put away beliefs and practices that had hitherto been a part of their lives, and to be true to their allegiance to Christ. In his letter, Paul reminded them of this, and entreated them not to forget that in order to keep their pledge they must put forth constant effort against the evils that would seek for mastery over them. 'If ye then be risen with Christ,' he said, 'seek those things which are above, where Christ sitteth on the right hand of God. Set your affection on things above, not on things on the earth. For ye are dead, and your life is hid with Christ in God.' "[1]

The Christian life is constant warfare against the propensity to do evil. Paul reminded the Colossians of those things they were to rid themselves of, "take off," and those things they were to "put on" when they became new creatures in Christ. The Christian does not participate in illicit sexual relationships, partake or view things that are impure or immoral, lust after those things not within their marriage vows. The Christian does not covet things belonging to another nor place the love of anything or anyone above love for God. The Christian is slow to anger, showing no malice toward others, watching lest his speech invoke foul language, curses, or lies. "The Christian must set a watch upon his lips (Ps. 141:3)."[2]

Christians are merciful, kind, humble, meek, longsuffering, forgiving, charitable, living at peace with others. Christians support, teach, and encourage each other with psalms and hymns. "As Christ is the express image of His Father (Heb. 1:3), so the Christian is to grow 'unto a perfect man [or woman], unto the measure of the stature of the fullness of Christ' (. . . Eph. 4:13)."[3] "The power of a higher, purer, nobler life is our great need. The world has too much of our thought, and the kingdom of heaven too little.[4]

"In his efforts to reach God's ideal for him [or her], the Christian is to despair of nothing. Moral and spiritual perfection, through the grace and power of Christ, is promised to all."[5]

---

1. Ellen G. White, *The Acts of the Apostles* (Mountain View, CA: Pacific Press®, 1911), 475, 476.
2. Francis D. Nichol, ed., *The Seventh-day Adventist Bible Commentary*, vol. 7 (Washington, DC: Review and Herald®, 1957), 211.
3. Nichol, *Seventh-day Adventist Bible Commentary*, vol. 7, 211.
4. White, *Acts of the Apostles*, 478.
5. White, *Acts of the Apostles*, 478.

Part 7: Develop Christlikeness

Therefore, as the elect of God, holy and beloved, put on tender mercies, kindness, humility,
meekness, longsuffering; bearing with one another, and forgiving one another.
—Colossians 3:12, 13

W hen did you last "honestly" assess how you measure up as a Christian? "Jesus Christ is . . . the goal for ultimate realization. He is 'the fulness of him that filleth all in all' (Eph. 1:23). Since His character is in all His people, how can there be any distinction among them? There can be no rivalry or enmity between members of the body of Christ. Jesus is the common heritage of His saints, their ideal, their goal in character building. He is also the means by which this brotherhood of victors is attained."[1] Did you catch the "no rivalry or enmity between church members" part? Do you promote harmony in your church?

"A heart of compassion is a distinguishing feature of true Christianity."[2] The Christian is "gentle, gracious, kindly [considerate], both in disposition and action, toward the needs of one's neighbor."[3] Are you cheerful and helpful around the house, the church, and the community? Are you a good Samaritan? The child of God "should labor constantly for humbleness of mind and that meek and quiet spirit which is in the sight of God of great price."[4] Do you live for the spotlight? Are you constantly agitating and vocalizing opinions? Christians should be slow to anger, "inwardly passing over the faults, wrongs, or weaknesses of others. This is true forgiveness."[5] "No matter how high may be the profession of the nominal Christian, if his soul is not filled with love for God and for his fellow men, he is not a true disciple of Christ (. . . 1 Cor. 13:1–3)."[6]

If you believe you are right and everyone else is wrong, if you can't stand certain people, if you say inconsiderate things about members of your church family, if you gossip, criticize, argue endlessly, find fault with others, refuse to forgive, have no charity or compassion for others who are struggling—if this sounds like you, then you might want to listen to Paul's admonition to the Colossians.

He is speaking to each of us! He is talking about the character that will mark the Christian.

---

1. Francis D. Nichol, ed., *The Seventh-day Adventist Bible Commentary*, vol. 7 (Washington, DC: Review and Herald®, 1957), 211, 212.
2. Nichol, *Seventh-day Adventist Bible Commentary*, vol. 7, 212.
3. Nichol, *Seventh-day Adventist Bible Commentary*, vol. 7, 212.
4. Ellen G. White, *Testimonies for the Church*, vol. 2 (Mountain View, CA: Pacific Press®, 1948), 288.
5. Nichol, *Seventh-day Adventist Bible Commentary*, vol. 7, 212.
6. Nichol, *Seventh-day Adventist Bible Commentary*, vol. 7, 212.

Part 8: Characters Built for Heaven

And whatever you do in word or deed, do all in the name of the Lord Jesus, giving thanks to God the Father through Him.

—Colossians 3:17

Our Saviour taught His disciples to pray: 'Forgive us our debts, as we forgive our debtors.' A great blessing is here asked upon conditions. We ourselves state these conditions. We ask that the mercy of God toward us may be measured by the mercy which we extend to others. Christ declares that this is the rule by which the Lord will deal with us. 'If ye forgive men their trespasses, your heavenly Father will also forgive you: but if ye forgive not men their trespasses, neither will your Father forgive your trespasses.' Wonderful terms! but how little are they understood or heeded. One of the most common sins, and one that is attended with most pernicious results, is the indulgence of an unforgiving spirit. How many will cherish animosity or revenge and then bow before God and ask to be forgiven as they forgive. Surely they can have no true sense of the import of this prayer or they would not dare to take it upon their lips. We are dependent upon the pardoning mercy of God every day and every hour; how then can we cherish bitterness and malice toward our fellow sinners! If, in all their daily intercourse, Christians would carry out the principles of this prayer, what a blessed change would be wrought in the church and in the world! This would be the most convincing testimony that could be given to the reality of Bible religion.

"God requires more of His followers than many realize. If we would not build our hopes of heaven upon a false foundation we must accept the Bible as it reads and believe that the Lord means what he says. He requires nothing of us that He will not give us grace to perform. We shall have no excuse to offer in the day of God if we fail to reach the standard set before us in His word."[1]

Actions seen in daily life have an impact for or against our personal plans for a future life in heaven. While sanctification is "the work of a lifetime," there should be steady, "daily" trending toward a more Christlike character. "The Christian should ever bear in mind that day by day he is building a character for eternity. He should constantly place himself under God's control. He must be guarded in all that he says and does.[2]

He must bear in mind that in his life 'religion is not merely one influence among others; it is to be an influence dominating all others.' "[3]

---

1. Ellen G. White, *Testimonies for the Church*, vol. 5 (Mountain View, CA: Pacific Press®, 1948), 170.

2. Francis D. Nichol, ed., *The Seventh-day Adventist Bible Commentary*, vol. 7 (Washington, DC: Review and Herald®, 1957), 214.

3. Nichol, *The Seventh-day Adventist Bible Commentary*, vol. 7, 214.

Part 9: Salty Speech

Let your speech always be with grace, seasoned with salt,
that you may know how you ought to answer each one.

—Colossians 4:6

Christians are to witness continuously for their faith before others. They are to win them to the Lord. "The most significant way to accomplish this is by the example of a virtuous Christian life. Against this there is no argument."[1] Those who profess to be Christians but do not live a life representative of their faith are worse than non-Christians, for they hold the gospel up to ridicule. Often the Christian is tempted to use the vernacular of those around him or her. Cursing for dramatic effect is never acceptable. Coarse and vile language, language peppered with innuendo and double meanings, are equally unacceptable. It goes without saying that lying lips are an abomination. James 3:5–8 speaks to the unbridled tongue. "A man's words reveal the general tenor of his thoughts. If he controls his thoughts to the extent that is words are consistently Christlike, the 'whole body' is safely under control."[2]

"Hand in hand with the Christian's manner of life go the words he [or she] speaks. Especially is this true in his [or her] contacts with those who 'are without' (v. 5). Not only the words he [or she] speaks, but the way he [or she] says them, and even the tone of his [or her] voice, make an impression for good or ill on those whom he [or she] meets. Hence his [or her] discourse and conversation should be well guarded."[3] "When Jesus spoke, those in His home-town synagogue were impressed by the 'gracious words' (literally, "words of grace") that fell from His lips (Luke 4:22). The words of the Christian should carry with them the power and influence of Heaven."[4]

"Salt renders food palatable. Here it is that which makes speech attractive, stimulating, and agreeable to listen to. The opposite would be stale, insipid, or idle speech. [...]When the Christian opens his mouth, pleasant, helpful, edifying words should flow forth.

"[...]It is the responsibility of each Christian to 'be ready always to give an answer to every man that asketh ... a reason of the hope that is in' him [or her] ([...]1 Peter 3:15). Personal witnessing is an essential part of the Christian life.[5]

In order to witness effectively, it is essential that our words be of the nature here described."[6]

---

1. Francis D. Nichol, ed., *The Seventh-day Adventist Bible Commentary*, vol. 7 (Washington, DC: Review and Herald®, 1957), 217.
2. Nichol, *Seventh-day Adventist Bible Commentary*, vol. 7, 525.
3. Nichol, *Seventh-day Adventist Bible Commentary*, vol. 7, 217.
4. Nichol, *Seventh-day Adventist Bible Commentary*, vol. 7, 217.
5. Nichol, *Seventh-day Adventist Bible Commentary*, vol. 7, 217
6. Nichol, *Seventh-day Adventist Bible Commentary*, vol. 7, 217.

Part 10: Final News

Now when this epistle is read among you, see that it is read also in the church of the Laodiceans, and that you likewise read the epistle from Laodicea.
—Colossians 4:16

Paul wraps up his letter to the church at Colossae by telling them he has entrusted their letter to Tychicus. "Tychicus was to explain to the members how Paul was doing, to encourage them to continue in the Christian way, and perhaps to obtain financial help to sustain Paul in prison."[1] Onesimus, the runaway slave of Philemon, was from Colossae. Paul was sending him back to them as a Christian who could be trusted. Paul mentions Aristarchus as being a fellow prisoner. Aristarchus was "a companion of Paul from Thessalonica (Acts 27:2). He had shared with the apostle the experiences connected with the tumult at Ephesus (Acts 19:29). When the apostolic delegation journeyed from Corinth to Jerusalem, Aristarchus probably carried the offering from Thessalonica to the mother church in Palestine (Acts 20:4). He also accompanied Paul at least part way on the apostle's journey as a prisoner from Jerusalem to Rome (Acts 27:2). In Philemon 24 he is included among Paul's 'fellow-labourers.'

". . . Some have conjectured that Aristarchus had voluntarily decided to share the discomforts of Paul's prison life, to minister to his needs, a practice which some allege the Romans allowed."[2]

Paul mentions John Mark, Justus, and Epaphras as being with him. "Epaphras was a native of Colossae, who had labored there and possibly at Laodicea and Hierapolis. He was Paul's informant regarding the situation in his home church (cf. [Colossians] 1:7, 8). Evidently he was remaining at Rome longer than he had planned at first, in order to assist Paul in his ministry. He joined Paul in sending greetings."[3] Luke, the physician, and Demas (2 Timothy 4:10) were also still with Paul. Paul wished both his letters read in the cities of the Lycus Valley (Colossians 4:16). "Paul wrote Ephesians at about the same time that he wrote Colossians, perhaps even on the same day. Both were entrusted to the same messenger, Tychicus (cf. Eph. 6:21; Col. 4:7). But this is only a conjecture."[4] Taking the quill "from the hand of his amanuensis [Paul] wrote his own farewell greeting. . . . The expression shows his affection, and adds a final touch of genuineness and personal authority to his letter."[5]

"Remember my chains. Grace be with you. Amen" (Colossians 4:18).

---

1. Francis D. Nichol, ed., *The Seventh-day Adventist Bible Commentary*, vol. 7 (Washington, DC: Review and Herald®, 1957), 217.
2. Nichol, *Seventh-day Adventist Bible Commentary*, vol. 7, 218.
3. Nichol, *Seventh-day Adventist Bible Commentary*, vol. 7, 218.
4. Nichol, *Seventh-day Adventist Bible Commentary*, vol. 7, 219.
5. Nichol, *Seventh-day Adventist Bible Commentary*, vol. 7, 219.

Part 1: To My Beloved Friend

Paul, a prisoner of Christ Jesus, and Timothy our brother,
To Philemon our beloved friend and fellow laborer, to the beloved Apphia,
Archippus our fellow soldier, and to the church in your house.
—Philemon 1:1, 2; emphasis added

Among the disciples who ministered to Paul at Rome was Onesimus, a fugitive slave from the city of Colosse. He belonged to a Christian named Philemon, a member of the Colossian church. But he had robbed his master and fled to Rome. Here this pagan slave, profligate and unprincipled, was reached by the truths of the gospel. He had seen and heard Paul at Ephesus, and now, in the providence of God, he met him again in Rome. In the kindness of his heart, the apostle sought to relieve the poverty and distress of the wretched fugitive, and then endeavored to shed the light of truth into his darkened mind. Onesimus listened attentively to the words of life which he had once despised, and was converted to the faith of Christ. He now confessed his sin against his master, and gratefully accepted the counsel of the apostle."[1]

Apparently, Philemon "was a person of considerable means and social prestige."[2] "Early Christians met in private homes for church services. . . . In large cities several church services would be conducted simultaneously in various homes."[3] The home of Philemon in Colossae was being used for just such a purpose. Perhaps that is why Paul calls him a "beloved friend and fellow laborer" (Philemon 1:2). Perhaps it was because Philemon had assisted Paul in his ministry at Ephesus. We do not know the nature of their labors together. For whatever reason, Paul knows that by using such an opening, "Philemon will find difficulty in ignoring counsel given in such sincerity and brotherly affection. Genuine affection is so rarely expressed, especially among men. Paul exemplifies the many tender traits as well as the sterner qualities that sincere Christian men will always exhibit."[4]

Paul also sends greetings to *Apphia*. Here is an oft-overlooked Christian woman of significance. "Paul grants Apphia equal status with himself and Philemon. The elevation of womanhood is one of Christianity's great contributions to the human race, this being one of the many instances in the New Testament where the dignity of a woman is emphasized."[5]

Paul is about to ask, not demand, a favor from a fellow Christian. Can you honestly call every member in your local church, your friend? If not, why not?

1. Ellen G. White, *Sketches From the Life of Paul* (Washington, DC: Review and Herald®, 1974), 284, 285.
2. Francis D. Nichol, ed., *The Seventh-day Adventist Bible Commentary*, vol. 7 (Washington, DC: Review and Herald®, 1957), 378.
3. Nichol, *Seventh-day Adventist Bible Commentary*, vol. 7, 379.
4. Nichol, *Seventh-day Adventist Bible Commentary*, vol. 7, 378.
5. Nichol, *Seventh-day Adventist Bible Commentary*, vol. 7, 378.

Part 2: A Slave No Longer

For perhaps he departed for a while for this purpose, that you might receive him forever, no longer as a slave but more than a slave—a beloved brother.
—Philemon 1:15, 16

Without an understanding of the slave problem as it existed in the Roman Empire of Paul's day the Epistle to Philemon cannot be fully appreciated. Slaves were a recognized part of the social structure and were considered members of their master's household. Between the years 146 B.C. and A.D. 235 the proportion of slaves to freedmen is said to have been three to one. . . .

"With so large a part of the population under bondage the ruling class felt obliged to enact severe laws to prevent escape or revolt. According to Roman law the master possessed absolute power of life and death over his slaves. . . . The punishment for running away was often death. . . .

"Some slave owners were more considerate than others, and some slaves showed great devotion to their masters. Certain tasks committed to slaves were relatively pleasant, and a number required a high degree of intelligence. Often teachers, physicians, and even philosophers became slaves as a result of military conquest. Many slaves ran shops or factories or managed estates for their masters. But always the slave was entirely subject to his master's will, whether wise or fickle. The institution of slavery was a school for cowardice, flattery, dishonesty, graft, immorality, and other vices, for above all else a slave had to cater to his master's wishes, however evil they might be."[1]

Paul was aware that whatever action Philemon took regarding his fugitive slave, it would "greatly influence his family, the group of Christians among whom he labored, and his pagan community."[2] Paul knew that had Onesimus not run away, he would not be a Christian. Being in prison, Paul had also come to highly appreciate the comfort of the slave's presence. Yet Paul felt Onesimus must return to his master and reconcile. "Paul would not allow his personal needs to interfere with the more important business of a spiritual triumph, or presume upon the rights of Philemon, legal owner of Onesimus."[3]

Onesimus in the Greek meant "useful," and while Philemon might have found him "useless," Onesimus had become as much a son to Paul as Philemon himself.

1. Francis D. Nichol, ed., *The Seventh-day Adventist Bible Commentary*, vol. 7 (Washington, DC: Review and Herald®, 1957), 376.
2. Nichol, *Seventh-day Adventist Bible Commentary*, vol. 7, 378.
3. Nichol, *Seventh-day Adventist Bible Commentary*, vol. 7, 381.

Part 3: Charge My Account

If then you count me as a partner, receive him as you would me. But if he had wronged you or owes anything, put that on my account. I, Paul, am writing with my own hand.
—Philemon 1:17–19

After a long and carefully worded preamble, Paul makes this definite request, which constitutes the climax of the epistle. Even in making this petition, which has been delayed by delicate and graceful tact, Paul appeals to a very real and tender motive in Philemon, that of personal friendship. From the standpoint of his legal rights Philemon could proceed with other action than that which Paul suggests. But Paul rises above mere justice and rests his case on the summit of love. Because of Philemon's unquestioned respect for Paul's judgment and his gratitude for the apostle's love, Onesimus will be received on the basis of Paul's estimate of him. For a man like Philemon that will be enough.

"... Onesimus had stolen from Philemon before departing and as a Christian he would be expected to make full restitution, without question. . . .

"Paul is here not making a veiled hint that Philemon should cancel Onesimus' financial debt because of Philemon's debt to Paul. Such a procedure contradicts the high ethical principles by which Paul guides his conduct.

"... [Rather,] Paul desires that no obstacle should hinder an unreserved reception of Onesimus when he arrives in Colossae. Paul would have the debt incurred by the runaway slave charged to him personally as a father covers the debts of his son."[1] No doubt, Paul was hopeful that Philemon would set Onesimus free, although he never forced that action on his friend. "The [New Testament] does not directly attack the institution of slavery, but it does outline principles that would eventually prove fatal to this institution."[2]

"Christ, like Paul, was not responsible for the failures of men. Yet He stands in man's stead, covering his debt with His own merits, so that the repentant sinner may be justified before all creation. Christ, like Paul, was willing to pay another's debt so that the sinner may be received by all as though he had committed no wrong."[3]

What do you owe the One who paid your debt to the Father, releasing you from your bondage to sin?

---

1. Francis D. Nichol, ed., *The Seventh-day Adventist Bible Commentary*, vol. 7 (Washington, DC: Review and Herald®, 1957), 382, 383.
2. Nichol, *Seventh-day Adventist Bible Commentary*, vol. 7, 384.
3. Nichol, *Seventh-day Adventist Bible Commentary*, vol. 7, 383.

Part 1: Paul's Bonds Work for Good

But I want you to know, brethren, that the things which happened to me have actually turned out for the furtherance of the gospel, so that it has become evident . . . that my chains are in Christ.
—Philippians 1:12, 13

M ore than ten years had passed since Paul had first preached the gospel at Philippi."[1] Things had not been easy for Lydia and the others since Paul and Silas had been beaten and thrown into prison for casting out the spirit of divination from the demon-possessed slave girl. Despite the midnight earthquake that had freed the prisoners, the conversion of the jailer and his entire family, and the subsequent abject apology by the city elders for falsely imprisoning Roman citizens, the church they had established was being persecuted. The church knew Paul was a prisoner in Rome. For this reason, they had sent Epaphroditus to him with support. Charity is the first of Christian graces.[2]

"From the letter [to the Philippians] one gains considerable insight into the situation at Philippi, the condition of Paul, and the relation between the apostle and the Philippian believers. The church at Philippi was led by bishops and deacons ([Philippians] 1:1). Its members were suffering persecution (v. 29). Apparently, there had been some tendency to discord, especially between two of the women members ([Philippians] 4:2), but there is no hint of moral corruption or erroneous doctrine. There is little to disturb the joy and thankfulness with which the apostle contemplates the Philippians' growth in grace. Their love for him is unchanged. They had sent Epaphroditus, one of their leaders, to convey their gifts and to minister to Paul in his affliction ([Philippians] 2:25). Paul thought that he might be released soon, and expressed a hope of shortly seeing them again ([Philippians] 1:26; 2:24). . . .

"The immediate occasion for the writing of the letter was that Epaphroditus, who had been seriously ill during part of his stay with Paul in Rome, was now well enough to return home to Philippi ([Philippians] 2:25–30). The church was eager to have Epaphroditus come to them, and Paul wished to take advantage of the opportunity to send a message thanking his friends for sending him gifts, telling them of his condition, and reminding them of his prayerful interest in them."[3] Despite being in prison, Paul saw good coming from his confinement.

Even in adversity, the Christian may rejoice in the strength of Christ.

---

1. Francis D. Nichol, ed., *The Seventh-day Adventist Bible Commentary*, vol. 7 (Washington, DC: Review and Herald®, 1957), 137.
2. For Paul's initial visit to Philippi, see the readings for April 20–26.
3. Nichol, *Seventh-day Adventist Bible Commentary*, vol. 7, 138.

Part 2: Exalt Christ

For to me, to live is Christ, and to die is gain.

—Philippians 1:21

All God's dealings with His people are intended as a discipline to ripen holy character in preparation for eternal life."[1] "Affliction, in itself, has no sanctifying power. It may embitter, harden, deaden the soul. On the other hand, it may become an instrument to chasten, deepen, and purify the Christian's spiritual experience (see Heb. 12:7–11). Our salvation will be affected by the way in which we avail ourselves of the potential benefits of affliction. If we resist and fight against the method of education and the teacher, the affliction will need to be prolonged or another sent to take its place. We should earnestly pray to learn spiritual lessons quickly, that we may move on from one phase of spiritual development to the next."[2]

"When the apostle Paul, through the revelation of Christ, was converted from a persecutor to a Christian, he declared that he was as one born out of due time. Henceforward Christ was all and in all to him. 'For to me to live is Christ,' he declared. This is the most perfect interpretation in a few words, in all the Scriptures, of what it means to be a Christian. This is the whole truth of the gospel. Paul understood what many seem unable to comprehend. How intensely in earnest he was! His words show that his mind was centered in Christ, that his whole life was bound up with his Lord. Christ was the author, the support, and the source of his life."[3]

Paul did not fear death. "But Paul's assertion is not that of a pessimist who says, 'Life is not worth living.' It is not that of one who is worn out, who has outlived the very sensation of enjoyment. Nor is it that of a holy man wearied with exhausting labors and anxious to be finished with trials and persecutions. Paul was not sour, morose, or cynical. He possessed hearty human sympathies and entered with spirit into the balanced activities of a true Christian life. But his present declaration deals with a higher topic than his own prospects. His is concerned with magnifying Christ."[4]

"The Christian has nothing worth while to lose by death, but he has much to gain. He loses temptation, trial, toil, sorrow. He gains, at the resurrection, glorious immortality."[5]

1. Francis D. Nichol, ed., *The Seventh-day Adventist Bible Commentary*, vol. 7 (Washington, DC: Review and Herald®, 1957), 146.
2. Nichol, *Seventh-day Adventist Bible Commentary*, vol. 7, 146.
3. Ellen G. White, "Words of Comfort," *Advent Review and Sabbath Herald*, October 19, 1897, 1.
4. Nichol, *Seventh-day Adventist Bible Commentary*, vol. 7, 147.
5. Nichol, *Seventh-day Adventist Bible Commentary*, vol. 7, 147.

Part 3: Humility

Let this mind be in you which was also in Christ Jesus.

—Philippians 2:5

Few things belie the Christian profession more than inability to live and work harmoniously with other Christians. When we accept Christ we become members of His body. To accomplish the greatest amount of good, the body must function as a unit. . . . The work of God will prosper if the people of God draw together and work in unity."[1] Paul points the Philippians to the example of Jesus. Jesus, "who, being in the form of God, did not consider it robbery to be equal with God, but made Himself of no reputation, taking the form of a bondservant, and coming in the likeness of men. And being found in appearance as a man, He humbled Himself and became obedient to the point of death, even the death of the cross" (Philippians 2:6–8).

"After Christ had condescended to leave His high command, step down from an infinite height and assume humanity, He could have taken upon Him any condition of humanity He might choose. But greatness and rank were nothing to Him, and He selected the lowest and most humble walk of life. The place of His birth was Bethlehem, and on one side His parentage was poor, but God, the Owner of the world, was His Father. No trace of luxury, ease, selfish gratification, or indulgence was brought into His life, which was a continual round of self-denial and self-sacrifice. In accordance with His humble birth, He had apparently no greatness or riches, in order that the humblest believer need not say Christ never knew the stress of pinching poverty. Had He possessed the semblance of outward show, of riches, of grandeur, the poorest class of humanity would have shunned His society; therefore He chose the lowly condition of the far greater number of the people."[2]

"This is the mystery into which angels desire to look. They desire to know how Christ could live and work in a fallen world, how He could mingle with sinful humanity. It was a mystery to them that He who hated sin with intense hatred felt the most tender, compassionate sympathy for the beings that committed sin."[3]

"We must come to the study of this subject with the humility of a learner, with a contrite heart. And the study of the incarnation of Christ is a fruitful field and will repay the searcher who digs deep for hidden truth."[4]

1. Francis D. Nichol, ed., *The Seventh-day Adventist Bible Commentary*, vol. 7 (Washington, DC: Review and Herald®, 1957), 153.
2. Ellen G. White, MS 9, 1896.
3. Ellen G. White, "The Way the Truth and the Life—No. 3," *Signs of the Times*, January 20, 1898.
4. Ellen G. White, MS 67, 1898.

Part 4: Partnering With God

Work out your own salvation with fear and trembling; for it is God
who works in you both to will and to do for His good pleasure.
—Philippians 2:12, 13

P aul wanted the Philippians to be humble examples of Christ to their neighbors. He wished they would be "children of God without fault in the midst of a crooked and perverse generation, among whom you shine as lights in the world, holding fast the word of life" (Philippians 2:15, 16). "Paul's words are appropriate for the last generation, who will live at a time when darkness will be greater than ever before. . . . With special brilliance God's children are then to 'arise, shine' (. . . Isaiah 60:1, 2)."[1]

"The apostle Paul felt a deep responsibility for those converted under his labors. Above all things, he longed that they should be faithful, 'that I may rejoice in the day of Christ,' he said, 'that I have not run in vain, neither labored in vain.' Philippians 2:16. He trembled for the result of his ministry. He felt that even his own salvation might be imperiled if he should fail of fulfilling his duty and the church should fail of cooperating with him in the work of saving souls."[2] If others might find salvation by the sacrifice of his life, Paul wanted the Philippians to rejoice with him. "The epistle lays great stress on joy, not only as a privilege, but as a duty, following from Christian faith and demonstrating its reality."[3]

When Paul told the Philippians to "work out [their] own salvation with fear and trembling" (verse 12), he was not preaching salvation by works. "We are saved by grace, through faith (. . . Rom. 3:20–22, 24, 28; Eph. 2:8). But this grace leads us to good works (. . . Rom. 6:11–16). Thus, such works are the outworking of the grace that has effected our salvation (Rom. 6:18; cf. 2 Cor. 6:1)."[4] "The work of gaining salvation is one of copartnership, a joint operation. There is to be co-operation between God and the repentant sinner. This is necessary for the formation of right principles in the character. Man is to make earnest efforts to overcome that which hinders him from attaining to perfection. But he is wholly dependent upon God for success. Human effort of itself is not sufficient. Without the aid of divine power it avails nothing. God works and man works. Resistance of temptation must come from man, who must draw his power from God."[5]

"Therefore submit to God. Resist the devil and he will flee from you" (James 4:7)

---

1. Francis D. Nichol, ed., *The Seventh-day Adventist Bible Commentary*, vol. 7 (Washington, DC: Review and Herald®, 1957), 159.
2. Ellen G. White, *The Acts of the Apostles* (Mountain View, CA: Pacific Press®, 1911), 206.
3. Nichol, *Seventh-day Adventist Bible Commentary*, vol. 7, 160.
4. Nichol, *Seventh-day Adventist Bible Commentary*, vol. 7, 158.
5. White, *Acts of the Apostles*, 482.

Part 5: Focus on What Counts

Forgetting those things which are behind and reaching forward to those things which are ahead, I press toward the goal for the prize of the upward call of God in Christ Jesus.
—Philippians 3:13, 14

Paul uses the metaphor of a footrace to illustrate his single-minded pursuit of the high calling of Christ Jesus. "When souls are converted their salvation is not yet accomplished. They then have the race to run; the arduous struggle is before them to do, what? 'To fight the good *fight of faith*,' to press forward to the mark for the prize of the high calling which is in Christ Jesus. There is no release in this warfare; the battle is lifelong, and must be carried forward with determined energy proportionate to the value of the object you are in pursuit of, which is eternal life. Immense interests are here involved."[1]

"In earthly races there could be only one winner (1 Cor. 9:24), but in the Christian race each has the opportunity to be a victor and receive the prize."[2] Paul paints the picture of the runner, leaning to reach "the goal with body bent forward and hand and foot outstretched. The figure vividly portrays Paul's single-minded dedication to the course laid out for him by Christ. Such dedication leaves no time for curious, regretful backward looks."[3] "To the runner in a race the only object worthy of attention is the winning post, and so it was with Paul in his spiritual course. He fixed his eyes on the goal of eternal life and an inheritance in the world beyond. A clear vision of this goal will stimulate the Christian faithfully and cheerfully to run the race that is set before him (Heb. 12:1, 2)."[4]

What is the nature of the race we run as Christians? We are told to occupy until He comes (Luke 19:13). "Christ commits to His followers an individual work—a work that cannot be done by proxy. Ministry to the sick and the poor, the giving of the gospel to the lost, is not to be left to committees or organized charities. Individual responsibility, individual effort, personal sacrifice, is the requirement of the gospel."[5] We are to walk ever closer and closer to the will of God. "The Christian needs a constant awareness of the fact that he is a citizen of heaven. . . . Keeping in mind the kind of life we expect to live in heaven, serves to guide us in our life on earth.[6]

The purity, humility, gentleness, and love we anticipate experiencing in the life to come may [nay, should] be demonstrated here below."[7]

---

1. Ellen G. White, *My Life Today* (Washington, DC: Review and Herald®, 1952), 313; emphasis in original.
2. Francis D. Nichol, ed., *The Seventh-day Adventist Bible Commentary*, vol. 7 (Washington, DC: Review and Herald®, 1957), 170.
3. Nichol, *Seventh-day Adventist Bible Commentary*, vol. 7, 170.
4. Nichol, *Seventh-day Adventist Bible Commentary*, vol. 7, 170.
5. Ellen G. White, *The Ministry of Healing* (Mountain View, CA: Pacific Press®, 1942), 147.
6. Nichol, *Seventh-day Adventist Bible Commentary*, vol. 7, 172
7. Nichol, *Seventh-day Adventist Bible Commentary*, vol. 7, 172.

Part 6: Rejoice in the Lord

Rejoice in the Lord always. Again I will say, rejoice!

—Philippians 4:4

Paul has been stressing unity to the brethren at Philippi. Philippians 4:2, 3 calls our attention to two *women* who were not getting along. Previously they had been "fellow laborers" helping Paul spread the gospel. Now there had been a parting of the ways. It would seem that the conflict was between *Euodias* and *Syntyche*. "*Euodias*," meaning "prosperous journey," and "*Syntyche*," meaning "pleasant acquaintance," were apparently not living up to the meanings of their respective Greek names. "It appears that there was a difference of opinion between Euodia and Syntyche, but we are not informed as to the cause of the contention. It may not have been an important matter so far as the church as a whole was concerned, but even a small problem in a peaceful and orderly community becomes disturbing to the group."[1] Paul admonished them to be "like-minded, having the same love, being of one accord, of one mind. Let nothing be done through selfish ambition or conceit, but in lowliness of mind let each esteem others better than himself" (Philippians 2:2, 3). "Today, in cases where church members are at variance, each should seek reconciliation with the other, without waiting for the other to take the initiative."[2]

Again Paul returns to the key message of his letter to the Philippians—joy in the Lord. "Paul never tires of repeating that holy joy is one of the chief duties and privileges of the Christian.

"...The Lord is always the same (...Mal. 3:6; Heb. 13:8; James 1:17). His love, His consideration, His power, are the same in times of affliction as in times of prosperity. Christ's ability to give peace to the heart does not depend on external circumstances; so the heart that is centered on Him may constantly rejoice."[3]

Have you ever wondered what is wrong with those Christians who are dour, stern, unhappy individuals? Is not the good news of salvation reason enough to rejoice? Yet many choose rather to deny their Lord by harboring the harshest feelings for others and wallowing in self-pity. They see no joy on this earth and wish to be whisked to heaven, where miraculously their temperament will be changed! Such will not be the case.

If we have not "rejoiced in the Lord" during trials on earth, we will not know joy in heaven.

---

1. Francis D. Nichol, ed., *The Seventh-day Adventist Bible Commentary*, vol. 7 (Washington, DC: Review and Herald®, 1957), 174.
2. Nichol, *Seventh-day Adventist Bible Commentary*, vol. 7, 174.
3. Nichol, *Seventh-day Adventist Bible Commentary*, vol. 7, 175.

Part 7: Think on This

Finally, brethren, whatever things are true, whatever things are noble, whatever things are just, whatever things are pure, whatever things are lovely, whatever things are of good report, if there is any virtue and if there is anything praiseworthy—meditate on these things.

—Philippians 4:8

P aul next tells the Philippians how to pray. "Be anxious for nothing, but in every-thing by prayer and supplication, with thanksgiving, let your requests be made known to God; and the peace of God, which surpasses all understanding, will guard your hearts and minds through Christ Jesus" (Philippians 4:6, 7). "There is nothing that in any way concerns the peace of the Christian that is too small for God to notice, just as there is nothing too great for Him to care for. He knows what we need. He wants us to have everything that is for our good. Then why should we be burdened with cares which may be laid on Him?

"... The Christian need not be worried over the affairs of this life: through prayer, he may discuss all his needs with God."[1]

Many Christians come to God with a laundry list of desires and perceived "needs." "We do not bring our requests to God simply to inform Him concerning our needs. He knows our necessities before we ask (... Matt. 6:8)."[2] We are to come to God with thanksgiving. How many forget to thank God for every breath we take, for each minute that His power sustains our bodies? Do we take for granted the vital spark that keeps our hearts beating second by second? " 'Thanksgiving' is a necessary accompaniment of prayer, and ought never to be absent from our devotions. It helps to remind us of past mercies and prepares us to receive further blessings. Paul himself sets an example of constant thankfulness."[3]

Finally, Paul is ready to put forward a proposal for the Philippi church. "If we will live right, we must think right. The development of Christian character requires right thinking. Therefore Paul outlines a constructive program of mental activity. Instead of thinking about differences with others, or being anxious about daily needs, we should exercise our minds on positive virtues."[4] "Dwell upon the good qualities of those with whom you associate, and see as little as possible of their errors and failings."[5]

"Let nothing but kind, loving words fall from your lips concerning the members of your family or of the church."[6]

---

1. Francis D. Nichol, ed., *The Seventh-day Adventist Bible Commentary*, vol. 7 (Washington, DC: Review and Herald®, 1957), 175.
2. Nichol, *Seventh-day Adventist Bible Commentary*, vol. 7, 176.
3. Nichol, *Seventh-day Adventist Bible Commentary*, vol. 7, 176.
4. Nichol, *Seventh-day Adventist Bible Commentary*, vol. 7, 177.
5. Ellen G. White, *Testimonies for the Church*, vol. 2 (Mountain View, CA: Pacific Press®, 1948), 437.
6. White, *Testimonies for the Church*, vol. 2, 438.

Part 8: A Thank-You

I can do all things through Christ who strengthens me. . . . And my God shall supply all your
need according to His riches in glory by Christ Jesus.
—Philippians 4:13, 19

P aul thanked the Philippians for the gift they had sent him by Epaphroditus. The
Philippians had been generous in the past with their support. They had sent funds
when Paul was in Thessalonica (Philippians 4:16) and again when he was in Corinth
(2 Corinthians 11:8, 9). Now they had sent him an additional gift.

"There are times when it seems to the servant of God impossible to do the work
necessary to be done, because of the lack of means to carry on a strong solid work.
Some are fearful that with the facilities at their command they cannot do all that they
feel it their duty to do. But if they advance in faith, the salvation of God will be revealed,
and prosperity will attend their efforts. He who has bidden His followers go into all
parts of the world will sustain every laborer who in obedience to His command seeks
to proclaim His message.

"In the upbuilding of His work the Lord does not always make everything plain
before His servants. He sometimes tries the confidence of His people by bringing
about circumstances which compel them to move forward in faith. Often He brings
him [or her] into strait and trying places, and bids them advance when their feet seem
to be touching the waters of Jordan. It is at such times, when the prayers of His servants
ascend to Him in earnest faith, that God opens the way before them and brings them
out into a large place."[1]

"Paul had accepted the offering as made, not to himself, but to the God whose
minister he was. Now he says in effect, 'God will accept your offerings as made to
Him. You have supplied my need; He will supply every need of yours.' Whether the
need be spiritual or temporal, God will withhold no good thing from the righteous
(see Ps. 84:11)."[2] It comes down to your attitude toward the salvation of others as
well as yourself. "The life of Christ was a life charged with a divine message of the
love of God, and He longed intensely to impart this love to others in rich measure.
Compassion beamed from His countenance, and His conduct was characterized by
grace, humility, truth, and love. Every member of His church militant must manifest
the same qualities, if he would join the church triumphant."[3]

"To do good to others out of a heart of love is to bring to God an acceptable sacrifice."[4]

---

1. Ellen G. White, *The Acts of the Apostles* (Mountain View, CA: Pacific Press®, 1911), 357.

2. Francis D. Nichol, ed., *The Seventh-day Adventist Bible Commentary*, vol. 7 (Washington, DC: Review and Herald®, 1957), 179.

3. Ellen G. White, *Fundamentals of Christian Education* (Nashville, TN: Southern Publishing, 1923), 179.

4. Nichol, *Seventh-day Adventist Bible Commentary*, vol. 7, 179.

Did Paul Write Hebrews?

*God, who at various times and in various ways spoke in time past to the fathers by the prophets,
has in these last days spoken to us by His Son, whom He has appointed heir of all things,
through whom also He made the worlds; who . . . when He had by Himself purged our sins,
sat down at the right hand of the Majesty on high.*

—Hebrews 1:1–3

The so-called 'Epistle of Paul the Apostle to the Hebrews' differs from the other thirteen Pauline letters in that the text nowhere contains the name of its author. Paul introduces every one of his other known letters with his name. . . . From early Christian times there has been much discussion as to whether Paul was really the writer of this epistle. The conclusion of this commentary [*The Seventh-day Adventist Bible Commentary*] is that while Paul may not himself have phrased the letter to the Hebrews, it contains, nevertheless, his teachings, and so may be counted among his epistles."[1]

"The evidences against the view that Paul wrote Hebrews have been drawn largely from considerations of the literary style and content of the book. . . .

"When compared with the generally accepted epistles of Paul, Hebrews differs markedly, especially in the small, common connective words with which its author binds together his clauses. Another distinctive difference is found in the handling of quotations from the OT [Old Testament]. The accepted epistles employ one group of more or less standard phrases to introduce OT quotations, whereas Hebrews uses another group."[2]

"It is generally agreed that Hebrews was written before the fall of Jerusalem. Now, the number of church leaders was very small in the years before A.D. 70. Which of those leaders might have set forth an argument as profound as that presented in the book of Hebrews? By all odds the most likely person is Paul. . . .

". . .The issue that produced probably a deeper cleavage in the apostolic church than any other was the question of the ceremonial law and its observance by Christians."[3] Paul could explain, by comparison and contrast, "the symbols by which God presented the plan of salvation to His chosen people in OT times and the reality of Christ's ministry on behalf of sinners since the cross."[4]

Here is a book crafted with the skill of a lawyer to defend the plan of salvation and righteousness by faith alone in the sacrifice of Christ! It ties together Old and New Covenants!

---

1. Francis D. Nichol, ed., *The Seventh-day Adventist Bible Commentary*, vol. 6 (Washington, DC: Review and Herald®, 1957), 106.

2. Francis D. Nichol, ed., *The Seventh-day Adventist Bible Commentary* , vol. 7 (Washington, DC: Review and Herald®, 1957), 387, 388.

3. Nichol, *Seventh-day Adventist Bible Commentary*, vol. 7, 388, 389.

4. Nichol, *Seventh-day Adventist Bible Commentary*, vol. 7, 390.

Part 1: Jesus Is Superior to Angels

Are they not all ministering spirits sent forth to minister for those who will inherit salvation?
—Hebrews 1:14

T he book of Hebrews takes the form of a general treatise on the ministry of Jesus Christ rather than an epistle to any specific church. "It is always a difficult task to change the customs of centuries, and to transform the habits of a nation in a few years is well-nigh impossible. In the case of the transition from Judaism to Christianity it was particularly difficult, in that the change had to be accomplished through the leadership of men who, in the estimation of most of the people, did not rank with those who had instituted the customs. The transition period was therefore a most trying one. Much wisdom and wise counsel were needed. The question would doubtless constantly recur that if God did not require sacrifices now, if in fact they were displeasing to Him, what about the great and good men of old who had taught them to Israel, and had themselves offered gifts to Him? Had these men not followed the specific directions of God? And who were Paul and the other apostles that they should presume to change ancient practices and institutions?"[1] One can readily see the problems Paul faced in putting forth an organized explanation of the Christian faith.

"The deity of Christ was a great stumbling block in the way of the Jews' acceptance of Christianity. Israel had for centuries prided itself on the worship of only one God, whereas the heathen had many gods. . . . The Jews needed to understand the nature of the Godhead, that the phrase 'one Lord' involved Father, Son, and Holy Spirit."[2] Paul wanted the Jews to understand that Jesus Christ was the Messiah, the Son of the Living God. God the Father exalted Him and caused Him to sit down (be inaugurated or installed) "at the right hand of the Majesty on high" (Hebrews 1:3). Jesus ranked higher than all the heavenly angels, "being made so much better than the angels" (verse 4, KJV). "The Jews highly regarded the angels; hence the argument in this chapter is an impressive one."[3]

"Man's salvation and the whole plan of redemption are based on the deity of Christ. If Christ is not God in the highest sense and in His own right, our faith is in vain and salvation becomes impossible."[4]

---

1. Francis D. Nichol, ed., *The Seventh-day Adventist Bible Commentary*, vol. 7 (Washington, DC: Review and Herald®, 1957), 395.
2. Nichol, *Seventh-day Adventist Bible Commentary*, vol. 7, 398.
3. Nichol, *Seventh-day Adventist Bible Commentary*, vol. 7, 401.
4. Nichol, *Seventh-day Adventist Bible Commentary*, vol. 7, 399.

Part 2: The Rest of Grace

There remains therefore a rest for the people of God.

—Hebrews 4:9

Paul is speaking in Hebrews chapters 3 and 4 about Jesus Christ, our High Priest. He says we must "come boldly" before Him to "obtain mercy and find grace to help in time of need" (Hebrews 4:16). "The Jews of Paul's time, whether Christian or non-Christian, were punctilious [conscientious] in their observance of the fourth commandment. Certainly, in writing to Jews, the author of Hebrews would not consider it necessary to prove to *them* that Sabbathkeeping 'remaineth'. . . . There would have been no point in so labored an effort to persuade the Jews to do what they were already doing—observing the seventh-day Sabbath. Furthermore, in apostolic times the seventh-day Sabbath was observed by all Christians, Jew and Gentile alike, and any argument to prove the validity of the Sabbath in those early Christian times would have been pointless."[1]

"The rest here spoken of is the rest of grace, obtained by following the prescription, 'Labor diligently.' Those who learn of Jesus His meekness and lowliness find rest in the experience of practicing His lessons. It is not in indolence, in selfish ease and pleasure-seeking, that rest is obtained. Those who are unwilling to give the Lord faithful, earnest, loving service will not find spiritual rest in this life or in the life to come. Only from earnest labor comes peace and joy in the Holy Spirit—happiness on earth and glory hereafter.

"Let us therefore labor. Speak often words that will be a strength and an inspiration to those who hear. We are altogether too indifferent in regard to one another. We forget that our fellow laborers are often in need of words of hope and cheer."[2]

"The Lord works in co-operation with the will and action of the human agent. It is the privilege and duty of every man to take God at His word, to believe in Jesus as his personal Saviour, and to respond eagerly, immediately, to the gracious propositions which He makes. He is to study to believe and obey the divine instruction in the Scriptures. He is to base his faith not on feeling but upon the evidence and the Word of God."[3]

Confidence in the saving grace of Jesus brings rest from striving to become saintly (righteous) by our own works. Rest confidently in Jesus' power to save you!

---

1. Francis D. Nichol, ed., *The Seventh-day Adventist Bible Commentary*, vol. 7 (Washington, DC: Review and Herald®, 1957), 423; emphasis in original.
2. Ellen G. White, MS 42, 1901.
3. Ellen G. White, MS 3, 1895.

Part 3: A Two-Edged Sword

For the word of God is living and powerful, and sharper than any two-edged sword,
piercing even to the division of soul and spirit, and of the joints and marrow,
and is a discerner of the thoughts and intents of the heart.

—Hebrews 4:12

At first sight [Hebrews 4, verses] 12 and 13 may appear to have no direct connection with the theme of [chapters] 3 and 4. However, as the word 'for' indicates, there is a close, logical relationship. Verses 12 and 13 explain how to avoid falling in unbelief ([verse] 11) and how to cease from one's 'own works' ([verse] 10), and set forth the means God has provided to enable His children to enter into His 'rest.'"[1] "It takes a living and active force to create in man a new heart and to renew a right spirit within him (cf. Ps. 51:10). The 'word' of God is living, and imparts life. Thus it was in the work of creation (Ps. 33:6, 9) and thus it is in the re-creation of the image of God in the soul of man."[2]

"Practical truth must be brought into the life, and the Word, like a sharp, two-edged sword, must cut away the surplus of self that there is in our characters."[3] "The Word makes the proud humble, the perverse meek and contrite, the disobedient obedient. The sinful habits natural to man are interwoven with the daily practice. But the Word cuts away the fleshly lusts. It is a discerner of the thoughts and intents of the mind. It divides the joints and marrow, cutting away the lusts of the flesh, making men willing to suffer for their Lord."[4] The Bible sets forth clear principles telling what is right and what is wrong, what is good and what is evil. Parsing the Word and choosing here a sentence and there a phrase to support human ideas is often a mechanism to deny direct condemnation of a treasured sin or belief. The follower of Christ must always rely on a "thus saith the Lord" and not on his or her own interpretation.

"Let your faith be substantiated by the Word of God. Grasp firmly the living testimony of truth. Have faith in Christ as a personal Saviour. He has been and ever will be our Rock of Ages."[5] "Keep a pocket Bible with you as you work, and improve every opportunity to commit to memory its precious promises."[6]

"None but those who have fortified the mind with the truths of the Bible will stand through the last great conflict."[7]

---

1. Francis D. Nichol, ed., *The Seventh-day Adventist Bible Commentary*, vol. 7 (Washington, DC: Review and Herald®, 1957), 424.
2. Nichol, *Seventh-day Adventist Bible Commentary*, vol. 7, 424.
3. Ellen G. White, Letter 5, 1897.
4. Ellen G. White, MS 42, 1901.
5. Ellen G. White, *Evangelism* (Washington, DC: Review and Herald®, 1946), 362.
6. Ellen G. White, "Instructions for Helpers and Students at Tacoma Park, DC," *Advent Review and Sabbath Herald*, April 27, 1905, 8.
7. Ellen G. White, *The Great Controversy* (Mountain View, CA: Pacific Press®, 1950), 593, 594.

Part 4: Our Great Heavenly High Priest

Seeing then that we have a great High Priest who has passed through the heavens, Jesus the Son of God, let us hold fast our confession. For we do not have a High Priest who cannot sympathize with our weaknesses, but was in all points tempted as we are, yet without sin. Let us therefore come boldly to the throne of grace, that we may obtain mercy and find grace to help in time of need.
—Hebrews 4:14–16

Christ as our great High Priest is the theme of the book of Hebrews. . . . Having introduced Christ in this role (ch. 3:1), [chapters] 3 and 4 develop the concept of our need for His ministry in the courts of heaven and of the experience of 'rest' of soul that comes when we avail ourselves of it. Chapters 5 through 10 are concerned with various aspects of His ministry on our behalf. The Christian system of salvation by faith finds its center in the person of Christ as our great High Priest."[1] "Christians must hold the beginning of their confidence firm unto the end. It is not enough to profess the faith. There must be a patient endurance of all trials and a brave resistance to all temptations."[2]

The Son of God "has fulfilled His pledge, and has passed into the heavens, to take upon Him the government of the heavenly host. He fulfilled one phase of His priesthood by dying on the cross for the fallen race. He is now fulfilling another phase by pleading before the Father the case of the repenting, believing sinner, presenting to God the offerings of His people. Having taken human nature, and in this nature having overcome the temptations of the enemy, and having divine perfection, to Him has been committed the judgment of the world. The case of each one will be brought in review before Him. He will pronounce judgment, rendering to every man according to his works."[3] "In all the Bible, God is presented not only as a being of mercy and benevolence, but as a God of strict and impartial justice."[4] "It is the glory of God to be merciful, full of forbearance, kindness, goodness, and truth. But the justice shown in punishing the sinner is as verily the glory of the Lord as is the manifestation of His mercy."[5]

"If we confess our sins, He is faithful and just to forgive us our sins and to cleanse us from all unrighteousness" (1 John 1:9).

---

1. Francis D. Nichol, ed., *The Seventh-day Adventist Bible Commentary*, vol. 7 (Washington, DC: Review and Herald®, 1957), 425.
2. Ellen G. White, MS 42, 1901.
3. White, MS 42, 1901.
4. Ellen G. White, "The Last Words of Moses," *Signs of the Times*, March 24, 1881, 1.
5. Ellen G. White, "Laborers Together With God," *Advent Review and Sabbath Herald*, March 10, 1904, 8.

Part 5: The Heavenly Holy Place

For Christ has not entered the holy places made with hands, which are copies of the true, but into heaven itself, now to appear in the presence of God for us.

—Hebrews 9:24

Consider the earthly tabernacle, a copy of the one in heaven. Earthly priests would take the blood offering from the sinner and present it to the Lord for forgiveness of sin. For without the shedding of blood, there can be no remission of sin. Now Jesus has shed His own blood for our sins. "Jesus stands in the holy of holies, now to appear in the presence of God for us. There He ceases not to present His people moment by moment, complete in Himself. But because we are thus represented before the Father, we are not to imagine that we are to presume upon His mercy, and become careless, indifferent, and self-indulgent. Christ is not the minister of sin. We are complete in Him, accepted in the Beloved, only as we abide in Him by faith."[1]

"The great truth taught by the stipulation that the shedding of blood was required for forgiveness, was that the salvation of man would one day require the death of the Son of God. . . . Every animal sacrifice pointed forward to the supreme sacrifice of the 'Lamb of God, which taketh away the sin of the world' (John 1:29)."[2]

Christ now ministers before God the Father on our behalf. "Therefore He is also able to save to the uttermost those who come to God through Him, since He always lives to make intercession for them" (Hebrews 7:25). "The reason we need someone to appear in the presence of God for us and to intercede for us is that we have sinned. Christ 'appeared to put away sin by the sacrifice of himself' ([Hebrews] 9:26). Now He is ministering the benefits of His atonement in the sinner's behalf."[3]

"Do not let your thoughts dwell upon yourselves. Think of Jesus. He is in His holy place, not in a state of solitude and grandeur, but surrounded by ten thousand times ten thousand of heavenly beings who wait to do their Master's bidding. And He bids them go and work for the weakest saint who puts his trust in God. High and low, rich and poor, have the same help provided."[4] How wonderful! First, He gave Himself for us, and now our Savior is pleading our cases before our Father.

"And if anyone sins, we have an Advocate with the Father, Jesus Christ the righteous" (1 John 2:1).

---

1. Ellen G. White, "Accepted in Christ," *Signs of the Times*, July 4, 1892.

2. Francis D. Nichol, ed., *The Seventh-day Adventist Bible Commentary*, vol. 7 (Washington, DC: Review and Herald®, 1957), 455.

3. Nichol, *Seventh-day Adventist Bible Commentary*, vol. 7, 455, 456.

4. Ellen G. White, Letter 134, 1899.

Part 6: Hold Fast Together

Not forsaking the assembling of ourselves together, as is the manner of some, but exhorting one another, and so much the more as you see the Day approaching.
—Hebrews 10:25

Things had never been easy for those Hebrews who became Christians. Paul himself had a hand in early persecution of the church. Then, as now, "Christian gatherings [were] for the purpose of worship and mutual encouragement, which in [New Testament] times were commonly held in the homes of believers. . . .

". . . Some were neglecting to fellowship with their brethren in seasons of worship and devotion, to their own detriment. In so doing they were living in contravention of the counsel of [Hebrews 10, verse] 24 to encourage their fellow believers in love and good works. In view of the political situation prevailing at the time the book of Hebrews was written, some may have absented themselves from fear of incurring governmental displeasure and possibly civil penalties. Others remained absent from religious services because of carelessness and indifference."[1]

The time will again come when it will be dangerous to worship on Saturday, the seventh day, the Sabbath of the Lord thy God (Exodus 20:8–11). "There will come a time when, because of our advocacy of Bible truth, we shall be treated as traitors."[2] "Those who honor the Bible Sabbath will be denounced as enemies of law and order, as breaking down the moral restraints of society, causing anarchy and corruption, and calling down the judgments of God upon the earth. Their conscientious scruples will be pronounced obstinacy, stubbornness, and contempt of authority. They will be accused of disaffection toward the government."[3] At such times we need to press together, encouraging each other and taking strength from each other. "Those who do not feel the necessity of seeking the assembly of the saints, with the precious assurance that the Lord will meet with them, show how lightly they value the help that God has provided for them. Satan is constantly at work to wound and poison the soul. In order to withstand his efforts we must breathe the atmosphere of heaven."[4]

"We must individually get hold and keep hold of Christ."[5] Despite what some profess, this is best done in "the company of believers."

---

1. Francis D. Nichol, ed., *The Seventh-day Adventist Bible Commentary*, vol. 7 (Washington, DC: Review and Herald®, 1957), 463, 464.
2. Ellen G. White, *Testimonies for the Church*, vol. 6 (Mountain View, CA: Pacific Press®, 1948), 394.
3. Ellen G. White, *The Great Controversy* (Mountain View, CA: Pacific Press®, 1950), 592.
4. Ellen G. White, MS 16, 1890.
5. White, MS 16, 1890.

Part 7: Jesus Will Not Tarry

"For yet a little while,
And He who is coming will come and will not tarry.
Now the just shall live by faith;
But if anyone draws back,
My soul has no pleasure in him."

—Hebrews 10:37, 38

We are told to persevere and remain faithful to the end. We have already discussed the letter Paul wrote to the brethren at Thessalonica. He wrote, "For this we say to you by the word of the Lord, that we who are alive and remain until the coming of the Lord will by no means precede those who are asleep" (1 Thessalonians 4:15). The Thessalonians misunderstood Paul to be saying Jesus' second advent was imminent, and many of them would see Him come. This prompted a correction from Paul in his second letter. "Now, brethren, concerning the coming of our Lord Jesus Christ and our gathering together to Him, we ask you, not to be soon shaken in mind or troubled, either by spirit or by word or by letter, as if from us, as though the day of Christ had come" (2 Thessalonians 2:1, 2). Paul goes on to describe a falling away that must first take place before Christ comes. Yet in Acts 20:28–30, Paul explains this event will occur after his death. He exhorts the Thessalonians to "stand fast and hold the traditions which you were taught, whether by word or our epistle" (2 Thessalonians 2:15).

Jesus has promised He will return for us. "Let not your heart be troubled; you believe in God, believe also in Me. In My Father's house are many mansions; if it were not so, I would have told you. I go to prepare a place for you. And if I go and prepare a place for you, I will come again and receive you to Myself; that where I am, there you may be also" (John 14:1–3). It may seem to us that Jesus is taking a long time to come back for us. "In the annals of human history, the growth of nations, the rise and fall of empires, appear as if dependent on the will and prowess of man; the shaping of events seems, to a great degree, to be determined by his power, ambition, or caprice. But in the word of God the curtain is drawn aside, and we behold, above, behind, and through all the play and counterplay of human interest and power and passions, the agencies of the All-merciful One, silently, patiently, working out the counsels of His own will."[1]

Take heart. Remain faithful. Trust Jesus' promises to the very end! (Mark 13:13).

---

1. Ellen G. White, *Prophets and Kings* (Mountain View, CA: Pacific Press®, 1943), 499, 500.

Part 8: What Is Faith?

Now faith is the substance of things hoped for, the evidence of things not seen.
—Hebrews 11:1

W e are called to be faithful. What is faith? "Faith and faithfulness are the supreme need of those who await the coming of the Lord. There is danger that some will cast away their confidence because the Lord appears to delay His coming. All such 'have need of patience' in order that they may 'live by faith.' "[1] "The faith in Christ which saves the soul is not what it is represented to be by many. 'Believe, believe,' is their cry; 'only believe in Christ, and you will be saved. It is all you have to do.' While true faith trusts wholly in Christ for salvation, it will lead to perfect conformity to the law of God. Faith is manifested by works. And the apostle John declares, 'He that saith, I know him, and keepeth not his commandments, is a liar.' "[2]

"Feeling and faith are as distinct as the east is from the west. Faith is not dependent on feeling. We must earnestly cry to God in faith, feeling or no feeling, and then live our prayers. Our assurance and evidence is God's Word, and after we have asked we must believe without doubting. I praise Thee, O God, I praise Thee. Thou hast not failed me in the performance of Thy Word. Thou hast revealed Thyself unto me and I am thine to do Thy will."[3] "Faith is simple in its operation and powerful in its results. Many professed Christians, who have a knowledge of the sacred word, and believe its truth, fail in the childlike trust that is essential to the religion of Jesus."[4]

So faith is not a feeling but rather a confident trust in the One who has promised to save you. "Faith is not the ground of our salvation, but it is the great blessing—the eye that sees, the ear that hears, the feet that run, the hand that grasps. It is the means not the end. If Christ gave His life to save sinners, why shall I not take that blessing? My faith grasps it, and thus my faith is the substance of things hoped for, the evidence of things unseen. Thus resting and believing, I have peace with God through the Lord Jesus Christ."[5]

"True faith consists in doing just what God has enjoined, not manufacturing things He has not enjoined. Justice, truth, mercy, are the fruit of faith."[6]

---

1. Francis D. Nichol, ed., *The Seventh-day Adventist Bible Commentary*, vol. 7 (Washington, DC: Review and Herald®, 1957), 471.
2. Ellen G. White, "The Conference in Sweden," *Advent Review and Sabbath Herald*, October 5, 1886, 2.
3. Ellen G. White, Letter 7, 1892.
4. Ellen G. White, *Redemption: Or the Miracles of Christ, the Mighty One* (1877), 97.
5. Ellen G. White, Letter 329a, 1905.
6. Ellen G. White, Letter 105, 1898.

Part 9: Take God at His Word

But without faith it is impossible to please Him, for he who comes to God must believe that He is,
and that He is a rewarder of those who diligently seek Him.

—Hebrews 11:6

S till, how do I develop a trusting attitude toward a God I have never seen? God is
so far beyond human comprehension that He must be taken on faith. "Whereas
the Creator is infinite, His creatures are irrevocably finite, and there are, accordingly,
things which they must take by faith. Indeed, to take God at His word is the most
exalted exercise of which the human mind is capable. Indeed, he must take God at
His word if he is to fill perfectly the place designed for him in a perfect universe, for
a realization of the love of God culminates in faith."[1]

"Belief that God really exists is the ultimate foundation of the Christian faith.
Through nature, through His Word, and through His providential leading God has
provided men with all the evidence of His existence that intelligent beings need and
can make use of."[2] If one does not believe in God, one cannot possibly come to love
God. If one does not love God, one does not keep His commandments. For "if you
love Me," Jesus says, "keep My commandments" (John 14:15). As with any relationship,
when you come to understand God's love for you, you will come to understand His
character and learn to trust Him. But to learn that trust is not the work of a moment.
It is built up over a lifetime of communion and close communication with your
Creator and Savior.

"Our faith must pierce beyond the veil, seeing things that are invisible. No one else
can look for you. You must behold for yourself. In the place of murmuring for blessings
that are withheld, let us remember and appreciate the blessings already bestowed."[3]
"There is no encouragement given for unbelief. The Lord manifests His grace and His
power over and over again, and this should teach us that it is always profitable under
all circumstances to cherish faith, to talk faith, to act faith."[4] God rewards those who
diligently seek Him. The key in this text is the word *diligently*. One defines *diligent*
as constant, industrious, hardworking, attentive. "Study" to show thyself approved
means digging deeply into the Word. There must be a constancy to our Bible study.
Comparing scripture with scripture is essential. A surface reading does not yield the
deeper-lying treasure that attentive, hard work reveals!

When was the last time you "diligently" sought the Lord through "study" of His Word?

---

1. Francis D. Nichol, ed., *The Seventh-day Adventist Bible Commentary*, vol. 7 (Washington, DC: Review and Herald®, 1957), 472, 473.
2. Nichol, *Seventh-day Adventist Bible Commentary*, vol. 7, 473.
3. Ellen G. White, MS 42, 1901.
4. Ellen G. White, Letter 97, 1898.

Part 10: The Faith Chapter

By faith Moses, when he became of age, refused to be called the son of Pharaoh's daughter, choosing rather to suffer affliction with the people of God than to enjoy the passing pleasures of sin, esteeming the reproach of Christ greater riches than the treasures in Egypt; for he looked to the reward.

—Hebrews 11:24–26

The eleventh chapter of Hebrews is known as the "faith chapter." In it are found examples of men and women who chose "by faith" to follow their Lord. It is encouraging to read the names recorded there, for many of these men and women had trials and difficulties in their walk with the Lord, yet they triumphed. Abraham, Isaac, Jacob, Joseph, Moses, Rahab, Gideon, Barak, Samson, Jephthah, David, Samuel, and the prophets. The list goes on. The Bible gives us stories of *real* people! Here are men and women who struggled with fear, anger, distrust, lust, adultery, prostitution, murder, pride, covetousness, theft, and deceit. How discouraging it would be if all we saw in the Bible were the stories of men and women who led perfect lives.

One of the key men listed in Hebrews 11 is Moses. Six verses speak to his faith. "The strength of Moses was his connection with the Source of all power, the Lord God of hosts. He rises grandly above every earthly inducement, and trusts himself wholly to God. He considered that he was the Lord's. While he was connected with the official interests of the king of Egypt, he was constantly studying the laws of God's government, and thus his faith grew. That faith was of value to him. It was deeply rooted in the soil of his earliest teachings, and the culture of his life was to prepare him for the great work of delivering Israel from bondage. He meditated on these things; he was constantly listening to his commission from God.

"After slaying the Egyptian, he saw that he had not understood God's plan, and he fled from Egypt and became a shepherd. He was no longer planning to do a great work, but he became very humble; the mists that were beclouding his mind were expelled, and he disciplined his mind to seek after God as his refuge."[1]

Consider the imperfect lives of the men and women listed in Hebrews 11. They are presented to give us hope and to strengthen our faith for, like them, we may triumph at last!

---

1. Ellen G. White, Letter 21a, 1893.

Part 11: The Author and Finisher of Our Faith

Looking unto Jesus, the author and finisher of our faith, who for the joy that was set before Him endured the cross, despising the shame, and has sat down at the right hand of the throne of God.
　　　　　　　　　　　　　　　　　　　　　　　　　　　　—Hebrews 12:2

As Peter found when he essayed to walk on the wind-tossed waves of Galilee (see Matt. 14:24–32), it is dangerous to turn one's eyes away from the Saviour, even for a moment. To keep the eye of faith fixed upon Jesus is to maintain uninterrupted contact with Him who is the source of power, Him who can strengthen us to endure and to overcome."[1] "Christ is the center of the plan of salvation and the source of every Christian grace. It is He who calls fallen men out of the dismal darkness of sin and into the glorious light of the gospel. It is He who cleanses them from their previous life of sin and qualifies them to become sons and daughters of God. It is He who justifies them by His grace, by virtue of His atonement on Calvary. It is He who plants their feet on the pathway to heaven."[2]

Yet, "the work of justification is only the beginning of the Christian experience. . . . We are to 'grow in grace, and in the knowledge of our Lord and Saviour Jesus Christ' (2 Peter 3:18). We are to gain victory after victory over our besetting sins . . . and to 'grow up into him [Christ] in all things' (Eph. 4:15). Our characters are to be 'transformed' by the renewing of our minds (Rom. 12:2). This is the work of the indwelling Christ (Gal. 2:20) as the 'perfecter' of faith. This is the work of sanctification."[3] "Christ 'endured the cross' in order that we might have strength to endure in our individual conflicts with the powers of darkness. He endured the cross that He might win the crown. The Captain of our salvation was made 'perfect through sufferings' ([Hebrews] 2:10), and as we learn to endure the cross we are called upon to bear we too may expect to be found perfect in Him at His coming. As a future joy inspired Christ to endure the cross, so in the difficult and trying experiences of life it is our privilege to look forward to the joy of eternity."[4] "Like Paul, we can count all earthly things but loss for the exquisite joy of knowing Christ Jesus as Lord (see Phil. 3:8)."[5]

Present sufferings are as nothing compared with the eternal weight of glory that awaits the saints.

---

1. Francis D. Nichol, ed., *The Seventh-day Adventist Bible Commentary*, vol. 7 (Washington, DC: Review and Herald®, 1957), 481.

2. Nichol, *Seventh-day Adventist Bible Commentary*, vol. 7, 481.

3. Nichol, *Seventh-day Adventist Bible Commentary*, vol. 7, 481.

4. Nichol, *Seventh-day Adventist Bible Commentary*, vol. 7, 482.

5. Nichol, *Seventh-day Adventist Bible Commentary*, vol. 7, 482.

Part 12: Jesus Never Changes

Jesus Christ is the same yesterday, today, and forever.

—Hebrews 13:8

Paul is wrapping up his letter to his fellow Jews. Yet one more admonishment is necessary. While those pioneers of the Jewish faith listed in chapter 11 were giants in the history of God's church, "there had also been faithful men in more recent times whose example might safely be followed."[1] Apparently, there were some who were drifting to and fro on the winds of doctrinal change listening first to one theory and then another. "Lacking spiritual discrimination, they [were] unable to differentiate between truth and error by comparing the new teaching with Scripture."[2] Hebrews 13:8 "was apparently intended to prepare the way for the warning of v. 9 ["Do not be carried about with various and strange doctrines."]. In view of the fact that Christ never changes, the message about Him can never change. Teachings that differ from the pure gospel already proclaimed may be dismissed without further examination."[3] How does one avoid false doctrine? "All Scripture is given by inspiration of God, and is profitable for *doctrine*, for reproof, for correction, for instruction in righteousness" (2 Timothy 3:16; emphasis added).

Paul previously confronted the issue of false doctrines in the churches of Galatia. "In almost every church [in Galatia] there were some members who were Jews by birth. To these converts the Jewish leaders found ready access, and through them gained a foot-hold in the churches. It was impossible, by scriptural arguments, to overthrow the doctrines taught by Paul; hence they resorted to the most unscrupulous measures to counteract his influence and weaken his authority. . . . Faith in Christ, and obedience to the law of ten commandments, were regarded as of minor importance. Division, heresy, and sensualism were rapidly gaining ground among the believers in Galatia.

"Paul's soul was stirred as he saw the evils that threatened speedily to destroy these churches."[4]

Paul closes Hebrews by writing that Timothy has been released from prison in Italy, "with whom I shall see you if he comes shortly.

"Greet all those who rule over you, and all the saints. Those from Italy greet you.

"Grace be with you all. Amen" (Hebrews 13:23–25).

Compare Scripture with Scripture to gain a clear understanding of God's will.

1. Francis D. Nichol, ed., *The Seventh-day Adventist Bible Commentary*, vol. 7 (Washington, DC: Review and Herald®, 1957), 491.
2. Nichol, *Seventh-day Adventist Bible Commentary*, vol. 7, 491.
3. Nichol, *Seventh-day Adventist Bible Commentary*, vol. 7, 491.
4. Ellen G. White, *Sketches From the Life of Paul* (Washington, DC: Review and Herald®, 1974), 188, 189.

At Liberty, Second Arrest, Imprisonment, Trial, and Death

AD 63–67 (68)
The Great Fire in Rome, AD 64

1 and 2 Timothy; Titus
The Acts of the Apostles, pp. 487–513
Sketches From the Life of Paul, pp. 301–334

At Liberty

You will keep him in perfect peace, whose mind is stayed on You, because he trusts in You.
—Isaiah 26:3

During the time Paul was held in Rome, a change took place in the government. "When, on his arrival at Rome, he was placed in charge of the captain of the imperial guards, the office was filled by a man of justice and integrity, by whose clemency he was left comparatively free to pursue the work of the gospel."[1] Now Nero was emperor. "Nero was more debased in morals, more frivolous in character, and at the same time capable of more atrocious cruelty, than any ruler who had preceded him. The reins of government could not have been intrusted to a more inhuman despot."[2] Things certainly looked bleak for Paul. "But the apostle felt that he had nothing to fear, so long as he preserved his loyalty and his love to God. His life was not in the hands of Nero, and if his work was not yet done, the Roman emperor would be powerless to destroy him. . . .

"And God did shield his servant. At Paul's examination the charges against him were not sustained, and, contrary to the general expectation,—with regard for justice wholly at variance with his character,—Nero declared the prisoner guiltless. Paul's fetters were struck off, and he was again a free man."[3]

Paul immediately left Rome. "The converts to Christianity had become so numerous during Paul's imprisonment as to attract the attention and arouse the enmity of the authorities. The ire of the emperor was especially excited by the conversion of members of his own household. . . . A terrible fire about this time occurred in Rome, by which nearly one-half the city was consumed. Nero himself caused the flames to be kindled, and then, to avert suspicion, he made a pretense of great generosity in assisting the homeless and destitute. He was, however, accused of the crime. The people were excited and enraged, and Nero determined to clear himself, and also to rid the city of a class whom he feared and hated, by charging the act upon the Christians.

"The Satanic device succeeded. Thousands of the followers of Christ—men, women, and children—were put to death in the most cruel manner."[4]

"From this terrible ordeal, Paul was spared."[5]

---

1. Ellen G. White, *Sketches From the Life of Paul* (Washington, DC: Review and Herald®, 1974), 301.
2. White, *Sketches From the Life of Paul*, 301.
3. White, *Sketches From the Life of Paul*, 302.
4. White, *Sketches From the Life of Paul*, 303, 304.
5. White, *Sketches From the Life of Paul*, 304.

Part 1: Challenging Timothy

As I urged you when I went into Macedonia—remain in Ephesus that you may charge
some that they teach no other doctrine, nor give heed to fables and endless genealogies,
which cause disputes rather than godly edification which is in faith.

—1 Timothy 1:3, 4

Paul would now write letters to friends, not churches. Paul's letter to Titus and his two letters to Timothy are known collectively as "the Pastorals." The first would go to Timothy. Paul had left Timothy as his personal representative to the church at Ephesus, and "though Paul seems to have felt himself closer to Timothy than to his other associates (see Phil. 2:19, 20), the inference may be drawn from this epistle that Timothy was a man of mild temperament and not so aggressive as Paul might have wished. Accordingly the apostle encourages his younger companion in the ministry to more vigorous leadership."[1] While Timothy wished to be at the side of his mentor in Rome, Paul told him his place was with his church in Ephesus instead. Paul advised him to keep the faith pure, avoid arguing over spurious doctrines, place no reliance on human fables, that genealogy means nothing, and that salvation comes only by believing in Jesus.

"God does not excuse sin in those in exalted positions any sooner than He does in those in more humble positions. Many professed Christians look upon men who do not reprove and condemn wrong, as men of piety and Christians indeed, while they think that those who stand boldly in defense of the right, and will not yield their integrity to unconsecrated influences, lack piety and a Christian spirit.

"Those who stand in defense of the honor of God and maintain the purity of truth at any cost will have manifold trials, as did our Saviour in the wilderness of temptation. While those who have yielding temperaments, who have not courage to condemn wrong, but keep silent when their influence is needed to stand in defense of the right against any pressure, may avoid many heartaches and escape many perplexities, they will also lose a very rich reward, if not their own souls. Those who are in harmony with God, and who through faith in Him receive strength to resist wrong and stand in defense of the right, will always have severe conflicts and will frequently have to stand alone. But precious victories will be theirs while they make God their dependence. His grace will be their strength."[2]

The church must take care not to change doctrine for popular teachings.

---

1. Francis D. Nichol, ed., *The Seventh-day Adventist Bible Commentary*, vol. 7 (Washington, DC: Review and Herald®, 1957), 285.
2. Ellen G. White, *Testimonies for the Church,* vol. 3 (Mountain View, CA: Pacific Press®, 1948), 302, 303.

Part 2: One Mediator

For there is one God and one Mediator between God and men,
the Man Christ Jesus, who gave Himself a ransom for all, to be testified in due time.
—1 Timothy 2:5, 6

Paul wants Timothy to understand that prayers offered to God are important. The measure of the Christian is often taken by the quality of his or her prayer life. We are not to confess our sins to other sinful human beings. There is only one Mediator between God the Father and us, Christ Jesus. "In His intercession as our Advocate Christ needs no man's virtue, no man's intercession. Christ is the only sin bearer, the only sin-offering. Prayer and confession are to be offered only to Him who has entered once for all into the holy place. Christ has declared, 'If any man sin, we have an advocate with the Father, Jesus Christ the righteous.' He will save to the uttermost all who come to Him in faith. He ever liveth to make intercession for us. This makes of no avail the offering of mass. . . .

"The so-called intercession of the saints is the greatest falsehood that can be invented. Priests and rulers have no right to interpose between Christ and the souls for whom He has died, as though invested with the Saviour's attributes, and able to pardon transgression and sin. They themselves are sinners. They are only human."[1]

"Christ represented His Father to the world, and He represents before God the chosen ones in whom He has restored the moral image of God. They are His heritage. To them He says, 'He that hath seen me hath seen the Father.' 'No man knoweth . . . the Father, save the Son, and he to whomsoever the Son will reveal him.' No priest, no religionist, can reveal the Father to any son or daughter of Adam.

"Men have only one Advocate, one Intercessor, who is able to pardon transgression."[2]

"Christ is the representative of God to man and the representative of man to God. He came to this world as man's substitute and surety, and He is fully able to save all who repent and return to their allegiance. Because of His righteousness, He is able to place man on vantage ground. Christ, our Passover, has been sacrificed for us."[3]

"He gave His precious, innocent life to save guilty human beings from eternal ruin, that through faith in Him they might stand guiltless before the throne of God."[4]

---

1. "Ellen G. White Comments—1 Timothy," in Francis D. Nichol, ed., *The Seventh-day Adventist Bible Commentary*, vol. 7 (Washington, DC: Review and Herald®, 1957), 913.
2. "Ellen G. White Comments—1 Timothy," 914.
3. Ellen G. White, MS 29, 1899.
4. Ellen G. White, MS 29, 1899.

Part 3: Speaking of Women

In like manner also, that the women *adorn themselves in modest apparel, with propriety and moderation, not with braided hair or gold or pearls or costly clothing, but, which is proper for women professing godliness, with good works.*
—1 Timothy 2:9, 10; emphasis added

Paul's first letter to Timothy is filled with solid counsel for the conduct of church members. Many find it interesting that he spends time discussing the deportment of women. One must remember the times in which Paul lived to understand his concern for the example Christian women set before the world. He had addressed many similar issues with the church at Corinth (1 Corinthians 14:34, 35). Apparently, the false teachers at Ephesus were having an impact upon the women of the church. Some of the women in the church were participating in idle gossip (1 Timothy 5:13). Some had gone so far as to throw off the restraints of Christian dignity and were misrepresenting their faith by copying the behavior of the heathen around them (1 Timothy 5:15).

Ellen White has some harsh words for those who put outward adornment before gifts to God. "There are many whose hearts have been so hardened by prosperity that they forget God, and forget the wants of their fellow-men. Professed Christians adorn themselves with jewelry, laces, costly apparel, while the Lord's poor suffer for the necessaries of life. Men and women who claim redemption through a Saviour's blood will squander the means intrusted to them for the saving of souls, and then grudgingly dole out their offerings for religion, giving liberally only when it will bring honor to themselves. These are idolaters."[1]

"I was shown the conformity of some professed Sabbathkeepers to the world. Oh, I saw that it is a disgrace to their profession, a disgrace to the cause of God. They give the lie to their profession. They think they are not like the world, but they are so near like them in dress, in conversation, and actions, that there is no distinction."[2] Paul urged women to dress modestly, not seductively like the heathen around them. "The most attractive and worthy adornment is a record of 'good works.'"[3]

"For the Christian, modesty, quality, appropriateness, and serviceability should determine what is worn and how it is worn. Expenditures that go beyond this ideal are incompatible with the principles of Christian stewardship."[4]

1. Ellen G. White, "The Victory at Ebenezer," *Signs of the Times,* January 26, 1882, 1.
2. Ellen G. White, *Testimonies for the Church,* vol. 1 (Mountain View, CA: Pacific Press®, 1948), 131.
3. Francis D. Nichol, ed., *The Seventh-day Adventist Bible Commentary,* vol. 7 (Washington, DC: Review and Herald®, 1957), 295.
4. Nichol, *Seventh-day Adventist Bible Commentary,* vol. 7, 295.

Part 4: Christianity in Simplicity

And without controversy great is the mystery of godliness:
[1]*God was manifested in the flesh,*
Justified in the Spirit,
[2]*Seen by angels,*
Preached among the Gentiles,
[3]*Believed on in the world,*
Received up in glory.

—1 Timothy 3:16

God's church is primarily the spiritual union of all its *converted* membership."[1] Notice the emphasis is placed upon those who are "converted." "It is not enough merely to assent to the principles of truth; they must be fully reflected in the life."[2] We are to be progressing daily in our walk with God.

In 1 Timothy 3:16, Paul shares what many commentators believe was an early first-century Christian hymn. This hymn consists of six Greek clauses that are rhythmic and lend themselves to song. Each is formed as a couplet that contrasts the work of Christ from a divine and then an earthly dimension with the central couplet being the inverse of the first and third. The first speaks of how Christ's mission was related to earth and in heaven, the second on heaven and on earth, the third on earth and in heaven again. The first gives reference to Christ's *incarnation*: (1) He appeared in the flesh (on earth) and was justified or declared to be righteous (sinless) in the spiritual things (in heaven). The second refers to His *witness* while on earth: (2) He witnessed both to angels (in heaven) and to earthly nations (on earth). The last refers to the *acceptance* of His sacrifice: (3) He was believed on by men who accepted the gospel here (on earth) and received in glory by His Father upon His ascension (to the heavenly courts above). All of creation watched His mission of mercy and sacrifice.

Here, in one verse, is a song for the ages. Oh, that it was put to music so that we might sing it together in our churches. The whole plan of salvation is embodied in this one verse. Heavenly angels, as well as human beings, witnessed "every phase of Christ's earthly life, from birth to resurrection and ascension."[3] Yet we have only scratched the surface of the greatest of all mysteries.

"Great is the mystery of godliness. There are mysteries in the life of Christ that are to be believed, even though they cannot be explained. The finite mind cannot fathom the mystery of godliness."[4]

---

1. Francis D. Nichol, ed., *The Seventh-day Adventist Bible Commentary*, vol. 7 (Washington, DC: Review and Herald®, 1957), 301; emphasis added.
2. Nichol, *Seventh-day Adventist Bible Commentary*, vol. 7, 301.
3. Nichol, *Seventh-day Adventist Bible Commentary*, vol. 7, 301.
4. Ellen G. White, Letter 65, 1905.

Part 5: Latter Times

Now the Spirit expressly says that in latter times some will depart from the faith,
giving heed to deceiving spirits and doctrines of demons, speaking lies in hypocrisy,
having their own conscience seared with a hot iron.

—1 Timothy 4:1, 2

Paul at Miletus had already warned the elders of the Ephesian church of the coming apostasy in the Christian church (see Acts 20:28–31)."[1] Now he reminds Timothy of that warning. "The most effective and deceptive opponents of the church are former members who set forth a cunning mixture of error and truth."[2] "The teachers of deception disseminate teachings that are inspired by Satan and his co-workers. . . . Satan works to control the minds of men, hence, the importance of a sound intellectual grasp of truth.

"Modern spiritualism, a prominent example of the 'doctrine of devils,' is merely a revival of the demon worship and witchcraft of the past. Its seductive influence will eventually sweep the world, Christian and non-Christian alike, and prepare the way for Satan's last great delusion."[3]

So how can we be safe and know what is truth? "None need be deceived. The law of God is as sacred as His throne, and by it every man who cometh into the world is to be judged. There is no other standard by which to test character. 'If they speak not according to this word, it is because there is no light in them.' Now, shall the case be decided according to the Word of God, or shall man's pretensions be credited? Says Christ, 'By their fruits ye shall know them.' If those through whom cures are performed, are disposed, on account of these manifestations, to excuse their neglect of the law of God, and continue in disobedience, though they have power to any and every extent, it does not follow that they have the great power of God. On the contrary, it is the miracle-working power of the great deceiver. He is a transgressor of the moral law, and employs every device that he can master to blind men to its true character. We are warned that in the last days he will work with signs and lying wonders. And he will continue these wonders until the close of probation, that he may point to them as evidence that he is an angel of light and not of darkness."[4]

"God's people will not find their safety in working miracles, for Satan will counterfeit the miracles that will be wrought."[5]

---

1. Francis D. Nichol, ed., *The Seventh-day Adventist Bible Commentary*, vol. 7 (Washington, DC: Review and Herald®, 1957), 302.

2. Nichol, *Seventh-day Adventist Bible Commentary*, vol. 7, 302.

3. Nichol, *Seventh-day Adventist Bible Commentary*, vol. 7, 302, 303.

4. Ellen G. White, "The Grace and Mercy of God," *Advent Review and Sabbath Herald*, November 17, 1885, 1, 2.

5. Ellen G. White, *Testimonies for the Church*, vol. 9 (Mountain View, CA: Pacific Press®, 1948), 16.

Part 6: What About Unclean Foods?

For every creature of God is good, and nothing is to be refused if it is received with thanksgiving; for it is sanctified by the word of God and prayer.
—1 Timothy 4:4, 5

To apply 1 Timothy 4:4, 5 to the matter of clean and unclean foods is to ignore the context of the letter. Paul was not talking here about clean versus unclean food. He was speaking to the beliefs of the false teachers who were confusing the church members at Ephesus. "God specified at creation what articles He intended man to use as food. This prescribed diet did not include the flesh of any animal, or even all types of vegetation (. . . Gen. 1:29, 31). They were created for a different purpose, and for that purpose they were 'good,' that is, perfectly adapted to meet the purpose for which God made them. After the Flood God permitted the use of 'clean' meats, but specifically forbade the eating of 'unclean' meats. The Bible nowhere removes that ban."[1] "Both food and marriage were part of God's original plan for man in Eden."[2] False teachers were perverting both.

Paul was still dealing with Judaizers, Gnostics, ascetics, and Docetists. All of these groups were attempting to permeate the Christian church with their teachings. "The Gnostics believed that all matter was evil, and that the human body, being material, must have its passions repressed and denied. According to this theory, marriage became a concession to the lusts of the flesh, and was therefore sinful. Paul makes clear that marriage is a God-given institution and that to attack this institution would be to assail the infinite wisdom and beneficent purposes of God."[3]

Likewise, Paul spoke to the relationship the Gnostics took to food. "For ceremonial, ritualistic reasons these ascetics considered the total prohibition of certain foods to be spiritually desirable. The prohibition of certain foods on particular religious days may also be included in the apostle's warning."[4] Some churches today still trace beliefs back to early Gnostic beliefs. "He who created man knows best what activities he should participate in so as to attain a balanced, happy life."[5]

"For man to deny himself the privileges of marriage and food necessary for proper health would be to question and defy the wisdom and will of God."[6]

---

1. Francis D. Nichol, ed., *The Seventh-day Adventist Bible Commentary*, vol. 7 (Washington, DC: Review and Herald®, 1957), 304.
2. Nichol, *Seventh-day Adventist Bible Commentary*, vol. 7, 303.
3. Nichol, *Seventh-day Adventist Bible Commentary*, vol. 7, 303.
4. Nichol, *Seventh-day Adventist Bible Commentary*, vol. 7, 303.
5. Nichol, *Seventh-day Adventist Bible Commentary*, vol. 7, 303.
6. Nichol, *Seventh-day Adventist Bible Commentary*, vol. 7, 303.

Part 7: Be an Example

Let no one despise your youth, but be an example to the believers in word,
in conduct, in love, in spirit, in faith, in purity.

—1 Timothy 4:12

Paul told Timothy to be an example to those around him. This would have been a strange command to give to one so young. Old age was revered in the first century, and young adults still had much to learn before they could be set forth as examples for others to emulate. Nevertheless, Paul saw Timothy as a model of what a genuine Christian should be. He should set an example through his refined speech, his charity, his faith, and his purity. "Thus the apostle challenges Timothy to continue to exemplify the Christian virtues and graces, so that his authority may be held in honor."[1] "Throw a pebble into the lake, and a wave is formed; and another and another; and as they increase, the circle widens, until it reaches the very shore. So with our influence. Beyond our knowledge or control it tells upon others in blessing or cursing. . . .

"And the wider the sphere of our influence the more good we may do. When those who profess to serve God follow Christ's example, practicing the principles of the law in their daily life; when every act bears witness that they love God supremely and their neighbor as themselves, then will the church have power to move the world."[2]

"Timothy was probably not 40 years old, and yet would have numerous elders under his charge. . . . From [1 Timothy] 4:12–16 some have concluded that Timothy was timid and reticent by nature, more given to obey than to command, and that Paul's counsel here was intended to correct this supposed defect. Youth is no barrier to a rich spiritual fellowship with God, and old age is not a guarantee of sound thinking or complete dedication. Men, according to Paul, are to be judged by their sanctified abilities and not by arbitrary standards such as age."[3]

"In the history of Timothy are found precious lessons. He was a mere lad when chosen by God as a teacher; but so fixed were his principles by a correct education that he was fitted for this important position. He bore his responsibilities with Christlike meekness. He was faithful, steadfast, and true, and Paul selected him to be his companion in labor and travel."[4]

"A godly example will tell more for the truth than the greatest eloquence unaccompanied by a well-ordered life."[5]

---

1. Francis D. Nichol, ed., *The Seventh-day Adventist Bible Commentary*, vol. 7 (Washington, DC: Review and Herald®, 1957), 306.
2. Ellen G. White, *Messages to Young People* (Nashville, TN: Southern Publishing, 1950), 418.
3. Nichol, *Seventh-day Adventist Bible Commentary*, vol. 7, 305, 306.
4. Ellen G. White, "God's Purpose for the Youth," *Youth's Instructor*, February 13, 1902, 2.
5. Ellen G. White, "Words to Ministers," *Advent Review and Sabbath Herald*, August 19, 1902, 7.

Part 8: Dealing With Elders

For the Scripture says, "You shall not muzzle an ox while it treads out the grain" [Deuteronomy 25:4], and, "The laborer is worthy of his wages" [Luke 10:7].
—1 Timothy 5:18

Paul next turns to compensation for and disciplining of ministers. There was a plan in place to provide support for the priests of old (Numbers 18:21). Paul had already spoken to this issue in his letter to the Corinthians (1 Corinthians 9:7–14). He had also spoken of it in his letter to the Hebrews (Hebrews 7:5). "The tribe of Levi was chosen by the Lord for the sacred offices pertaining to the temple and the priesthood. Of the priest it was said, 'The Lord thy God hath chosen him . . . to stand to minister in the name of the Lord.' (Deuteronomy 18:5.) One-tenth of all the increase was claimed by the Lord as His own, and to withhold the tithe was regarded by Him as robbery."[1]

Some elders needed to be disciplined. "It is a serious moment when one church member accuses another of sin. Consequently, any charge should be thoroughly validated by reliable witnesses before it is made public. . . . Such counsel forbids reckless accusations whereby the reputations of innocent people are damaged and their confidence in the brethren weakened."[2] Two or three witnesses needed to come forward to endorse the charges (Deuteronomy 17:6; 19:15). As these were public figures, their rebuke must be made in public as well. It would have been difficult for one as young as Timothy to rebuke a more senior elder, yet impartiality must prevail. No matter who the offender, justice must be done.

Certain inexperienced men had perhaps been ordained by the laying on of hands. Such haste was now being seen as a mistake. Haste should also not be taken to reinstate those who had been disciplined. "The office of elder was too sacred and important for a hasty admission or readmission of anyone who had not proved himself worthy. The candidate for eldership must first be carefully examined as to his qualifications (. . . [1 Timothy] 3:1–7)."[3] Sometimes mistakes are made. Hidden sins surface only after the fact. In time the truth will come out. Even the most rigorous scrutiny cannot keep leadership pure. Sanctimonious candidates for church office can often fool a congregation. Eventually, good and evil become a habit, and past actions again arise. The church must then act to purge the sinner from leadership.

Note our text. Paul "places the words of Jesus on the same plane as [Old Testament] Scripture."[4]

---

1. Ellen G. White, *The Acts of the Apostles* (Mountain View, CA: Pacific Press®, 1911), 336.
2. Francis D. Nichol, ed., *The Seventh-day Adventist Bible Commentary*, vol. 7 (Washington, DC: Review and Herald®, 1957), 313.
3. Nichol, *Seventh-day Adventist Bible Commentary*, vol. 7, 314.
4. Nichol, *Seventh-day Adventist Bible Commentary*, vol. 7, 313.

Part 9: Medicinal Wine?

No longer drink only water, but use a little wine for
your stomach's sake and your frequent infirmities.

—1 Timothy 5:23

Apparently Timothy was frequently ill. A body frequently beset with infirmities is not an attractive advertisement for any kind of health reform."[1] "In Paul's day, as now, the water of the Near East was often unsafe for use. Physical ailments such as dysentery, often due to contaminated water, were common occurrences. Consequently, other ways to quench thirst were often recommended.

"... Some commentators believe that Paul here advocates the temperate use of fermented wine for medicinal purposes. They call attention to the fact that wine has, through the centuries, thus been used.

"Others hold that Paul refers to unfermented grape juice, their reasoning being that he would not give advice inconsistent with the rest of Scripture, which warns against the use of intoxicating beverages. . . .

"... The purpose of Paul's counsel is that Timothy should be physically fit for the heavy duties that rest upon him as administrator of the churches in Asia Minor. Mental and moral alertness are closely related to physical fitness."[2]

It would be inconsistent to believe Paul was telling Timothy to drink fermented beverages after what he wrote on the subject. He wrote the Ephesians saying, "And do not be drunk with wine, in which is dissipation; but be filled with the Spirit" (Ephesians 5:18). He wrote the Galatians, "Now the works of the flesh are evident which are: adultery, fornication, uncleanness, lewdness, idolatry, sorcery, hatred, contentions, jealousies, outbursts of wrath, selfish ambitions, dissensions, heresies, envy, murders, *drunkenness*, revelries, and the like" (Galatians 5:19–21; emphasis added).

"Wine is a mocker, strong drink is a brawler, and whoever is led astray by it is not wise" (Proverbs 20:1). "Whatever injures the health not only lessens physical vigor, but tends to weaken the mental and moral powers. Indulgence in any unhealthful practice makes it more difficult for one to discriminate between right and wrong, and hence more difficult to resist evil."[3]

"Pure air, sunlight, abstemiousness, rest, exercise, proper diet, the use of water, trust in divine power—these are the true remedies."[4]

---

1. Francis D. Nichol, ed., *The Seventh-day Adventist Bible Commentary*, vol. 7 (Washington, DC: Review and Herald®, 1957), 314.
2. Nichol, *Seventh-day Adventist Bible Commentary*, vol. 7, 314.
3. Ellen G. White, *The Ministry of Healing* (Mountain View, CA: Pacific Press®, 1942), 128.
4. White, *Ministry of Healing*, 127.

Part 10: Dealing With Money

For we brought nothing into this world, and it is certain we can carry nothing out. And having food and clothing, with these we shall be content. . . . For the love of money is a root of all kinds of evil, for which some have strayed from the faith in their greediness, and pierced themselves through with many sorrows.

—1 Timothy 6:7, 8, 10

Here Paul illustrates the temporary nature of material possessions. Only that which is spiritual and is deposited with God will endure forever. . . .

". . . Because a man cannot take any of his material possessions with him beyond the grave, his chief pursuit while on earth should be for character development. After obtaining the essentials that sustain life, man has acquired all that he will ever need. To crave more than the essentials breeds a discontented spirit, a competitive zeal that is never satisfied.

". . . Those who strive for riches are nurturing within themselves a fire of passion that will eventually destroy the finer qualities of the soul. Man cannot serve God and mammon simultaneously."[1]

It is not money that is bad; it is the *love* of money that we are warned against. "The perils of prosperity are self-created. Balaam (2 Peter 2:15) and Judas Iscariot (Matt. 27:3; John 12:4–6) illustrate the lure of riches and its inevitable disillusionment and sorrow. Neither man was forced to submit to the seductive appeal of quick wealth. The agony of sinking in one's own pit defies imagination. Many parents awaken too late, after years of acquiring wealth, to find that their children are strangers within their own home, their affections rooted elsewhere. No amount of money in the bank will buy back the neglected years, and the comfort of being loved and appreciated in old age will often be denied such parents, regardless of their tears of anguish. Extensive land ownings and a more pretentious home are not balm enough for spent health that has lost its vigor to enjoy the acquired possessions. Countless are the 'sorrows' that are self-induced in man's quest for material security."[2]

"Instead of directing his energy and time to the pursuit of riches, the Christian should use them in the pursuit of Christlike virtues. God has promised that our material needs will be provided when we seek His service first (. . . Matt. 6:33)."[3]

1. Francis D. Nichol, ed., *The Seventh-day Adventist Bible Commentary*, vol. 7 (Washington, DC: Review and Herald®, 1957), 318.
2. Nichol, *Seventh-day Adventist Bible Commentary*, vol. 7, 318, 319.
3. Nichol, *Seventh-day Adventist Bible Commentary*, vol. 7, 319.

Part 11: Fighting the Good Fight

Fight the good fight of faith, lay hold on eternal life, to which you were also called and have confessed the good confession in the presence of many witnesses.
—1 Timothy 6:12

Again we see Paul using the athletic contests he witnessed during his lifetime as a metaphor for the Christian life. Paul had watched athletes in training. "Victory was the result of determined perseverance and rigid self-control. Once the race began there was no time for side issues or divided thinking, nor does a runner stop halfway in the race to compliment himself on how well he has run."[1] "All who entered the Greek races put forth their best efforts to win the prize. They used all the skill and stamina they had acquired as a result of their intensive training. None of them was indifferent, lethargic, or careless. The crown of life eternal is offered to all, but only those who subject themselves to strict training will obtain the prize. This means that at all times the Christian will be guided in word, thought, and deed by the high standards found in the Bible, and will not be controlled by the desires and inclinations of his own heart. He will ask at every step of the journey: 'What would Jesus do? Will this course of action, this plan of work, or this form of recreation increase my spiritual strength or lessen it?' Everything that in any way interferes with spiritual progress must be rejected; otherwise victory is not possible."[2]

"Because the Christian race is a lifelong experience, it calls for patience and perseverance—perseverance in the face of successive difficulties and disappointments and patience to await the reward at the end of the course."[3] Paul is talking about character development. Paul wants Timothy to consider that righteousness, godliness, faith, love, patience, and meekness are of more value than envy, strife, arguments, covetousness, and lust. "Before all the competing religions of the world the Christian defends the gospel in two ways—by a consistent Christian life and by an able, logical presentation of Christian truth."[4] Christian character is a qualification for Christian service.

"The most winsome argument for Christianity is not unanswerable logic but the fragrance of a Christlike life. . . .

". . . The preaching of the gospel is hindered or hastened by the lives lived by professing Christians."[5]

1. Francis D. Nichol, ed., *The Seventh-day Adventist Bible Commentary*, vol. 7 (Washington, DC: Review and Herald®, 1957), 319.
2. Francis D. Nichol, ed., *The Seventh-day Adventist Bible Commentary*, vol. 6 (Washington, DC: Review and Herald®, 1957), 735.
3. Nichol, *Seventh-day Adventist Bible Commentary*, vol. 7, 481.
4. Nichol, *Seventh-day Adventist Bible Commentary*, vol. 7, 319.
5. Nichol, *Seventh-day Adventist Bible Commentary*, vol. 7, 307.

Part 12: Protect the Gospel

O Timothy! Guard what was committed to your trust, avoiding the profane
and vain babblings and contradictions of what is falsely called knowledge.
—1 Timothy 6:20

Paul used the Greek phrase "guard the deposit" to explain how important it was for Timothy to remain true to the gospel message. Just as a bank must protect the assets of those who place their trust in it, so the Christian must be true to his or her calling. "Paul knew that the purity of the gospel message would depend upon the faithfulness of the next generation of workers, represented by young Timothy."[1] Paul encouraged Timothy to turn away from "secular, empty talk. One way to preserve the purity and power of the gospel is to shun trivial subjects and to use one's time for teaching truth, not for discussing irrelevancies. Paul thus ends his letter by summarizing the theme begun in [1 Timothy] 1:3–7."[2]

"Many exalt human reason, idolize human wisdom, and set the opinions of men above the revealed wisdom of God. . . .

". . . The maxims of the world, that know not God, have been worked into the theories of the church. In the eyes of men, vain philosophy and science, falsely so-called, are of more value than the word of God. The sentiment prevails to a large extent that the divine Mediator is not essential to the salvation of man. A variety of theories advanced by the so-called worldly-wise men for man's elevation, are believed and trusted in more than is the truth of God, as taught by Christ and His apostles."[3]

"As we near the end of time, falsehood will be so mingled with truth, that only those who have the guidance of the Holy Spirit will be able to distinguish truth from error.

"We need to make every effort to keep the way of the Lord. We must in no case turn from His guidance to put our trust in man. The Lord's angels are appointed to keep strict watch over those who put their faith in the Lord, and these angels are to be our special help in every time of need. Every day we are to come to the Lord with full assurance of faith and to look to Him for wisdom."[4]

"Those who are guided by the Word of the Lord will discern with certainty between falsehood and truth, between sin and righteousness."[5]

---

1. Francis D. Nichol, ed., *The Seventh-day Adventist Bible Commentary*, vol. 7 (Washington, DC: Review and Herald®, 1957), 321.
2. Nichol, *Seventh-day Adventist Bible Commentary*, vol. 7, 321.
3. Ellen G. White, "Imperative Necessity of Searching for Truth," *Advent Review and Sabbath Herald*, November 8, 1892, 2.
4. Ellen G. White, MS 43, 1907.
5. White, MS 43, 1907.

Part 1: Background—Crete

To Titus, a true son in our common faith.

—Titus 1:4

It is generally believed Paul wrote to Titus while at liberty between his first and second imprisonments in Rome. Titus was "an intimate friend, traveling companion, and assistant of the apostle Paul. . . . Paul considered Titus his 'own son after the common faith' (v 4)—evidently because he was one of his own converts. That Titus was a Gentile is indicated by Paul's refusal to circumcise him in order to appease overzealous Jewish Christians at Jerusalem—perhaps on the occasion when he visited that city as a member of the Antioch delegation to the council held to resolve the issue of Gentile converts (Gal 2:1–5; cf. Acts 15). Possibly he was a native of Antioch. In any case, he was apparently a member of the Gentile church in that city (Gal 2:1) and probably accepted Christianity during Paul's early ministry there. When some in the Corinthian church turned against Paul about AD 57, he sent Titus to effect a reconciliation. Paul's anxiety for the success of this mission is evident from his perplexity at not meeting Titus at Troas as planned (2 Cor 2:12, 13; 7:6, 13, 14). A little later he met Titus in Macedonia, joyfully received his glowing report of success . . . , and sent him back to Corinth with the 2d Epistle to the Corinthians . . . , and to supervise the collection of funds for the poor at Jerusalem. . . . Several years later, apparently not long before his second imprisonment in Rome, Paul wrote the Epistle to Titus. He had left Titus on the island of Crete to organize the churches there and to instruct the believers more thoroughly ([Titus] 1:4, 5)."[1]

But what was happening in Crete? "From the epistle it appears that there were groups of Christians in a number of places in Crete. The general church organization, however, was incomplete, and trouble was brewing because of false teachers, who may have been half-converted Jews. These false teachers were laying great emphasis on myths, genealogies, and the law. They were wasting much time and energy, both their own and that of other church members, on pointless argument. Titus was responsible for straightening matters out, and Paul sends him counsel and encouragement."[2]

"When the mind is absorbed with religious trivia, too often the really important questions of morality and integrity are ignored and religion deteriorates into a matter of form and theory."[3]

1. Siegfried H. Horn, *Seventh-day Adventist Bible Dictionary*, ed. Don F. Neufeld, Commentary Reference Series, vol. 8 (Washington, DC: Review and Herald®, 1960), s.v. "Titus."
2. Francis D. Nichol, ed., *The Seventh-day Adventist Bible Commentary*, vol. 7 (Washington, DC: Review and Herald®, 1957), 356.
3. Nichol, *Seventh-day Adventist Bible Commentary*, vol. 7, 356.

Part 2: Set Things in Order!

*For this reason I left you in Crete, that you should set in order the things
that are lacking, and appoint elders in every city as I commanded you.*

—Titus 1:5

O ne of the challenges confronting Titus was the appointment of leaders for the
various churches on Crete. Paul gave him guidance on what he should look
for in a candidate for church office: "If a man is blameless, the husband of one wife,
having faithful children not accused of dissipation or insubordination. For a bishop
[elder] must be blameless, as a steward of God, not self-willed, not quick-tempered,
not given to wine, not violent, not greedy for money, but hospitable, a lover of what
is good, sober-minded, just, holy, self-controlled, holding fast the faithful word as he
has been taught, that he may be able, by sound doctrine, both to exhort and convict
those who contradict" (Titus 1:6–9). Paul's stipulations mirror those he gave Timothy
(1 Timothy 3:1–7). Added emphasis was given to select persons who could deal with
dissent—"not self-willed, not quick-tempered, . . . but . . . self-controlled, holding fast
the faithful word" (verses 7, 8). "In any organization, secular or ecclesiastical, there are
moments when ideas clash and misunderstandings develop. The efficiency of a church
under the strain of divergent opinions depends upon the stabilizing influence of a self-
possessed leader, whose self-discipline inspires patience and a spirit of understanding."[1]

Titus had a daunting, highly responsible job to perform. He, like Timothy, was
young. Without his mentor by his side, Titus had to bring order to churches that might
not accept his authority. Paul knew the issues Titus would face. He knew the Cretan
reputation for being lazy prevaricators. He knew Titus would have to confront false
doctrines and personal agendas. Titus needed special men! "The ministry demands
more of those who give themselves to it than would other professions, and the need
to continue learning never ceases. Indeed, the ministry is more than a profession; it is
a calling—a divine calling.

". . . With a humility born of an honest view of himself the genuine minister realizes
his own shortcomings and the immense task before him.[2]

*Such a man is not overwhelmed, but challenged, by the possibilities confronting him, and he seeks,
prayerfully and diligently, to improve the talents lent to him by God."[3]*

---

1. Francis D. Nichol, ed., *The Seventh-day Adventist Bible Commentary*, vol. 7 (Washington, DC: Review and Herald®,
1957), 360.

2. Nichol, *Seventh-day Adventist Bible Commentary*, vol. 7, 361.

3. Nichol, *Seventh-day Adventist Bible Commentary*, vol. 7, 361.

Part 3: Stopping False Teachers

This testimony is true. Therefore rebuke them sharply, that they may be sound in the faith, not giving heed to Jewish fables and commandments of men who turn from the truth.

—Titus 1:13, 14

The Cretan church apparently had an above average number of false teachers who accentuated some of the basic weaknesses of the Cretan inhabitants. . . .

". . . Nominal church members who refused cooperation were factious, opinionated, and insubordinate."[1] "In the ancient world the phrase, 'to Cretanize,' meant to lie, or deceive, like a Cretan. This offensive Cretan trait was now apparent in the perverse religious teachers and the 'unruly' members of various congregations. . . .

". . . What had been written of the Cretans 600 years before was still true—their basic character had not changed. This lack of moral integrity that permeated much of the Cretan population posed a grave danger to the young churches on the island."[2]

We are not told who the false teachers were that were troubling the Cretan church, but it would seem they were Jews. Paul referred to them as being members of "the circumcision." With the Cretans, these Jews found fertile ground to practice their trade of religion for hire. "Similar problems confronted both Titus and Timothy (. . . 1 Tim. 1:4–7). The Jewish practice of interpreting the [Old Testament] by the allegorical method obscured the truth and produced speculation and strife. . . . Jewish fables gave rise to word battles (2 Tim. 2:14) and lacked the regenerating power of the Holy Spirit."[3]

Paul had dealt with Judaizers and orthodox Jews during his entire ministry. He was way beyond using smooth words to counter their insidious influence. "Because of their emphasis upon intellectual speculations these unconverted teachers claim[ed] to know God, perhaps even better than the Christians. However, their behavior reveal[ed] their true master; they [did] not the works of God."[4] "Apparently many of the Cretan believers went to teachers of this kind for instruction in Christian doctrine and practice. Paul had no choice but to speak frankly concerning both the teachers and their followers."[5] "Rebuke them sharply!"

"Satan can always do more damage to the advancement of truth by working within the church than by attacking it from without."[6]

---

1. Francis D. Nichol, ed., *The Seventh-day Adventist Bible Commentary*, vol. 7 (Washington, DC: Review and Herald®, 1957), 361.
2. Nichol, *Seventh-day Adventist Bible Commentary*, vol. 7, 362.
3. Nichol, *Seventh-day Adventist Bible Commentary*, vol. 7, 362.
4. Nichol, *Seventh-day Adventist Bible Commentary*, vol. 7, 363.
5. Nichol, *Seventh-day Adventist Bible Commentary*, vol. 7, 363.
6. Nichol, *Seventh-day Adventist Bible Commentary*, vol. 7, 362.

Part 4: Character in Old Age

*That the older men be sober, reverent, temperate, sound in faith, in love,
in patience, the older women likewise, that they be reverent in behavior,
not slanderers, not given to much wine, teachers of good things.*
                                                            —Titus 2:2, 3; emphasis added

P aul writes much the same type of pastoral letter to Titus that he earlier had written
     to Timothy. Included is a plan for church leaders to follow. In chapter 2 of his Epistle
to Titus, Paul summarizes the instruction given to Timothy (1 Timothy 2:8–6:2). He
instructs Titus to be sure older men and women are solemn (sober), reverent, temperate;
sound in faith, in love, and in patience; not slanderers, not given to much wine, teachers
of good things. Thus when we review the instruction Paul gave elders (bishops), deacons,
and women in 1 Timothy 3:1–10, we find nearly an identical list. He told Timothy that
leaders must be blameless, husband of one wife, vigilant, serious, of good behavior, given
to hospitality, apt to teach, not given to wine, no striker, patient. Women were admonished
in 1 Timothy 3 to be grave, not slanderers, sober, faithful in all things (verse 11). "Older
men in the church ought to be respected for their wise counsel. When one is disciplined
by God, such counsel should not be taken lightly."[1]

Why mention women given to wine? "Because the church at Crete was newly
established the 'aged women' were those who had lived most of their lives by the
standards and habits of a pagan society. The drinking of wine is a common practice
in the Middle East and the Orient. After a long life of such practice, enslavement to
wine would be the rule, not the exception."[2] Perhaps this was more of a problem with
older women than men.

Women were to teach "good things," not gossip or slander. "The virtues of womanhood are best transmitted from one generation to another by emotionally mature
women who have learned well the lessons of self-discipline and personal piety. It
is tragic for women to assume the duties of wifehood and motherhood without
having been properly taught by precept and example the responsibilities of Christian
womanhood. . . .

". . . The sound-minded wife realizes that the harmony and strength of the home
depends upon her role as a helper to her husband, not as a competitor."[3]

*"Paul's special care was to establish the church on right principles, knowing that the moral and
spiritual tone of the home and community is largely determined by its women."*[4]

---

1. Francis D. Nichol, ed., *The Seventh-day Adventist Bible Commentary*, vol. 7 (Washington, DC: Review and Herald®, 1957), 364.
2. Nichol, *Seventh-day Adventist Bible Commentary*, vol. 7, 364.
3. Nichol, *Seventh-day Adventist Bible Commentary*, vol. 7, 364.
4. Nichol, *Seventh-day Adventist Bible Commentary*, vol. 7, 365.

Part 5: The Virtues of *Womanhood*

That they admonish the young women *to love their husbands, to love*
their children, to be discreet, chaste, homemakers, good, obedient to their
own husbands, that the word of God may not be blasphemed.
                                                —Titus 2:4, 5; emphasis added

Christianity elevated the status of womanhood to a position hitherto unknown. However, this new status required a corresponding response from Christian women. They were to fulfill God's original purpose as bulwarks of tenderness and devotion. Thus, Christian women were to set the pattern of purity and devotion to home and children, both for their own daughters as well as for their pagan neighbors."[1] "Paul's description of a Christian *woman* compares with the classic portraiture of the honorable mother and wife in Prov. 31:10–31."[2]

> Who can find a virtuous wife?
> For her worth is far above rubies.
> The heart of her husband safely trusts her;
> So he will have no lack of gain.
> She does him good and not evil
> All the days of her life.
> She seeks wool and flax,
> And willingly works with her hands.
> She is like the merchant ships,
> She brings her food from afar.
> She also rises while it is yet night,
> And provides food for her household,
> And a portion for her maidservants.
> She considers a field and buys it;
> From her profits she plants a vineyard.
> She girds herself with strength,
> And strengthens her arms.
> She perceives that her merchandise is good,
> And her lamp does not go out by night.
> She stretches out her hands to the distaff,
> And her hand holds the spindle.
> She extends her hand to the poor,
> Yes; she reaches out her hands to the needy.
> She is not afraid of snow for her household,
> For all her household is clothed with scarlet.
> She makes tapestry for herself;

(*continued on next page*)

Her clothing is fine linen and purple.
Her husband is known in the gates,
When he sits among the elders of the land.
She makes linen garments and sells them,
And supplies sashes for the merchants.
Strength and honor are her clothing;
She shall rejoice in time to come.
She opens her mouth with wisdom,
And on her tongue is the law of kindness.
She watches over the ways of her household,
And does not eat the bread of idleness.
Her children rise up and call her blessed;
Her husband also, and he praises her:
"Many daughters have done well,
But you excel them all."
Charm is deceitful and beauty is passing,
But a woman who fears the LORD, she shall be praised.
Give her of the fruit of her hands,
And let her own works praise her in the gates.
  (Proverbs 31:10–31)

God surely blesses those who marry a Christian woman with a taste for heaven on earth!

---

1. Francis D. Nichol, ed., *The Seventh-day Adventist Bible Commentary*, vol. 7 (Washington, DC: Review and Herald®, 1957), 364.

2. Nichol, *Seventh-day Adventist Bible Commentary*, vol. 7, 365.

Part 6: Titus, Set an Example!

Likewise, exhort the young men to be sober-minded, in all things showing
yourself to be a pattern of good works; in doctrine showing integrity,
reverence, incorruptibility, sound speech that cannot be condemned.

—Titus 2:6–8

Young men were urged to be steady and levelheaded (Titus 2:6). This attribute was required of all: older men (verse 2), older women (verse 4), and younger women (verse 5). In verses 7 and 8, Paul urges Titus to be a role model for the young men of the congregation. Again we see a parallel to the advice Paul gave to Timothy (1 Timothy 4:11–12). If Titus practices these character traits, his opponents will have nothing evil to say about him or his behavior. By removing all cause for criticism, the church will deprive those who seek to find fault. There will be a lack of ammunition that can be used to hold Christianity up to ridicule. If more Christians "practiced what they preached," the world would indeed be a better place.

"Both the Christians of Crete and their pagan neighbors had the right to expect that the Christian pastor would faithfully exemplify the principles of Christianity.

"In all probability Titus had been reared in a pagan home, possibly in the luxurious and wicked city of Antioch. He had been drawn to the Master's service in the freshness of his youth. He had been tested in the furnace of trial and difficulty. Here Paul reminds Titus that for him to set an example by his own self-restrained and disciplined Christian manhood would provide the most effective inspiration possible for the Cretan believers."[1]

"Those who are ever pressing a little closer to the world, and becoming more like them in feelings, in plans, in ideas, have left a space between them and the Saviour, and Satan has pressed his way into this space, and low, worldly-tainted, selfish plans become interwoven with their experience."[2] "Those who walk even as Christ walked, who are patient, gentle, kind, meek and lowly in heart, those who yoke up with Christ and lift His burdens, who yearn for souls as He yearned for them—these will enter into the joy of their Lord. They will see with Christ the travail of his soul, and be satisfied.[3]

Heaven will triumph, for the vacancies made in heaven by the fall of Satan and his angels will be filled by the redeemed of the Lord."[4]

---

1. Francis D. Nichol, ed., *The Seventh-day Adventist Bible Commentary*, vol. 7 (Washington, DC: Review and Herald®, 1957), 365.
2. Ellen G. White, "Losing Our First Love," *Advent Review and Sabbath Herald*, June 7, 1887, 1, 2.
3. Ellen G. White, "Christ's Ambassadors," *Advent Review and Sabbath Herald*, May 29, 1900, 2.
4. Ellen G. White, "Christ's Ambassadors," *Advent Review and Sabbath Herald*, May 29, 1900, 2.

Part 7: The Blessed Hope

For the grace of God that brings salvation has appeared to all men, teaching us that, denying ungodliness and worldly lusts, we should live soberly, righteously, and godly in the present age, looking for the blessed hope and glorious appearing of our great God and Savior Jesus Christ.
—Titus 2:11–13

The Lord saw our fallen condition; he saw our need of grace, and because he loved our souls, he has given us grace and peace. Grace means favor to one who is undeserving, to one who is lost. The fact that we are sinners, instead of shutting us away from the mercy and love of God, makes the exercise of His love to us a positive necessity in order that we may be saved."[1]

"The Lord purifies the heart very much as we air a room. We do not close the doors and windows and throw in some purifying substance; but we open the doors and throw wide the windows and let heaven's purifying atmosphere flow in. The Lord says, 'He that doeth truth cometh to the light.' The windows of impulse, of feeling, must be opened up toward heaven, and the dust of selfishness and earthliness must be expelled. The grace of God must sweep through the chambers of the mind, the imagination must have heavenly themes for contemplation, and every element of the nature must be purified and vitalized by the Spirit of God."[2]

"God's plan is to restore in lost men the original image in which they were created. Sin will not be overlooked, but eradicated. The process of sanctification consists of the grace of God acting upon the fully dedicated will of man, so that every trace of sin may be completely removed from the life. . . . To deliver man from the alluring power of sin and to lead him into habits of righteousness demands nothing less than the power of God. Because of sinful habits etched deeply within his life man has no other resort than to grasp the rescuing hand of God for complete deliverance. Yet, though the whirling worlds respond instantly to the directions of God, man, the climax of all creation, often limits the power and designs of God by his rebellious will."[3]

"The hope of Christ's return has been the grand incentive of the Christian faith for nearly 2,000 years, buoying the believer's spirit and steeling his courage amid all the vicissitudes of life."[4]

---

1. Ellen G. White, "Transformation Through Faith and Obedience," *Signs of the Times,* June 5, 1893.

2. Ellen G. White, Ms. 8c, 1891.

3. Francis D. Nichol, ed., *The Seventh-day Adventist Bible Commentary,* vol. 7 (Washington, DC: Review and Herald®, 1957), 367.

4. Nichol, *Seventh-day Adventist Bible Commentary,* vol. 7, 366.

Part 8: A Civics Lesson

Remind them to be subject to rulers and authorities, to obey, to be ready for every good work.
—Titus 3:1

Probably this counsel was specially needed in Crete. Crete had been under Roman rule for over a century, and its people fretted under foreign domination, as did the Jews. Paul's counsel on loyalty to the government was most appropriate. . . .

". . . Christians are to be known for their loyalty to the civil authorities in matters such as tax collections and community projects. Neglect of civic responsibilities brings needless reproach upon the church. Peace and order are an integral part of the Christian message. Disloyalty and sedition would not commend Christianity to the pagan world.

"Paul's counsel testifies to his own nobility of character. His experience with the Roman government had not been pleasant. Paul had been imprisoned, fettered, hindered, beaten, and threatened because Roman officials had listened to the malicious stories invented by his implacable Jewish enemies."[1] Nevertheless, Paul counseled that Christians should join with government when the government was doing "good works." "A genuine Christian should be recognized as an upright, patriotic citizen, who eagerly supports every governmental program designed to relieve hardship and to establish equity. At the same time the Christian is conscience bound to refrain from any governmental activity that denies basic rights to any man or that encourages evil practices."[2]

The Christian must draw the line when it comes to disobeying God's laws to obey the government's laws. As Paul wrote in Romans 13:1, "Let every soul be subject to the governing authorities. For there is no authority except from God, and the authorities that exist are appointed by God." That is not to say that these rulers are always right. In Romans Paul is not implying "that God always approves the conduct of civil governments. Nor does Paul mean that it is the Christian's duty always to submit to them. The requirements of government may at times be contrary to the law of God, and under such circumstances the Christian is 'to obey God rather than men' (Acts 4:19; 5:29)."[3]

As Christians, we are to pray for our elected officials (1 Timothy 2:1, 2) and obey them (Titus 3:1). He who breaks man-made laws finds it easy to break God's!

---

1. Francis D. Nichol, ed., *The Seventh-day Adventist Bible Commentary*, vol. 7 (Washington, DC: Review and Herald®, 1957), 369.

2. Nichol, *Seventh-day Adventist Bible Commentary*, vol. 7, 369.

3. Francis D. Nichol, ed., *The Seventh-day Adventist Bible Commentary*, vol. 6 (Washington, DC: Review and Herald®, 1957), 626.

Part 9: Justified by Mercy

But when the kindness and the love of God our Savior toward man appeared, not by works of righteousness which we have done, but according to His mercy He saved us.
—Titus 3:4, 5

Paul very plainly sets before Titus the pitiful nature of sinful man. Humans can do nothing to save themselves from the sentence of death for transgressing God's law. "All have sinned and fall short of the glory of God" (Romans 3:23). Yet many religions teach that humans can atone for their mistakes through contrition and good works. This is a fallacy. "Let no one take the limited narrow position that any of the works of man can help in the least possible way to liquidate the debt of his transgression. This is a fatal deception."[1]

"The grace of Christ is freely to justify the sinner without merit or claim on his part. Justification is a full, complete pardon of sin. The moment a sinner accepts Christ by faith, that moment he is pardoned. The righteousness of Christ is imputed to him, and he is no more to doubt God's forgiving grace.

"There is nothing in faith that makes it our saviour. Faith cannot remove our guilt. Christ is the power of God unto salvation to all them that believe. The justification comes through the merits of Jesus Christ. He has paid the price for the sinner's redemption. Yet it is only through faith in His blood that Jesus can justify the believer.

"The sinner cannot depend upon his own good works as a means of justification."[2]

"If we were defective in character, we could not pass the gates that mercy has opened to the obedient; for justice stands at the entrance and demands holiness, purity, in all who would see God.

"Were justice extinct, and were it possible for divine mercy to open the gates to the whole race, irrespective of character, there would be a worse condition of disaffection and rebellion in heaven than before Satan was expelled. The peace, happiness, and harmony of heaven would be broken up. The change from earth to heaven will not change men's characters; the happiness of the redeemed in heaven results from the characters formed in this life, after the image of Christ. The saints in heaven will first have been saints on earth."[3]

"The salvation that Christ made such a sacrifice to gain for man is that which is alone of value, that which saves from sin."[4]

---

1. Ellen G. White, MS 50, 1900.
2. Ellen G. White, "Faith and Good Works," *Signs of the Times*, May 19, 1898.
3. Ellen G. White, Letter 1f, 1890.
4. White, Letter 1f.

Part 10: Sanctified by the Holy Spirit

Through the washing of regeneration and renewing of the Holy Spirit,
whom He poured out on us abundantly through Jesus Christ our Savior.

—Titus 3:5, 6

A s the penitent sinner, contrite before God, discerns Christ's atonement in his behalf, and accepts this atonement as his only hope in this life and the future life, his sins are pardoned. This is justification by faith. Every believing soul is to conform his will entirely to God's will, and keep in a state of repentance and contrition, exercising faith in the atoning merits of the Redeemer, and advancing from strength to strength, from glory to glory.

"Pardon and justification are one and the same thing."[1]

"Justification by faith in Christ will be made manifest in transformation of character. This is the sign to the world of the truth of the doctrines we profess. The daily evidence that we are a living church is seen in the fact that we are practicing the word. A living testimony goes forth to the world in consistent Christian action."[2] "Because the Holy Spirit does not operate without man's consent, spiritual progress depends upon the Christian's daily commitment to God's way of life. Thus, the process of sanctification calls for a partnership between God and man. After man chooses God's way, the Holy Spirit energizes his weakened will, so that he is empowered to do God's will."[3]

"God requires at this time just what He required of the holy pair in Eden, perfect obedience to his requirements. His law remains the same in all ages. The great standard of righteousness presented in the Old Testament is not lowered in the New. It is not the work of the gospel to weaken the claims of God's holy law, but to bring men up where they can keep its precepts.

"The faith in Christ which saves the soul is not what it is represented to be by many. 'Believe, believe,' is their cry; 'only believe in Christ, and you will be saved. It is all you have to do.' While true faith trusts wholly in Christ for salvation, it will lead to perfect conformity to the law of God. Faith is manifested by works. And the apostle John declares, 'He that saith, I know him, and keepeth not his commandments, is a liar.' "[4] "The Father gave us the law, and the Son died to magnify it and make it honorable."[5]

"The enemy has ever labored to disconnect the law and the gospel. They go hand in hand."[6]

---

1. Ellen G. White, MS 21, 1891.
2. Ellen G. White, Letter 83, 1896.
3. Francis D. Nichol, ed., *The Seventh-day Adventist Bible Commentary*, vol. 7 (Washington, DC: Review and Herald®, 1957), 370.
4. Ellen G. White, "The Conference in Sweden," *Advent Review and Sabbath Herald*, October 5, 1886, 2.
5. Ellen G. White, MS 5, 1885.
6. Ellen G. White, MS 11, 1893.

Part 11: Heirs of the Kingdom

That having been justified by His grace we should
become heirs according to the hope of eternal life.

—Titus 3:7

Is the sinner who commits sin every day with impunity, regarded of God with the same favor as the one who through faith in Christ tries to work in his integrity? The Scripture answers, 'We are his workmanship, created in Christ Jesus unto good works, which God hath before ordained that we should walk in them' [Ephesians 2:10]. In His divine arrangement, through His unmerited favor, the Lord has ordained that good works shall be rewarded. We are accepted through Christ's merit alone; and the acts of mercy, the deeds of charity, which we perform, are the fruits of faith; and they become a blessing to us; for men are to be rewarded according to their works. . . . Our works in and of themselves have no merit. When we have done all that it is possible for us to do, we are to count ourselves as unprofitable servants. We deserve no thanks from God. We have only done what it was our duty to do, and our works could not have been performed in the strength of our own sinful natures."[1]

Yet "the atonement that has been made for us by Christ is wholly and abundantly satisfactory to the Father. God can be just, and yet the justifier of those who believe."[2] "As the bow in the cloud is formed by the union of the sunlight and the shower, so the rainbow encircling the throne represents the combined power of mercy and justice. It is not justice alone that is to be maintained; for this would eclipse the glory of the rainbow of promise above the throne; man could see only the penalty of the law. Were there no justice, no penalty, there would be no stability to the government of God. It is the mingling of judgment and mercy that makes salvation full and complete. It is the blending of the two that leads us, as we view the world's Redeemer and the law of Jehovah, to exclaim, 'Thy gentleness hath made me great.'

"We know that the gospel is a perfect and complete system, revealing the immutability of the law of God."[3]

"Mercy invites us to enter through the gates into the city of God, and justice is satisfied to accord to every obedient soul full privileges as a member of the royal family, a child of the heavenly King."[4]

---

1. Ellen G. White, "The Grace of God Manifested in Good Works," *Advent Review and Sabbath Herald*, January 29, 1895, 1.
2. Ellen G. White, MS 28, 1905.
3. Ellen G. White, Letter 1f, 1890.
4. White, Letter 1f, 1890.

Part 12: Perverted Bible Study

But avoid foolish disputes, genealogies, contentions,
and strivings about the law; for they are unprofitable and useless.

—Titus 3:9

The 'vain talkers and deceivers' ([Titus] 1:10) who had endeavored to lead astray the Cretan church designed their teachings to favor the natural impulses of the church members, with a view to monetary advantage. . . . Paul, however, was interested solely in their character transformation. . . . Paul's gospel disturbed the Cretans, as it did others elsewhere, but it was this very disturbance that led men to examine themselves and to appropriate the cleansing mercy and restoring grace of God."[1]

"Because of his early training in the fanciful reasonings of Jewish lore, Paul resisted any tendency toward similar developments within the Christian church. The apostle had seen the effect on Judaism of the malignant growth of senseless and perverted teachings. He purposed that Christianity should not be so afflicted."[2] There were those on Crete who enjoyed speculating in areas where a clear "thus saith the Lord" did not exist. They "sought to pervert Bible study into a discussion of strange and bizarre topics. Such theoretical speculations led to no character improvement, nor were they conducive to Christian fellowship."[3] Paul gave Timothy a similar warning against perverted Bible study. In 1 Timothy 1:4, he made "reference to a Jewish practice in which an attempt was made to trace family ancestries back to a Davidic or priestly heritage. Much of Jewish teaching and preaching was based on finely spun allegories that pleased the fancies of the people without feeding their souls."[4]

There are four "approved" ways, found in 2 Timothy 3:16, to use the Bible: (1) For doctrine or teaching. "The Bible alone is man's textbook of salvation."[5] (2) For reproof or censure. It refutes false teachings. (3) For correction or improvement. "Ever since its first page was written, the Bible has manifested its re-creative, transforming power in the lives of men."[6] (4) For instruction or training.

"The Christian finds in the Scriptures those principles that will help him to grow up to the 'perfect man, unto the measure of the stature of the fulness of Christ' (Eph. 4:13). This process of growing up to be like Christ is known as sanctification, a training that continues throughout life."[7]

---

1. Francis D. Nichol, ed., *The Seventh-day Adventist Bible Commentary*, vol. 7 (Washington, DC: Review and Herald®, 1957), 371.
2. Nichol, *Seventh-day Adventist Bible Commentary*, vol. 7, 371.
3. Nichol, *Seventh-day Adventist Bible Commentary*, vol. 7, 371.
4. Nichol, *Seventh-day Adventist Bible Commentary*, vol. 7, 288.
5. Nichol, *Seventh-day Adventist Bible Commentary*, vol. 7, 345.
6. Nichol, *Seventh-day Adventist Bible Commentary*, vol. 7, 345.
7. Nichol, *Seventh-day Adventist Bible Commentary*, vol. 7, 345.

Part 13: Gospel Workers

*When I send Artemas to you, or Tychicus, be diligent to come to
me at Nicopolis, for I have decided to spend the winter there. Send Zenas
the lawyer and Apollos on their journey with haste, that they may lack nothing.*
—Titus 3:12, 13

Paul closed his letter to Titus, urging him to come to Nicopolis when he could find a replacement for him on Crete. That replacement was to be either Artemas or Tychicus. Artemas we have met before. Tychicus was "a Christian, probably Gentile, who, with Trophimus, represented the church of Asia when a gift was presented to the Jerusalem church (Acts 20:4). He was with Paul in Rome during the apostle's 1st imprisonment and was the bearer of Paul's letters to the Colossians and Ephesians (Col 4:7; Eph 6:21), who were told that Tychicus could give them additional information concerning Paul's condition. It was probably he whom Paul sent to Crete ([Titus] 3:12). Later he was sent to Ephesus (2 [Timothy] 4:12). Paul characterized him as a beloved brother and faithful minister in the Lord (Col 4:7)."[1]

"The Nicopolis of the [New Testament] is probably the city in Epirus, near Actium . . . , which Augustus founded in commemoration of his victory over Antony at Actium in 31 B.C. Under the patronage of the emperor it became a magnificent cultural center with many beautiful buildings, some of them built by Herod the Great. . . . Athletic games held every 4 years in honor of the Actian Apollo ranked with the other 4 athletic festivals of Greece. . . . Paul . . . planned to spend the winter at Nicopolis, and requested his younger fellow worker to come there to meet him. Paul apparently considered Nicopolis a good center from which to evangelize western Greece. It is generally believed that the pastoral epistles, to which the letter to Titus belongs, were written after Paul's 1st Roman imprisonment; hence his stay at Nicopolis must be placed in one of the winters between A.D. 63 and 66, the probable year of his last arrest."[2]

"According to Clement of Rome, perhaps the friend to whom Paul referred in Phil. 4:3, Paul preached in both East and West. . . . Clement states that Paul went to the 'limits' of the West, which probably meant Spain. If this visit was made, it was in keeping with the intention he had earlier expressed to the Romans (Rom. 15:28). . . . The pastoral epistles suggest that he went also to Crete, Ephesus, and to Nicopolis and Troas in Macedonia."[3]

Paul made good use of the limited "free" time he was given.

---

1. Siegfried H. Horn, *Seventh-day Adventist Bible Dictionary*, ed. Don F. Neufeld, Commentary Reference Series, vol. 8 (Washington, DC: Review and Herald®, 1960), s.v. "Tychicus."
2. Horn, *Seventh-day Adventist Bible Dictionary*, s.v. "Nicopolis."
3. Francis D. Nichol, ed., *The Seventh-day Adventist Bible Commentary*, vol. 6 (Washington, DC: Review and Herald®, 1957), 30.

The Final Arrest

Blessed are you when they revile and persecute you,
and say all kinds of evil against you falsely for My sake.

—Matthew 5:11

Paul was granted a brief reprieve from the terrible persecution that broke out in Rome following his departure. "This last precious interval of freedom was earnestly improved in laboring among the churches. He sought to establish a firmer union between the Greek and Eastern churches which he had raised up, and to guard them against the subtle heresies that were creeping in to corrupt the faith. The trials and anxieties which he had endured, had preyed upon his physical and mental energies. The infirmities of age were upon him. He felt that his work was nearly accomplished.

"At Jerusalem and at Antioch he had defended Christianity against the narrow restrictions of Judaism. He had preached the gospel to the pagans of Lycaonia, to the fanatics of Galatia, to the colonists of Macedonia, to the frivolous art-worshipers of Athens, to the pleasure-loving merchants of Corinth, to the half-barbarous nations of Dalmatia, to the islanders of Crete, and to slaves, soldiers, and men of rank and station, in the multitudes at Rome. Now he was doing his last work."[1]

"Though Paul's labors were chiefly among the churches, he could not escape the observation of his enemies. Since Nero's persecution, Christians were everywhere the objects of hatred and suspicion. Any evil-disposed person could easily secure the arrest and imprisonment of one of the proscribed sect. And now the Jews conceived the idea of seeking to fasten upon Paul the crime of instigating the burning of Rome. Not one of them for a moment believed him guilty; but they knew that such a charge, made with the faintest show of plausibility, would seal his doom. An opportunity soon offered to execute their plans. At the house of a disciple in the city of Troas, Paul was again seized, and from this place he was hurried away to his final imprisonment.

"The arrest was effected by the efforts of Alexander the coppersmith, who had so unsuccessfully opposed the apostle's work at Ephesus, and who now seized the opportunity to be revenged on one whom he could not defeat."[2]

Paul's trials would soon end.

---

1. Ellen G. White, *Sketches From the Life of Paul* (Washington, DC: Review and Herald®, 1974), 304.
2. White, *Sketches From the Life of Paul*, 304, 305.

Back in Rome

Beloved, do not avenge yourselves, but rather give place to wrath; for it is written, "Vengeance is Mine, I will repay," [Deuteronomy 32:35] says the Lord.

—Romans 12:19

No warm-hearted disciples now met Paul and his companions at Appii Forum and Three Taverns as before, when he was constrained to thank God and take courage. There was now no one like the courteous and kindly Julius, to say a word in his favor, no statement from Festus or Agrippa to attest his innocence."[1] Nero was persecuting Roman Christians. He cleverly placed blame on Christians as those who set the devastating fire that had recently burned large portions of Rome. To visit Paul now "was to visit one who was the object of universal hatred, who was accused of instigating the basest and most terrible crime against the city and the nation. Whoever ventured to show him the slightest attention, thereby made himself the object of suspicion, and endangered his own life. Rome was now filled with spies, who stood ready to bring an accusation against any one on the slightest occasion. None but a Christian would visit a Christian; for no other would incur the odium of a faith which even intelligent men regarded as not merely contemptible, but treasonable."[2]

"The prospect before him was far less favorable than at the time of his former imprisonment. The persecution under Nero had greatly lessened the number of Christians in Rome. Thousands had been martyred for their faith, many had left the city, and those who remained were greatly depressed and intimidated. At Paul's first arrival, the Jews of Rome had been willing to listen to his arguments; but through the influence of emissaries from Jerusalem, and also because of the received charges against Christians, they had become his bitter enemies.

"...The change which had taken place in the city and its inhabitants—the city still scarred and blackened from the terrible conflagration, and the people, by tens of thousands, reduced to the most squalid poverty—seemed to harmonize with the change in his own condition and prospects."[3]

"Through the surging crowds that still thronged the streets of Rome, and that looked upon him and his fellow-Christians as the authors of all their misery, Paul passed, not now to his own hired house, but to a gloomy dungeon, there to remain, chained night and day, until he should finish his course."[4]

1. Ellen G. White, *Sketches From the Life of Paul* (Washington, DC: Review and Herald®, 1974), 307.
2. White, *Sketches From the Life of Paul*, 307, 308.
3. White, *Sketches From the Life of Paul*, 306, 307.
4. White, *Sketches From the Life of Paul*, 307.

Paul Before Nero

Therefore whoever resists the authority resists the ordinance of God,
and those who resist will bring judgment on themselves.

—Romans 13:2

I t was the practice among the Greeks and Romans to allow an accused person an advocate to present his case in a court of justice, and to plead in his behalf. . . . But no man ventured to act as Paul's counsel or advocate; no friend was at hand, even to preserve a record of the charges brought against him by his accusers, or of the arguments which he urged in his own defense. Among the Christians at Rome, there was not one who came forward to stand by him in that trying hour."[1] "Paul and Nero face to face!—the youthful monarch bearing upon his sin-stamped countenance the shameful record of the passions that reigned within; the aged prisoner's calm and benignant face telling of a heart at peace with God and man. The results of opposite systems of training and education stood that day contrasted,—the life of unbounded self-indulgence and the life of utter self-sacrifice."[2]

"The vast hall which was the place of trial was thronged by an eager, restless crowd that surged and pressed to the front to see and hear all that should take place. . . .

"Again the Jews urged against the prisoner the old charges of sedition and heresy, while both Jews and Romans accuse him of instigating the burning of the city. While his enemies were vehemently urging their accusations, Paul preserved a quiet dignity; no shade of fear or anger disturbed the peaceful serenity that rested upon his countenance. The people and even the judges beheld him with surprise. They had been present at many trials, and had looked upon many a criminal; but never had they seen a man wear such a look of holy calmness as did the prisoner before them. The keen eyes of the judges, accustomed as they were to read the countenances of their prisoners, searched the face of Paul for some hidden trace of crime, but in vain. When he was permitted to speak in his own behalf, all listened with eager interest to his words."[3]

If you have been a student of Scripture, God will bring to your mind the words to speak in defense of the gospel. Seek to be found in favor with both God and man (see Luke 2:52).

---

1. Ellen G. White, *Sketches From the Life of Paul* (Washington, DC: Review and Herald®, 1974), 310.
2. White, *Sketches From the Life of Paul,* 312.
3. White, *Sketches From the Life of Paul,* 313.

Like a Shout of Victory

Also I say to you, whoever confesses Me before men,
him the Son of Man also will confess before the angels of God.

—Luke 12:8

On the day of his trial, Paul stands not as an accomplished lawyer but as an envoy for Christ. "Once more Paul had an opportunity to raise aloft before a wondering multitude the banner of the cross of Christ. With more than human eloquence and power, he that day urged home upon their hearts the truths of the gospel. . . .

"As Paul gazed upon the throng before him,—Jews, Greeks, Romans, with strangers from many lands,—his soul was stirred with an intense desire for their salvation. He lost sight of the occasion, of the perils which surrounded him, of the terrible fate which seemed so near. He looked above all this, to Jesus, the Divine Intercessor, the Advocate pleading before the throne of God in behalf of sinful men. Earnestly he pointed his hearers to the great Sacrifice made in behalf of the fallen race, and presented before them man in his true dignity and value. An infinite price had been paid for man's redemption; provision had been made that he might be exalted to share the throne of God and to become the heir of immortal riches. . . .

". . . There is no trace of fear, sadness, or discouragement in countenance or manner. . . . His words are like a shout of victory above the roar of battle. The cause of truth to which he has devoted his life, he makes appear as the only cause that can never fail. Though he may perish for the truth's sake, the gospel will not perish. God lives, and the truth will triumph.

"His countenance glows with the light of Heaven, as though reflecting the rays of the sun. Many who looked upon him in that hall of judgment 'saw his face as it had been the face of an angel.' Tears dimmed many eyes that had never before been seen to weep. The gospel message found its way to the minds and hearts of many who would never have listened to it but for the imprisonment of Paul."[1]

The outcome of Paul's trial had never been in doubt. "From the judgment-hall of Caesar, Paul returned to his prison-house, knowing that he had gained for himself only a brief respite; his enemies would not rest until they had secured his death.[2]

Yet he knew that truth had triumphed for the time, and that to have proclaimed a crucified and risen Saviour before the vast throng who had listened to his words, was in itself a victory."[3]

---

1. Ellen G. White, *Sketches From the Life of Paul* (Washington, DC: Review and Herald®, 1974), 313–315.
2. White, *Sketches From the Life of Paul*, 318, 319
3. White, *Sketches From the Life of Paul*, 319.

Part 1: My Son

Paul, an apostle of Jesus Christ by the will of God,
according to the promise of life which is in Christ Jesus,
To Timothy, a beloved son:
Grace, mercy, and peace from God the Father and Christ Jesus our Lord.

—2 Timothy 1:1, 2

The apostle's speech had gained him many friends, and he was visited by some persons of rank, who accounted his blessing of greater value than the favor of the emperor of the world. But there was one friend for whose sympathy and companionship he longed in those trying days. That friend was Timothy, to whom he had committed the care of the church at Ephesus, and who had therefore been left behind when he made his last voyage to Rome. The affection between this youthful laborer and the apostle began with Timothy's conversion through the labors of Paul; and the tie had strengthened as they had shared together the hopes and perils and toils of missionary life, until they seemed to be as one. The disparity in their age and the difference in their character made their interest and love for each other more earnest and sacred. The ardent, zealous, indomitable spirit of Paul found repose and comfort in the mild, yielding, retiring character of Timothy. . . .

"And now, sitting day after day in his gloomy cell, knowing that at a word or nod from the tyrant Nero his life may be sacrificed, Paul thinks of Timothy, and determines to send for him. Under the most favorable circumstances, several months must elapse before Timothy can reach Rome from Asia Minor. Paul knows that his own life, for even a single day, is uncertain, and he fears that Timothy may arrive too late, or may hesitate through fear of the dangers to be encountered. He has important counsel and instruction for the young man to whom so great responsibility is intrusted, and while urging him to come without delay, he dictates the dying testimony which he may not be spared to utter."[1] Paul looked upon Timothy as his own beloved son. He had seen Timothy grow up and mature as a Christian. Now he wanted to leave him with his last words of advice. What would you have told Timothy? Paul told him, Preach the Word! Tell others about Jesus Christ. That is the most important thing one can do here on earth.

"As a 'herald' for God the minister must preach nothing but the Word, otherwise he is an impostor."[2]

---

1. Ellen G. White, *Sketches From the Life of Paul* (Washington, DC: Review and Herald®, 1974), 319, 320.
2. Francis D. Nichol, ed., *The Seventh-day Adventist Bible Commentary*, vol. 7 (Washington, DC: Review and Herald®, 1957), 347.

Part 2: Do Not Be Ashamed

For this reason I also suffer these things; nevertheless I am not ashamed, for I know whom I have believed and am persuaded that He is able to keep what I have committed to Him until that Day.
—2 Timothy 1:12

Paul stood indicted by the highest Roman court for crimes against the empire. Yet he was not ashamed. "Even though Paul faced the disgrace of execution as a criminal, and the sneers of an empire, his confidence in the message he preached buoyed up his spirit and strengthened his courage. This same kind of nobility steeled the hearts of the Hebrew worthies when they faced the fury of Babylon's king (see Dan. 3:16–18); Christ also gave the universe an example of unashamed confidence in the overruling providence of the Father when He faced the disgrace of the cross. . . .

". . .[Paul was] convinced of Christ's personal concern for his welfare, and his gratitude for this is revealed in his unashamed witness."[1]

Paul had walked with Jesus since he met Him on the road to Damascus. His Christian experience was one of faith and trust. He did not have to develop confidence in his Savior this late in life. He trusted Jesus with his life and future. There are two schools of thought among commentators as to what Paul is telling Timothy here. "The first view considers Paul's personal salvation, his character, his future, to be the deposit that Christ will faithfully keep until the day of resurrection, when life is restored to the sleeping saints. Even though death hides men from earthly view, Christ has marked the graves of all who will one day receive the gift of eternal life.

"Those who set forth the second view find difficulty in thinking that Paul would use the same words found in 1 Tim. 6:20 and 2 Tim. 1:14, but in a different sense. In these passages the meaning clearly denotes the deposit entrusted to Timothy as a Christian minister. These commentators contend that Paul here shares with Timothy the confidence that even though he himself would soon die, the gospel would not perish."[2]

"Christ is able to guard the Christian witness until the task is done. Other men, like Timothy, will be entrusted with the same commission that was given to Paul."[3]

1. Francis D. Nichol, ed., *The Seventh-day Adventist Bible Commentary*, vol. 7 (Washington, DC: Review and Herald®, 1957), 330.
2. Nichol, *Seventh-day Adventist Bible Commentary*, vol. 7, 331.
3. Nichol, *Seventh-day Adventist Bible Commentary*, vol. 7, 331.

Part 3: Onesiphorus

*The Lord grant mercy to the household of Onesiphorus, for he often refreshed me,
and was not ashamed of my chain; but when he arrived in Rome,
he sought me out very zealously and found me.*

—2 Timothy 1:16, 17

An unexpected encouragement was granted the apostle at this time, by the visit of Onesiphorus, an Ephesian Christian who came to Rome not long after Paul's arrival. He knew that Paul was somewhere in that city as a prisoner, and he determined to find him. This was no easy matter in a city crowded with prisoners, where suspicion was everywhere, and had only to fasten upon an unfortunate victim to consign him to prison and perhaps to death. But notwithstanding the difficulties, Onesiphorus searched for Paul until he found him. Not satisfied with one visit, he went again and again to his dungeon, and did all in his power to lighten the burden of his imprisonment. The fear of scorn, reproach, or persecution, was powerless to terrify this true-hearted Ephesian, when he knew that his beloved teacher was in bonds for the truth's sake, while he himself, in every respect far less worthy, walked free.

"The visit of Onesiphorus, testifying to his loving fidelity at a time of loneliness and desertion, was a bright spot in Paul's prison experience. . . .

"The desire for love and sympathy was implanted in the heart by God himself. Christ in his hour of agony in Gethsemane, while bearing the guilt of sinful men, longed for the sympathy of his disciples. And Paul, though almost indifferent to hardship and suffering, yearned for sympathy and companionship. God would have his people cherish love and sympathy for one another. . . . The sons and daughters of God will be tenderhearted, pitiful, courteous, to all men, 'especially unto them who are of the household of faith.' But Paul was bound to his fellow-disciples by a stronger tie than even that of Christian brotherhood."[1]

"The Lord had revealed himself to Paul in a special manner, and had made him instrumental in the salvation of many souls. Many churches might in truth regard him as their father in the gospel. Such a man, who had sacrificed every earthly consideration in the service of God, had a special claim upon the love and sympathy of his converts and fellow-laborers."[2]

1. Ellen G. White, *Sketches From the Life of Paul* (Washington, DC: Review and Herald®, 1974), 308–310.
2. White, *Sketches From the Life of Paul*, 310.

Part 4: Teach Faithfully

And the things that you have heard from me among many witnesses,
commit these to faithful men who will be able to teach others also.
—2 Timothy 2:2

This letter was written to Timotheus, the first bishop of the church at Ephesus, after Paul had been brought before Nero the second time to witness with his life to the faith he held. In placing on record this account of his trials through men who turned from the faith, Paul speaks words which should encourage our hearts as we pass over the same ground."[1] "The affection between Paul and Timothy began with Timothy's conversion; and the tie had strengthened as they had shared in the hopes, the perils, and the toils of missionary life, till they seemed to be as one. The disparity in their age and the difference in their character made their love for each other more earnest. The ardent, zealous, indomitable spirit of Paul found repose and comfort in the mild, yielding, retiring disposition of Timothy. The faithful ministration and tender love of this tried companion had brightened many a dark hour in the apostle's life. All that Melanchthon was to Luther, all that a son could be to a loved and honored father, the youthful Timothy was to the tried and lonely Paul."[2] Paul's concern now was that the gospel should be handed down to faithful stewards who would continue the work he had started.

We have a responsibility to faithfully pass the truth of the gospel to the next generation. Repeatedly we see examples of gospel mentoring taking place in the history of the early church. Had Barnabas not mentored Paul (Acts 4:36, 37; 9:26–30; 11:22–30), we might not be reading this devotional. Barnabas also worked with his nephew, the young and frightened John Mark, building his confidence so that later Paul could say John Mark was "useful to me for ministry" (2 Timothy 4:11). Priscilla and Aquila took Apollos under their wing and coached him, expanding his gospel understanding (Acts 18:1–3, 24–28). Paul edified Timothy, putting finishing touches on the firm biblical foundation already laid by his faithful mother, *Eunice*, and grandmother, *Lois* (2 Timothy 1:5).

Being a gospel teacher is equally as important as being a gospel herald (minister) or apostle (missionary).

---

1. Ellen G. White, "A Message to the Churches," *Advent Review and Sabbath Herald*, July 18, 1907, 9.
2. Ellen G. White, "A Faithful Witness," *Youth's Instructor*, July 10, 1902, 1.

Part 5a: The Ideal Minister

You therefore must endure hardship as a good soldier of Jesus Christ.

—2 Timothy 2:3

Paul certainly had the opportunity to observe Roman soldiers up close and personally! "All the devotion and loyalty and physical stamina of a real soldier are prerequisite to genuine Christian leadership."[1] Paul has already written Timothy telling him they are involved in a warfare for good against evil. "This charge I commit to you, son Timothy, according to the prophecies previously made concerning you, that by them you may wage the good warfare, having faith and a good conscience" (1 Timothy 1:18, 19).

"Timothy's endeavor, both to provide strong leadership as Paul's representative, and to campaign against sin, may be likened to a warfare of righteousness against evil."[2] One cannot help thinking back to the letter Paul wrote the Ephesians in which he described the Christian life in terms of a battle against strong foes. "Finally, my brethren, be strong in the Lord and in the power of His might. Put on the whole armor of God, that you may be able to stand against the wiles of the devil. For we do not wrestle against flesh and blood, but against principalities, against powers, against the rulers of the darkness of this age, against spiritual hosts of wickedness in the heavenly places. Therefore take up the whole armor of God, that you may be able to withstand in the evil day, and having done all, to stand" (Ephesians 6:10–13). "If we have on the heavenly armor, we shall find that the assaults of the enemy will not have power over us. Angels of God will be round about us to protect us."[3]

"We must put on every piece of the armor, and then stand firm. The Lord has honored us by choosing us as his soldiers. Let us fight bravely for Him, maintaining the right in every transaction. Rectitude in all things is essential to the welfare of the soul. As you strive for victory over your own inclinations, he will help you by his Holy Spirit to be circumspect in every action, that you may give no occasion for the enemy to speak evil of the truth. Put on as your breastplate that divinely protected righteousness which it is the privilege of all to wear. This will protect your spiritual life."[4]

Hardships may come, but all who wear the armor of Christ are promised protection and ultimate victory!

---

1. Francis D. Nichol, ed., *The Seventh-day Adventist Bible Commentary*, vol. 7 (Washington, DC: Review and Herald®, 1957), 334.
2. Nichol, *Seventh-day Adventist Bible Commentary*, vol. 7, 291.
3. Ellen G. White, "The Work for This Time," *Advent Review and Sabbath Herald*, May 25, 1905, 17.
4. Ellen G. White, "Conquering Temptation," *Youth's Instructor*, September 12, 1901, 6.

Part 5b: The Ideal Minister

And also if anyone competes in athletics, he is not crowned unless he competes according to the rules. The hardworking farmer must be first to partake of the crops.

—2 Timothy 2:5, 6

P aul has already compared the ministry to being a soldier. Now he compares it to being an athlete and a farmer. "Any athlete who violates the rules of the contest is disqualified. Again Paul allows Timothy to deduce the intended parallel with the Christian minister. Regardless of the quantity of sermons preached and people visited, if the minister does not teach 'sound words' ([2 Timothy] 1:13) or does not clothe his message with the winsomeness and love of Christ, all his labors will prove to have been in vain."[1] Every Christian is called to be a living example to others of how the gospel changes lives.

In verse 6, Paul "compares the minister with a farmer, as he already has to an athlete (v. 5) and a soldier (vs. 3, 4).

"...The farmer's produce feeds both himself and the rest of the world. If the farmer did not share in his produce, he would die and the rest of his world would go hungry. Hence, the minister must first partake of the Christian graces (... Gal. 5:22, 23) before he is able to share these graces with others. No one can share something he does not have. The world needs both the produce of the farmer and a genuine exhibit of the fruits of Christianity, but if the farmer does not eat the food he produces and the minister does not exhibit the truths he preaches, the world suffers."[2]

Despite the tremendous effort needed to succeed, ministering to others offers great rewards. Each of us is to minister within our own sphere of influence. Remember, "the Christian is a spectacle to the world, to angels, and to men. Singular? Yes; he has a most singular, peculiar character, because his life is worked out after the divine similitude [image]."

"The inhabitants of unfallen worlds and of the heavenly universe are watching with an intense interest the conflict between good and evil. They rejoice as Satan's subtleties one after another are discerned and met with 'It is written,' as Christ met them in His conflict with the wily foe."[3]

"Every victory gained is a gem in the crown of life."[4]

---

1. Francis D. Nichol, ed., *The Seventh-day Adventist Bible Commentary*, vol. 7 (Washington, DC: Review and Herald®, 1957), 334.

2. Nichol, *Seventh-day Adventist Bible Commentary*, vol. 7, 334.

3. Ellen G. White, Letter 5, 1900.

4. White, Letter 5, 1900.

Part 6: An Unashamed Workman

Be diligent to present yourself approved to God, a worker who does not need to be ashamed,
rightly dividing the word of truth.

—2 Timothy 2:15

Since Paul himself was a tentmaker (. . . Acts 18:3), he well knew how important it was for a workman to labor so efficiently that he need not be 'ashamed' of his efforts. . . .

". . . The truths of the Bible must be rightly interpreted so that no part of the Scriptures will be set in opposition to the picture presented by the Bible as a whole. Each passage of Scripture must be given its true meaning even as every brick in the wall of a building must be in its proper place, or the whole wall suffers. In v. 14 Paul warns against 'word battles,' an example of the improper use of Scripture. To cut the Bible straight suggests that every phase of truth must receive its proper emphasis. Irrelevancies and secondary issues are to be subordinated to the principles that actually prepare men to conquer sin and enable them to live triumphantly in Christ."[1]

Paul had concerns that Timothy would need to stand up against false teachers at Ephesus. Hymenaeus and Philetus were again parsing doctrine and words, creating divisions among the faithful. Paul had already put Hymenaeus out of the church once (1 Timothy 1:20). The situation was grave, and Paul was not on site. Paul had this advice: study, Timothy; get it right! "This is a warning appropriate for this time. Then comes a charge which will often need to be given: 'Study to show thyself approved unto God, a workman that needeth not to be ashamed, rightly dividing the word of truth.' Learn to take the truths that have been revealed, and to handle them in such a way that they will be food for the flock of God.

"We shall meet those who allow their minds to wander into idle speculations about things of which nothing is said in the word of God. God has spoken in the plainest language upon every subject that affects the salvation of the soul. But He desires us to avoid all day-dreaming, and He says, Go work to-day in my vineyard. The night cometh wherein no man can work. Cease all idle curiosity; watch, and work, and pray. Study the truths that have been revealed. Christ desires to break up all vacant reveries, and He points us to the fields ripe for the harvest. Unless we work earnestly, eternity will overwhelm us with its burden of responsibility."[2]

Any way Timothy looked at it, he was to use the Bible as his guide and not deviate from its path of righteousness. That is still great advice for each of us today!

---

1. Francis D. Nichol, ed., *The Seventh-day Adventist Bible Commentary*, vol. 7 (Washington, DC: Review and Herald®, 1957), 336, 337.
2. Ellen G. White, "A Warning for This Time," *Advent Review and Sabbath Herald*, February 5, 1901, 1.

Part 7: Gentleness/Meekness

And a servant of the Lord must not quarrel but be gentle to all, able to teach, patient, in humility correcting those who are in opposition.

—2 Timothy 2:24, 25

The essential business of Christianity . . . is character development."[1] "The restoring is to be done, not in a proud, officious, masterly manner, but in the spirit of meekness. Do not cast your brother aside, saying, He has disappointed me, and I shall not try to help him."[2] This is difficult to do when those who oppose you are quarrelsome, combative, and divisive. Remaining meek, patient, and humble when personally wronged is extremely difficult. It is human nature to strike back at those who would do you harm and completely surrender the high ground of principle. "Even the best of men, if left to themselves, will make grave blunders. The more responsibilities placed upon the human agent, the higher his position to dictate and control, the more mischief he is sure to do in perverting minds and hearts if he does not carefully follow the way of the Lord. At Antioch Peter failed in the principles of integrity. Paul had to withstand his subverting influence face to face. This is recorded that others may profit by it, and that the lesson may be a solemn warning to the men in high places, that they may not fail in integrity, but keep close to principle."[3]

Even truth, when delivered in a contentious spirit, can divide. Truth spoken in love has the potential to disarm stubborn antagonists. "The 'servant of the Lord' will teach others as He did. The unenlightened were thus captivated by Christ's willingness to meet the common man on his own ground. Although Jesus spoke with earnestness and authority, He never embarrassed or coerced His listeners. He gently varied His presentations of truth to suit His hearers. The educated and the ignorant alike were drawn by His winsomeness and love, because they felt that Christ identified Himself with their wants and interests."[4]

"A godly example will tell more for the truth than the greatest eloquence unaccompanied by a well-ordered life. Trim the lamp of the soul, and replenish it with the oil of the Spirit. Seek from Christ that grace, that clearness of comprehension, which will enable you to do successful work. Learn from him what it means to labor for those for whom he gave his life."[5]

"The most talented worker can do little unless Christ is formed within, the hope and strength of the life."[6]

---

1. Francis D. Nichol, ed., *The Seventh-day Adventist Bible Commentary*, vol. 7 (Washington, DC: Review and Herald®, 1957), 339.
2. Ellen G. White, MS 117a, 1901.
3. Ellen G. White, MS 122, 1897.
4. Nichol, *Seventh-day Adventist Bible Commentary*, vol. 7, 339.
5. Ellen G. White, "Words to Ministers," *Advent Review and Sabbath Herald*, August 19, 1902, 7.
6. White, "Words to Ministers," 7.

Part 8: Perilous Times Ahead

But know this, that in the last days perilous times will come.

—2 Timothy 3:1

Paul had warned the believers at Thessalonica and Ephesus to expect wolves to come into their churches trying to destroy them from within, thus causing apostasy. Now he writes the same admonishment to Timothy. Jesus knew such attacks would come, and He warned against them (Matthew 7:15) as did John the beloved, who, "in the last moments of the first apostolic century, saw apostasy as a danger current in his day (1 John 4:1), and in the Revelation he relates visions he was given of appalling decay and paganizing of the church (Rev. 2:12–24; 6:3–11; 17; 18)."[1]

"In these days of peril we are not to accept everything that men bring to us as truth. As professed teachers from God come to us declaring that they have a message from God, it is proper to inquire carefully, How do we know that this is truth? Jesus told us that 'false prophets shall arise and shall deceive many.' But we need not be deceived; for the word of God gives us a test whereby we may know what is truth. The prophet says, 'To the law and to the testimony: if they speak not according to this word, it is because there is no light in them.'

"From this statement it is evident that it becomes us to be diligent Bible students, that we may know what is according to the law and the testimony. We are safe in no other course of action. Jesus says, 'Beware of false prophets, which come to you in sheep's clothing, but inwardly they are ravening wolves. Ye shall know them by their fruits.' "[2]

"I would say to our dear brethren who have been so eager to accept everything that came in the form of visions and dreams, Beware that you be not ensnared. Read the warnings that have been given by the world's Redeemer to His disciples, to be given again by them to the world. The Word of God is solid rock, and we may plant our feet securely upon it. Every soul must needs be tested, every faith and doctrine must needs be tried by the law and the testimony."[3]

"Take heed that no man deceive you. The warnings of Christ on this matter are needed at this time; for delusions and deceptions will come in among us and will multiply as we near the end."[4]

1. Francis D. Nichol, ed., *The Seventh-day Adventist Bible Commentary*, vol. 6 (Washington, DC: Review and Herald®, 1957), 393.
2. Ellen G. White, "Sanctify Them Through Thy Truth," *Advent Review and Sabbath Herald*, February 23, 1892, 1.
3. Ellen G. White, Letter 27, 1894.
4. White, Letter 27, 1894.

Part 9a: The Unconverted

For men will be lovers of themselves, lovers of money, boasters, proud,
blasphemers, disobedient to parents, unthankful, unholy, unloving, unforgiving,
slanderers, without self-control, brutal, despisers of good.

—2 Timothy 3:2, 3

Ever since the entrance of sin the evils enumerated in 2 Tim. 3:1–5 have been rampant in the world. Thus it was in the days of Noah (see Gen. 6:5, 11) and in New Testament days . . . , and thus it will continue to be to the very close of time. Elsewhere Paul speaks of 'this present evil world,' and John declares that 'the whole world lieth in wickedness' (1 John 5:19). Thus, the presence of evil is not a unique characteristic of 'the last days.' Nevertheless, the progressive moral depravity of the human race testifies to the utter inability of man to save himself. But with the increasing activity of the prince of evil (cf. Rev. 7:1; 12:12), it is to be expected that the agelong course of evil will reach a climax of intensity in 'the last days.' In contradiction to the bland assertions of a myriad of misguided religionists who teach that man is getting better and better and that eventually the entire world will be converted, the Scriptures declare that evil men will 'wax worse and worse' (2 Tim. 3:13). It is in this setting that the words of the apostle concerning 'the last days' take on their full and complete meaning."[1]

This list is most closely related to the one Paul offered the Christians in Rome (Romans 1:29–31). Eighteen self-centered traits are here condemned. The false teachers were putting on a pious front, but they were not fooling Paul. Their external show of godliness did not hide their agenda for selfishness. Isaiah summed up these men very neatly:

"Inasmuch as these people draw near with their mouths
And honor Me with their lips,
But have removed their hearts far from Me,
And their fear toward Me is taught by the commandment of men"
(Isaiah 29:13).

Here, unfortunately, is an accurate depiction of many twenty-first-century lives. These selfish individuals are bent on personal gain at all costs. They "are ruled by personal impulses and not by principle. The selfish person wants his impulses satisfied when and how he chooses."[2]

We are warned to shun individuals who say they are Christians, but their lives contradict that fact!

---

1. Francis D. Nichol, ed., *The Seventh-day Adventist Bible Commentary*, vol. 7 (Washington, DC: Review and Herald®, 1957), 341.
2. Nichol, *Seventh-day Adventist Bible Commentary*, vol. 7, 342.

Part 9b: The Unconverted

[For men will be] traitors, headstrong, haughty, lovers of pleasure rather than lovers of God, having a form of godliness but denying its power. And from such people turn away!
                                                   —2 Timothy 3:4, 5

Paul's list of attributes of those who are enemies of the truth continues in verses 4 and 5 of 2 Timothy 3. Of particular interest is Paul's warning against those who have a "form of godliness" but deny the power it brings. These "would-be Christians" exhibit "external characteristics of religion, such as church attendance, church gifts, and even personal service for the church [yet cherish the sinful tendencies Paul mentions in these verses]. . . .

". . . Paul counsels Timothy and all future leaders to be alert to the dangers confronting the church. Besides a personal vigilance lest he succumb to the evil practices here described (vs. 2–5), Timothy was to point out publicly these insidious tendencies and practices, which were curtailing the influence of Christianity. Through the years the behavior of nominal church members, that is, those who profess loyalty to God's way of life and yet reveal no tangible evidence of a development in Christlikeness, has been a greater handicap to the progress of the gospel than any other factor."[1]

"If religious teaching does not produce godly lives, it stands self-condemned. The worth of all spiritual instruction is measured by the degree of spiritual health enjoyed by its adherents."[2] Christ's parable of the wheat and tares (Matthew 13:24–30) tells us that not everyone in the church is what they appear to be. The wheat and tares will grow together within the church until the final harvest. Many know they are living a sham Christian life, while others smugly think themselves on the high road to heaven and needing no help.

"Many who think themselves Christians will at last be found wanting. Many will be in heaven who their neighbors supposed would never enter there. Man judges from appearance, but God judges the heart."[3]

"Christ Himself will decide who are worthy to dwell with the family of heaven. He will judge every man according to his words and his works. Profession is as nothing in the scale. It is character that decides destiny."[4]

1. Francis D. Nichol, ed., *The Seventh-day Adventist Bible Commentary*, vol. 7 (Washington, DC: Review and Herald®, 1957), 342.
2. Nichol, *Seventh-day Adventist Bible Commentary*, vol. 7, 316.
3. Ellen G. White, *Christ's Object Lessons* (Washington, DC: Review and Herald®, 1941), 72.
4. White, *Christ's Object Lessons*, 74.

Part 10: You Know Me!

*But you have carefully followed my doctrine, manner of life, purpose, faith, longsuffering, love,
perseverance, persecutions, afflictions, which happened to me at Antioch, at Iconium, at Lystra—
what persecutions I endured. And out of them all the Lord delivered me.*
—2 Timothy 3:10, 11

The Greek emphasizes Timothy's special acquaintance with Paul's life, which stands in striking contrast with the behavior pattern of the pseudo teachers described in [2 Timothy 3:]2–9. If there were any inconsistencies in Paul's life, any hidden deeds that betrayed his sincerity and integrity, Timothy would surely be aware of them. Paul's life would ever be a challenge and a guide for Timothy to emulate in the difficult days after Paul's leadership ended."[1]

"Personal confidence in the love and daily guidance of God provided Paul with perspective amid the oppressive problems that surrounded him."[2]

"Paul's aim after his conversion had always been the glorification of Christ, in order that all men might be drawn to Him. This purpose controlled his teaching and conduct."[3]

And what problems those had been! Paul mentions just three of the many tribulations he confronted in his ministry for Christ. Timothy would have been well acquainted with these because they occurred in the district near where he grew up. In Antioch, the Jews had "stirred up the devout and prominent women and the chief men of the city, raised up persecution against Paul and Barnabas, and expelled them from their region" (Acts 13:50).

At Iconium, "the multitude of the city was divided: part sided with the Jews, and part with the apostles. And when a violent attempt was made by both the Gentiles and Jews, with their rulers, to abuse and stone them, they became aware of it and fled to Lystra and Derbe" (Acts 14:4–6). At Lystra, the apostles refused the worship of the pagans after healing the crippled man. "Then Jews from Antioch and Iconium came there; and having persuaded the multitudes, they stoned Paul and dragged him out of the city, supposing him to be dead" (verse 19). "Such a witness to God's personal care would be a great source of encouragement to Timothy when the same persecutions and sufferings would sweep over his life."[4]

Strengthen each other by sharing stories of God's providence.

---

1. Francis D. Nichol, ed., *The Seventh-day Adventist Bible Commentary*, vol. 7 (Washington, DC: Review and Herald®, 1957), 343.
2. Nichol, *Seventh-day Adventist Bible Commentary*, vol. 7, 343.
3. Nichol, *Seventh-day Adventist Bible Commentary*, vol. 7, 343.
4. Nichol, *Seventh-day Adventist Bible Commentary*, vol. 7, 343.

Part 11: Persecution Will Come

Yes, and all who desire to live godly in Christ Jesus will suffer persecution.
                                                              —2 Timothy 3:12

Not only the ministers of the church, but all who dedicate themselves to follow Christ's way of life, must expect to be misunderstood, maligned, and subjected to suffering of every kind."[1] "As with Job, God permits Satan to test the character of His faithful ones. God knew Job's endurance, and ever since then those who suffer have been strengthened by his example of steadfastness under a 'fiery trial.' Life's sufferings are not sent by God but by Satan. However, God overrules by making them the means of developing character in His children."[2]

"God did not spare Paul from the trials of life, neither did He spare Jesus. But God helps us to endure such trials. The stones of life become pillows. The tried saints are able, like Christ, to see 'the joy' that is set before them (cf. Heb. 12:2), thus witnessing to the keeping power of the grace of God amid adverse circumstances."[3] "In the face of unparalleled persecution (2 Cor. 4:8–12; 11:23–28) Paul could say, 'For our light affliction, which is but for a moment, worketh for us a far more exceeding and eternal weight of glory' (2 Cor. 4:17). Fearful that afflictions would overwhelm the infant church at Thessalonica, Paul wrote to the believers, 'That no man should be moved by these afflictions: for yourselves know that we are appointed thereunto' (1 Thess. 3:3 . . .)."[4]

"What lessons of humility and faith may we not learn as we trace the dealings of God with his creatures. The Lord can do but little for the children of men, because they are so full of pride and vain glory. They exalt self, magnifying their own strength, learning, and wisdom. It is necessary for God to disappoint their hopes and frustrate their plans, that they may learn to trust in him alone. All our powers come from God; we can do nothing independent of the strength which he has given us. . . .

". . . He would have us make him our protector and our guide in all the duties and affairs of life."[5]

We must learn to trust our Creator and Redeemer. "Nothing is beneath the notice of the infinite God, nothing too small for his attention."[6]

1. Francis D. Nichol, ed., *The Seventh-day Adventist Bible Commentary*, vol. 7 (Washington, DC: Review and Herald®, 1957), 343.
2. Nichol, *Seventh-day Adventist Bible Commentary*, vol. 7, 581.
3. Nichol, *Seventh-day Adventist Bible Commentary*, vol. 7, 343.
4. Francis D. Nichol, *Seventh-day Adventist Bible Commentary*, vol. 5 (Washington DC: Review and Herald®, 1956), 1044.
5. Ellen G. White, "Victory at Last," *Signs of the Times*, July 14, 1881, 1.
6. Ellen G. White, "God in Nature," *General Conference Daily Bulletin*, February 18, 1897.

Part 12: Salvation's Beacon

*And that from childhood you have known the Holy Scriptures, which are able
to make you wise for salvation through faith which is in Christ Jesus.*
—2 Timothy 3:15

Timothy's *mother* and *grandmother* were united in their efforts to train him for God. What was his lesson book? The Bible. Paul, his father in the gospel, declares, 'From a child thou hast known the holy scriptures.' The faith of the mother and grandmother in the oracles of God was a constant illustration to Timothy of the blessing of doing God's will.

"When Timothy was little more than a boy, Paul took him with him as his companion in labor. Those who had taught Timothy in his childhood were rewarded by seeing the son of their care linked in close fellowship with the great apostle."[1]

Paul wanted Timothy to understand that his training in the Holy Scriptures was the most important beacon to traverse seas of popular opinion and false philosophy successfully. "God committed the preparation of His divinely inspired Word to finite man. This Word, arranged into books, the Old and New Testaments, is the Guidebook to the inhabitants of a fallen world; bequeathed to them, that by studying and obeying the directions not one soul would lose its way to heaven.

"Those who think to make the supposed difficulties of Scripture plain, in measuring by their finite rule that which is inspired and that which is not inspired, had better cover their faces as Elijah when the still small voice spoke to him; for they are in the presence of God and holy angels, who for ages have communicated to men light and knowledge, telling them what to do and what not to do unfolding before them scenes of thrilling interest, waymark by waymark in symbols and signs and illustrations.

"And He has not, while presenting the perils clustering about the last days, qualified any finite man to unravel hidden mysteries, or inspired on man or any class of men to pronounce judgment as to that which is inspired or is not. When men, in their finite judgment, find it necessary to go into an examination of Scriptures to define that which is inspired and that which is not, they have stepped before Jesus to show Him a better way than He has led us."[2]

---

1. Ellen G. White, MS 117a, 1901; emphasis added.
2. Ellen G. White, MS 16, 1888.

Part 13: The Bible Standard

All Scripture is given by inspiration of God, and is profitable for doctrine,
for reproof, for correction, for instruction in righteousness.

—2 Timothy 3:16

Ellen White has this to say about the Bible: "There are some that may think they are fully capable with their finite judgment to take the Word of God and to state what are the words of inspiration and what are not the words of inspiration. I want to warn you off that ground, my brethren in the ministry. 'Put off thy shoes from off thy feet, for the place whereon thou standest is holy ground.' There is no finite man that lives, I care not who he is or whatever is his position, that God has authorized to pick and choose in His Word.

"It is true that the apostle has said that there are some things that are hard to be understood in the Scriptures. So there are. And if it were not that there are subjects that are difficult and hard to be understood, well might the skeptic who now pleads that God has given a revelation that cannot be understood, well might he, I say, have something else to plead.

"God's infinity is so much higher than we are, that it is impossible for man to comprehend the mystery of godliness. Angels of God looked with amazement upon Christ, who took upon Himself the form of man and humbly united His divinity with humanity in order that He might minister to fallen man. It is a marvel among the heavenly angels. God has told us that He did do it, and we are to accept the Word of God just as it reads.

"And although we may try to reason in regard to our Creator how long He has had existence, where evil first entered into our world, and all these things, we may reason about them until we fall down faint and exhausted with the research when there is yet an infinity beyond. We cannot grasp it, so what man is there that dares to take that Bible and say this part is inspired and that part is not inspired? . . .

"Never attempt to search the Scriptures unless you are ready to listen, unless you are ready to be a learner, unless you are ready to listen to the Word of God as though His voice were speaking directly to you from the living oracles. Never let mortal man sit in judgment upon the Word of God or pass sentence as to how much of this is inspired and how much is not inspired and that this is more inspired than some other portion."[1]

---

1. Ellen G. White, MS 13, 1888.

Part 14: Preach Jesus!

Preach the word! Be ready in season and out of season.
Convince, rebuke, exhort, with all longsuffering and teaching.
—2 Timothy 4:2

P aul now charges Timothy to do his duty. And first on the list is—preach the Word! "Christ's method of communicating the truth constitutes the pattern for every Christian. Christ concentrated on revealing the truth; He refused to waste time either in discussing erroneous theories or in refuting their proponents. Jesus emphasized the practical duties that touched the life experiences of His hearers. He wanted men to be strengthened for the daily requirements of life. Consequently, He did not preach fanciful doctrines or sensational suppositions designed to gratify the curious or to establish His own prestige with the fickle crowd. So, today, ministers are not to include mere human traditions and opinions in their sermons. Only the Word is adequate to meet the needs of sin-weakened men and women. Pleasing stories, which merely attract attention and create a laugh, are incompatible with the sober responsibility of a minister professing to represent Christ.

"The expression 'preach the word' suggests content designed to aid men and women in meeting temptation and in solving life's problems day by day. This command bars all levity, all fanciful interpretations based on inaccurate exegesis, and all trifling subjects. The Holy Spirit will cooperate with the minister's efforts only when truth is being communicated. As a 'herald' for God the minister must preach nothing but the Word, otherwise he is an imposter."[1]

Every Christian should be ready to tell others about Jesus. Timothy was also to identify sins, condemning outrageous ones using Scripture as his guide. He was to encourage the troubled, teaching others about God and His plan of salvation. "Every phase of the minister's task, whether reproving, rebuking, or exhorting, should be clothed with the grace of patience and compassion. Severe, cold condemnation will never bring sinners to Christ."[2]

Christians have a responsibility to preach the Word to their friends and neighbors. "Unless the truth is planted in the heart, it cannot control the life."[3]

---

1. Francis D. Nichol, ed., *The Seventh-day Adventist Bible Commentary*, vol. 7 (Washington, DC: Review and Herald®, 1957), 347.
2. Nichol, *Seventh-day Adventist Bible Commentary*, vol. 7, 347.
3. Ellen G. White, Letter 13, 1893.

Part 15: The Finish Line in Sight

I have fought the good fight, I have finished the race, I have kept the faith. Finally, there is laid up for me the crown of righteousness, which the Lord, the righteous Judge, will give to me on that Day, and not to me only but also to all who have loved His appearing.

—2 Timothy 4:7, 8

Once again, we see Paul using athletic ideas and phrases to explain the Christian experience. He had faithfully borne his testimony of Jesus Christ and preached the gospel to the Gentiles. "Paul has almost finished his course, and he desires Timothy to take his place, guarding the churches from the fables and heresies with which Satan and his agents would endeavor to lead them from the truth. He admonishes him to shun temporal pursuits and entanglements, which would prevent him from giving himself wholly to God's work. He is to endure with cheerfulness the opposition, reproach, and persecution to which his faithfulness would expose him. He is to make full proof of his ministry, employing every means of doing good to his fellow men."[1]

"Paul does not expect the 'crown' of victory to be awarded him at death; it is 'laid up' to be given him at that future day, the day of Christ's 'appearing.' "[2] "Paul knows of no immediate entrance into heaven at death; the second advent is 'that day' when the redeemed will be rewarded with eternal life."[3]

Paul assured Timothy that the crown of righteousness is "not for me only" (2 Timothy 4:8). "Paul here gives further evidence that he expected no immediate entrance to heaven at death. The righteous, both dead and living, will receive their reward of eternal life at the same time, 'at that day.' (. . . 1 Corinthians 15:51–54)."[4]

"There are living upon our earth, men who have passed the age of four score and ten. The natural results of old age are seen in their feebleness. But they believe God, and God loves them. The seal of God is upon them, and they will be among the number of whom the Lord has said, 'Blessed are the dead which die in the Lord.' With Paul they can say, 'I have fought a good fight, I have finished my course, I have kept the faith; henceforth there is laid up for me a crown of righteousness, which the Lord, the righteous judge, shall give me at that day, and not to me only, but unto all them also which love his appearing.'[5]

There are many whose gray hairs God honors because they have fought a good fight and kept the faith. "[6]

---

1. Ellen G. White, "A Faithful Witness II," *Youth's Instructor*, July 10, 1902, 1, 2.
2. Francis D. Nichol, ed., *The Seventh-day Adventist Bible Commentary*, vol. 7 (Washington, DC: Review and Herald®, 1957), 349.
3. Nichol, *Seventh-day Adventist Bible Commentary*, vol. 7, 349.
4. Nichol, *Seventh-day Adventist Bible Commentary*, vol. 7, 349.
5. Ellen G. White, Letter 207, 1899
6. Ellen G. White, Letter 207, 1899.

Part 16: Luke and Mark

Only Luke is with me. Get Mark and bring him with you, for he is useful to me for ministry.
—2 Timothy 4:11

One by one, Paul saw his friends leaving him. The first to depart were Phygellus and Hermogenes. Then Demas, dismayed at the thickening clouds of difficulty and danger, forsook the persecuted apostle to seek for ease and security in a worldly life. Crescens was sent on a mission to the churches of Galatia, Titus to Dalmatia, Tychicus to Ephesus. Luke, the beloved physician and faithful friend, was still with him. This was a great comfort to Paul, who had never needed the companionship and ministration of his brethren more than now, enfeebled as he was by age, toil, and infirmities, and confined in the damp, dark vaults of a Roman prison. And, as he was dependent upon the aid of an amanuensis, the services of Luke were of great value, enabling him still to communicate with his brethren and the world without."[1] Forsaking prestige and wealth as a physician, "Luke counted fellowship with Paul in suffering the higher honor."[2]

"Some time after the unfortunate episode at Perga (Acts 13:13) Mark readjusted himself to meet the requirements of the ministry, and the record reveals his new usefulness as one of Paul's faithful assistants (see Col. 4:10; Philemon 24). At the present time he was Timothy's assistant in Asia Minor. He had been with Paul during his first imprisonment in Rome, and this previous experience would make him especially valuable in this last tragic ordeal."[3] Here we see "the magnanimous spirit of Paul, who held no grudge against Mark because of his previous failure (. . . Acts 13:13; 15:37)."[4] Paul wanted to see Mark one last time.

Paul also asked Timothy to "bring the cloak that I left with Carpus at Troas when you come—and the books, especially the parchments" (2 Timothy 4:13). "At his second arrest, Paul was seized and hurried away so suddenly that he had no opportunity to gather up his few 'books and parchments,' or even to take with him his cloak. And now winter was coming on, and he knew that he would suffer with cold in his damp prison-cell. He had no money to buy another garment, he knew that his end might come at any moment, and with his usual self-forgetfulness and fear to burden the church, he desired that no expense should be incurred on his account."[5]

"After Paul's death, Mark worked with Peter in Rome."[6]

---

1. Ellen G. White, *Sketches From the Life of Paul* (Washington, DC: Review and Herald®, 1974), 308.
2. Francis D. Nichol, ed., *The Seventh-day Adventist Bible Commentary*, vol. 7 (Washington, DC: Review and Herald®, 1957), 350.
3. Nichol, *Seventh-day Adventist Bible Commentary*, vol. 7, 350.
4. Nichol, *Seventh-day Adventist Bible Commentary*, vol. 7, 350.
5. White, *Sketches From the Life of Paul*, 327.
6. Nichol, *Seventh-day Adventist Bible Commentary*, vol. 7, 350.

Part 17: Alexander the Coppersmith

Alexander the coppersmith did me much harm. May the Lord repay him according to his works.
You also must beware of him, for he has greatly resisted our words.
—2 Timothy 4:14, 15

Alexander the coppersmith was the reason Paul had been arrested. "The arrest was effected by the efforts of Alexander the coppersmith, who had so unsuccessfully opposed the apostle's work at Ephesus, and who now seized the opportunity to be revenged on one whom he could not defeat. Paul in his second Epistle to Timothy afterward referred to the machinations of this enemy of the faith: 'Alexander the coppersmith did me much evil. The Lord reward him according to his works.' In his first epistle he spoke in a similar manner of Hymeneus and Alexander as among those who 'concerning faith have made shipwreck;' 'whom,' he says, 'I have delivered unto Satan, that they may learn not to blaspheme.' These men had departed from the faith of the gospel, and furthermore had done despite to the Spirit of grace by attributing to the power of Satan the wonderful revelations made to Paul. Having rejected the truth, they were filled with hatred against it, and sought to destroy its faithful advocate.

". . . Paul had faithfully reproved their sin,—the vice of licentiousness so prevalent in that age,—but they had refused to be corrected. He had proceeded according to the instructions of Christ regarding such cases, but the offenders had given no token of repentance, and he had therefore excommunicated them. They had then openly apostatized from the faith, and united with its most bitter opponents. When they rejected the words of Paul, and set themselves to hinder his labors, they were warring against Christ; and it was by the inspiration of the Spirit of God, and not as an expression of personal feeling, that Paul pronounced against them that solemn denunciation."[1]

Paul now warned Timothy to beware of Alexander. If the coppersmith would travel all the way from Ephesus to Troas just to report Paul to the authorities as a Christian and have him arrested, then he would certainly go to any lengths to capture Paul's friends as well. "Alexander gained momentary advantage, but he lost his eternal inheritance."[2]

He made a bad bargain in settling his grudge against Paul!

1. Ellen G. White, *Sketches From the Life of Paul* (Washington, DC: Review and Herald®, 1974), 305, 306.
2. Francis D. Nichol, ed., *The Seventh-day Adventist Bible Commentary*, vol. 7 (Washington, DC: Review and Herald®, 1957), 351.

Part 18: Forsaken

At my first defense no one stood with me, but all forsook me. May it not be charged against them.
—2 Timothy 4:16.

T he emperor's malice against Paul was heightened by the fact that members of the imperial household, and also other persons of distinction, had been converted to Christianity during his first imprisonment. For this reason he made the second imprisonment much more severe than the first, granting him little opportunity to preach the gospel; and he determined to cut short his life as soon as a plausible pretext could be found for so doing."[1] During his trial, Paul had "no one of influence to intercede. Luke, Titus, Crescens, or Tychicus would have been of no help to Paul in this respect. Apparently, there were some men of stature and influence who could have spoken a word in favor of Paul, but did not. Perhaps the severe persecution of Nero had made it extremely hazardous even to admit friendship. . . .

". . . God never failed to be Paul's 'refuge and strength, a very present help in trouble' (Ps. 46:1). Even though Paul was denied the support of influential friends (2 Tim. 4:16), his courage remained strong because of One greater than all, who remained by his side."[2]

"Oh, taste and see that the LORD is good; blessed is the man who trusts in Him!" (Psalm 34:8).

We have already seen Paul urge Timothy, "Do your utmost to come before winter" (2 Timothy 4:21). "Paul longed for Timothy's companionship even as Christ longed for the fellowship of His closest friends in the dark hours prior to His execution (Matt. 26:38)."[3] Paul asked Timothy to bring his cloak, for he had left in such a hurry he had not brought it with him. He had no money to buy another. It was cold and damp in the prison, and Paul could use the simple covering to offset the chill. Did Timothy make it in time? What became of Timothy? "According to Heb. 13:23 Timothy was 'set at liberty' after being imprisoned, but when and where this imprisonment occurred is not known. Tradition has it that Timothy suffered martyrdom under either Domitian (A.D. 81–96) or Trajan (A.D. 98–117)."[4]

"The angel of the Lord encamps all around those who fear Him, and delivers them" (Psalm 34:7).

---

1. Ellen G. White, *Sketches From the Life of Paul* (Washington, DC: Review and Herald®, 1974), 328, 329.
2. Francis D. Nichol, ed., *The Seventh-day Adventist Bible Commentary*, vol. 7 (Washington, DC: Review and Herald®, 1957), 351.
3. Nichol, *Seventh-day Adventist Bible Commentary*, vol. 7, 350.
4. Nichol, *Seventh-day Adventist Bible Commentary*, vol. 7, 326.

Condemned to Death

Then they will deliver you up to tribulation and kill you,
and you will be hated by all nations for My name's sake.

—Matthew 24:9

The closing scenes in the life of Paul are graphically portrayed by Ellen White. Her words take us to the place of his execution and draw down the curtain upon a life of service.

"Nero's mind was so impressed with the force of the apostle's words at his last trial that he deferred the decision of the case, neither acquitting nor condemning him. But the sentence was only deferred. It was not long before the decision was pronounced which consigned Paul to a martyr's grave. Being a Roman citizen, he could not be subjected to torture, and was therefore sentenced to be beheaded. . . .

"Paul was led in a private manner to the place of execution. His persecutors, alarmed at the extent of his influence, feared that converts might be won to Christianity, even by the scenes of his death. Hence few spectators were allowed to be present. But the hardened soldiers appointed to attend him, listened to his words, and with amazement saw him cheerful and even joyous in prospect of such a death. His spirit of forgiveness toward his murderers, and his unwavering confidence in Christ to the very last, proved a savor of life unto life to some who witnessed his martyrdom. . . .

". . . As he stood at the place of martyrdom, he saw not the gleaming sword of the executioner, or the green earth so soon to receive his blood; he looked up through the calm blue heaven of that summer's day to the throne of the Eternal. . . .

"The Captain of our salvation has prepared his servant for the last great conflict. Ransomed by the sacrifice of Christ, washed from sin in his blood, and clothed in his righteousness, Paul has the witness in himself that his soul is precious in the sight of his Redeemer. His life is hid with Christ in God, and he is persuaded that He who has conquered death is able to keep that which is committed to his trust. His mind grasps the Saviour's promise, 'I will raise him up at the last day.' His thoughts and hopes are centered in the second advent of his Lord."[1]

"And as the sword of the executioner descends, and the shadows of death gather about the martyr's soul, his latest thought springs forward, as will his earliest thought in the great awakening, to meet the Lifegiver who shall welcome him to the joy of the blest."[2]

---

1. Ellen G. White, *Sketches From the Life of Paul* (Washington, DC: Review and Herald®, 1974), 329–333.
2. White, *Sketches From the Life of Paul*, 333.

Keep the Faith!

And this is the will of Him who sent Me, that everyone who sees the Son and believes in Him may have everlasting life; and I will raise him up at the last day.

—John 6:40

Until the latest hour the life of Paul testified to the truth of his words to the Corinthians: 'God, who commanded the light to shine out of darkness, hath shined in our hearts, to give the light of the knowledge of the glory of God in the face of Jesus Christ. But we have this treasure in earthen vessels, that the excellency of the power may be of God, and not of us. We are troubled on every side, yet not distressed; we are perplexed, but not in despair; persecuted, but not forsaken; cast down, but not destroyed; always bearing about in the body the dying of the Lord Jesus, that the life also of Jesus might be made manifest in our body.' 2 Corinthians 4:6–10. His sufficiency was not in himself, but in the presence and agency of the divine Spirit that filled his soul and brought every thought into subjection to the will of Christ. The prophet declares, 'Thou wilt keep him in perfect peace, whose mind is stayed on Thee: because he trusteth in Thee.' Isaiah 26:3. The heaven-born peace expressed on Paul's countenance won many a soul to the gospel."[1] Reflecting back over decades of service, Paul might have considered the martyrdom of Stephen and the peace on Stephen's face as he asked God to forgive his murderers. Saul had come far from the day he held the coats of those who killed Stephen.

"Well-nigh a score of centuries have passed since Paul the aged poured out his blood as a witness for the word of God and for the testimony of Christ. No faithful hand recorded for the generations to come, the last scenes in the life of this holy man; but inspiration has preserved for us his dying testimony. Like a trumpet peal has his voice rung out through all the ages, nerving with his own courage thousands of witnesses for Christ, and wakening in thousands of sorrow-stricken hearts the echo of his own triumphant joy: 'I am now ready to be offered, and the time of my departure is at hand. I have fought a good fight, I have finished my course, I have kept the faith. Henceforth there is laid up for me a crown of righteousness, which the Lord, the righteous Judge, shall give me at that day; and not to me only, but unto all them also that love his appearing.' "[2]

Now unite with your church family. Vow to set the world on fire for Christ! Your crown awaits! "The Lord Jesus Christ be with your spirit. Grace be with you. Amen" (2 Timothy 4:22).

---

1. Ellen G. White, *The Acts of the Apostles* (Mountain View, CA: Pacific Press®, 1911), 510.
2. Ellen G. White, *Sketches From the Life of Paul* (Washington, DC: Review and Herald®, 1974), 334.